U.S. Department of Labor

Annual report of the Commissioner general of Immigration to the

Secretary of Labor

U.S. Department of Labor

Annual report of the Commissioner general of Immigration to the Secretary of Labor

ISBN/EAN: 9783741140860

Manufactured in Europe, USA, Canada, Australia, Japa

Cover: Foto ©Suzi / pixelio.de

Manufactured and distributed by brebook publishing software (www.brebook.com)

U.S. Department of Labor

Annual report of the Commissioner general of Immigration to the Secretary of Labor

ANNUAL REPORT

OF THE

COMMISSIONER GENERAL OF IMMIGRATION

TO THE

SECRETARY OF LABOR

FOR THE

FISCAL YEAR ENDED JUNE 30

1913

WASHINGTON
GOVERNMENT PRINTING OFFICE
1914

REPORT

OF THE

COMMISSIONER GENERAL OF IMMIGRATION.

DEPARTMENT OF LABOR,
BUREAU OF IMMIGRATION,
Washington, July 1, 1913.

SIR: On the date of this report, July 1, 1913, I have occupied the position of Commissioner General of Immigration for one month only. During 11 months of the fiscal year covered Hon. Daniel J. Keefe was the incumbent of said office. It was my intention to ask Mr. Keefe either to sign this report jointly with me or himself make a separate report covering the period of his incumbency; but before the text could be prepared Mr. Keefe had left the United States for an extended tour in the Orient and Europe. The best I can do under the circumstances is to call attention to the fact that most of the work mentioned and accomplishments shown were done and attained during his able and effective administration, and to give place herein to some of the views heretofore expressed by him regarding important phases of the enforcement of the several laws under which the bureau and service operate. In this connection there is inserted as Appendix IV (pp. 257–260, post) a statement made by him when retiring from office, to which attention is directed for his views on the subjects treated therein.

During the past fiscal year immigration to the United States, amounting to 1,197,892 aliens, has been much larger than in any fiscal year since 1907, and has been less than that shown for said year, the total for which was 1,285,349, by only 87,457, and exceeded that for the fiscal year 1912 by 359,720 and the average per year from 1908 to 1912 by 339,295. When it is remembered that during a considerable portion of the year a war was in progress in which a very large percentage of the able-bodied men of Turkey and the Balkan States were engaged, the number of immigrants entering this country seems the more remarkable. The year's net increase in population from immigration is 815,303, as compared with a net increase for the preceding year of 401,863, and for 1911 of 512,085. The aliens have not only come, but have remained in larger numbers than heretofore.

It was found necessary and possible under the provisions of the immigration law to exclude 19,938 aliens during the year, amounting to 1.38 per cent of the total number (1,447,165) applying for entry. The principal grounds of rejection were: Likely to become a public charge, of which class 7,941 were excluded; afflicted with physical or mental defects affecting ability to earn a living, 4,208; contract

3

laborers, 1,624; afflicted with contagious diseases or tuberculosis, 2,564; and afflicted with serious mental defects, 753.

Simultaneously with the rejection at the ports of the number of aliens above mentioned belonging to classes declared by the law to be inadmissible, it has been necessary to remove from the United States at considerable expense and trouble 3,461 aliens found here in violation of law. This total was composed principally of 714 who became public charges within three years after landing, 464 who entered without inspection, 1,262 who were likely to become public charges at time of entry, and 551 who belonged to the immoral classe at times of entry or engaged in immoral practices after landing.

When it is remembered that the foregoing results, in addition to other important labors of the bureau, have been accomplished during the past year with an appropriation of $2,225,000 (only about 53 per cent of the amount collected as head tax on admitted aliens during the year), and that therefore the force of inspectors, doctors, interpreters, and other employees available to the service has necessarily been kept at a number wholly inadequate properly to perform the work required, no one can fail to realize that the year's results have been secured only by the most painstaking and thorough administration and constant application of the employees of the service to the particular duties assigned them.

This bureau, in its present situation, may be likened to a great manufacturing plant, fully equipped, with the major cost of operation fixed and unavoidable and with an output limited by failure to utilize its powers of production owing to insufficiency of funds to secure all the labor and material required to attain its maximum capacity. An institution so conducted operates at a loss, just as our service is doing, notwithstanding its thoroughness of organization and ability to approximate maximum efficiency in administration.

Increased appropriations and a larger force of officers in the several stations as well as at the main office, and more Public Health surgeons, with the necessary interpreters, to make possible a thorough inspection and a more strict enforcement of the law, are as important considerations in the effort to deal with immigration problems as the passage of new laws. New laws, no matter how well drawn, will not in the future, any more than such have in the past, accomplish the end sought unless necessary appropriations are made available for exercising the ample powers of the bureau to lessen the opportunity for the entry, as well as to facilitate the deportation, of the physically, mentally, and morally defective.

The full exercise of the powers of the bureau through the means above suggested would effectively regulate immigration, even under existing laws, as it would debar more aliens on primary inspection as well as after examination by boards of special inquiry, check illegal entries, and deport all in the country not entitled to remain.

As a consequence immigration would be much reduced, directly through these methods and indirectly by preventing the coming of those not clearly admissible who, warned thereby, would not risk the expense and loss of time required to come to our ports of entry. The latter are not deterred now, owing to the small percentage of debarments.

The congested conditions in our cities, the result mainly of the concentration of our own people from interior sections and that of the numerous aliens who come from foreign lands, requires attention. The "back-to-the-land" movement has not had any appreciable effect in correcting the unfavorable conditions, labor and other, that often disturb our populous centers.

Regulation of and reduction in volume of immigration from foreign lands are the ready expedients to remedy, particularly in the cities, an already difficult situation.

We can not by law prevent our people from flocking to the cities, nor can we under the existing system, in order to overcome the same tendency in a large majority of immigrants, direct them after landing to certain localities where they may remain. We can, however, regulate their coming.

But how and in what way?

Some advocate the "illiteracy test," which, notwithstanding all that can be offered in its favor, has also, it must be conceded, its drawbacks.

After all, manhood should be the test of admission and would constitute the ideal way of sifting immigration so as to admit none except altogether desirable aliens with the requisite physical, mental, and moral qualifications.

As a rule the admitted aliens must, because of lack of knowledge of the English language and of existing conditions, earn their livelihood by manual labor. It is important, therefore, that they should be physically sound. In the bureau's judgment, the adoption of a physical test similar to that which recruits for the Army undergo would insure a suitable standard. The fact that more than 6,000 applicants during the past 12 months were rejected as physically unfit under the existing law, notwithstanding that the requirements thereof and the funds and facilities for its enforcement were wholly inadequate, indicates that the physical standard now prevailing is far below what it should be.

Irrespective of whether or not the illiteracy test is adopted, the standards of the law regarding physical and moral qualifications should be materially raised and the machinery for their enforcement extensively improved.

Only in the event of more physicians and interpreters being provided for the Public Health Service can the present law regarding mentally defective aliens be effectively administered. This subject is further considered later in this report.

Except that section 2 of the present law should be made to apply to male as well as female aliens of the sexually immoral classes, and should otherwise in its provisions relating to the sexually immoral be brought into exact agreement with section 3, the law has been made sufficiently strict in its requirements regarding the sexually immoral. But criminals and anarchists are not reached as effectively as they should be. With regard to both the three-year limitation on the Government's right to deport should be removed from the law; and with respect to criminals, rejection should be predicated upon the alien's having *committed* a crime or misdemeanor involving moral turpitude, rather than upon his having been convicted of or admitting its commission. Many members of the criminal classes come to the United States who have not been convicted or even indicted or arrested, though guilty, or of whose conviction no record can be produced by immigration officials; hence the necessity for this amendment.

Moreover, the law should provide for the deportation at any time of any alien who becomes an anarchist or commits a crime involving moral turpitude subsequent to his admission to the United States, and the definition of the term "anarchist" in the law should be made broad enough to include all aliens who advocate the destruction of property.

STATISTICS OF IMMIGRATION.[1]

The statistical tables form Appendix I of this report (pp. 37–148). These tables are so arranged and the data therein supplied is so extensive and detailed in its character that almost any branch of the immigration problem can readily be studied, in so far as affected by statistics, by carefully perusing and comparing the results indicated by them. The information furnished in several of these tables is worthy of particular note in the text. Some of the more important items have been mentioned, but are repeated for the sake of comparison with others here given.

Tables I to V show, among other things, the following: Immigration for the past fiscal year amounted to 1,197,892, which is more than the total for the preceding year (838,172) by 359,720 aliens. The increase has occurred principally in the months from July to November, 1912, each of those months recording more than 50 per cent increase, and June of last year, 91 per cent. Some increase was shown, however, for each month of the year, the smallest being 6 per cent in March, 1913. In addition to the 1,197,892 aliens of the immigrant class above mentioned, 229,335 of the nonimmigrant class entered, making a total of 1,427,227. The departures during the year embraced 611,924 aliens, 308,190 of whom were of the emigrant and 303,734 of the nonemigrant class. The net gain in population by immigration, therefore, was 815,303, as compared with 512,085 for the fiscal year 1911, and 401,863 for the fiscal year 1912. While immigration has increased in the past year 43 per cent over the total for the preceding year, the rejections (shown by Table XVII) for 1913 were 19,938 as compared with 16,057 for 1912, an increase of only 24 per cent, or, to make a more accurate and lucid comparison, 1.55 per cent of applying aliens were rejected in 1912, while in 1913 only 1.38 per cent were rejected.

Table VI shows the occupations of aliens entering and leaving the country in three groups—professional, skilled, and miscellaneous. Of common, unskilled laborers, 251,542 (220,992 immigrant and 30,550 nonimmigrant) entered and 278,115 (191,604 emigrant and 86,511 nonemigrant) departed, as against arrivals of members of skilled trades aggregating 192,978 (160,108 immigrant and 32,870 nonimmigrant) and departures of the same aggregating 74,449 (31,563 emigrant and 42,886 nonemigrant).

Information with respect to sex, age, literacy, financial condition, how passage was paid, and whether coming to join a relative or friend are given in Table VII with respect to admitted aliens; while

---

[1] In the classification of aliens the terms (1) immigrant and emigrant and (2) nonimmigrant and nonemigrant, respectively, relate (1) to permanent arrivals and departures and (2) to temporary arrivals and departures. In compiling the statistics under this classification the following rule is observed: Arriving aliens whose permanent domicile has been outside the United States who intend to reside permanently in the United States are classed as immigrant aliens; departing aliens whose permanent residence has been in the United States who intend to reside permanently abroad are classed as emigrant aliens; all alien residents of the United States making a temporary trip abroad and all aliens residing abroad making a tempoary trip to the United States are classed as nonemigrant aliens on the outward journey and nonimmigrant on the inward.

there are given in its counterpart, Table VII A, data regarding sex, age, and how long in the United States with respect to emigrant aliens leaving the country.

Of the total number of immigrant aliens admitted (1,197,892), 808,144 were males and 389,748 females; 986,355 were between the ages of 14 and 44, while 147,158 were under 14 and 64,379 were 45 or over.

Of those admitted, 269,988 (185,872 males and 84,116 females) could neither read nor write and 5,326 (2,842 males and 2,484 females) could read but not write. This does not include any aliens under 14 years of age. The percentage of admitted aliens shown by these figures to have been illiterate is, therefore, 26 per cent.

The total amount of money shown to inspection officers by arriving aliens was $40,890,197, or an average of about $34 per person. There is no way of determining what portion of this consisted of money sent applicants by relatives or friends in this country. Of those admitted 755,097 showed amounts of less than $50 each, so that of those able to demonstrate the possession of money, namely, 906,917, about 83 per cent had in their possession less than $50 each.

Of the aliens entering, 811,151 claimed to have paid their own passage, while 375,947 admitted that their passage had been paid by relatives and 10,794 admitted that it had been paid by persons other than relatives. From this information (known not to be absolutely correct) it appears that over 32 per cent of the total number admitted were assisted to reach this country.

Table XVII shows that during the year 19,938 aliens were refused admission. The following comparative statement as to the principal grounds on which they were rejected is prepared for convenience and as a continuation of a similar illustration given in previous reports:

Cause of rejection.	1907	1908	1909	1910	1911	1912	1913
Idiots	29	20	18	16	12	10	18
Imbeciles		45	42	40	26	44	54
Feeble-minded persons		121	121	125	126	110	483
Insanity (including epileptics)	189	184	167	198	144	133	198
Likely to become a public charge (including paupers and beggars)	6,866	3,741	4,458	15,927	12,048	8,182	7,956
Afflicted with contagious diseases	3,822	2,847	2,308	3,033	2,735	1,674	2,457
Afflicted with tuberculosis		59	82	95	111	74	107
Physically or mentally defective		870	370	312	3,055	2,288	4,208
Criminals	341	136	273	580	644	592	808
Prostitutes and other immoral aliens	18	124	323	316	253	263	367
Procurers of prostitutes	1	43	181	179	141	192	253
Contract laborers	1,434	1,932	1,172	1,786	1,336	1,333	1,624

Table XVIII covers aliens expelled from the country, segregated into the three general classes, "Deportation compulsory within three years," "Deportation compulsory without time limit," and "Public charges within one year after entry, from subsequent causes," and under such general classification into specific causes for deportation. The total number of aliens expelled on deportation warrants was 3,461, compared with 2,456 in 1912. All but 8 of these aliens were of the mandatorily excluded classes, said 8 having been deported by their own consent. Only 79 aliens were deported who had been in the United States more than three years, all of whom, of course, belonged to the sexually immoral classes. Of the remaining 3,374 expelled aliens, 2,019 were members of the excluded classes at time of entry, 714 had become public charges from causes existing prior to entry, 116 had become prostitutes after entry, 61 were found to be supported by or receiving the proceeds of prostitution, and 464 had entered without inspection. Of the 79 who had been here more than three years, 36 were immoral women, 4 were procurers, and 39 were being supported by the proceeds of prostitution.

Tables XIX and XIX A cover appeals and applications for admission under bond. During the year 6,947 appeals from excluding decisions were reviewed by the bureau and submitted to the department for final decision, 2,130 of the aliens being admitted outright, 678 admitted on bond, and 4,139 ordered deported by affirming the decision of the board of inquiry. Dissenting board members took 55 appeals from admitting decisions, in 34 of which the aliens were admitted outright, 2 admitted on bond, and 19 deported. In 101 instances aliens applied direct for admission on bond, the cases not being technically appealable, 68 of which applications were granted and 33 denied.

SOURCES OF IMMIGRATION.

Referring to Table III (pp. 40, 41), it will be found that 182,886 immigrant aliens came from northern and western Europe during the past year, divided as follows: Belgium, 7,405; Denmark, 6,478; France, 9,675; German Empire, 34,329; Netherlands, 6,902; Norway, 8,587; Sweden, 17,202; Switzerland, 4,104; England, 43,363; Ireland, 27,876; Scotland, 14,220; Wales, 2,745. The total of these figures constitutes about 15 per cent of the entire immigration. On the other hand, 896,553, or about 75 per cent, came from eastern and southern Europe and western Asia, divided as follows: Italy, 265,542; Russia (principally southern), including Finland, 291,040; Austria, 137,245; Hungary, 117,580; Greece, 22,817; Turkey in Europe, 14,128; Turkey in Asia, 23,955; Portugal, 14,171; Spain, 6,167; Bulgaria, Servia, and Montenegro, 1,753; Roumania, 2,155.

Attention should also be directed to the fact that immigration from Asia (not including the extreme western portion included in the foregoing figures) amounted to 11,403, constituted of 8,281 from Japan, 2,105 from China, 179 from India, and 838 from other portions of Asia. This is 1 per cent of the total immigration. In 1912 this class of immigration was 1; in 1911, 0.8; in 1910, 0.8; in 1909, 0.7; in 1908, 2.4; in 1907, 2.5; and in 1906, 1.4 per cent of the total immigration shown for those respective years. People from these sections are of such widely different racial type from the main stock of our population that racial assimilation is extremely difficult, and, in addition, the races to which they belong are incapable of assimilation in the political sense, members thereof not being eligible for naturalization.

ALIENS WITH PHYSICAL, MENTAL, OR MORAL DEFECTS.

In a few respects immigration has been regarded in laws heretofore passed as undesirable on economic grounds. These economic reasons are discussed hereinafter. Aside from these grounds the existing law excludes from the country only those who do not attain certain physical, mental, or moral standards. Illustrations of this consist of the inclusion in the excluded classes of aliens suffering from loathsome and dangerous contagious diseases, from insanity, imbecility, epilepsy, or feeble-mindedness, and those who are morally defective in the sense of being anarchists, criminals, or sexually immoral.

Under section 9 of the act a fine of $100 is assessed against any steamship line that brings to the United States an alien afflicted with a loathsome or dangerous contagious disease, tuberculosis, or certain mental defects (idiocy, imbecility, or epilepsy). This fine has been assessed in 302 cases in the past year, the sum collected being $30,200, of which $28,300 was on account of loathsome or dangerous contagious diseases, $600 on account of tuberculosis, and the balance on account of the mentally defective.

During the past year 10,629 aliens physically, mentally, or morally below the legal standard have been returned to the country of origin. Of these, 8,999 were excluded at the ports, divided into 2,564 with grave physical defects, 753 with grave mental defects, 4,208 with physical or mental defects not so serious but affecting ability to earn a living, and 1,474 morally defective. There were arrested and expelled from the country 1,630 such aliens, divided into 272 physically, 677 mentally, and 681 morally defective. See Tables XVII and XVIII (pp. 106–113). In 1912, 6,653 aliens physically, mentally, or morally below standard were returned, 5,427 of whom were rejected at the ports and 1,226 arrested within the country. The 5,427 defectives rejected in 1912 constituted 34 per cent of the total number debarred, while the 8,999 rejected at the ports during the past year constituted 45 per cent of the total number debarred. Those shown to have been rejected for grave physical causes, viz, 2,564, are divided into 107 for tuberculosis and 2,457 for loathsome or dangerous contagious diseases; the corresponding figures for 1912 being 74 and 1,674.

Regarding mentally defective aliens the statistics show that during 1913, 753 aliens suffering from serious defects of that nature were turned back at the ports, divided into 18 idiots, 175 insane, 54 imbeciles, 23 epileptics, and 483 feeble-minded. The corresponding statistics for 1912 were 10 idiots, 105 insane, 44 imbeciles, 28 epileptics, and 110 feeble-minded, a total of 297. What the rejection of even this comparatively small number of the mentally defective means to the country can hardly be overstated. Yet it can readily be understood that here is a field in which much more might be accomplished if Congress would only furnish sufficient funds to make the examination for mental defects more thorough. This must be accomplished, if at all, by detailing more Public Health surgeons to the duty of examining aliens for mental defects, and by providing the law and the means for more complete opportunity for observation for mental defects either before embarkation or on shipboard.

Attention has been directed in previous reports to a misapprehension regarding one provision of the law that relates to physically defective aliens. There seems to be a somewhat common impression that an alien suffering from a physical defect can not be excluded from the country unless there is evidence indicating that he is likely to become a public charge. Those who hold this view overlook the fact that the act of 1907 contained a new excluded class, described therein as persons who are found to be, and are certified by the examining surgeon as being, mentally or physically defective to an extent that interferes with their earning a livelihood. It will be noted that of this class 4,208 were rejected in 1913, compared with 2,288 in 1912.[1]

The criminal and the sexually immoral classes of aliens constitute a particularly difficult element to handle successfully under the law. It may be seen by examining the statistics (Table XVII) that 808 "criminals," 367 immoral women, 253 procurers of women, and 4 persons supported by the proceeds of prostitution were rejected in 1913; also (Table XVIII) that 124 "criminals," 330 immoral women, 121 procurers of women, and 100 persons supported by the proceeds of prostitution were apprehended in the country and deported. The total is 2,107, compared with a total of 1,457 for 1912, and 1,555 for 1911.

Anarchists are even more difficult to detect; but it is shown (same tables) that during the past year 2 were rejected and 4 arrested and deported. Although these numbers are small, it is commonly known that there are many alien anarchists in the United States. Such aliens are usually familiar with the provisions of the immigration law and keep under cover for three years after entry. When the limitation has run against the Government often their presence becomes known. The three-year limitation has been removed from the law in so far as the sexually immoral classes enumerated in section 3 of the act are concerned (Bugajewitz v. Adams, 228 U. S., 585); and the bureau suggests like action concerning the anarchist, the criminal, and also all of the sexually immoral classes named in section 2 of the act, thus making it possible for the Immigration Service to remove them to the country of origin whenever apprehended. In this connection it should be remarked that 79 of the sexually immoral aliens deported during 1913 could not have been expelled from the country except for the removal from the law of the three-year limitation; and now that the Supreme Court has passed upon the question it will be possible materially to increase deportations in cases of this kind.

Wherever possible, efforts have been made to prosecute those who have been connected with the importation and exploitation of the sexually immoral classes; and in this respect, as well as with regard to the expulsion of the aliens from the country the efforts of the immigration officials have been rewarded with a marked degree of success.

HOSPITAL TREATMENT.

Section 19 of the immigration act specifies that—

"no alien certified * * * to be suffering from tuberculosis or from a loathsome or dangerous contagious disease other than one of quarantinable nature shall be permitted to land for medical treatment thereof in any hospital in the United States, unless with the express permission of the Secretary of (Commerce and) Labor."

The words "unless with the express permission of the Secretary of (Commerce and) Labor" were not contained in the act of 1903. Section 37, as it appeared in the act of 1903, was a reasonable measure, allowing the Secretary to exercise discretion with regard to the deten-

---

[1] In connection with the foregoing so much of the report of the commissioner at New York as relates to the physically and mentally defective should be read. (Appendix III, pp. 180–187.)

tion and treatment of wives and minor children of aliens who had declared their intention to become citizens provided it appeared that the disease with which afflicted had been contracted on shipboard while en route to this country; but as this section was worded in the act of 1907, and with the change above noted in section 19, as it appeared in that act, a situation has been created which frequently causes embarrassment.

The law absolutely prohibits the admission to this country of aliens afflicted with a disease of this class, and penalizes the steamship lines if they bring to a United States port an alien so afflicted when it appears that the disease might have been detected by competent medical examination at the time of foreign embarkation. The spirit and intent of the law are opposed to the bringing of such diseased persons in the ships on which travel those who are physically sound, and the dictates of common humanity as well object to such action on the part of steamship lines. All afflicted aliens should be cured beyond doubt before they are allowed to start on a journey to this country. Yet, the provisions in sections 19 and 37 above mentioned are distinctly calculated to encourage physically defective aliens to come to the United States in the hope of escaping detection at the port, or, if detected, of being allowed treatment here until cured on the plea that undue hardship is involved in deportation. This practice has a tendency to make steamship officials careless in the conduct of the medical examination on the other side. Appreciating this paradoxical condition of the law, and the severe hardship which results to the aliens, as well as the danger of spread of contagion resulting to the entire country, the bureau has always endeavored to reduce to a minimum cases in which hospital treatment is allowed. Liberality in such cases might be exercised when the treatment would be of short duration and the expense slight; but generally the diseases most frequently encountered (trachoma, favus, tinea tonsurans, etc.) are of such a stubborn nature that the doctors will not even venture an approximate estimate of the time required to effect a cure. Sometimes treatment is continued for many months with no appreciable effect upon the patient. All the while the expenses are accumulating, and, as in most instances the aliens' relatives or friends are in ordinary circumstances, the burden becomes very onerous. Besides in many cases, as the nature of the disease is such as not to require the patient to remain in bed, he soon becomes impatient and restless, and as a consequence is a disturbing element where quiet should prevail for the welfare of others who are bedridden. As the purpose of the Public Health Service is to detect disease rather than treat the afflicted excepting under unavoidable circumstances, treatment should not be allowed unless most urgent reasons are shown to exist for not returning the alien to the country whence he came. If treatment is given, it should be only in hospitals at the immigration stations under the direct supervision of the Public Health surgeons.

With a view clearly to illustrate this matter, the bureau has compiled from reports submitted by the officers in charge of the principal ports of entry the table following showing the hospital-treatment cases arising during the past fiscal year.

CASES IN WHICH HOSPITAL TREATMENT WAS GRANTED UNDER SECTIONS 19 AND 37 OF THE IMMIGRATION LAW, FISCAL YEAR ENDED JUNE 30, 1913.

NEW YORK.

Aliens.	Race.	Age.	Sex.	Disease.	Length of treatment.		By whom expenses paid.	Final disposition.
		Yrs.			*M.*	*D.*		
1 2	Syrian	9–6	M., F...	Trachoma	11	15	Father	Futile; deported.
1 1	Hebrew	16	F	...do	11	15	...do	Cured and admitted.
1 1	Hungarian	8	F	Tinea tonsurans	7	19	...do	Futile; deported.
1 1	Hebrew	7	M	...do	16	24	...do	Under treatment.
1 1	Italian	11	F	...do	4	11	...do	Futile; deported.
1 1	...do	13	F	Trachoma	4	16	...do	Cured and admitted.
1 2	Syrian	11–10	M	...do	{ 11 / 1	25 / 26 }	}...do	Do.
1 1	German	52	F	...do	1	11	Husband	Do.
1 1	Syrian	11	M	Favus	12	5	Father	Under treatment.
1 1	Hebrew	20	M	Trachoma	2	12	Relatives	Cured and admitted.
1 1	...do	22	F	...do	3	20	...do	Do.
1 1	...do	9	F	Tinea tonsurans	13	9	Father	Under treatment.
1	Italian	15	F	Trachoma	2	27	...do	Do.
1	...do	10	F	...do	5	29	...do	Cured and admitted.
1	...do	11	F	...do	1	28	...do	Do.
1	Polish	4	M	Tinea tonsurans	5	22	...do	Futile; deported.
1	Italian	6	F	Trachoma		19	...do	Cured and admitted.
1	Hebrew	20	F	...do	2	16	Relatives	Do.
1	Swedish	24	F	...do	1	18	Husband	Do.
1	Armenian	22	F	...do	2	20	Father	Do.
1	Hebrew	3	M	Tinea tonsurans	5	2	...do	Futile; deported.
2	Greek	6–7	F	Trachoma	6	1	...do	Cured and admitted.
1	Armenian	17	F	...do	10		Relatives	Under treatment.
1	Syrian	7	F	...do	1	22	Father	Cured and admitted.
1	Armenian	21	F	...do	4	20	Relatives	Do.
1	Hebrew	7	M	...do	2	24	...do	Do.
1	...do	7	F	...do	1	3	...do	Do.
1	Syrian	17	F	...do	5	28	Red Cross Society.	Under treatment.
1	...do	20	F	...do	5	3	Relatives	Futile; deported.
1	Arabian	13	M	...do	4	17	Father, Government.	Payment defaulted; deported.
1	Italian	9	F	...do	5	26	Father	Under treatment.
1	...do	9	M	...do	4	6	...do	Do.
1	Brazilian	24	M	Gonorrhœa	1	4	Brazilian consul.	Cured and admitted.
1	Italian	8	M	Trachoma	7	24	Relatives	Under treatment.
1	Greek	20	F	...do	1	17	...do	Do.
1	Hebrew	14	M	...do	1	17	Father	Do.
1	Italian	9	F	...do	11	25	...do	Do.
1	...do	15	F	...do	6		...do	Do.
1	Syrian	9	M	...do	7	14	Relatives	Do.
1	Lithuanian	9	M	...do		25	Father	Do.
1	Hebrew	37	F	...do		6	Husband	Do.
1	Italian	29	M	...do	3	20	Relatives	Payment defaulted; deported.

BALTIMORE.

1 1	Hebrew	8	F	Favus	21		Parents and bondsmen	Under treatment.
1 1	...do	11	M	...do	18		Father	Cured and admitted.
1 1	...do	10	M	...do	11	13	Friends	Do.
1 3	...do	{11,9 / 6}	2 F., 1 M	...do	18		...do	Do.
1 2	German	10,5	M., F	Trachoma	8		Father	Do.
1 1	Hebrew	9	M	...do	9		...do	Do.
1 3	...do	{15, / 9}	2 M., 1 F	...do	10	16	...do	Do.
1 2	German	10,8	M., F	...do	7		Friends	Do.
1	Polish	35	F	...do		16	...do	Do.
3	Hebrew	{8,7 / 4}	2 F., 1 M	Tinea tonsurans	12		Father	Under treatment.
1	Polish	26	F	Trachoma	11		Husband	Do.
2	Bohemian	6,4	F	Favus	2	29	Father	Cured and admitted.
1	Polish	6	M	Trachoma	8	21	Parents and bondsmen	Under treatment.
2	...do	11,7	M	Tinea tonsurans	9	2	Father and bondsmen	Do.
1	German	20	M	Trachoma	3	18	Father	Cured and admitted.

¹ Pending from last year.

CASES IN WHICH HOSPITAL TREATMENT WAS GRANTED UNDER SECTIONS 19 AND 37 OF THE IMMIGRATION LAW, FISCAL YEAR ENDED JUNE 30, 1913—Continued.

BOSTON.

Aliens.	Race.	Age.	Sex.	Disease.	Length of treatment.	By whom expenses paid.	Final disposition.
		Yrs.			*M. D.*		
¹1	English	5	M	Tinea tonsurans	5 2	Father	Cured and admitted.
1	Syrian	11	M	Trachoma	3 7	Mother	Payment defaulted; deported.
1	Hebrew	11	F	....do	10 21	Father	Under treatment.
1	Portuguese	8	M	Tinea tonsurans	10 13	...do	Futile; deported.

PHILADELPHIA.

Aliens.	Race.	Age.	Sex.	Disease.	Length of treatment.	By whom expenses paid.	Final disposition.
¹1	Polish	40	F	Trachoma	16	Husband	Cured and admitted.
¹1	....do	9	F	....do	16	Father	Do.
¹1	Hebrew	8	M	....do	24		Do.
¹1	....do	8	M	....do	16	Brother	Do.
1	Italian	20	M	Tuberculosis		Relatives	Escaped from hospital, surrendered by bondsmen, and deported.
1	German	16	M	Trachoma	16	Sister	Cured and admitted.
1	Polish	11	F	....do	24	Brother	Do.
1	Syrian	7	M	....do	17	Father	Do.
1	Armenian	6	M	....do	19	Uncle	Do.
1	Hebrew	18	M	....do	10	Father	Do.
1	German	30	M	....do	18	Self	Do.
1	Syrian	6	M	....do	17	Mother	Do.
1	German	11	F	....do	13	Uncle	Do.
1	....do	3	F	....do	24	....do	Do.
1	....do	2	M	....do	24	....do	Do.
1	Polish	17	M	....do	19	Father	Do.
1	....do	15	F	....do	17	....do	Do.
1	Hebrew	10	F	....do	10	....do	Do.
1	....do	10	M	....do	17	....dc	Do.
1	....do	11	F	....do	15	....do	Do.
1	....do	20	F	....do	14	Cousin	Do.
1	Polish	27	F	....do	12	Husband	Do.
1	Hebrew	10	M	....do	15	Father	Do.
1	....do	10	M	....do	16	....do	Do.
1	Polish	10	F	....do	23	....do	Do.
1	Italian	16	M	....do	20	Brother	Do.
1	Russian	28	M	....do	17	....do	Do.
1	Hebrew	11	M	....do	15	Mother	Do.
1	....do	10	F	....do	15	Brother	Do.
1	....do	19	M	....do	18	....do	Do.
1	Italian	10	F	....do	17	Uncle	Do.
1	Hebrew	45	M	....do	14	Daughter	Do.
1	....do	8	F	....do	16	Brother	Do.
1	German	19	M	....do	20	Friend	Do.
1	....do	11	F	....do	19	Father	Do.
1	Hebrew	3	F	....do	19	....do	Do.
1	Polish	9	M	....do	18	....do	Do.
1	German	43	M	....do	15	Wife	Do.
1	Syrian	15	M	....do	14	Father	Do.
1	Polish	28	M	....do	24	Cousin	Do.
1	German	33	F	....do	17	Brother-in-law.	Do.
1	....do	10	M	....do	17	Uncle	Do.
1	....do	7	M	....do	17	....do	Do.
1	....do	22	M	....do	15	....do	Do.
1	....do	17	F	....do	15	....do	Do.
1	Lithuanian	14	M	....do	16	Father	Do.
1	....do	9	M	....do	16	....do	Do.
1	Hebrew	8	M	....do	19	....do	Do.
1	....do	30	F	....do	9	Husband	Do.
1	Polish	30	F	....do	16	....do	Do.
1	German	25	F	....do	19	Intended husband.	Do.
1	....do	8	F	....do	19	Intended stepfather.	Do.
1	Polish	9	F	....do	15	Father	Do.
1	Italian	14	F	....do	12	Mother	Do.

¹ Pending from last year.

CASES IN WHICH HOSPITAL TREATMENT WAS GRANTED UNDER SECTIONS 19 AND 37 OF THE IMMIGRATION LAW, FISCAL YEAR ENDED JUNE 30, 1913—Continued.

NEW ORLEANS.

Aliens.	Race.	Age.	Sex.	Disease.	Length of treatment.	By whom expenses paid.	Final disposition.
		Yrs.			M. D.		
[1] 1	Syrian.....	15	F.......	Trachoma..........	12	Father....	Under treatment.
[1] 1	Hebrew.....	15	M.........	.....do............	3 12	...do......	Cured and admitted.
1	....do.....	16	M.........	.....do............	5 15	...do......	Do.
1	Syrian.....	16	M.........	.....do............	6	...do......	Under treatment.

GALVESTON.

[1] 1	Bohemian...	48	F.......	Trachoma..........	2 24	Son-in-law.	Cured and admitted.

SAN FRANCISCO.

	Male.	Female.	Total.
Aliens treated for uncinariasis (hookworm):[2]			
Japanese......	96	377	473
Chinese......	339	20	359
Hindu......	6	....	6
Aliens treated for trachoma:[2]			
Japanese......	10	11	21
Chinese......	12	2	14
Total......	463	410	[3] 873

SEATTLE.

	Male.	Female.	Total.
Aliens treated for uncinariasis (hookworm):			
Japanese......	41	296	337
Chinese......	21	....	21
Hindu......	1	....	1
Aliens treated for trachoma:			
Japanese......	....	2	2
Total......	63	298	[3] 361

[1] Pending from last year.
[2] Average length of treatment for trachoma, 1.8 weeks; for uncinariasis, 1.5 weeks.
[3] In two of the above cases the same patient was treated for both trachoma and uncinariasis.

From an analysis of the figures for New York, which may be said to represent average conditions, it will be observed that of the 42 cases reported (involving 45 aliens) 18 were cured and the aliens landed, while 16 are still under treatment, and in 8 cases treatment was found to be futile or the relatives became unable or unwilling to bear further expenses. The average length of time required to effect a cure in the 18 cases wherein that result was attained was 4 months. Among the cases still pending 1 has now been treated for over 16 months; 2 for over 12 months; 2 from 10 to 12 months; and 6 for 5 months or more, and it is impossible to state how much longer treatment will have to be continued in order to effect cures; while 6 of the 8 cases deported had been under treatment from 5 to 11 months. The above clearly shows that in many of the cases it would have been more satisfactory to all concerned to have insisted that the aliens return to their native countries for treatment, where it can be secured at home or in public clinics at a less cost than at our hospitals.   When the privilege of undergoing treatment has once been accorded and the funds available to the aliens or their friends have been exhausted, the service finds itself in a somewhat embarrassing position, and the aliens are much worse off than they would have been had their petition been denied.   Moreover, denial of such petitions materially aids good administration by discouraging aliens and steamship lines from taking action which produces these embarrassing cases.[1]

. It will be noted that at Philadelphia, where 55 cases of trachoma were under treatment during the year, "cures" were effected much more rapidly than elsewhere.   In most of those cases the "grattage operation" for the "radical cure" of trachoma was performed.   Surgeons located at other ports do not advocate the use of said operation; and the bureau, from all the information it has so far been able to obtain, is exceedingly skeptical concerning these so-called cures.

ALIENS EXCLUDABLE OR SUBJECT TO DEPORTATION ON ECONOMIC GROUNDS.

Aliens who by the terms of the law fall under this heading consist of those found on arrival to be paupers, persons likely to become a public charge, contract laborers, induced immigrants, and assisted immigrants.   Unlike those discussed under the two preceding headings, they are undesirable principally for economic reasons, ranging all the way from interference with labor conditions in this country to becoming a burden on the taxpayers thereof.

One of the chief objections to an abnormally large immigration is the effect it has upon the American standard of wages and living obtaining among the laboring classes, both skilled and unskilled. As the economic welfare of a country must be measured ultimately to a very large degree by the success of its laboring classes, it is a patriotic appreciation of this axiom rather than selfishness that makes the laboring elements and those interested in their behalf, advocates of restriction of immigration.

PAUPERS AND ALIENS LIKELY TO BECOME PUBLIC CHARGES.

The rejection of paupers and persons likely to become public charges is based upon the principle that the State and municipal governments in this country ought not to maintain, at the expense of their taxpayers, the indigent and destitute belonging to other countries.   In the view of the law it makes no difference whether the aliens are actually paupers when they are brought here or become such within so short a time after entry as to show that their destitution here is the result, not of local conditions and environment, but of their own inherent inability to maintain themselves.   Formerly the period within which deportation to country of origin could be effected if an alien became a public charge was fixed at one year. Since 1903 it has been fixed at three years.   In view of the extent to which immigration has increased, even three years falls considerably short of what might be regarded a reasonable time limit within

---

[1] In connection with the foregoing, so much of the reports of the commissioners at New York and Baltimore as relates to hospital treatment should be read (Appendix III, pp. 180-187 and 194-199).

which it could be held that the public-charge status was the result of conditions existing prior to entry; and the bureau has suggested on several occasions that the time should be increased. It should be raised at least to correspond to the period of residence required under the naturalization law, to wit, five years.

In the fiscal year 1913, 7,941 aliens, or about 40 per cent of the entire number rejected, were excluded at United States ports as likely to become public charges, compared with 8,152, or 51 per cent, in 1912 (Table XVII, pp. 106–109). Moreover, in 1913, 714 aliens who had become public charges were arrested and deported, while 1,262 others were removed from the country on the ground that they were likely to become public charges at the time of admission (a fact not then discovered)—a total of 1,976 (Table XVIII, pp. 110–113). Under rule 24 of the immigration regulations 8 aliens were removed to their native countries at their own request and in accordance with authority conferred by the statute upon the Commissioner General to extend assistance and protection to admitted aliens (Table XVIII, pp. 110–113). The advantages derived from this rule are that the communities in which the aliens have become public charges are relieved of the burden of their maintenance, and simultaneously the desire of the alien to be repatriated is satisfied. These were, of course, cases in which it appeared that the causes of the aliens' distress had arisen subsequent to entry.

ALIEN CONTRACT LABORERS.

The debarment during the past fiscal year of 1,624 alien contract laborers (Table XVII, pp. 106–109) compared with 1,333 in 1912, and the arrest and expulsion from the United States of 54 such aliens (Table XVIII, pp. 110–113), compared with 31 in 1912, is only a very meager indication of the good work which has been done under the provision of law relating to this subject.

If space permitted, there could be incorporated at this point (as was done in several of the former reports of the bureau) a number of concrete illustrations showing not only the facts that led to the deportation of the aliens involved, but valuable results attained in the courts, where many prosecutions and suits have been brought, with varying but on the whole satisfactory results. No pains are spared with a view to see that these provisions of the law relating to contract laborers are given effect to the end that the protection Congress has provided shall be extended to the laborers, skilled and unskilled, resident in this country. There are now engaged exclusively upon the work of enforcing these particular provisions of the law 16 inspectors, employed in accordance with section 24 of the immigration act, and, of course, all of the regular inspectors enforce said provisions as well as the other provisions of the law.

It should be stated here that during the past fiscal year fines have been collected under the alien contract labor provisions which almost equaled the $50,000 specially appropriated for this purpose under section 24 of the act.

It is sometimes found advisable in cases in which suit has been instituted to recover the statutory penalty for violating the alien contract labor provisions to compromise with the defendants. In agreeing to compromises of this nature all the facts are carefully considered and the compromise is not authorized unless this bureau, with the approval of the Secretary and the Department of Justice conclude that substantial justice will be administered. The principal determinative factors are: (a) Whether the violation was deliberate and premeditated, or unintentional and technical; (b) whether the sum offered in compromise practically equals the statutory penalty, less the expense which the Government would have to incur in pressing the suit to trial; (c) whether the case is in such condition, with respect to possibility of introducing evidence, etc., as to make a compromise advisable from the Government's point of view. In illustration of this, the bureau might mention the case of Francis Willey & Co., a manufacturing concern of New England, by which a number of aliens were imported, the suit against which was compromised by accepting the sum of $20,000 from the firm, a number of the aliens involved being deported.

INDUCED IMMIGRATION.

Vigilance to prevent the entry of the induced classes of immigration has not been relaxed in the least during the past year; and many of the 7,941 shown (Table XVII) to have been excluded as likely to become a public charge, as well as of the 1,624 rejected as contract laborers, fell within said classes. But, notwithstanding the continuous efforts to detect cases of this kind, it is confidently believed that many of the aliens who gain admission really belong to the induced classes. The inducement is not always an offer of employment by a transportation company or others selfishly intending to exploit the immigrant, but frequently is merely the extension of financial assistance—mentioned more particularly under the next heading—or the raising of false hopes in the alien's breast, or even an incident to efforts, not of the alien himself but of some person or organization interested in him. And here is found the origin of one of the most difficult tasks of the Immigration Service, as it is not always possible to show by the actual production of evidence that the inducement to the immigrant has been an offer or promise of employment. If our immigration is to be kept upon a natural, unstimulated plane—and such is the evident purpose and spirit of the law—the law must be made to reach these branches of induced immigration as well as that induced directly by a promise of employment. In other words, our immigration should be voluntary—the result of a personal desire on the part of the alien to better his condition—and all inducements to immigrants not strictly of a family nature should be discouraged or absolutely prohibited.

ASSISTED IMMIGRATION.

If a corporation, association, society, municipality, or foreign Government assists an alien to immigrate, by either direct or indirect means, the alien is excluded by the terms of the law. Assistance by an individual merely operates to place the alien in a situation where his proofs of eligibility to enter must be of an affirmative and satisfactory nature. The law regards assisted immigration as undesirable,

7686°—14——2

not only because assistance is another means and method of induce-ment, but because, generally speaking, the fact that an alien has to be assisted to meet the comparatively small expense involved in immigrating under modern conditions carries with it an imputation of penury and undesirableness. Nevertheless, a great deal of the present-day immigration is of this assisted character. Thus of the aliens who entered during the past fiscal year, 811,151 claimed to have paid their own passage, while 375,947 stated that their passage had been paid by relatives, and 10,794 that it had been paid by persons other than relatives. In the previous fiscal year the corre-sponding figures were 536,802, 289,657, and 11,713. While informa-tion obtained as this is can not be regarded as absolutely reliable, the percentage of inaccuracy therein is not sufficient to destroy the value of the figures, and it may be safely assumed that the statistics under-state rather than overstate the number of aliens assisted. It will be observed that according to these figures over 32 per cent of the immi-gration during the past year was assisted, compared with 36 per cent in the fiscal year 1912; 33⅓ per cent in 1911, and 25 per cent in 1910.

So far as the figures given above merely illustrate the kindness and philanthropy of aliens living in this country in sending for relatives or friends poorly situated abroad, they constitute a cred-itable fact; but that is not the principal point involved, which is that they show that a considerable part of our immigration is of a class that could not migrate at all unless aided by relatives or friends already here or by others interested to obtain the services of the aliens at wages lower than the American standard. Of course, where the assistance is extended by, an individual, exclusion is never based solely on that fact, but the assisted alien is merely required to make an affirmative showing, which frequently he can easily do. But where the assistance is rendered by a corporation or other like con-cern or is merely a part of a plan to induce and stimulate immigra-tion, it is given great weight in enforcing the law, and is usually considered sufficient of itself to exclude.

Assistance of immigration and inducement thereof are clearly re-lated subjects, and if our immigration is to be kept upon a healthful voluntary plane assistance other than that of a strictly family nature should be prohibited, and even where an alien located here sends for a relative and pays his passage, admission, if otherwise admissible, should occur only upon a very clear showing that the alien will be able to get along in the United States, or upon bond in proper instances where any doubt exists.

NATURALIZATION.

Under the act of Congress establishing the Department of Labor the branch of the Government service charged with the duty of enforcing the naturalization laws, which was formerly a division of this bureau, has been made a separate bureau, the title of the chief thereof having been changed to Commissioner of Naturalization. The prac-tice heretofore obtaining of publishing the report of that officer as an appendix to the report of this bureau is of course abandoned, and for information regarding all naturalization questions reference should be had to the report of the Commissioner of Naturalization, which, under the law, will be published separately. The bureau proper, at any rate, never took an active part in the enforcement of those laws, but left the conduct of the division almost entirely to the supervision of the chief thereof, and the provision of law constituting the division a separate bureau is welcomed as a wise adjustment of the public business.

DISTRIBUTION OF IMMIGRANTS.

With respect to the distribution of aliens, attention is directed to the report of the Chief of the Division of Information, printed as Appendix II hereof. This is a very important phase of the immigration problem. There can be no question but that many of the evils that grow out of our present excessive immigration would be remedied, or at least alleviated, if the congestion of aliens in our large centers of population could be broken up. Distribution of admitted aliens, therefore, even from this standpoint, is a thing much to be desired. Moreover, there are still certain sections of the United States that need accretions to their population, especially of laboring classes, more particularly of those who will work on the farms. If some detailed plan could be devised whereby aliens could be directed to those places without disturbing labor conditions elsewhere, a great good would be accomplished. Three chief difficulties exist, however, to the success of plans of this kind: (1) The labor required is to a considerable extent merely seasonal, and usually neither aliens no more than natives care to go to any great distance to accept temporary employment even though high wages are offered; (2) opportunities for using any plans having in view the distribution of foreign laborers are always more or less open to the objection that labor conditions, already uncertain in many ways, are disturbed by any action that involves artificial interference with the "natural operation" of the law of supply and demand; (3) in many sections of the country in need of immigration to aid development of agricultural and promote other industrial pursuits, the desire seems to be for settlers who will invest in lands and establish homes rather than for laborers.

It will be seen from the report of the Chief of the Division of Information that, along certain conservatively restricted lines, considerable has been accomplished, despite the aforementioned difficulties, toward placing admitted aliens advantageously to themselves and to others concerned.

JAPANESE IMMIGRATION.

The general provisions of the immigration law apply to Japanese in the same manner as to all other aliens. Separate statistics are kept of Japanese only so far as some special provisions of the law regarding alien laborers leaving their native countries with passports of a limited nature make the keeping of such statistics necessary and desirable. A proviso to section 1 of the immigration act authorized the President, whenever satisfied that passports issued by any foreign Government to its citizens to go to any country other than the United States are being used for the purpose of enabling the holders to come to the continental territory of the United States to the detriment of labor conditions therein, to refuse to permit such foreign laborers to enter the continental territory of the United

States. The President's proclamation on this subject was reissued, in slightly revised form, on February 24, 1913, and reads as follows:

Whereas, by the act entitled "An act to regulate the immigration of aliens into the United States," approved February 20, 1907, whenever the President is satisfied that passports issued by any foreign Government to its citizens to go to any country other than the United States or to any insular possession of the United States or to the Canal Zone, are being used for the purpose of enabling the holders to come to the continental territory of the United States to the detriment of labor conditions therein, it is made the duty of the President to refuse to permit such citizens of the country issuing such passports to enter the continental territory of the United States from such country or from such insular possession or from the Canal Zone;

And whereas, upon sufficient evidence produced before me by the Department of Commerce and Labor, I am satisfied that passports issued by certain foreign Governments to their citizens or subjects who are laborers, skilled or unskilled, to proceed to countries or places other than the continental territory of the United States, are being used for the purpose of enabling the holders thereof to come to the continental territory of the United States to the detriment of labor conditions therein;

I hereby order that such alien laborers, skilled or unskilled, be refused permission to enter the continental territory of the United States.

It is further ordered that the Secretary of (Commerce and) Labor be, and he hereby is, directed to take, through the Bureau of Immigration and Naturalization, such measures and to make and enforce such rules and regulations as may be necessary to carry this order into effect.

For purposes of easy comparison the plan followed in previous reports in presenting comment on the statistics regarding Japanese immigration is again adopted here:

Table A shows an increase in the number of Japanese admitted to both the continent and the Territory of Hawaii. However, the figures shown by said table should be compared also with those for 1908, the first year the system under the proclamation and Rule 11 of the Immigration Regulations and understanding with Japan became operative, in which year 9,544 Japanese were admitted to continental United States and 8,694 to Hawaii, with 643 debarred at the ports of the former and 60 at the ports of the latter. In 1911 the corresponding figures were 4,282, 2,159, 46, and 34; while those for 1912 were 5,358, 3,231, 103, and 63, respectively, and those for 1913 are 6,771, 4,901, 88, and 180. Therefore, the number of Japanese admitted to the mainland and Hawaii, respectively, in 1913 was about 71 and 56 per cent of the number for the year 1908, and about 26 and 52 per cent, respectively, more than the number shown for 1912.

Table B furnishes a means of comparing the immigration and emigration of Japanese in 1912 with that of the past year, by months.

Table C gives in some detail the occupations of Japanese who have entered and left the country during the year, divided roughly into professional, skilled, miscellaneous, which includes common laborers and those having no occupations (including women and children). The total number admitted to the mainland, for each of these classes, respectively, is 309, 301, 3,477, and 2,684; to Hawaii, 209, 126, 4,062, and 504.

A comparison of the records of Japanese immigration and emigration kept by the bureau with similar records compiled by the Japanese Government is given in Table D. The variation between this and other tables is partially explained by the fact that this table is compiled from records of embarkation and debarkation, whereas the others relate to entries and departures recorded at United States ports

Table E shows that during the past year 6,859 Japanese applied for admission to continental United States, of whom 6,771 were admitted and 88 debarred. Of the total number applying, 6,715 were and 144 were not in possession of proper passports. Of the 6,715 holding proper passports, 6,673 were found on examination to belong to the classes entitled by the understanding to receive passports and the remaining 42 were found on examination not to fall within such classes. The 6,673 entitled to passports consisted of 2,837 former residents, 3,083 parents, wives, and children of residents, and 739 new arrivals, who were nonlaborers, together with 14 settled agriculturists. The 42 in possession of passports, although apparently not entitled thereto, were found to be laborers and not to be former residents, parents, wives, or children of residents, or settled agriculturists. Of the 6,859 applying for admission, 4,087 were males, and 2,772 were females. Of those applying for admission on the claim of relationship, 44 were "parents," 642 were "children," and 2,397 were "wives" of residents. Of the passports presented, 1,192 gave the holders' occupation as of a nonlaboring character, 184 gave such occupation as laboring, and 5,339 failed to state occupation. This table also furnishes other interesting pertinent details regarding the passports and the aliens presenting them, which it is not necessary to emphasize in the text.

Information similar to the above regarding the Territory of Hawaii is supplied by Table F. During the year 5,081 Japanese applied at Honolulu, 4,901 of whom were admitted and 180 debarred. All but 12 of the 5,081 applicants had passports. Of the 5,069 holding passports, 4,902 were entitled thereto under the definitions set forth in the table and 167 were found upon examination not to fall within such definitions. Of the 4,902 entitled to passports, 1,281 were former residents and 3,621 were parents, wives, or children of residents. The 167 not entitled to passports consisted of 20 laborers and 147 nonlaborers who were neither former residents nor parents, wives, or children of residents.

Of the total number of Japanese shown by Tables E and F to have been admitted to the country during the year (11,672), 6,237 were nonlaborers and 5,435 were laborers.

In connection with the statistics similar to the foregoing furnished in the last annual report, particular attention was directed to the fact that 4,328, or over 50 per cent, of the Japanese admitted during 1912 were females. During the past year 5,484, or 47 per cent, of those admitted were females. The following contained in the last annual report on this subject needs to be repeated and emphasized:

Many of these were what are known as "proxy" or "photograph" brides, i. e., women who have been married, under a custom existing and recognized as legal in Japan, to men living in this country whom in many instances they have never seen, the marriage being arranged between the heads of the families of the bride and bridegroom. Of the aliens treated in hospital for dangerous contagious diseases, mentioned under a previous heading of this report (p. 7), 681 were Japanese females,[1] the majority of whom were "proxy" or "photograph" brides. Passports are given these women on the ground that they are coming to continental United States to join a husband, the arrangement with Japan contemplating that where a Japanese laborer is migrating for the purpose of joining a member of his immediate family the passport may be issued. Most of the women, while they do join the husband, are farm laborers and immediately become colaborers with their husbands on the farms where

---

[1] The figures for this year are 684.

the latter are employed or which they are conducting. As these "proxy" or "photograph" marriages would not, of course, be recognized as valid in any of the States of this country, the men to whom these women are going are required to meet them at a seaport and go through a ceremony of marriage legal in the United States. * * * But the bureau feels that two facts growing out of this situation should not be overlooked by those interested in the economic phases of the immigration problem: (1) The practice of furnishing the passport to these women and admitting them on the basis of the passport and a marriage performed at the port opens the way for the introduction into continental United States of large bodies of common laborers—females, it is true, but none the less competitors of the laborers of this country; and (2) this practice must necessarily result in constituting a large native-born Japanese population—persons who, because of their birth on American soil, will be regarded as American citizens, although their parents can not be naturalized, and who, nevertheless, will be considered (and will probably consider themselves) subjects of the Empire of Japan under the laws of that country, which holds that children born abroad of parents who are Japanese subjects are themselves subjects of the Japanese Empire.[1]

CHINESE EXCLUSION.

To understand and appreciate how inadequate are the so-called Chinese-exclusion laws to prevent the entry of Chinese laborers to the United States it is only necessary to examine and analyze the statistics on this subject furnished in Tables 1 to 8 (pp. 142–148). All possible under existing law is done to prevent the entry of Chinese not entitled to be in the United States; but despite these efforts Chinese laborers are constantly gaining admission, in the guise of "minor sons of merchants," "students," "natives," or "sons of natives." There is no doubt that a considerable number of those shown by the tables to have entered under these designations were, as a matter of fact, not what they claimed to be, but laborers desirous of earning a livelihood here despite the prohibition of the law. When the laborer is old or ignorant, or otherwise unable fraudulently to assume a "lawful" status, smuggling across the land boundaries or from ships on which they are employed as "seamen" is resorted to. There seems to be no lack of money with which to carry out these schemes, however costly they may be. Under these circumstances, it can readily be seen that the enforcement of the law becomes a very difficult matter.

In Table 1 a comparison is made between the number of Chinese applying for admission during the years 1908 to 1913 inclusive. In the past year 5,662 Chinese were admitted, as compared with 5,374 in 1912, 5,107 in 1911, 5,950 in 1910, 6,395 in 1909, and 4,624 in 1908, the admissions for the past year being 5.3 per cent greater than for the preceding year, 11 per cent greater than for 1911, 4.8 per cent less than for 1910, 11 per cent less than for 1909, and 22 per cent greater than for 1908. In the past year 384 Chinese were deported, as against 400 in the preceding year, 692 in 1911, 969 in 1910, 564 in 1909, 364 in 1908, and 259 in 1907.

[1] The foregoing views of Commissioner General Keefe seem to the signer of this report especially significant, for they are the result of the retiring Commissioner General's experience in the enforcement of the law and are in exact accord with the writer's observations, both before and since his induction into office. The writer desires, however, to state that he does not agree with the notion that any such marriage is binding upon the United States in the administration of immigration laws; and also that there is no treaty with Japan, or other arrangement whatsoever, that provides for the recognition by the United States of the so-called marriage of a woman in Japan with a man who may be in the United States at the alleged date of the same. The doctrine of *lex loci*, in his judgment, is not applicable to cases of this kind for the above reason, as well as that such marriage is not consummated entirely and completely in the country permitting it, as it is apparent that a part of the so-called marriage is initiated in one jurisdiction or nation, and it is completed in another and entirely foreign jurisdiction or nation. Further comments on this, as well as other matters connected with Japanese immigration, is deferred owing to his brief incumbency.

In Table 2 will be found a statement of the disposition, preliminary and final, of every application of a Chinese for admission. New applications to the number of 6,250 were made during the year, and 242 were pending from the previous year, a total of 6,492. Of these 5,594 were admitted at the ports, 67 by the department on appeal, and 1 by the courts, a total of 5,662, while 384 were deported, 1 escaped, and 445 remain pending. The recapitulation by ports given at the bottom of Table 2 shows that 3,896 Chinese arrived at San Francisco, 1,286 at Seattle, 407 at Vancouver, and 797 at Honolulu, the balance being scattering cases at ports of less importance.

Of the section 6 exempt classes, 559 applied for admission, compared with 809 in the preceding year. Of these only 28 were deported. The applicants were composed of 122 merchants, 345 students, 33 teachers, and 19 travelers, together with 40 officials who are for convenience placed in this class. The number of "students" applying increased from 247 in 1911 to 477 in 1912, but in the past year dropped back to 345. No one would dispute the propriety and advisability of permitting young men of the Chinese race to obtain a higher education in this country, provided the privilege is so safeguarded as to prevent its abuse. But this claim of a student status, now adopted much more frequently than formerly, is often used as a mere cloak for the introduction into this country, in violation of the spirit of the law, of young Chinese laborers. The difficulty is that many of these so-called students have actually been engaged in study in China, and it is really intended by them, and by the good but often misled people who take an interest in having them brought to this country, that they shall enter institutions of learning in the United States; indeed, they usually do take up a course of study after arrival here, but soon leave the institution in which placed and remove to distant localities, where they enter laboring pursuits or join relatives or clansmen who are engaged in conducting stores or restaurants, and live with them and attend the public day or night schools, working for their living during such time as they are not intermittently engaged in study. The law never intended that young Chinese laborers should come to this country for any such purpose as this, and the bureau is determined that, to the fullest extent possible, such evasions of the law shall be prevented.

It is shown by Table 2 that 1,011 domiciled merchants applied for readmission, 14 cases having been pending from the previous year, making a total of 1,025, of whom 986 were admitted, 13 deported, and 1 escaped, while 26 remain pending. Of those claiming to be "minor sons of merchants," 583 entered and 86 were deported. Of "wives of merchants," 179 applied, 155 being admitted and 6 deported; while of "wives of natives," 158 applications were considered, in 126 of which admission was ordered and in 9 deportation effected.

Table 3 contains a special discussion of the "United States citizen" class, which falls into two general divisions—(1) those of native birth and (2) those born abroad of native-born parents. Of these there were admitted 2,048 (about 36 per cent of all Chinese entering), of whom 1,553 belong to the first, and 495 to the second. In 1912 the corresponding figures were 1,396 and 258, respectively. The 1,553 belonging to the first division are segregated further into 241 of whose claimed departure from this country there was no record (raw natives), and 1,312 of whose departure there was a record (returning natives). Of the latter, status had been determined previously in 1,080 and was determined for the first time in 232 cases. The number of Chinese adjudicated "citizens" for the first time therefore was 968, compared with 585 for the previous year, 534 for 1911, and 1,295 for 1910. In this connection, it should be noted from Table 6 that of the Chinese arrested and brought before courts or court commissioners during the past year 117 were discharged, practically all on the claim of birth in the United States. The corresponding figures for 1912, 1911, and 1910 are 108, 156, and 190, respectively. It should also be noted from Table 2 that 126 alleged wives of natives were admitted, compared with 88 in 1912, 80 in 1911, and 109 in 1910. Adding these several sets of figures relating to admissions as United States citizens and wives of citizens, it will be observed that the total is 4,356, or an average of 1,089 per year for the four years compared. Thus it may be demonstrated that the number of United States citizens of the Chinese race is increasing at a very rapid rate, although persons of the Mongolian race can not acquire citizenship by naturalization.

The present law permitting United States commissioners to make citizens should be repealed. American citizenship is a proud privilege of inestimable value and of the highest dignity and should not be granted except upon clear evidence of right thereto and the title to same passed upon either by a court of record or by the Bureau of Immigration, with the approval of the Department of Labor.

Table 4 shows that during the past year 245 appeals of Chinese were considered by the department, in 178 of which the decisions of the officers of the ports were sustained and in 67 overruled.

Table 5 presents a concise summary of the granting of return certificates to Chinese residents of this country who applied for the privilege of going abroad with the assurance of prompt admission on return. Applications for these certificates to the number of 3,163 were submitted, divided into 1,261 natives, 1,055 exempts, and 847 laborers, of which applications the officers at the ports of proposed departure granted 2,996 and denied 167. Of those denied 55 appealed, 10 of the appeals being sustained and 45 dismissed by the bureau. During the year, therefore, return certificates were refused in 157 cases (of which 75 were natives, 62 exempts, and 20 laborers) and granted in 3,006 cases (1,186 natives, 993 exempts, and 827 laborers).

Tables 6 and 7 are compiled from statements furnished by United States marshals. During the year 191 Chinese were arrested on judicial warrants, compared with 616 in the fiscal year 1912. There remained pending from the previous year 371 cases, so that the total number of cases considered was 562. These were disposed of as follows: In 12, Chinese died or escaped; in 117, the court or commissioner ordered defendants' discharge; in 165, deportation was ordered; and 268 cases remain pending. Table 7 shows that, as in previous years, most of the arrests were made in districts contiguous to the land boundaries or readily reached therefrom. That deportation orders were obtained in so large a percentage of the cases as here shown (59 per cent of those actually brought to trial) is due mainly to this fact; for experience has demonstrated that it is extremely difficult to obtain orders of deportation in the cases of Chinese arrested at interior points, where it is not easy to persuade a United States commissioner that a Chinese has entered the country in violation of law, or, even if the Government is successful in proving such a case before a commissioner, in the interim between the issuance by him of an order of deportation and the rehearing of the case (de novo) before a district judge, the Chinese manage to manufacture enough evidence to insure discharge. It is recommended, for the reasons above set forth, that all proceedings of this nature shall be conducted in the United States courts or by the Bureau of Immigration, with the approval of the Department of Labor.

In connection with these tables, attention should be directed to Table XVIII (pp. 110–113), from which it will be observed that during the last fiscal year 409 aliens of the Chinese race were arrested and deported under the immigration law without resort to the provisions of the exclusion laws. These figures show that the decision finally obtained in 1912 from the Supreme Court of the United States, to the effect that Chinese, like all other aliens, who enter surreptitiously are subject to deportation by the administrative process provided in the general immigration laws (Wong You v. United States, 223 U. S., 67), is now producing most valuable results. Incidentally, also, these figures partly explain why there has been a decrease in arrests of Chinese before United States commissioners from 616 in 1912 to 191 in 1913; i. e., this decrease, so far as it is not offset by the increase in arrests of Chinese under the administrative process from 185 in 1912 to 409 in 1913, is due largely to the discouragement of smuggling operations incident to the more summary and effective enforcement of the law possible under the administrative method of arrest, hearing, and deportation. To justify proceeding under the immigration law, however, it must appear that three years have not elapsed since the alien Chinese entered unlawfully, and a full measure of success in the enforcement of the exclusion laws need not be expected unless and until Congress adopts the recommendations so often urged by the bureau, that those laws be consolidated with the general immigration act, and the three-year limitation on the right to deport removed in so far as it affects Chinese.

When the limitations of the existing law are understood and appreciated, a review of the year's work is not altogether discouraging, notwithstanding the disclosures of the statistics regarding the admission of Chinese claiming American citizenship, already alluded to, so many of which claims are false in the belief of our officers, but the Government, owing to the peculiar conditions surrounding cases of this kind, often finds itself helpless.

Table 8 is presented this year for the first time. In it are furnished some interesting items of information that can not conveniently be furnished in the same form in the preceding tables. The only items thereof needing any special comment are those regarding Chinese granted the privilege of proceeding through the United States, in bond, in transit to nearby countries. Such privilege was allowed 2,944 Chinese and denied 270 during the year. As many Chinese secure this privilege with the ulterior purpose of gaining unlawful entry to the United States from the near-by country to which ostensibly emigrating, it may soon become necessary materially to curtail said privilege and to hedge it about with additional safeguards.[1]

---

[1] In connection with the foregoing regarding enforcement of the Chinese-exclusion laws, see reports of the commissioners at Montreal, Seattle, and San Francisco and of the supervising inspector, El Paso (Appendix III, pp. 167–178, 224–236, 237–242, and 250–255.)

CERTIFICATES OF RESIDENCE.

Copies of the certificates of residence issued under the registration acts of 1892 and 1893 are on file in the bureau. Verification was had of the certificates presented by the 847 Chinese laborers shown by Table 5 to have applied for return certificates during the year and of many others desired for use as evidence in cases pending in court or elsewhere, and it was necessary to furnish for like purposes a large number of certified copies of duplicate certificates or of applications therefor, while under the provisions of rules 20 and 21 of the Chinese regulations applications for certificates of residence were considered and disposed of as follows:

Cases pending	95
Cases reopened	12
Applications	175
Total	282

Duplicate certificates of residence issued	127
Original certificates found	2
Applications denied	79
Applications dropped	23
Applications pending	51
Total	282

ALIENS EMPLOYED ON VESSELS.

The employment of aliens on vessels entering United States ports, whether such vessels are of American or foreign register, has always led, directly or indirectly, to numerous and flagrant violations of both the immigration and the Chinese-exclusion laws. It will be observed by referring to Table XX (p. 116), that a record has been secured during the past year of the desertion in United States ports of 9,136 alien "seamen." In the fiscal year 1912 a record was made of the desertion of 6,384. These figures are not complete by any means; nor is it possible to state how many of these deserters reshipped, although it is true, of course, that many of them did, for the bona fide sailor does not usually desert with any intent of remaining in the United States otherwise than as a coastwise seaman. But the difficulty arises out of the fact that many aliens who, by reason of being diseased or otherwise objectionable, can not enter in regular manner, ship or are deliberately shipped for a consideration by conniving petty ships' officers, for the purpose of evading inspection under the law, availing themselves of this ready means of landing at our ports undetected. It must be remembered also that Chinese (and other Asiatics as well) are now extensively used to man both steam and sailing vessels. During the year from 35,000 to 40,000 Chinese sailors entered United States ports, and while the regulations require the giving of bonds if such sailors are allowed shore leave in our ports, the rule is honored in the breach as much as in the observance, and in several judicial districts the decisions of the courts have been such as to make its enforcement very difficult.

This subject of deserting foreign seamen calls for very careful consideration by Congress, and as there are now pending before that body several bills affecting the matter directly or indirectly, the bureau offers the following comment upon it, for in its various phases and ramifications it touches the enforcement of the immigration and Chinese-exclusion laws, and the "seamen's bill," on the one hand, and the immigration and Chinese-exclusion laws, on the other, can not be properly enforced unless their terms are brought into substantial and practical accord.

One of the main purposes of the now pending seamen's bill is to place laborers who earn their livelihood by following the sea in a situation where, by eliminating the element of practically involuntary servitude that attaches to the sailor's calling under the laws and customs that have gradually hedged him about, he will be accorded better treatment and better wages and his calling be made more responsive than at present to the economic principle of supply and demand. Its purpose is not limited as to either place or time, but is of world-wide applicability. In other words, the broad and underlying purpose of the seamen's bill—the basis upon which rest all of the minor advantages that it would secure for seafaring men—extends to all quarters of the globe, because the occupation affected is not limited to any particular country, but is the primary element in sea industries, just as the tilling of the soil is the primary element in land industries.

The unloosening of the seafaring man's bonds—bonds that are the result of so extending the "common hazard" principle of life on the high seas as to have it apply where it is not necessary, i. e., while the vessel is in port—and the bringing of the occupation within reach of the rules that govern in all other lines of labor—so far as possible when the "common hazard" principle is accorded its necessary and proper field of action, i. e., the vessel while actually on the high seas—are objects worthy of the Nation that has always stood for liberty, on sea as well as on land, and is becoming more and more interested in the commerce of the world, which can not be carried on successfully and with a proper regard for the Nation's ultimate welfare unless the men whose personal manual labor is the basis thereof are treated in a fair and equitable manner. Therefore, so much of this subject as affects the immigration, alien contract labor, and Chinese-exclusion laws of this country must be adjusted upon broad lines; otherwise a destructive conflict between the several laws will arise.

If the condition and wages of American seamen are to be improved and raised, it is necessary that, either simultaneously or as a close-following result, the condition and wages of European seamen shall also be improved and raised; and if American and European seamen are to be benefited in this manner, there is no escape from the conclusion that aliens from Asiatic countries following the sea must be allowed the same chance to bring themselves and their part of the seafaring occupation up to the same level. Unless this is done, the Chinese, Japanese, and Lascar seamen, already great in numbers, and now working for lower wages than the white sailor, will not only continue to render service for less recompense, but will crowd the labor market, and eventually push the seamen who demand higher compensation out of the seafaring occupations. Moreover, the owners of the vessels on which the sailor must find employment would adopt the flag of the country in which they could man their vessels at the lowest rate, and a further purpose of the seamen's bill, the building up of a merchant marine, would be defeated.

It seems rather immaterial how many alien sailors come to our ports, provided they are free from mental or physical disease, and provided, if they belong to any class regarded under our immigration law and policy as undesirable, they come here about their business only and depart. The chief difficulty in this connection arises from the Chinese, for laborers of that race are absolutely excluded from admission into the United States, and that very fact increases the incentive for, and the profit to be gained from, their surreptitious entry to the country, and one of the favorite modes of entering surreptitiously is to adopt the guise of a seaman. To a certain extent, also, seamen of other Asiatic races fall into the same category as the Chinese.

So far as the European is concerned, while the law has been extensively violated in the past by European aliens of inadmissible classes falsely claiming to be seamen, the difficulty of controlling the situation with respect to them is by no means as great as that arising in the cases of Asiatics.

The European phase of the seamen question, in so far as it affects the immigration law, it is believed can readily be met by inserting in that law a provision requiring that all alien seamen arriving at United States ports shall be examined in substantially the same manner and, of course, for the same purpose as alien passengers are examined, the department to be given a broad discretion for the adoption of regulations having in view the prevention of violations of the immigration law without undue interference with navigation or conflict with the purpose of the seamen's bill. By this means, provided Congress furnished sufficient appropriations for the employment of the necessary additional inspectors and medical examiners, the principal objects of the immigration law, to wit, the prevention of the admission of aliens physically or mentally deficient, could be effected with respect to seamen almost as thoroughly as with respect to passengers, and violations of that law by the entry of other excluded classes (such as contract laborers, persons likely to become a public charge, etc.) could be materially curtailed, especially if the authority to promulgate regulations included authority to require detailed descriptions or even photographs of sailors to be used in identifying those who might enter, despite the efforts of the immigration officers to prevent, and later be found unlawfully in the country.

To allow the liberty of movement on the part of Asiatic sailors necessary to the accomplishment of the objects of the seamen's bill, and at the same time prevent evasion and violation of the immigration policy of this country regarding such aliens, is a much more difficult undertaking than that last above mentioned. If the policy is to be maintained, the law excluding certain classes of Asiatic laborers on the ground that they are such must be rigidly enforced. There are in many of our cities, particularly on the Pacific coast, large colonies of these foreigners. As soon as such an alien escapes into the country he goes to one of these colonies, and once there, it is practically impossible to discover him and effect his deportation. If a law were enacted requiring all Asiatics lawfully here to have in their possession a certificate of identification, those who entered unlawfully would not have such a certificate, and would thus be identified as subject to deportation. Then if the provisions of law regarding arrest and deportation were strictly enforced, the introduction of the Asiatic into the country by surreptitious methods would soon become too expensive to be profitable, and it would be almost as easy to control this phase of the proposition as that regarding Europeans.

In the bureau's judgment, therefore, this matter should be approached in its every ramification from a broad point of view; that is to say, the seamen's bill ought not to be modified either within itself or by legislation dealing with immigration so as to prevent its operating in a world-wide manner, and the immigration law ought to be so worded as to permit of the most thorough accomplishment of its provisions dealing with both Europeans and Asiatics that is possible, and in so far as it relates to the latter should be made more effective by requiring the registration of all such aliens now in the country.   To accomplish this the bureau suggests that a section reading as follows should be inserted in whatever immigration measure is eventually passed by Congress after the committees of the two Houses have used the various bills before them in preparing a composite draft of new legislation:

SECTION —. That aliens arriving at United States ports as employees of vessels shall be examined under the provisions of this act and of the act hereby amended, in accordance with rules prescribed by the Commissioner General of Immigration, with the approval of the Secretary of Labor, to prevent violations of the immigration law and at the same time avoid, so far as possible, interference with navigation and commerce and conflict with the purpose of the act of Congress approved ————, entitled "An act to abolish the involuntary servitude imposed upon seamen in the merchant marine of the United States while in foreign ports and the involuntary servitude imposed upon seamen in the merchant marine of foreign countries while in ports of the United States, to prevent unskilled manning of American vessels, to encourage the training of boys in the American merchant marine, for the further protection of life at sea, and to amend the laws relative to seamen."   The rules adopted under this section shall be such as may be deemed necessary to insure a proper enforcement of the various provisions of the act hereby amended and the provisions of this act excluding from the United States Asiatic laborers, and include the requirement that masters of vessels shall furnish detailed personal descriptions and photographs of all aliens employed on vessels arriving in United States ports for the use of immigration officials in identifying such aliens in the event they attempt to remain permanently in the United States: *Provided*, That nothing in this act or the act hereby amended shall be construed to deny to aliens who are bona fide seamen the privilege of going ashore or of being discharged in United States ports, so long as they are not afflicted with idiocy, imbecility, feeble-mindedness, epilepsy, insanity, tuberculosis, or a loathsome or dangerous contagious disease, nor to deprive such aliens of the privilege of hospital treatment when entitled thereto under any provisions of existing law.

REPORTS OF COMMISSIONERS AND INSPECTORS IN CHARGE.

There are submitted herewith, as Appendix III (pp. 165-255), the reports (or extracts therefrom) of the commissioners of immigration and inspectors in charge of the 22 districts into which, for convenience of administration, the United States are divided.   They should be carefully perused by all who are interested in the immigration problem or in the enforcement of the important laws having in view the regulation and restriction of immigration.   The following four in particular are interesting: That of the commissioner at New York (pp. 180–187) because through that port over 70 per cent of the aliens enter; that of the commissioner for Canada (pp. 167–178) and that of the supervising inspector for the Mexican border (pp. 250–255) because the control of immigration from and through these contiguous countries is the most difficult and diverse, and in some respects the most important, part of the work done under the bureau's supervision; and that of the commissioner at San Francisco (pp. 237–242) because that is the largest Pacific station and the principal port for the admission of aliens from the Orient. The interest that attaches to these reports, however, is due merely to said peculiar facts and the magnitude of the work performed under the direction of the signers; at other ports and interior stations just as important work is being done, some of it of a similar and other of a quite dissimilar nature. All the reports should be read, therefore, to gain a really comprehensive view of the affairs of the service. The work done in the interior is well illustrated, but not fully shown, by the reports of the inspectors in charge of districts Nos. 11 and 13, with headquarters at Chicago and St. Louis, respectively (pp. 210–215 and 217–219).

Hon. William Williams, twice commissioner of immigration at New York, whose resignation was recently tendered to take effect at the close of the fiscal year, is regarded by the bureau and recognized everywhere as an authority on immigration. The bureau is glad once more to be able to insert in its annual report his views on certain phases of the intricate problem with the application of the law to which it is constantly engaged. And it is the bureau's desire to call very particular attention to all that is said in his report, reproduced in full (pp. 180–187). At various points herein Mr. Williams's report and those of the other commissioners and inspectors in charge are cited in support or explanation of points made by the bureau; therefore no extended digest of them is here attempted.

"THE IMMIGRANT FUND."

"The immigrant fund" was created by section 1 of the original immigration act approved August 3, 1882 (22 Stat., 214), assessing a duty of 50 cents "for each and every passenger not a citizen of the United States who shall come * * * to any port within the United States," and providing that

The money thus collected shall be paid into the United States Treasury, and shall constitute a fund to be called the immigrant fund, and shall be used, under the direction of the Secretary of the Treasury, *to defray the expenses of regulating immigration* under this act and *for the care of immigrants* arriving in the United States, for the relief of such as are in distress, and for *the general purposes and expenses* of carrying this act into effect.

In upholding the above-quoted provision of law, the Supreme Court, in December, 1884, in its decision of the "Head-money cases" (112 U. S., 580) pointed out (pp. 590–594) that said provision constituted a "valid exercise of the power to regulate commerce with foreign nations"; and, in answer to the contention (p. 594) that in passing the law Congress was exercising the taxing power conferred by section 8 of Article I of the Constitution, and that the exercise thereof was subject to all the restraints and qualifications thereto attached, the Supreme Court said (pp. 595–596):

If it were necessary to prove that the imposition of this contribution on owners of ships is made for the general welfare of the United States, it would not be difficult to show that it is so, and particularly that it is among the means which Congress may deem necessary and proper for that purpose; and beyond this we are not permitted to inquire.

But the true answer to all these objections is that the power exercised in this instance is not the taxing power. The burden imposed on the shipowner by this statute is the mere incident of the regulation of commerce—of that branch of foreign commerce which is involved in immigration. The title of the act, "An act to regulate immigration," is well chosen. It describes, as well as any short sentence can describe it, the real purpose and effect of the statute. Its provisions, from beginning to end, relate to the subject of immigration, and they are aptly designed to mitigate the evils inherent in the business of bringing foreigners to this country, as those evils affect both the immigrant and the people among whom he is suddenly brought and left to his own resources.

It is true not much is said about protecting the shipowner; but he is the man who reaps the profit from the transaction, who has the means to protect himself and knows well how to do it, and whose obligations in the premises need the aid of the statute for their enforcement. The sum demanded of him is not, therefore, strictly speaking, a tax or duty within the meaning of the Constitution. The money thus raised, though paid into the Treasury, is appropriated in advance to the uses of the statute and does not go to the general support of the Government. It constitutes a fund, raised from those who are engaged in the transportation of these passengers and who make profit out of it, for the temporary care of the passengers whom they bring among us and for the protection of the citizens among whom they are landed.

By the sundry civil appropriation act of August 18, 1894 (28 Stat., 391), the "head tax" was increased to $1. By the immigration act of March 3, 1903 (32 Stat., 1213), said "tax" was increased to $2, the integrity and purpose of the "immigrant fund" being maintained therein in the following language:

The money thus collected shall be paid into the United States Treasury and shall constitute a permanent appropriation to be called the "immigrant fund," to be used under the direction of the Secretary of the Treasury to defray the expense of regulating the immigration of aliens into the United States under this act, including the cost of reports of decisions of the Federal courts and digests thereof for the use of the Commissioner General of Immigration, and the salaries and expenses of all officers, clerks, and employees appointed for the purpose of enforcing the provisions of this act.

By the immigration act of February 20, 1907 (34 Stat., 898), the "head tax" was increased to $4, and the "immigrant fund" was made to include also moneys collected as "fines and rentals," as follows:

The money thus collected, together with all fines and rentals collected under the laws regulating the immigration of aliens into the United States, shall be paid into the Treasury of the United States, and shall constitute a permanent appropriation to be called the "immigrant fund," to be used under the direction of the Secretary of Commerce and Labor to defray the expense of regulating the immigration of aliens into the United States under said laws, including the contract labor laws, the cost of reports of decisions of the Federal courts, and digest thereof for the use of the Commissioner General of Immigration, and the salaries and expenses of all officers, clerks, and employees appointed to enforce said laws.

But by the appropriation act approved March 4, 1909 (35 Stat., 945, 981-2), the "immigrant fund" was abolished, and the "head tax" receipts are now covered into the Treasury in the same manner as other "revenue receipts." While the tax did not quite pay expenses in some of the early years of Federal control of immigration, the Immigration Service has always, on the average, been more than supported by the "immigrant fund;" the "regulation of immigration" has not cost the taxpayers of the United States anything. Since the abolishment of the "immigrant fund" the service has become a revenue producer, and the regulation of immigration has had to be accomplished, as best it could be, on such annual allowances from the Treasury as Congress has seen fit to make. The theory upon which the "tax" was originally created and has been from time to time increased, and one of the grounds on which the assessment was upheld by the Supreme Court is that the money is collected, not as a revenue for the support of the Government in general but as a fund held in trust by the Government to be expended for the protection of the country from the evils of an unrestricted immigration and to provide for the comfort and convenience of detained aliens. While the head tax is paid by the transportation companies, it of course comes out of the pockets of the aliens themselves.

Now, let us see to what extent the moneys collected as "head tax" have been used to discharge the trust and to what extent, on the other hand, such moneys have been converted to uses other than the enforcement of the law and the protection of aliens. This is clearly shown by the following table, in which round but approximately correct figures are given:

STATEMENT OF RECEIPTS AND EXPENDITURES FOR THE IMMIGRATION SERVICE DURING THE FOLLOWING FISCAL YEARS.

Fiscal year.	Rate.	Receipts.	Expenditures.	Deficiency.	Balance.
1894	$1	$225,328.26	$258,788.18	$33,459.92	
1895	1	315,113.16	278,060.96		$37,052.20
1896	1	451,503.68	290,424.65		161,079.03
1897	1	317,170.31	359,327.83	42,157.52	
1898	1	326,644.47	275,809.32		50,835.15
1899	1	421,457.64	288,002.26		133,455.38
1900	1	576,688.50	1,103,867.25	527,178.75	
1901	1	619,463.60	905,487.05	286,023.45	
1902	1	806,399.67	1,023,941.69	217,542.02	
1903	1	1,416,515.14	826,314.66		590,200.48
1904	2	1,599,472.25	1,296,808.85		302,663.40
1905	2	2,082,873.50	1,508,901.13		573,972.37
1906	2	2,290,901.56	1,571,280.01		719,621.55
1907	2	2,782,103.68	1,645,373.21		1,136,730.47
1908	4	3,442,330.57	2,657,779.86		784,550.71
1909	4	3,300,068.52	3,237,669.08		62,399.44
1910	4	4,227,285.43	2,759,671.08		1,467,614.35
1911	4	3,759,174.97	2,841,330.31		917,844.66
1912	4	3,457,010.91	2,927,009.99		530,000.92
1913	4	4,818,505.28	[1]2,898,754.06		1,919,751.22
Total, 20 years		37,236,011.10	28,954,601.43	1,106,361.66	9,387,771.33
Net balance					8,281,409.67

[1] Estimated.

Prior to 1907 appropriations for the enforcement of the Chinese-exclusion laws were made from "moneys in the Treasury not otherwise appropriated." From 1907 to 1911, inclusive, annual appropriations of $500,000 were made for this purpose, the money, however, being taken from the immigrant fund, and said amounts were practically exhausted each year in paying the expenses of enforcing the exclusion laws; while in 1912 and 1913 no specific amount was named, all of said expenses were paid out of the immigrant fund and no doubt were approximately the same as in previous years.

It will be observed that during the 20 years covered by the above statement there has accumulated in the Treasury (or should have accumulated if not used for other purposes) $8,281,409.67, all of which has come out of the pockets, not of the taxpayers of this country, but of aliens who were applying for admission. Also that over $3,000,000 of the amount expended has been used in enforcing the Chinese-exclusion laws—a purpose which, while indirectly related to the regulation of immigration, was not in contemplation when the fund was created. It is not difficult to support, on the basis of these figures, an argument to the effect that a proper and judicious expenditure of even half of this accumulated surplus would in no way be to the disadvantage of the people of the United States and the aliens of the right sort concerned, but on the contrary would place the country in much better condition in so far as the presence here of the morally, mentally, and physically undesirable is concerned, and would simultaneously afford to the aliens seeking admission better protection and greater comfort than we can extend to them under existing conditions.

Why should this money, so urgently needed for the proper enforcement of the law, be retained in the Treasury or devoted to uses never intended and to which, in fairness to those from whom collected and to those supposed to be protected by its collection and proper expenditure, it ought not to be devoted? In this connection the reports of the various commissioners and inspectors in charge should be read, for they show under what dreadful handicaps the officers of the service have been proceeding in their efforts to make the law reasonably effective and to extend to the aliens who must be inspected at least fairly decent treatment and accommodation. The following facts shown by some of the reports demonstrate that the implied trust connected with this "head tax" has not been observed in either letter or spirit:

Commissioner Williams points out (Appendix III, pp. 180–187) that while at the Ellis Island station many improvements have in recent years been made in the buildings and plant funds are still very urgently needed for several important improvements and for the upkeep in a business-like manner of the buildings, grounds, and equipment of the station, and that "Even with the best of facilities the work at Ellis Island will always be a difficult one to transact, and the executive officers should not be hampered by the lack of any tools they may require." The commissioner for Canada (Id., pp. 167–178) shows that the lack of funds has been such that "for many months our staff of help at the seaports has been inadequate to meet the needs of the situation, and as a consequence at times our service has all but broken down"; that "long hours of duty have almost invariably characterized the inspection at Quebec and Halifax, the officers at these ports on numerous occasions having been compelled to work 36 consecutive hours with no period for rest, and on account of the mental and physical exhaustion which must result from such a strain it is obvious that it has been simply impossible to enforce that careful inspection of aliens which the immigration laws and regulations and the interests of our country demand"; that "during recent months, owing to the congestion at Quebec, aliens held for board of special inquiry hearing have been compelled to undergo detention in the crowded hospitals for periods of from six to eight days before their cases could be heard, and thus for the prompt inspection that should have been accorded arriving aliens was substituted what amounted to annoying hardships, which were keenly felt particularly in the cases of women and children, who, wearied from weeks of travel from their foreign homes, were anything but prepared cheerfully to endure such vexatious delay"; that in the district under his control it has been impossible with the money and men allowed him properly to enforce either the immigration or the Chinese-exclusion laws.

Quotations might be made from many other reports, some of which appear in Appendix III, to illustrate the bureau's point, which is that the greatest impediment to a proper enforcement of the law is the very one which, in view of the fact that the service is not only self-supporting but a producer of extensive revenues for the Government, would the least be expected to exist; to wit, the lack of sufficient funds, men, and facilities to properly and humanely enforce the law. Especially surprising is this in view of the fact that in the very body from which there came, as recently as last February, a most emphatic demand for immigration legislation of a much more restricted nature than the existing law, lies the power to make, from funds which are collected from the aliens themselves sufficient provision for a thoroughly effective and at the same time humane application of the law and regulations affecting aliens.

When aliens must be held at our ports unreasonable periods of time before their cases can be passed upon, and often detained in inadequate and uncomfortable quarters; when officers, who are efficient, painstaking, conscientious men, are required to work long hours daily and Sunday, often under conditions that would not be tolerated even by one of our "soulless corporations;" when improvements and corrections in practice obviously needed must go unmade; and when steps clearly demanded to meet some new or changing condition must be left untaken—all because the money necessary has not been provided—when conditions of this kind confront the bureau, is there not sufficient excuse for a feeling of discouragement? And let it not be forgotten, as has already been shown, that ample financial provision to meet the conditions here portrayed could be made by Congress without one cent of cost being charged against the taxpayers of the United States, the money collected from the aliens as head tax being more than sufficient to pay all expenses of conducting the service properly and with appropriate regard for the aliens and those who are attempting to carry out the repeatedly expressed desire of Congress that immigration shall be "regulated."

In the bureau's opinion the "immigrant fund" was intended to be used and should be used for the following objects: (1) To protect the people of the United States against the evils of unrestricted or unregulated immigration; (2) to provide protection and a reasonable degree of comfort for alien immigrants; (3) to relieve the various States of the burden of maintaining aliens in their public institutions, and communities of the economic social menace of having in their midst aliens of the classes described by the law as undesirable, especially the mentally or morally defective or degenerate.

NEW IMMIGRATION STATIONS.

Stations, for which provision was made by Congress some time ago for the ports of Galveston, New Orleans, and Charleston, have been completed. Those at Galveston and New Orleans have been occupied and are being put to the use for which intended; but, as no immigration comes to Charleston, it has not been necessary to put the station there to any use, and it is standing idle and unoccupied, but protected as fully as possible from decay and deterioration in value by employing two watchmen to guard it day and night.

With regard to the proposed new station for Boston, the bureau regrets to report that after plans had been prepared by the Office of the Supervising Architect, it was found that the money available was not sufficient. The Secretary of the Treasury has been requested to endeavor to secure an additional appropriation, and also to have authorized the transfer of that now existing to the Treasury Department, so that the delays and embarrassments arising from having the work controlled by one department and the appropriation therefor by another may be avoided.

At Gloucester City, N. J., where the new Philadelphia immigration station has been occupied for some time, a landing pier is being constructed. It is proposed to place on said pier an inpsection building, but the erection of said building can not be undertaken unless and until a further appropriation is made by Congress.[1]

CONCLUSION.

There is no field of endeavor in which "standing still" would be "moving backward" more truly than in the enforcement of the statutes regulating immigration. The difficulties inherent in the administration of these laws are so great and so constantly changing with change of conditions or circumstances that eternal vigilance and ready inventiveness are required if the varying and often astute or even cunning schemes for the defeat of the purposes of the laws are to be met with even a reasonable degree of success. Many of the details of administration must of course be left to the officers exercising supervisory powers throughout the service, and in turn by them to their subordinates. Fortunate indeed is the bureau in having on the whole, so able and conscientious a corps of officers and employees as has gradually been built up, improved, and fitted into proper places of responsibility and duty. To the untiring and ably directed efforts of the individuals who man and officer the service, supplemented, as they so thoroughly are, by the work of the Public Health surgeons, is due so large a measure of success as has heretofore attended the bureau's endeavors. It is the well directed, intelligent, conscientious, and patriotic manner in which the individual officer has performed his individual duty which produces progress in the aggregate results of the year, that makes it possible to claim that there has been no "standing still," or "marking time," but, on the contrary, constant improvement in the enforcement of the law.

The foregoing is written, however, with the full realization that the accomplishments of the past—whether of the remote or the immediate past—notwithstanding the fact that there has been a constant evolution of improvement, have fallen far short of the ideal. It is the constant striving for quick and all-inclusive improvements and attaining thereby only slow and nonextensive betterment of methods and results which, to some extent at least, explains the note of pessimism pervading some of the reports submitted to the bureau, for instance those of the commissioners at Montreal and San Francisco (Appendix III, pp. 167–178 and 237–242). When officers in charge of districts become discouraged, as a result of their comparatively limited observation of the administration and operation of the laws, is it any cause for wonder that the bureau, wherein to a large extent centers the work of the entire service, is sometimes inclined to

---

[1] See also reports of commissioners of immigration at Boston, Philadelphia, and New Orleans, and inspector in charge at Galveston (Appendix III, pp. 178–180, 190–194, 201–205, and 205–207.

become pessimistic ?   The slow, if sure, progress, the criticism so often encountered as the reward for earnest efforts exerted under adverse conditions, and the proneness of those from whom commendation and assistance rightfully ought to come to withhold their financial and sometimes even their moral support when most needed, all tend to discourage if we allow our consideration of the matter to become too restricted—to cover too short a time to be fair to ourselves and the conditions under consideration.   But when the condition of the service to-day is compared, not with its condition on yesterday, but with the situation shown by previous reports to have existed four, three, or even two years ago, and proper allowances made for adverse conditions, the bureau is confident that all others, like itself, must find some cause for gratulation, and also for somewhat optimistic anticipations for the future.

Respectfully submitted.

A. CAMINETTI,
Commissioner General. -

To Hon. W. B. WILSON,
Secretary of Labor.

APPENDIX I

STATISTICAL TABLES

TABLE I.—ALIENS ADMITTED, DEPARTED, DEBARRED, AND RETURNED, FISCAL YEARS ENDED JUNE 30, 1912 AND 1913, AND CITIZENS ARRIVED AND DEPARTED, FISCAL YEAR ENDED JUNE 30, 1913, BY PORTS.

Port	Aliens 1912 Admitted — Immigrant aliens	Aliens 1912 Admitted — Non-immigrant aliens	Aliens 1912 Departed — Emigrant aliens	Aliens 1912 Departed — Non-emigrant aliens	Aliens 1912 De-barred	Aliens 1912 Returned after landing	Aliens 1913 Admitted — Immigrant aliens	Aliens 1913 Admitted — Non-immigrant aliens	Aliens 1913 Departed — Emigrant aliens	Aliens 1913 Departed — Non-emigrant aliens	Aliens 1913 De-barred	Aliens 1913 Returned after landing	Citizens 1912 Arrived	Citizens 1912 Departed	Citizens 1913 Arrived	Citizens 1913 Departed
New York, N.Y.	605,151	112,268	259,209	181,316	8,294	1,364	892,653	139,937	227,151	171,291	10,720	1,889	179,358	219,357	166,686	195,094
Boston, Mass.	38,782	10,008	10,758	11,980	337	87	54,740	11,049	9,003	13,216	384	99	10,517	11,020	11,894	13,839
Philadelphia, Pa.	43,749	3,606	9,981	2,974	293	89	59,466	4,271	7,514	2,294	420	125	3,983	4,942	3,999	4,837
Baltimore, Md.	21,667	814	1,836	1,620	162	46	32,833	763	1,303	581	220	67	1,136	1,431	1,104	1,855
Portland, Me.	2,058	12,511	605	3,040	51	3	3,874	22,505	653	4,511	43	5	28	11	199	232
New Bedford, Mass.	1,017	302	281	28	50	7	3,983	139	464	39	1	1	413	219	28	8
Providence, R.I.	5,178	692	1,517	503	63	1	11,101	1,002	1,605	644	100	10			533	444
Newport News, Va.							249	116		2	11	1			68	1
Norfolk, Va.	280	97			32	2	18	4	15	10	7	1	52	2	2	5
Savannah, Ga.	6				2	1	7						11		28	
Miami, Fla.	1,406	1,410		1,542	25	4				1,326	15		1,173	1,048	270	290
Key West, Fla.	1,435	2,437	538	5,029	21	3	1,312	1,525	723	5,938	38	9	11,265	12,746	14,627	14,673
Knights Key, Fla.	11	54	2,167	75	1		1,165	3,140	1,432				587	749		
Other Atlantic ports.	47	9	2	1	15	1		7	1	3	3	1	116	1	33	3
Tampa, Fla.	1,224	1,583	1	3	24	3	26	1,289	2	6	16	6	2,709	6	1,886	7
Pensacola, Fla.	18												32		25	
Mobile, Ala.	98	122	6	58	8	1	82	126	12	79	15	2	309	158	303	184
New Orleans, La.	1,284	2,135	496	1,783	46	10	1,344	1,941	516	1,037	62	4	8,215	6,959	8,634	8,955
Galveston, Tex.	4,758	311	503	299	346	18	1,446	281	603	304	249	14	859	594	1,263	827
Other Gulf ports.	27	4	6	2	2		50				1	40	10		4	
San Francisco, Cal.	3,958	4,108	2,007	6,213	363	60	5,554	3,381	2,455	6,186	266	1	5,567	5,994	5,909	5,699
Portland, Oreg.	9	1			1		31	1		1		170				
Seattle, Wash.	2,113	1,392	1,136	2,007	101	13	2,405	2,020	633	2,280	100	2	712	852	801	776
Alaska.	125	30			7		359	44			5	38	2,075		3,470	
Mexican border ports.	22,892	3,849	225	1,314	1,538	398	11,273	4,390	741	1,300	1,822	529	2,115	1,467	1,484	1,206

Region	Imm. aliens 1912	Nonimm. aliens 1912	Emig. aliens 1912	Nonemig. aliens 1912	Debarred 1912	Deported 1912	Imm. aliens 1913	Nonimm. aliens 1913	Emig. aliens 1913	Nonemig. aliens 1913	Debarred 1913	Deported 1913	1911	1912	1913
Through Canada: Atlantic ports	15,443	7,745	6,488	2,926	145	5	28,776	18,314	4,920	2,947	333		5,345	3,261	3,938
Pacific ports	230	723	496	918			211	646	440	1,134			526	427	541
Border stations	57,154	9,396	33,080	55,548	3,951	339	75,837	9,043	46,646	83,216	4,780	446	54,497	78,322	90,129
Honolulu, Hawaii	6,616	1,342	924	2,266	141		5,797	1,516	681	3,351	298		1,198	1,751	2,110
Porto Rico	1,386	1,974	410	1,579	38	1	823	1,284	676	1,148	22		1,788	2,294	2,049
Total	838,172	178,983	333,262	282,030	16,057	2,456	1,197,892	229,335	308,190	303,734	19,938	3,461	286,604	353,890	347,702
Philippine Islands	2,536	6,932	729	8,776	130	205	4,408	8,238	768	9,138	194	184			

TABLE II.—NET INCREASE OF POPULATION BY ARRIVAL AND DEPARTURE OF ALIENS, FISCAL YEARS ENDED JUNE 30, 1912 AND 1913, BY MONTHS.

Month	1912 Admitted Immigrant aliens	Nonimmigrant aliens	Total	1912 Departed Emigrant aliens	Nonemigrant aliens	Total	Increase (+) or decrease (–)	1913 Admitted Immigrant aliens	Nonimmigrant aliens	Total	1913 Departed Emigrant aliens	Nonemigrant aliens	Total	Increase (+) or decrease (–)
July	51,737	9,989	61,726	40,749	29,074	69,823	−8,097	78,101	12,417	90,518	24,673	18,189	42,862	+47,656
August	50,110	13,242	63,352	31,915	20,589	52,504	+10,848	82,377	15,424	97,801	25,725	20,710	46,435	+51,366
September	62,599	16,194	78,793	29,630	20,770	50,400	+28,393	105,611	22,855	128,466	23,728	19,559	43,287	+85,179
October	69,418	17,470	86,888	30,728	20,465	51,213	+35,675	108,300	20,288	128,588	27,153	22,133	49,286	+79,302
November	61,765	12,382	74,147	45,804	26,620	72,424	+1,723	94,739	13,348	108,087	41,444	28,683	70,127	+37,960
December	61,620	10,061	71,687	42,822	29,060	71,882	−195	76,315	11,293	87,608	45,048	30,797	75,845	+11,763
January	38,453	8,367	46,820	17,415	13,791	31,206	+15,614	46,441	8,794	55,235	29,730	27,305	57,035	−1,800
February	45,380	9,521	54,901	14,949	14,365	29,314	+25,587	59,156	12,199	71,355	15,253	14,866	30,119	+41,236
March	91,185	19,763	110,948	19,930	23,211	43,141	+67,807	96,958	24,283	121,241	15,044	15,823	30,867	+90,374
April	99,839	27,162	127,001	18,088	27,995	46,083	+80,918	136,371	38,808	175,179	18,331	27,195	45,526	+129,653
May	113,635	19,022	132,657	17,999	24,381	42,380	+90,277	137,262	27,430	164,692	19,131	43,218	62,349	+102,343
June	92,425	15,810	108,235	23,233	31,689	54,922	+53,313	176,261	22,196	198,457	22,930	35,256	58,186	+140,271
Total	838,172	178,983	1,017,155	333,262	282,030	615,292	+401,863	1,197,892	229,335	1,427,227	308,190	303,734	611,924	+815,303

TABLE III.—NET INCREASE OR DECREASE OF POPULATION BY ARRIVAL AND DEPARTURE OF ALIENS, FISCAL YEARS ENDED JUNE 30, 1912 AND 1913, BY COUNTRIES.

Country	1912 Coming from — Immigrant aliens	1912 Coming from — Nonimmigrant aliens	1912 Coming from — Total aliens admitted	1912 Going to — Emigrant aliens	1912 Going to — Nonemigrant aliens	1912 Going to — Total aliens departed	1912 Increase (+) or decrease (−)	1913 Coming from — Immigrant aliens	1913 Coming from — Nonimmigrant aliens	1913 Coming from — Total aliens admitted	1913 Going to — Emigrant aliens	1913 Going to — Nonemigrant aliens	1913 Going to — Total aliens departed	1913 Increase (+) or decrease (−)
Austria	85,834	5,842	91,696	46,137	3,142	49,279	+42,417	137,245	11,403	148,648	28,760	3,064	31,824	+116,824
Hungary	93,028	1,280	94,308	42,423	2,862	45,285	+49,023	117,580	1,233	118,813	29,904	2,851	32,755	+86,058
Belgium	4,169	786	4,955	1,103	823	1,926	+3,029	7,405	1,382	8,787	803	688	1,491	+7,296
Bulgaria, Servia, and Montenegro	4,447	958	5,405	3,577	222	3,799	+1,606	1,753	205	1,958	9,664	1,757	11,421	−9,463
Denmark	6,191	332	6,523	665	415	1,080	+5,443	6,478	369	6,847	608	356	964	+5,883
France, including Corsica	8,628	2,327	10,955	3,473	3,551	7,024	+3,931	9,675	2,484	12,159	3,430	2,406	5,836	+6,323
German Empire	27,788	3,500	31,288	5,785	5,472	11,257	+20,031	34,329	4,784	39,113	4,759	5,209	9,968	+29,145
Greece	21,449	452	21,901	11,461	783	12,244	+9,657	22,817	528	23,345	30,603	4,289	34,892	−11,547
Italy, including Sicily and Sardinia	157,134	10,988	168,122	108,388	10,101	118,489	+49,633	265,542	21,713	287,255	88,021	8,242	96,263	+190,992
Netherlands	6,619	581	7,200	564	878	1,442	+5,758	6,902	924	7,826	599	859	1,458	+6,358
Norway	8,675	1,155	9,830	2,310	613	2,923	+6,907	8,587	1,368	9,955	1,710	637	2,347	+7,608
Portugal, including Cape Verde and Azore Islands	10,230	61	10,291	1,916	222	2,138	+8,153	14,171	56	14,227	1,965	241	2,206	+12,021
Roumania	1,997	100	2,097	550	105	655	+1,442	2,155	183	2,338	319	77	396	+1,942
Russian Empire and Finland	162,395	5,902	168,357	34,681	4,911	39,592	+128,765	291,040	14,120	305,160	26,923	4,410	31,333	+273,827
Spain, including Canary and Balearic Islands	6,327	1,127	7,454	1,581	870	2,451	+5,003	6,167	2,060	8,227	2,029	925	2,954	+5,273
Sweden	12,088	1,087	13,175	2,490	719	3,209	+9,966	17,202	725	17,927	1,989	474	2,463	+15,464
Switzerland	3,505	263	3,768	510	360	870	+2,898	4,104	406	4,510	449	381	830	+3,680
Turkey in Europe	14,481	374	14,855	5,926	350	6,276	+8,579	14,128	217	14,345	4,809	547	5,356	+8,989
United Kingdom: England	40,408	18,139	58,547	6,700	15,602	22,302	+36,245	43,363	23,296	66,659	5,969	14,843	20,812	+45,847
Ireland	25,879	1,170	27,049	3,082	1,793	4,875	+22,174	27,876	1,477	29,353	2,894	1,467	4,361	+24,992
Scotland	14,578	2,472	17,050	2,195	2,853	5,048	+12,002	14,220	3,304	17,524	2,179	2,701	4,880	+12,644
Wales	2,162	395	2,557	185	217	402	+2,155	2,745	632	3,377	157	190	347	+3,030
Other Europe	243	31	274	22	18	40	+234	371	209	580	16	17	33	+547
Total Europe	718,875	58,762	777,657	285,724	56,882	342,606	+435,051	1,055,855	93,078	1,148,933	248,559	56,631	305,190	+843,743

China	1,765	1,148	2,913	2,609	891	3,500	+587	2,105	751	2,856	2,303	407	2,710	+146
Japan	6,114	412	6,526	1,485	424	1,909	+4,617	8,281	373	8,654	731	374	1,105	+7,549
India	175	137	312	182	136	318	+6	179	151	330	240	106	346	+16
Turkey in Asia	12,788	175	12,963	1,551	335	1,886	+11,077	23,955	265	24,220	1,313	292	1,605	+22,615
Other Asia	607	67	674	104	36	140	+534	838	118	956	103	34	137	+819
Total Asia	21,449	1,939	23,388	5,931	1,822	7,753	+15,635	35,358	1,658	37,016	4,690	1,213	5,903	+31,113
Africa	1,009	242	1,251	266	322	588	+663	1,409	334	1,743	209	287	496	+1,247
Australia, Tasmania, and New Zealand	794	189	983	645	1,180	1,825	+158	1,229	1,596	2,825	645	1,399	2,044	+781
Pacific islands, not specified	104	188	292	43	247	290	+2	111	191	302	29	208	237	+65
British North America	55,990	11,556	67,546	33,506	63,326	96,832	+29,286	73,802	14,165	87,967	46,981	94,010	140,991	+53,024
Central America	1,242	1,875	3,117	328	1,842	2,170	+947	-1,473	1,926	3,399	991	1,982	2,464	+935
Mexico	23,238	1,946	25,184	605	2,231	2,836	+22,348	11,926	2,134	14,060	482	2,302	3,293	+10,767
South America	2,999	2,093	5,082	1,319	2,387	3,706	+1,376	4,248	2,502	6,750	1,367	2,321	3,688	+3,062
West Indies	12,467	8,299	20,766	4,864	12,829	17,693	+3,073	12,458	8,591	21,049	4,223	12,410	16,633	+4,416
United States		90,854	90,854		138,930	138,930	-48,076		103,150	103,150		130,946	130,946	+27,796
Other countries	15	20	35	31	32	63	-28	23	10	33	14	25	39	-6
Grand total	838,172	178,983	1,017,155	333,262	282,030	615,292	+401,863	1,197,892	229,335	1,427,227	308,190	303,734	611,924	+815,303

TABLE IV.—NET INCREASE OR DECREASE OF POPULATION BY ARRIVAL AND DEPARTURE OF ALIENS, FISCAL YEAR ENDED JUNE 30, 1913, BY RACES OR PEOPLES.

Race or people.	Admitted.			Departed.			Increase (+) or decrease (−).
	Immigrant aliens.	Nonimmigrant aliens.	Total.	Emigrant aliens.	Nonemigrant aliens.	Total.	
African (black)	6,634	3,100	9,734	1,671	2,385	4,056	+ 5,678
Armenian	9,353	201	9,554	676	357	1,033	+ 8,521
Bohemian and Moravian (Czech)	11,091	761	11,852	871	757	1,628	+ 10,224
Bulgarian, Servian, and Montenegrin	9,087	996	10,083	13,525	5,359	18,884	− 8,801
Chinese	2,022	1,465	4,382	2,250	3,499	5,749	− 1,367
Croatian and Slavonian	42,499	2,255	44,754	10,209	3,726	13,935	+ 30,819
Cuban	3,099	3,022	6,121	1,264	6,128	7,392	− 1,271
Dalmatian, Bosnian, and Herzegovinian	4,520	255	4,775	849	521	1,370	+ 3,405
Dutch and Flemish	14,507	4,239	18,746	2,145	5,619	7,764	+ 10,982
East Indian	188	45	233	213	122	335	− 102
English	55,522	44,540	100,062	10,794	61,168	71,962	+ 28,100
Finnish	12,756	2,164	14,920	3,053	3,071	6,124	+ 8,796
French	20,652	5,857	26,509	4,019	6,218	10,237	+ 16,272
German	80,865	20,899	101,764	11,871	23,160	35,031	+ 66,733
Greek	38,644	2,289	40,933	31,556	19,321	50,877	− 9,944
Hebrew	101,330	4,496	105,826	6,697	4,841	11,538	+ 94,288
Irish	37,023	11,080	48,103	4,458	13,256	17,714	+ 30,389
Italian (north)	42,534	11,637	54,171	10,995	14,335	25,330	+ 28,841
Italian (south)	231,613	32,735	263,453	79,057	40,075	119,132	+144,321
Japanese	8,302	3,370	11,672	733	7,707	8,440	+ 3,232
Korean	64	10	74	44	19	63	+ 11
Lithuanian	24,647	882	25,529	3,276	1,343	4,619	+ 20,910
Magyar	30,610	2,951	33,561	11,496	4,596	16,092	+ 17,469
Mexican	10,954	4,541	15,495	910	1,883	2,793	+ 12,702
Pacific Islander	11	16	27	4	16	20	+ 7
Polish	174,365	10,842	185,207	24,107	11,705	35,812	+149,395
Portuguese	13,566	1,065	14,631	1,583	1,916	3,499	+ 11,132
Roumanian	13,451	1,329	14,780	3,156	2,022	5,178	+ 9,602
Russian	51,472	6,908	58,380	10,548	8,910	19,458	+ 38,922
Ruthenian (Russniak)	30,588	8,817	39,405	5,327	7,038	12,365	+ 27,040
Scandinavian (Norwegians, Danes, and Swedes)	38,737	12,913	51,650	9,291	14,211	23,502	+ 28,148
Scotch	21,293	10,141	31,434	4,118	12,302	16,420	+ 15,014
Slovak	27,234	1,860	29,094	9,854	3,237	13,091	+ 16,003
Spanish	9,042	5,975	15,017	3,181	5,503	8,684	+ 6,333
Spanish-American	1,363	2,046	3,409	457	1,980	2,437	+ 972
Syrian	9,210	809	10,019	797	1,335	2,132	+ 7,887
Turkish	2,015	117	2,132	1,297	681	1,978	+ 154
Welsh	2,820	1,102	3,922	298	1,073	1,371	+ 2,551
West Indian (except Cuban)	1,171	1,131	2,302	584	1,382	1,966	+ 336
Other peoples	3,038	474	3,512	1,118	957	2,075	+ 1,437
Not specified [1]				19,838		19,838	− 19,838
Total	1,197,892	229,335	1,427,227	308,190	303,734	611,924	+815,303
Admitted in and departed from Philippine Islands	4,408	8,238	12,646	768	9,138	9,906	+ 2,740

[1] Departed via Canadian border. Reported by Canadian Government as Canadians.

REPORT OF COMMISSIONER GENERAL OF IMMIGRATION.   43

TABLE V.—INTENDED FUTURE PERMANENT RESIDENCE OF ALIENS ADMITTED AND LAST PERMANENT RESIDENCE OF ALIENS DEPARTED, FISCAL YEAR ENDED JUNE 30, 1913, BY STATES AND TERRITORIES.[1]

State or Territory.	Admitted.		Departed.	
	Immigrant aliens.	Nonimmigrant aliens.	Emigrant aliens.	Nonemigrant aliens.
Alabama	1,170	107	375	210
Alaska	618	89	106	114
Arizona	3,945	1,020	613	228
Arkansas	353	49	56	34
California	32,277	4,107	8,120	7,938
Colorado	5,673	372	1,664	1,030
Connecticut	35,138	2,529	6,259	2,791
Delaware	1,810	103	242	56
District of Columbia	1,717	319	354	275
Florida	5,352	2,353	2,520	2,216
Georgia	787	127	158	196
Hawaii	5,837	1,123	682	3,011
Idaho	1,082	142	385	376
Illinois	107,060	7,449	24,178	10,932
Indiana	13,005	832	3,860	892
Iowa	8,666	588	1,387	1,237
Kansas	3,663	249	595	357
Kentucky	761	90	176	131
Louisiana	1,774	309	423	240
Maine	6,624	307	655	483
Maryland	8,168	504	1,146	461
Massachusetts	101,674	9,155	17,070	12,503
Michigan	59,192	3,391	7,529	3,970
Minnesota	18,693	1,457	2,933	2,732
Mississippi	415	40	41	39
Missouri	11,504	937	3,386	2,196
Montana	5,796	464	955	869
Nebraska	6,266	370	695	696
Nevada	1,000	87	402	321
New Hampshire	8,230	311	1,622	723
New Jersey	61,358	5,589	12,401	5,671
New Mexico	758	84	246	140
New York	330,531	31,903	83,608	32,577
North Carolina	429	66	80	68
North Dakota	4,285	259	229	463
Ohio	63,007	3,745	13,238	6,244
Oklahoma	1,018	103	235	68
Oregon	4,994	587	1,385	1,297
Pennsylvania	182,744	11,897	43,836	12,501
Philippine Islands	17	12	2	5
Porto Rico	894	601	741	286
Rhode Island	13,678	1,296	2,593	1,848
South Carolina	258	36	53	48
South Dakota	1,641	171	196	255
Tennessee	818	102	134	113
Texas	11,214	2,835	806	435
Utah	2,932	318	1,349	890
Vermont	3,608	236	557	292
Virginia	1,822	180	407	241
Washington	18,313	1,698	2,827	3,239
West Virginia	10,472	634	3,492	935
Wisconsin	23,091	1,149	4,037	1,557
Wyoming	1,160	123	505	294
Outside United States		126,731		177,010
Unknown[2]			46,646	
Total	1,197,892	229,335	308,190	303,734

[1] For permanent residences of aliens arriving in and departing from the Philippine Islands, see Tables IX, IXA, XIV, and XIVA.
[2] Left United States via Canadian border. Figures reported by Canadian Government.

TABLE VI.—OCCUPATIONS OF ALL ALIENS ADMITTED AND DEPARTED, FISCAL YEAR
ENDED JUNE 30, 1913.[1]

Occupation.	Admitted.		Departed.	
	Immigrant aliens.	Nonimmigrant aliens.	Emigrant aliens.	Nonemigrant aliens.
PROFESSIONAL.				
Actors	911	757	333	1,171
Architects	299	330	97	547
Clergy	1,051	1,023	335	1,086
Editors	207	228	28	269
Electricians	941	328	103	394
Engineers (professional)	1,917	2,457	408	2,825
Lawyers	290	638	42	860
Literary and scientific persons	493	512	73	483
Musicians	1,254	495	284	636
Officials (Government)	365	763	98	846
Physicians	508	933	137	1,254
Sculptors and artists	676	333	139	427
Teachers	2,389	1,510	484	1,624
Other professional	2,168	1,395	364	1,313
Total professional	13,469	11,702	2,925	13,735
SKILLED.				
Bakers	4,256	749	475	874
Barbers and hairdressers	3,213	554	537	648
Blacksmiths	5,431	761	292	743
Bookbinders	543	52	25	43
Brewers	240	64	29	93
Butchers	3,748	597	298	628
Cabinetmakers	501	119	62	131
Carpenters and joiners	15,035	3,089	1,529	4,232
Cigarette makers	64	5	4	10
Cigar makers	899	906	760	1,680
Cigar packers	86	35	9	11
Clerks and accountants	14,025	5,492	1,804	6,731
Dressmakers	6,411	737	482	810
Engineers (locomotive, marine, and stationary)	1,594	1,091	158	889
Furriers and fur workers	607	86	80	97
Gardeners	1,516	666	198	766
Hat and cap makers	805	65	45	87
Iron and steel workers	1,728	441	263	612
Jewelers	404	107	89	160
Locksmiths	2,811	180	28	99
Machinists	2,725	1,115	817	1,970
Mariners	4,979	2,399	696	1,661
Masons	7,377	1,731	616	1,783
Mechanics (not specified)	1,853	573	6,758	775
Metal workers (other than iron, steel, and tin)	793	142	47	159
Millers	804	68	11	40
Milliners	1,193	124	71	144
Miners	9,510	2,121	8,280	5,344
Painters and glaziers	3,888	765	366	977
Pattern makers	106	51	33	90
Photographers	389	113	48	137
Plasterers	418	264	85	334
Plumbers	778	290	76	300
Printers	1,104	293	114	324
Saddlers and harness makers	616	66	24	66
Seamstresses	8,723	373	217	335
Shoemakers	11,578	1,036	838	1,025
Stokers	1,112	428	606	535
Stonecutters	1,111	303	254	558
Tailors	22,934	1,626	1,850	1,765
Tanners and curriers	487	47	40	56
Textile workers (not specified)	1,179	287	711	1,171
Tinners	879	84	72	123
Tobacco workers	52	43	12	44
Upholsterers	262	46	14	70
Watch and clock makers	611	83	51	88
Weavers and spinners	3,909	623	457	973
Wheelwrights	380	40	15	27
Woodworkers (not specified)	358	70	50	108
Other skilled	6,083	1,870	1,169	2,560
Total skilled	160,108	32,870	31,563	42,886

[1] For occupations of aliens arriving in and departing from Philippine Islands, see Tables XI and XIA.

TABLE VI.—OCCUPATIONS OF ALL ALIENS ADMITTED AND DEPARTED, FISCAL YEAR ENDED JUNE 30, 1913—Continued.

Occupation.	Admitted.		Departed.	
	Immigrant aliens.	Nonimmigrant aliens.	Emigrant aliens.	Nonemigrant aliens.
MISCELLANEOUS.				
Agents...	1,148	1,646	136	1,914
Bankers..	293	736	72	1,302
Draymen, hackmen, and teamsters........................	933	236	140	435
Farm laborers..	320,105	48,613	3,948	30,543
Farmers...	13,180	5,197	6,120	8,758
Fishermen...	1,174	251	261	386
Hotel keepers...	315	328	106	482
Laborers..	220,992	30,550	191,604	86,511
Manufacturers...	454	776	66	1,132
Merchants and dealers...................................	13,919	11,391	5,979	14,248
Servants..	140,218	18,686	16,220	20,187
Other miscellaneous.................................. ..	14,396	7,368	3,654	10,748
Total miscellaneous.................................	727,127	125,778	228,306	176,646
No occupation (including women and children)..............	297,188	58,985	45,396	70,467
Grand total...	1,197,892	229,335	308,190	303,734

TABLE VII.—SEX, AGE, LITERACY, FINANCIAL CONDITION, ETC., OF IMMIGRANT

Race or people.	Number admitted.	Sex.		Age.			Literacy, 14 years and over.				
		Male.	Female.	Under 14 years.	14 to 44 years.	45 years and over.	Can read but can not write.		Can neither read nor write.		Total.
							Male.	Female.	Male.	Female.	
African (black)...	6,634	3,691	2,943	565	5,804	265	11	14	666	239	930
Armenian.........	9,353	7,893	1,460	718	8,309	326	4	3	1,835	415	2,257
Bohemian and Moravian......	11,091	6,328	4,763	2,006	8,539	546	2	1	50	43	96
Bulgarian, Servian, and Montenegrin.......	9,087	7,834	1,253	560	8,044	483	6	1	2,510	423	2,940
Chinese.........	2,022	1,692	330	189	1,530	303	.....	.....	16	205	221
Croatian and Slovenian.........	42,499	31,590	10,909	3,422	37,362	1,715	24	11	6,679	2,368	9,082
Cuban...........	3,099	2,126	973	396	2,368	335	.....	1	16	22	39
Dalmatian, Bosnian, and Herzegovinian......	4,520	3,938	582	159	4,168	193	6	1	1,851	208	2,066
Dutch and Flemish..............	14,507	9,471	5,036	2,675	10,896	936	3	5	157	68	233
East Indian.......	188	184	4	1	181	6	.....	.....	23	.....	23
English.............	55,522	31,320	24,202	8,915	40,296	6,311	23	18	137	123	301
Finnish...........	12,736	8,219	4,537	888	11,651	217	11	5	43	26	85
French...........	20,652	11,620	9,032	3,831	14,402	2,419	36	25	919	342	1,322
German..........	80,865	45,974	34,891	15,450	59,627	5,788	62	103	1,929	2,059	4,153
Greek............	38,644	35,143	3,501	1,269	36,591	784	10	.....	7,164	1,558	8,732
Hebrew...........	101,330	57,148	44,182	22,378	72,218	6,734	222	96	5,563	10,009	15,980
Irish..............	37,023	19,072	17,951	2,543	32,441	2,039	12	18	176	142	348
Italian (North)...	42,534	32,428	10,106	4,248	36,645	1,641	18	2	1,974	563	2,557
Italian (South)...	231,613	176,472	55,141	27,302	190,795	13,516	49	10	75,256	24,146	99,461
Japanese.........	8,302	3,157	5,145	437	7,290	575	.....	.....	548	1,876	2,424
Korean...........	64	15	49	13	51	.....	.....	.....	3	9	12
Lithuanian.......	24,647	16,069	8,578	1,760	22,438	449	491	441	5,826	4,420	11,178
Magyar..........	30,610	16,637	13,973	5,670	22,410	2,530	6	9	1,177	1,271	2,463
Mexican..........	10,954	6,359	4,595	3,048	6,931	975	13	24	1,998	1,657	3,692
Pacific Islander...	11	8	3	.....	8	3	.....	.....	.....	.....	.....
Polish............	174,365	115,772	58,593	17,253	152,988	4,124	1,597	1,579	31,308	17,152	51,636
Portuguese.......	13,566	8,696	4,870	2,301	10,366	899	4	8	4,562	2,398	6,972
Roumanian......	13,451	10,373	3,078	992	10,539	1,920	7	2	3,191	1,185	4,385
Russian..........	51,472	45,633	5,839	1,747	48,906	819	100	28	14,792	2,837	17,757
Ruthenian (Russniak)............	30,588	18,980	11,608	2,365	27,250	973	59	36	6,746	4,453	11,294
Scandinavian.....	38,737	25,243	13,494	3,038	34,056	1,643	10	15	60	31	116
Scotch...........	21,293	11,545	9,748	3,521	15,406	2,366	4	5	39	43	91
Slovak...........	27,234	16,242	10,992	4,205	22,048	981	22	11	1,985	1,273	3,291
Spanish..........	9,042	7,240	1,802	926	7,568	548	20	5	1,059	398	1,482
Spanish - American......	1,363	978	385	203	1,065	95	2	2	3	10	17
Syrian...........	9,210	6,177	3,033	1,341	7,448	421	4	2	2,359	1,769	4,134
Turkish..........	2,015	1,866	149	70	1,903	42	.....	.....	1,203	75	1,278
Welsh............	2,820	1,771	1,049	443	2,128	249	1	.....	5	8	14
West Indian (except Cuban)....	1,171	655	516	125	938	108	.....	2	10	3	15
Other peoples.....	3,038	2,585	453	185	2,751	102	3	1	1,034	199	1,237
Total......	1,197,892	808,144	389,748	147,158	986,355	64,379	2,842	2,484	185,872	84,116	275,314
Admitted in Philippine Islands..	4,408	3,865	543	964	3,323	121	.....	.....	682	158	840

ALIENS ADMITTED, FISCAL YEAR ENDED JUNE 30, 1913, BY RACES OR PEOPLES.

Money.			By whom passage was paid.			Going to join—		
Aliens bringing—		Total amount of money shown.	Self.	Relative.	Other than self or relative.	Relative.	Friend.	Neither relative nor friend.
$50 or over.	Less than $50.							
1,059	4,494	$167,191	4,884	1,497	253	4,317	847	1,470
786	7,215	260,074	7,881	1,412	60	7,142	2,089	122
1,923	5,822	455,907	6,638	4,388	65	8,680	2,150	261
1,153	6,831	307,147	7,709	1,351	27	4,493	3,866	728
571	1,180	69,784	845	1,074	103	1,189	513	320
2,661	34,883	1,066,699	34,898	7,434	167	28,310	12,973	1,216
1,820	576	164,944	1,922	1,152	25	974	258	1,867
334	3,770	128,967	4,046	448	26	2,816	1,542	162
3,815	5,501	745,603	8,699	5,626	182	9,646	3,723	1,138
145	21	41,878	169	15	4	32	75	81
22,101	15,769	4,352,365	33,580	20,357	1,585	33,838	10,356	11,328
1,861	9,238	470,932	8,708	3,587	461	7,128	4,823	805
6,533	6,373	1,332,572	11,981	7,988	683	13,758	2,524	4,370
19,285	32,526	4,309,865	46,501	32,959	1,405	59,192	15,417	6,256
3,403	31,751	1,230,553	35,790	2,838	16	25,423	12,323	898
7,805	41,536	2,307,345	36,423	64,400	507	94,591	4,837	1,902
7,121	23,006	1,985,703	22,852	13,689	482	30,588	3,262	3,173
6,977	26,968	1,437,640	33,305	8,948	281	31,857	9,012	1,665
17,697	168,463	5,938,521	175,817	55,391	405	219,102	11,043	1,468
3,578	3,644	290,635	1,630	6,600	72	6,802	439	1,061
8	24	1,219	7	56	1	54	4	6
1,166	17,916	504,884	13,833	10,681	133	22,796	1,747	104
2,644	18,686	775,515	18,530	11,979	101	25,353	4,545	712
1,134	3,620	189,873	5,102	5,675	177	5,361	711	4,882
7	2	3,360	6	3	2	2		7
7,839	130,569	4,033,440	119,633	54,306	426	155,011	17,785	1,569
953	8,549	292,824	7,260	6,046	260	10,823	2,270	473
685	10,582	316,465	10,639	2,771	41	9,443	3,654	354
2,054	44,397	1,279,412	45,628	5,538	306	29,898	20,573	1,001
690	24,349	627,904	22,971	7,526	91	25,511	4,448	629
8,003	25,190	2,084,546	29,124	8,959	654	24,496	10,065	4,176
7,397	7,580	1,775,314	13,689	7,291	313	13,960	3,714	3,619
1,575	19,879	627,518	19,834	7,352	48	24,287	2,690	257
2,740	3,673	439,783	6,455	1,393	1,194	3,867	2,238	2,937
1,021	119	130,231	807	462	94	324	243	796
1,207	5,231	305,782	6,383	2,817	10	7,925	1,055	230
180	1,584	65,356	1,791	220	4	1,504	398	113
1,105	854	190,225	1,746	1,037	37	1,878	573	369
496	404	82,968	838	305	28	661	150	360
288	2,342	99,273	2,597	376	65	1,899	983	156
151,820	755,097	40,890,197	811,151	375,947	10,794	954,931	179,920	63,041
1,867	1,895	43,589	2,658	1,662	88	1,808	587	2,013

TABLE VII A.—SEX, AGE, AND LENGTH OF RESIDENCE IN UNITED STATES OF EMIGRANT ALIENS DEPARTED, FISCAL YEAR ENDED JUNE 30, 1913, BY RACES OR PEOPLES.

Race or people.	Number departed.	Sex.		Age.			Continuous residence in the United States.					
		Male.	Female.	Under 14 years.	14 to 44 years.	45 years and over.	Not over 5 years.	5 to 10 years.	10 to 15 years.	15 to 20 years.	Over 20 years.	Unknown.
African (black)	1,671	1,127	544	137	1,431	103	1,245	301	77	18	10	20
Armenian	676	640	36	4	556	116	415	209	31	10	9	2
Bohemian and Moravian	871	545	326	30	721	120	504	263	47	6	13	38
Bulgarian, Servian, Montenegrin	13,525	13,222	303	66	12,547	912	10,638	2,458	147	20	5	267
Chinese	2,250	2,204	46	2	564	1,684	227	226	264	222	1,309	2
Croatian and Slovenian	10,209	9,098	1,111	146	8,868	1,195	6,144	2,788	319	24	30	904
Cuban	1,264	835	429	163	980	121	1,072	123	45	13	5	6
Dalmatian, Bosnian, Herzegovinian	849	824	25	5	775	69	590	240	16	1	2	—
Dutch and Flemish	2,148	1,600	548	207	1,724	217	1,004	287	59	4	21	773
East Indian	213	212	1	—	185	28	104	106	3	—	—	—
English	10,794	6,797	3,997	1,104	8,447	1,243	5,033	1,189	254	79	106	4,133
Finnish	3,053	2,221	832	124	2,734	195	1,285	515	98	11	17	1,127
French	4,019	2,550	1,469	191	3,390	438	2,610	508	160	25	52	664
German	11,871	7,613	4,258	751	9,606	1,514	6,615	2,260	392	74	164	2,366
Greek	31,556	31,115	441	113	30,193	1,250	18,054	12,107	1,147	50	18	180
Hebrew	6,697	5,215	1,482	315	5,501	881	3,812	1,252	241	21	34	1,337
Irish	4,458	2,439	2,019	188	3,788	482	1,646	965	235	74	160	1,378
Italian (North)	10,995	9,378	1,617	299	9,585	1,111	6,324	3,260	738	91	115	467
Italian (South)	79,057	70,619	8,438	2,198	69,035	7,824	54,853	19,062	3,521	415	297	909
Japanese	733	561	172	18	505	210	235	316	115	41	19	7
Korean	44	38	6	—	35	9	—	34	6	4	—	—
Lithuanian	3,276	2,412	864	191	2,719	366	2,585	552	113	9	17	—
Magyar	11,496	8,225	3,271	567	9,905	1,024	7,887	3,063	431	44	34	37
Mexican	910	773	137	47	765	98	816	70	15	3	2	4
Pacific Islander	4	3	1	—	—	—	4	—	—	—	—	—
Polish	24,107	18,886	5,221	701	20,623	2,783	18,770	3,585	850	80	50	772
Portuguese	1,583	1,128	455	105	1,308	170	1,067	416	67	16	14	3
Roumanian	3,156	2,811	345	52	2,661	443	2,432	604	51	1	1	67
Russian	10,548	9,040	1,508	622	9,153	773	7,635	848	99	14	6	1,946
Ruthenian (Russniak)	5,327	4,643	684	105	4,706	516	2,599	497	79	6	103	2,043
Scandinavian	9,291	6,989	2,302	400	8,012	879	1,812	1,229	293	54	29	5,874
Scotch	4,118	2,706	1,412	433	3,249	436	1,796	435	52	26	39	1,780
Slovak	9,851	7,678	2,173	294	8,276	1,281	7,092	2,172	477	71	39	—
Spanish	3,181	2,692	489	134	2,748	299	2,349	556	201	15	13	47
Spanish-American	457	310	147	52	364	41	368	69	10	3	2	5
Syrian	797	616	181	30	674	93	409	260	70	9	6	43

Turkish	1,297	1,266	31	13	1,196	88	907	43	22	1	3	22
Welsh	208	231	67	11	258	29	139	31	6	1	6	118
West Indian (except Cuban)	584	299	285	48	471	65	338	95	35	1	5	109
Other peoples	1,118	1,050	68	29	1,017	72	776	171	17	6		143
Not specified[1]	19,838	11,197	8,641	3,348	15,460	1,030						19,838
Total	308,190	251,808	56,382	13,245	264,137	30,808	182,985	63,471	10,803	1,559	2,726	46,646
Departed from Philippine Islands	768	566	202	107	539	122	508	142	61	18	39	

[1] Departed via Canadian border. Reported by Canadian Government as Canadians.

TABLE VII b.—CONJUGAL CONDITION OF IMMIGRANT ALIENS

[Abbreviations: S., single;

Race or people	Under 14 years (total).[1]	14 to 44 years.					45 years and over.				
		S.	M.	W.	D.	Total.	S.	M.	W.	D.	Total.
African (black)	237	2,478	861	10	....	3,349	16	80	9	....	105
Armenian	413	4,110	3,168	24	....	7,302	5	158	15	....	178
Bohemian and Moravian	1,008	3,263	1,764	21	1	5,049	12	229	30	....	271
Bulgarian, Servian, and Montenegrin	295	3,108	3,961	51	....	7,120	15	377	26	1	419
Chinese	162	782	461	....	....	1,243	1	286	....	....	287
Croatian and Slovenian	1,684	14,382	13,992	97	1	28,472	47	1,344	43	....	1,434
Cuban	218	1,354	347	11	....	1,712	27	147	22	....	196
Dalmatian, Bosnian, Herzegovinian	98	2,082	1,564	15	....	3,661	7	162	10	....	179
Dutch and Flemish	1,337	4,713	2,854	42	2	7,611	64	416	42	1	523
East Indian	1	111	59	7	....	177	1	5	....	....	6
English	4,503	15,197	8,372	190	5	23,764	368	2,333	350	2	3,053
Finnish	400	5,837	1,775	32	....	7,644	17	83	15	....	115
French	1,922	5,488	2,752	102	4	8,346	178	981	192	1	1,352
German	7,707	22,234	12,736	144	18	35,132	234	2,572	262	7	3,075
Greek	755	24,097	9,672	51	....	33,820	35	510	23	....	568
Hebrew	11,186	27,072	15,539	140	11	42,762	53	2,793	352	2	3,200
Irish	1,281	14,559	2,181	75	1	16,816	226	602	147	....	975
Italian (North)	2,210	16,994	11,869	131	....	28,994	109	1,047	68	....	1,224
Italian (South)	14,356	78,351	74,517	343	1	153,212	322	8,161	421	....	8,904
Japanese	280	1,448	979	4	2	2,433	8	418	18	....	444
Korean	6	7	2	....	....	9	....	....	....	....	....
Lithuanian	887	11,548	3,346	17	....	14,911	20	241	10	....	271
Magyar	2,857	4,486	7,396	74	2	11,958	16	1,715	89	2	1,822
Mexican	1,608	2,557	1,605	59	....	4,221	37	404	89	....	530
Pacific Islander	....	4	2	....	....	6	....	2	....	....	2
Polish	8,603	61,555	42,533	211	1	104,300	80	2,691	98	....	2,869
Portuguese	1,200	3,612	3,379	40	1	7,032	19	416	29	....	464
Roumanian	528	2,443	5,529	64	4	8,040	19	1,705	81	....	1,805
Russian	880	20,296	23,658	102	....	44,056	18	654	25	....	697
Ruthenian (Russniak)	1,145	8,304	8,667	37	....	17,008	11	799	17	....	827
Scandinavian	1,566	20,115	2,649	55	3	22,822	230	546	78	1	855
Scotch	1,766	6,099	2,459	56	3	8,617	188	811	163	....	1,162
Slovak	2,052	6,308	7,167	28	1	13,594	7	551	38	....	596
Spanish	508	4,208	2,094	29	....	6,331	58	312	31	....	401
Spanish-American	121	643	142	4	....	789	8	56	4	....	68
Syrian	766	3,963	1,177	58	....	5,198	13	169	31	....	213
Turkish	43	1,144	648	4	....	1,796	4	21	2	....	27
Welsh	201	946	463	11	....	1,420	18	111	21	....	150
West Indian (except Cuban)	62	394	139	3	....	536	1	51	5	....	57
Other peoples	89	1,554	869	7	....	2,430	5	61	....	....	66
Total	75,061	407,936	283,347	2,349	61	693,693	2,497	34,020	2,856	17	39,390

[1] None divorced; 62 married, as follows: Bohemian and Moravian, Bulgarian, Servian, and Montenegrin, Croatian and Slovenian, Dalmatian, Bosnian, Herzegovinian, Dutch and Flemish, French, Lithuanian, Mexican, Roumanian, Scandinavian, Scotch, Slovak, and Welsh, 1 each; Portuguese, 3; English, 4; Greek and Polish, 5 each; German, 6; Hebrew, 7; and Italian (South), 19; and 3 widowed—Hebrew, Italian (South), and Scandinavian, 1 each.

ADMITTED, FISCAL YEAR ENDED JUNE 30, 1913, BY RACES OR PEOPLES.

M., married; W., widowed; D., divorced.]

Under 14 years (to-tal).²	14 to 44 years.					45 years and over.					Single females.			
	S.	M.	W.	D.	Total.	S.	M.	W.	D.	Total.	14-21 years.	22-29 years.	30-37 years.	38-44 years.
328	1,719	635	100	1	2,455	29	60	71	...	160	761	725	173	60
305	459	476	71	1	1,007	1	63	84	...	148	340	95	17	7
998	2,245	1,181	63	1	3,490	3	150	122	...	275	1,507	632	94	12
265	215	660	45	4	924	3	45	16	...	64	153	56	6	.....
27	22	264	1	....	287	1	12	3	...	16	16	6	....	.....
1,738	5,005	3,619	264	2	8,890	15	171	95	...	281	3,330	1,446	200	29
178	299	317	40	....	656	16	66	57	...	139	157	111	28	3
61	316	182	9	....	507	.....	6	8	...	14	160	138	18	.....
1,338	1,195	2,054	32	4	3,285	20	271	120	2	413	573	451	130	41
......	......	1	3	....	.....	4	.....	.....	...	.....	1	.....	.....	.....
4,412	8,398	7,661	462	11	16,532	444	1,642	1,171	1	3,258	2,885	3,446	1,531	536
428	3,163	800	43	1	4,007	13	50	38	1	102	1,922	1,040	172	29
1,909	3,238	2,688	126	4	6,056	120	575	370	2	1,067	1,637	1,032	423	146
7,683	13,920	9,962	553	54	24,495	243	1,384	1,075	11	2,713	8,412	4,190	1,032	292
514	1,517	1,194	60	....	2,771	3	118	95	...	216	1,006	450	52	9
11,192	18,159	10,436	813	48	29,456	32	1,822	1,666	14	3,534	15,015	2,861	245	38
1,262	13,597	1,855	172	1	15,625	191	422	451	...	1,064	7,746	4,665	933	253
2,038	3,228	4,321	100	2	7,651	23	196	197	1	417	1,839	1,124	223	42
12,946	16,077	20,754	751	1	37,583	123	2,610	1,877	2	4,612	10,658	4,412	795	212
157-	296	4,556	4	1	4,857	1	111	18	1	131	251	35	8	2
7	5	37	....	....	42	.....	.....	.....	...	...	2	3	.....	.....
873	5,919	1,520	88	....	7,527	2	70	106	...	178	4,311	1,449	143	16
2,813	4,825	5,046	541	40	10,452	9	354	340	5	708	3,596	957	237	35
1,440	785	1,726	199	....	2,710	12	188	245	...	445	543	165	54	23
......	......	1	1	....	.....	2	.....	1	...	.....	1	.....	.....	.....
8,650	34,269	13,549	870	....	48,688	21	656	577	1	1,255	28,534	5,159	498	78
1,101	1,849	1,396	85	4	3,334	29	209	196	1	435	1,305	422	96	26
464	712	1,529	244	14	2,499	3	76	36	...	115	404	276	27	5
867	2,873	1,873	104	....	4,850	3	80	39	...	122	2,016	788	64	5
1,220	7,459	2,516	267	....	10,242	1	88	57	...	146	6,399	906	120	34
1,472	9,184	1,928	118	4	11,234	147	351	289	1	788	5,083	3,212	676	213
1,755	4,385	2,257	145	2	6,789	189	579	436	...	1,204	1,444	1,972	754	215
2,153	4,732	3,496	225	1	8,454	4	150	231	...	385	4,055	622	47	8
418	556	658	23	....	1,237	11	78	58	...	147	291	200	49	16
82	151	113	12	....	276	4	12	11	...	27	81	45	18	7
575	1,003	1,017	230	....	2,250	4	84	120	...	208	807	168	24	4
27	58	45	4	....	107	.....	6	9	...	15	42	14	2	.....
242	378	324	6	....	708	9	63	27	...	99	140	172	47	19
63	279	109	13	1	402	9	29	13	...	51	140	105	23	11
96	157	150	14	....	321	1	19	16	...	36	107	45	3	2
72,097	172,655	112,908	6,897	202	292,662	1,739	12,867	10,340	43	24,989	117,670	43,595	8,962	2,428

² None divorced; 40 married, as follows: Armenian, Dutch and Flemish, French, Irish, Japanese, Russian, and Scotch, 1 each; Greek and Mexican, 2 each; Hebrew and Magyar, 3 each; English and German, 4 each; Italian (South), 5; and Polish, 10; and widowed—Hebrew, 1.

TABLE VIII.—IMMIGRANT ALIENS ADMITTED, FISCAL YEAR ENDED JUNE 30, 1913, BY COUNTRIES OF LAST PERMANENT RESIDENCE AND RACES OR PEOPLES.

Country of last permanent residence	African (black)	Armenian	Bohemian and Moravian	Bulgarian, Servian, and Montenegrin	Chinese	Croatian and Slovenian	Cuban	Dalmatian, Bosnian, and Herzegovinian	Dutch and Flemish	East Indian	English	Finnish	French	German	Greek	Hebrew	Irish	Italian (North)	Italian (South)	Japanese	Korean
Austria	1	2	10,362	1,096		17,797	1	4,120	21		13	1	9	8,113	8	11,531	3	1,937	25		
Hungary		10	179	3,213		22,970		144	24		5		3	16,002	4	3,371	1	48	22		
Belgium	2	15		1,528					6,340		24	11	636	147	5	162	4	7	6		
Bulgaria, Servia, and Montenegro						4									27	14		2			
Denmark				26					18		240		1	47		82					
France, including Corsica	3	37		34	1			7	7		66	13	6,423	452	52	693		566	349	3	
German Empire	1	8	14	42	1	21		2	148	4			72	28,037	3	806		216	50	5	
Greece		96		3		30	5	11	87	1	58	2	4	5	22,437	60		6	14		
Italy, including Sicily and Sardinia				1	2	263	2	7	7		7	3	59	87	15	16		37,531	227,624		
Netherlands	1		177						6,681		2		6	114	1	56		7	10		
Norway												6	3	16		4					
Portugal, including Cape de Verde and Azore Islands	972					42	16	6	1		11	25	4	1				2	1		
Roumania		12		5		1		1	2		37			51	21	1,640		1	1		
Russian Empire		909	73	21		39		11	11		10	11,156	4	17,857	30	74,033	2	469	8		
Spain, including Canary and Balearic Islands											1		5	9	2			3	5		
Sweden						5		1	3		37	31		18		90			3		
Switzerland			6			8		1	30	1	10	1	510	2,910		51	2	469	15		
Turkey in Europe		442	3	1,589		7		4	1	15	7			16	9,374	1,007	1	3	10		
United Kingdom	22	140	14	13	3			6	62	1	36,018	30	239	639	31	4,001	29,930	250	174	23	1
Other Europe		7		14					2	1	35		4	1	76	9	1	15	125		
Total Europe	1,002	1,678	10,831	7,535	6	41,197	25	4,321	13,446	22	36,574	11,279	7,992	74,530	32,086	97,930	30,019	41,063	228,443	31	1
China	3	1			1,981	1	1	1	1	1	30		4	18	1	12	4	1	2	4	
Japan					17					6	18		2	5			2			8,212	
India	1			38					1	104	40			6		2	7	2	17		
Turkey in Asia		7,369				4				6	10		4	7	5,192	1,046	4	5	2		
Other Asia		46	4						6	2	14			1	4	30	1			1	57
Total Asia	4	7,415	4	38	2,000	5	1	1	9	113	112		10	37	5,197	1,090	18	8	22	8,217	57
Africa	26	95				3	1	1	27	1	206		23	51	109	330	19	98	85		

Immigrant aliens admitted, by race or people and country of last permanent residence — *(continued; races Lithuanian through West Indian)*

Country of last permanent residence	Lithuanian	Magyar	Mexican	Pacific Islander	Polish	Portuguese	Roumanian	Russian	Ruthenian	Scandinavian	Scotch	Slovak	Spanish	Spanish-American	Syrian	Turkish	Welsh	West Indian (except Cuban)	Other peoples	Total
Austria	53	399			54,997		484	366	24,700	23	1	911	1			10			16	137,245
Hungary	15	29,422			336		11,955	37	3,879	8	1	25,923							6	117,580
Belgium					13			16	2	1	5	3					2		2	7,405
Bulgaria, Servia, and Montenegro		2			195		75	29				10		3		1			29	1,753
Denmark	72	28			74		28	85	1	6,063	18	105							3	6,478
France, including Corsica			4			8		74		34	8		157						32	9,675
German Empire			3		3,658	2	4	1	252	105	18	10	5							34,329
Greece	1					1	3							1						22,817
Italy, including Sicily and Sardinia					15					2	7		6			6				265,542
Netherlands					5			3	2	9	5									6,902
Norway								2		8,511	1									8,587
Portugal, including Cape Verde and Azore Islands				2		13,164														14,171
Roumania		10			12		375	3		5	3				1	6			5	2,155
Russian Empire	23,873	30		1	112,345	8	21	48,472	1,074	892	226	24		15	6				100	291,040
Spain, including Canary and Balearic Islands						8							6,028							6,167
Sweden	3	9			13					17,007	6									17,202
Switzerland					24		101	1	6	7	4		3		4				53	4,104
Turkey in Europe	340	34		1	156	12	8	72	2	189	1	3	46	15	48	303				14,128
United Kingdom				1		2				7	13,226				55	33	2,367	10	1,187	88,294
Other Europe											6				2	1			17	371
Total Europe	24,361	30,025	11	2	171,844	13,198	13,163	49,190	29,918	32,903	13,290	26,988	6,318	77	213	404	2,375	20	1,544	1,055,855
Australia, Tasmania, and New Zealand		114	226								9	18	50	7	29		130		2	
Pacific Islands, not specified	1	1	4	1,443	10			935	6	24		7	20	1		3	3	21	2	
British North America		47	24	3	5	8	11	7	21	898	1,453	2,362	406	946	467	6,763	1,070	89	56	
Central America	1			61	1	3	1	8	10	157	5	21	90	151	20	11	21	155	33	
Mexico	47	2	1	1	1	27	1	22	1	97	4	67	114	60	409	8	89	90	494	
South America						6	14	43	14	128	4	53	457	1	39	21	155	94	39	
West Indies						46				582		98	110		6	31	27	39		
Other countries																				
Grand total	24,634	9,353	11,091	9,087	2,022	3,099	4,520	14,507	188	55,522	12,756	20,652	80,865	38,644	101,330	37,023	42,534	231,613	8,302	
Admitted in Philippine Islands					1,864	1		15	603	118		37	77	2		9		21	1,273	

TABLE VIII.—IMMIGRANT ALIENS ADMITTED, FISCAL YEAR ENDED JUNE 30, 1913, BY COUNTRIES OF LAST PERMANENT RESIDENCE AND RACES OR PEOPLES—Continued.

Country of last permanent residence.	Lithuanian.	Magyar.	Mexican.	Pacific Islander.	Polish.	Portuguese.	Roumanian.	Russian.	Ruthenian.	Scandinavian.	Scotch.	Slovak.	Spanish.	Spanish-American.	Syrian.	Turkish.	Welsh.	West Indian (except Cuban).	Other peoples.	Total.
China		1			1			8		8	12		1		1		1		7	2,106
Japan								5		2	4				2				3	8,281
India		1				2	1			1	11		2		1		1			179
Turkey in Asia								2			3				8,224	1,385			635	23,955
Other Asia					1			68		1	1	4	4		41	3		1	554	838
Total Asia	1	2			2	3	1	83		12	31		7		8,269	1,388	2	1	1,199	35,358
Africa	2				8			6	2	6	38		10		144	27	3	1	88	1,409
Australia, Tasmania, and New Zealand					7			16		19	132	224	1	5	2		12		18	1,229
Pacific Islands, not specified				6						6	5	1	7						4	111
British North America	251	558	7	3	2,226		253	1,981	656	5,595	7,712		95	437	134	1	414	3	146	73,802
Central America	2	6	8			10	1	8		28	16		118	52	20	173	1	38	2	1,473
Mexico	28	14	10,908		35	2	3	17	1	22	13		203	652	52	1	1	2	6	11,926
South America		2	20		239	239	26	169	11	73	20	16	325	140	253	5	4	32	25	4,248
West Indies					2	102	4	1		69	36		1,957		111	8	8	1,074	2	12,458
Other countries										4			1		4	8			4	23
Grand total	24,647	30,610	10,954	11	174,365	13,566	13,451	51,472	30,588	38,737	21,293	27,234	9,042	1,363	9,210	2,015	2,820	1,171	3,038	1,197,892
Admitted in Philippine Islands		1	1			25		4		8	34		276	5	2	24			6	4,408

TABLE VIII A.—EMIGRANT ALIENS DEPARTED, FISCAL YEAR ENDED JUNE 30, 1913, BY COUNTRIES OF INTENDED FUTURE RESIDENCE AND RACES OR PEOPLES.

Country of intended future residence.	African (black).	Armenian.	Bohemian and Moravian.	Bulgarian, Servian, and Montenegrin.	Chinese.	Croatian and Slovenian.	Cuban.	Dalmatian, Bosnian, and Herzegovinian.	Dutch and Flemish.	East Indian.	English.	Finnish.	French.	German.	Greek.	Hebrew.	Irish.	Italian (North).	Italian (South).	Japanese.	Korean.
Austria			787	749		6,473		838	9		3	2	7	969	11	955	1	108	12		1
Hungary			18	822	2	2,773		4	2		7	1	92	2,915	2	256	1	4	10		
Belgium		1							684		1			9		4					
Bulgaria, Servia, and Montenegro				9,593					3		1			3	3	3					
Denmark			1	1		15			13		1			4		2		1	3		
France, including Corsica		11	6	13	1	5		1	9		31	1	3,018	46	11	47		57	20	1	
German Empire				21		9					10		7	4,445	2	32		32	4		
Greece				1		10	9								30,531				8		
Italy, including Sicily and Sardinia						5		3			8				16			10,197	77,717	3	
Netherlands									582												
Norway				1					2												
Portugal, including Cape Verde and Azore Islands	464	2												21		1			3		
Roumania		22		1							2			6	2	2					
Russian Empire					1				1			1,906	1			94	3		2		
Spain, including Canary and Balearic Islands		1		6			11		2		2		1					1	1		
Sweden									1			4		4		1					
Switzerland									1		5		4	5	2	2					
Turkey in Europe		20							4				1		2						
United Kingdom		1		1					1		5,452		59	396	746	48	2,971	39	13		1
Other Europe			9					3	6		1		30	332	2	206		2,16			
Total Europe	464	64	825	13,223	4	9,293	20	846	1,320	1	5,527	1,916	3,228	9,211	31,328	5,166	2,982	10,428	77,795	13	1
China					2,232				1	1	26			8		1		1		1	
Japan				19	5					1	9		13		4	10	1	1	15	704	
India										209	15				3						
Turkey in Asia		599							2					8	7	11		2			
Other Asia		1				1			3		2		6		8	37	46	1			1
Total Asia		600		19	2,237					211	52	2		8	15				9	705	1
Africa	5	5							4		39			8		3		8			40
Australia, Tasmania, and New Zealand		2	2	2		1		1	6		369			21							41

TABLE VIII A.—EMIGRANT ALIENS DEPARTED, FISCAL YEAR ENDED JUNE 30, 1913, BY COUNTRIES OF INTENDED FUTURE RESIDENCE AND RACES OR PEOPLE—Continued.

Country of intended future residence	Korean	Japanese	Italian (South)	Italian (North)	Irish	Hebrew	Greek	German	French	Finnish	English	East Indian	Dutch and Flemish	Dalmatian, Bosnian, and Herzegovinian	Cuban	Croatian and Slovenian	Chinese	Bulgarian, Servian, and Montenegrin	Bohemian and Moravian	Armenian	African (black)
Pacific Islands, not specified								7	8		6										
British North America		8	916	471	1,339	1,340	185	2,374	608	1,131	4,377		777		6	905	2	277	36	4	20
Central America		2	19	6	73	5	6	47	5	1	37	1	2		3	2	1	4	1	3	15
Mexico		1	5		1	134	2	17	4		27		9		5	4	2		4		
South America		1	280	65	7	1	3	111	30	1	65		27	1	1	4	4		3		14
West Indies		3	18		6		1	67	57	2	291				1,230						
Other countries							1				4										1,153
Grand total		733	79,057	10,995	4,458	6,097	31,556	11,871	4,019	3,053	10,794	213	2,148	849	1,264	10,209	2,250	13,525	871	676	1,671
Departed from Philippine Islands	44	198		12			1	51	17		54	64	2				44				

Country of intended future residence	Total	Not specified	Other peoples	West Indian (except Cuban)	Welsh	Turkish	Syrian	Spanish-American	Spanish	Slovak	Scotch	Scandinavian	Ruthenian (Russniak)	Russian	Roumanian	Portuguese	Polish	Pacific Islander	Mexican	Magyar	Lithuanian
Austria	28,760		3			2	1	1		1,004	3	6	2,379	392	134		13,325		3	575	9
Hungary	29,904		3			5	9			8,831	1	6	763	55	2,677	3	103			10,647	1
Belgium	803										1	2		3		1	2				
Bulgaria, Servia, and Montenegro	9,664										1	1									
Denmark	608										1	595									
France, including Corsica	3,430						4	7			1	3		19			3		19	4	1
German Empire	4,759		8			13		7		3	1	14		37	4		3			8	
Greece	30,603		4	1		12	1			1	1						2			4	
Italy, including Sicily and Sardinia	88,021		20	1		17			72	3	2	7		2	4		7		4	4	1
Netherlands	599		1			3			3			7			1						
Norway	1,710						2					1,698		3	2		146			2	

	Total
Portugal, including Cape Verde and Azore Islands	1,965
Roumania	319
Russian Empire	26,923
Spain, including Canary and Baleare Islands	2,029
Sweden	1,989
Switzerland	449
Turkey in Europe	4,809
United Kingdom	11,199
Other Europe	16
Total Europe	248,559
China	2,303
Japan	731
India	240
Turkey in Asia	1,313
Other Asia	103
Total Asia	4,690
Africa	209
Australia, Tasmania, and New Zealand	645
Pacific Islands, not specified	29
British North America	46,981
Central America	482
Mexico	991
South America	1,367
West Indies	4,223
Other countries	14
Grand total	308,190
Departed from Philippine Islands	768

[1] Departed via Canadian border. Reported by Canadian Government as Canadians.

TABLE IX.—IMMIGRANT ALIENS ADMITTED, FISCAL YEAR ENDED JUNE 30, 1913, BY STATES OF INTENDED FUTURE RESIDENCE AND RACES OR PEOPLES.[1]

Race or people.	Ala.	Alaska.	Ariz.	Ark.	Cal.	Colo.	Conn.	Del.	D.C.	Fla.	Ga.	Hawaii.	Idaho.	Ill.	Ind.	Iowa.	Kans.	Ky.
African (black)	45		1		15		37		39	1,446	5	1		32	7	1	3	3
Armenian	8	3			694	7	246		1	2				790	8	7	1	1
Bohemian and Moravian (Czech)	36	67	8	17	115	59	77		9	1	6		6	3,055	63	310	83	2
Bulgarian, Servian, and Montenegrin	16		43	2	57	13	23		2	7			8	1,018	656	83	7	3
Chinese	1		13		1,362	7		2	28		3	143	4	26		3		2
Croatian and Slovenian	33	18	54	33	287	466	432	1	15		13		21	4,192	983	222	401	10
Cuban	11				17	1	10		4	839	18			12	19			4
Dalmatian, Bosnian, and Herzegovinian	4	10	33		440	39	5		1				2	618	172	9	3	1
Dutch and Flemish	10	12	7	4	308	37	34		20	57	3		44	2,442	461	937	57	6
East Indian					48					9								
English	72	74	330	35	3,863	273	1,108	81	172	435	107	6	268	3,130	386	628	172	41
Finnish	5	33	26	5	268	36	76		9	20	14	6	59	241	8	8	1	1
French	18	17	17	6	989	73	568	4	69	75	10	81	66	893	131	48	124	10
German	74	18	49	74	2,405	2,060	1,170	33	178	141	93	1	222	9,773	696	1,213	1,431	128
Greek	169	9	6	30	531	244	857	6	98	352	178	3	66	3,448	487	971	58	37
Hebrew	58			11	477	139	1,591	74	209	50	162	19	6	7,579	272	469	87	35
Irish	21	30	57	23	1,338	98	1,005	84	97	76	24	1	77	2,173	158	187	50	34
Italian (North)	62	90	138	26	6,082	565	1,919	17	55	15	26	1	103	4,773	273	334	283	84
Italian (South)	323	14	32	1	3,130	663	9,503	404	383	304	26	8	49	12,704	772	398	107	1
Japanese	2	5	12		2,616	59	5		10	3		4,062	59	47	1	2	1	
Korean					15							45						
Lithuanian	2	9		2	39	13	1,628	15	5	3	5		3	5,415	363	207	5	26
Magyar					44	32	1,117	4	5	5			8	1,838	1,016	43	12	
Mexican	1		2,465	1	874	3	2		6	23	8			18	6	3	40	
Pacific Islander		1			2						3		5					
Polish	31		9	4	87	87	7,298	783	17	7		3	4	25,658	2,632	184	212	32
Portuguese			4		1,839	1	76		5	11	3	228		32				1
Roumanian				1	11	128	54	49					3	1,091	1,295	90	3	105
Russian	9	33	7	2	556	5	2,539	215	35	5	11	99		4,930	556	331	126	10
Ruthenian (Russniak)	1		2		10		988		7	4	32			1,275	185	15	28	1
Scandinavian (Norwegians, Danes, and Swedes)	44	91	44	14	1,050	223		18	42	34		7	293	4,982	190	1,589	156	7
Scotch	33	52	49	14	1,371	152	889	10	54	83	3	73	101	1,260	336	184	49	20
Slovak	26	5	4	6	35	53	452	4	2	3			4	2,501	435	36	19	11
Spanish	13		502		937	53	653		15	1,111	28	1,043	144	47	9	33	84	
Spanish-American	2	2	1		125	1	4		88		2			21	12	2		
Syrian	24		13	15	55	11	367	4	19	40	1		1	298	206	58	18	40
Turkish	2	1	4		10		25		4				3	176	58	10	5	3
Welsh	3		7		107	58	32		3	10				178	29	31	31	11
West Indian (other than Cuban)	9	23		8	4		13	1	10	171	2		37	6	2		1	2
Other peoples	2		5	3	74	6	248		9			3		322	119	11	1	2
Total	1,170	618	3,945	353	32,277	5,673	35,138	1,810	1,717	5,352	787	5,837	1,689	107,060	13,005	8,666	3,663	761

Race or people.	La.	Me.	Md.	Mass.	Mich.	Minn.	Miss.	Mo.	Mont.	Nebr.	Nev.	N.H.	N.J.	N. Mex.	N.Y.	N.C.	N. Dak.	Ohio.	Okla.
African (black)	30	16	22	1,173	101	4	8	5				6	269		2,688	4	1	43	12
Armenian		55	6	2,367	321		1	132			1	84	374		2,813	5		60	
Bohemian and Moravian (Czech)	4	2	202	61	416	207		175	48	453			273	5	1,708		45	1,310	32
Bulgarian, Servian, and Montenegrin		4	51	42	972	426		198	55	53		9	126	8	1,044	2	21	1,397	2
Chinese	6	18	6	45	30	8	7	6	5		4		1	1	8			17	1
Croatian and Slovenian	24	3	130	57	2,070	2,066	11	513	234	95	5	7	526	103	3,880	1	8	6,391	12
Cuban	59		44	30	1	1		8			43	2	32		1,786	14		8	
Dalmatian, Bosnian, and Herzegovinian	38	2	8	19	104	274	15		38				123		697			130	10
Dutch and Flemish	27	10	22	653	3,738	394	3	80	199	136		1	802	1	1,931	28	4	222	
East Indian	3			9								75					76	3	
English	118	1,114	192	6,541	5,388	649	44	323	920	144	9	308	2,113	1	12,756	66	250	2,103	67
Finnish	7	114	1	2,239	2,641	2,130	5	101	177	14	1	144	211	3	2,177		24	404	
French	178	2,102	33	3,318	907	206	6	1,599	229	2	69	2,414	278		4,242	17	44	140	30
German	118	66	775	938	4,471	1,352	25	1,024	1,071	2,455	14	54	4,333	51	18,013	35	1,307	6,060	315
Greek	58	312	99	5,919	449	210	16		33	143	49	1,861	908	1	10,279	56	33	2,073	
Hebrew	106	129	1,534	6,109	1,674	870	22	1,363	11	302	42	80	3,771	8	59,029	13	79	2,453	45
Irish	21	470	117	6,607	1,557	372	5	251	580	61	56	241	1,164	24	11,961	7	127	705	5
Italian (North)	12	82	70	2,739	1,747	502	48	603	236	70	1	101		20	9,398	2	6	845	168
Italian (South)	510	526	1,359	21,030	5,546	930	76	2,156	147	801	304	191	13,398	4	91,223	41	33	9,944	36
Japanese		1		24	3	8		4	40	8	123		5	20	163			11	
Korean											10			4					
Lithuanian	2		275	3,957	538	52	6	93	11	34		214	1,185		3,259	13	17	583	15
Magyar	17	257	66	81	1,575	105	2	237	53	35	1	2	3,957	136	4,921		11	6,646	2
Mexican	26	7	4	24				13	1		1	1		128	569			5	7
Pacific Islander																			
Polish	9	313	1,309	13,627	16,071	1,150	18	1,054	100	259	1	1,054	14,433	1	39,505	15	134	8,692	98
Portuguese	3	3		9,002	3			7			6	3	23	2	905			5	
Roumanian		142	59	32	1,345	185	4	210	32	37			692	51	929	2	9	4,396	
Russian	22	22	1,485	5,266	2,532	412	5	286	37	96	1	686	2,444		14,420	2	138	1,520	4
Ruthenian (Russniak)			73	965	729	308	3	227	52	13		159	3,327		7,642		79	1,467	22
Scandinavian (Norwegians, Danes, and Swedes)	45	169	54	2,374	852	5,194	18	133	939	835	26	115	827	2	6,380	7	1,694	370	14
Scotch	14	422	54	3,090	2,060	293	5	136	462	45	28	148	1,168	1	4,000	43	110	682	68
Slovak	160	76	45	132	484	221	1	201	20	20		6	2,209		3,264	4	5	3,333	13
Spanish	102	5	22	203	26	4	4	47	2	6	152	1	17	3	3,118	5	1	23	1
Spanish-American	36		14	26	192	2	8	86		9	1		285	29	751			9	
Syrian	1	53	11	1,692	440	61	43	12	6	30	3	146	21	15	2,638	38	5	540	19
Turkish	4	16	1	658	101	8		16	1			31	45	5	319	3	2	163	1
Welsh		10	9	89	98	36	1		45	25		5	39	1	530	2	17	3	10
West Indian (other than Cuban)	3	1	11	67			5				20	1	58	5	676	4		98	
Other peoples	2	96	5	469		13		108	9	12		77		27	768		5		2
Total	1,774	6,624	8,168	101,674	59,192	18,693	415	11,504	5,796	6,266	1,000	8,220	61,358	758	330,531	429	4,285	63,007	1,018

1 Also 4,408 immigrant aliens were admitted to the Philippine Islands for future permanent residence therein.

TABLE IX.—IMMIGRANT ALIENS ADMITTED, FISCAL YEAR ENDED JUNE 30, 1913, BY STATES OF INTENDED FUTURE RESIDENCE AND RACES OR PEOPLES—Continued.

Race or people.	Oreg.	Pa.	P. I.	P. R.	R. I.	S. C.	S. Dak.	Tenn.	Tex.	Utah.	Vt.	Va.	Wash.	W. Va.	Wis.	Wyo.	Total.
African (black)	4	128		164	281	1		10	6	3	2	11	10		1		6,634
Armenian	20	239		1	673	2	1	12	8		16	13	12	8	385	1	9,353
Bohemian and Moravian (Czech)		774			3		42	1	812	4	16	36	67	17	482	20	11,091
Bulgarian, Servian, and Montenegrin		1,740			17		1	1	35	9	5	4	415	89	325	16	9,087
Chinese	40	30		2	1		2	19	6	139		9	88		3	2	2,022
Croatian and Slovenian	108	117	2	15	3	2	9	3	78		11	24	966	878	2,020	99	42,499
Cuban		937			3				15			7	1		1		3,099
Dalmatian, Bosnian, and Herzegovinian	77	211		8			17	16	5	14	3		238		188		4,520
Dutch and Flemish	111	15	2	18	88	7	133	16	62	108	3	7	333	188	512	8	14,507
East Indian	6		3		1						7	13	17	5	3	4	188
English	561	4,197		51	1,582	22	134	73	353	515	342	215	2,217	239	496	93	55,522
Finnish	238	250		16	14	6	44	1	15	54	70	6	614	38	256	50	12,756
French	117	591	1	1	949	1	6	32	53	25	786	10	459	29	87	34	20,652
German	925	8,032	1		199	24	332	53	674	180	50	105	1,593	143	5,639	53	80,865
Greek	202	3,097		1	435	55	34	87	156	521	34	259	887	830	832	106	38,644
Hebrew	113	9,797		16	482	64	10	151	622	17	54	193	186	47	637	7	101,330
Irish	247	4,104		2	573	7	19	13	113	51	91	49	881	27	119	33	37,023
Italian (North)	227	6,135		1	189	5	21	166	274	428	267	51	834	327	392	200	42,534
Italian (South)	316	41,996		3	3,775	5	13	90	229	334	459	202	985	3,876	1,975	67	231,613
Japanese	272	10	3	2			1		7	68		2	747		2	29	8,302
Korean	14												108				64
Lithuanian	9	5,543			97		3	8	5	4	66	5	36	130	462	1	24,647
Magyar	36	7,286			4	2	3	2	33	7	39	85	4	586	616	12	30,610
Mexican	4	35	2					7	6,749	6		3			2		10,954
Pacific Islander	5									3			4				11
Polish	191	32,249	1	1	1,232	2	20	8	120		485	80	283	1,232	3,604	118	174,365
Portuguese	5	30		3	1,333				6		9	7	74		129	1	13,566
Roumanian		2,398			7	7	10	2	18		9	5	483	201			27,234
Russian	581	9,715	2	5	275		7	4	167	1	249	118	201	636	684	15	51,472
Ruthenian (Russniak)	392	12,007		1	337	3	1	3	51		33	22	4	201	83	2	30,588
Scandinavian (Norwegians, Danes, and Swedes)	581	850	1	5	251	5	738	10	207	294	90	71	4,354	11	1,499	51	38,737
Scotch	392	1,520		1	275	13	26	27	77	55	226	64	1,086	79	173	96	21,293
Slovak	31	12,200	1		15	1	1	3	3	4	15	28	60	274	657	13	27,234
Spanish	42	86		437	1	3		2	128	31	130	22	33	250	5	15	9,042
Spanish-American	8	84		40		24	7	2	9	1		9	11		2		1,363
Syrian	1	1,091	1	17	296		4	16	9	17	21	68	38	132	37	3	9,210
Turkish		90		1	256	1	1	1	3	1		1	8	8	14		2,015
Welsh	38	745			10			1	6	28	36	5	158	26	67	8	2,820
West Indian (other than Cuban)		40		93	4	1	1	2	3	6	2	1		14	53	2	1,171
Other peoples	31	203			17	1			4			3	11				3,038
Total	4,994	182,744	17	894	13,678	258	1,641	818	11,214	2,932	3,608	1,822	18,313	10,472	23,091	1,160	1,197,892

TABLE IX A.—EMIGRANT ALIENS DEPARTED, FISCAL YEAR ENDED JUNE 30, 1913, BY STATES OF LAST PERMANENT RESIDENCE AND RACES OR PEOPLES.[1]

Race or people.	Ala.	Alaska	Ariz.	Ark.	Cal.	Colo.	Conn.	Del.	D.C.	Fla.	Ga.	Hawaii	Idaho	Ill.	Ind.	Iowa.	Kans.	Ky.
African (black)	22				4		9		6	719				3	2	23	8	1
Armenian					18	1	15	1	1		1			56	6			5
Bohemian and Moravian (Czech)					7		9	2						198		150	128	1
Bulgarian, Servian, and Montenegrin				4			8				3			3,313	1,023		89	
Chinese	60	18	358	9	301	354	2	1	14	6	2	230	36	84	3	4	3	8
Croatian and Slovenian		8	23		1,142	187	107		5	3			21	1,018	237	67	5	1
Cuban	39		18		220				6	776	3			4		1		
Dalmatian, Bosnian, and Herzegovinian	2				4		1						28	111	3			
Dutch and Flemish	6	2			46	13	7		3	5		1	2	226	13	4		
East Indian					41	12							1	3				
English	11	5	7	3	160	37	167	15	17	37	12	49	25	400	96	68	11	24
Finnish		3	5		411	26	2	5	14	8	1	3	10	68	42	45	1	13
French	7				69	8	17	4	37	2			4	179	5	11		3
German	8				287	48	120	3	80	14	1	16	3	964	4	87	49	8
Greek	108	25	31	5	249	362	187	15	5	235	95	1	117	4,235	70	384	114	59
Hebrew	2	2	12	11	1,159	9	24	12	7	3	5		30	213	476	1	5	1
Irish		4	3	2	15	10	134		12	3	2	6	15	112	10	18	9	9
Italian (north)	12		10		76	170	432				4	1	7	1,178	13	82	13	8
Italian (south)	49		8	7	1,324	282	2,463	57	78	107	5		3	4,131	66	152	2	15
Japanese		5		6	614	2	8		1	1		216	3	17	216	14	3	2
Korean					226							32	1	1				
Lithuanian		1			8	1	250	4	1				1	738	27	21		2
Magyar						9	350	1	1					883	378	13		
Mexican	1		2		13	15								3	272	12	46	
Pacific Islander					757							15						
Polish	2	8	24			1	1,163	56	5	6	3			2,970	400	28	2	2
Portuguese	8		10		26	20	15					90		2	103	2		
Roumanian	1				158	2	19	7	5	1				166	9			
Russian					1	50	298	43	12	6	5	1		1,090	15	141	67	1
Ruthenian (Russniak)					77		49							53	44			
Scandinavian (Norwegians, Danes, and Swedes)	9		2	2	2	12	116	5	7				22	666	79	16	11	
Scotch	2	19	1	2	178	6	72	6	10	5	2	17	1	201	2	27	10	4
Slovak	15	1	10	1	84	13	158	2	4		1		1	598	37	1	8	
Spanish	6	2	8	2	6	6	1	2	16	512	1	3	52	56	64	3	3	
Spanish-American	3		77		323		23		6					5				
Syrian			1		28		28		1	2	2			25	7	4	1	
Turkish		1			3		3							92				
Welsh		1			13	2	2	1	1			1	1	18		1		
West Indian (other than Cuban)					8					68				3				
Other peoples					61			1	3				2	95	137	5	3	2
Total	375	106	613	56	8,120	1,664	6,259	242	354	2,520	158	682	385	24,178	3,860	1,387	595	176

[1] Also 768 emigrant aliens whose last permanent residence was the Philippine Islands departed therefrom.

TABLE IX A.—EMIGRANT ALIENS DEPARTED, FISCAL YEAR ENDED JUNE 30, 1913, BY STATES OF LAST PERMANENT RESIDENCE AND RACES OR PEOPLES—Continued.

Race or people.	La.	Me.	Md.	Mass.	Mich.	Minn.	Miss.	Mo.	Mont.	Nobr.	Nev.	N. H.	N. J.	N. Mex.	N. Y.	N. C.	N. Dak.	Ohio.	Okla.
African (black)	3	3	5	372	1		1	1				3	21		319	1		2	4
Armenian		28	1	146	77		1	15		1		8	5		132		1	4	
Bohemian and Moravian (Czech)			18	6	11	10		18		29			15		234	10	1	48	
Bulgarian, Servian, and Montenegrin																			
Chinese	11	2	40	65	681	439	4	419	443	24	65	5	36	17	872		2	1,997	73
Croatian and Slovenian	17	1	8	79	4	8	1	20	23	1	7		8	7	281			9	1
Cuban	17		39	32	388	481	6	283	91	17	10	1	96	50	887	1	6	893	3
Dalmatian, Bosnian, and Herzegovinian			2	8	1			2					3		349			6	
Dutch and Flemish	11	1	2	3	202	4		61	5	2			57		217	9		27	
East Indian	11			61		26		12							11		8	33	13
English	37	19	22	678	218	68	5	53	33	15	13	3	380	10	2,249	9	10	190	
Finnish	1	13		380	387	250		2	25		4	26	55		260			49	
French	38	2	132	221	38	9	1	3	7	1	9	1	56	3	2,159	3		18	11
German	28	5	38	150	435	96	1	229	88	79	4	1	651	49	2,906	2	17	683	11
Greek	12	83		3,296	262	200	1	870		191	112	937	190		12,035	15	23	690	14
Hebrew		2		128	39	14		42	6	6			95	47	1,275	1		47	2
Irish	2	10	1	367	19	15		28	13	2		14	195		1,287	1	1	27	
Italian (north)	25	6	22	596	305	173		146	60	13	76	16	340	47	2,699	6	1	269	76
Italian (south)	78	214	412	5,232	1,140	367	13	513	50	134	53	269	4,110	44	34,382		9	2,623	6
Japanese	1	1		9					5	2	2		1		1			1	
Korean																			
Lithuanian		33	33	528	48	4		11	2	2	1	47	180	3	698			55	2
Magyar		10	21	32	619	88		147	9	16		3	1,603		1,856		7	1,793	1
Mexican	5		1	3				1		1			2	3	98				
Pacific Islander															1				
Polish	1	23	160	1,931	1,650	116	1	103	6	40	2	117	2,095	1	5,598		7	864	7
Portuguese				943	1						1				213			2	
Roumanian			10	11	242	39		80	10	12		2	66	1	211		2	1,224	10
Russian	4	17	108	459	280	66		34	4	18		70	356	1	3,291	1	25	143	1
Ruthenian (Russniak)		2	2	26	30	7		24	1			4	432		566		4	106	
Scandinavian (Norwegians, Danes, and Swedes)	13	15	10	223	96	398	2	20	50	72	5	6	169	6	1,081	2	102	40	1
Scotch	4	26	16	240	79	22		20	13	5	1	8	183	2	663	13	7	68	3
Slovak	41	45	15	41	135	30		98	5	4			867	4	1,118			1,071	3
Spanish	55	2	1	137	3	3		23	2	1	37		9	6	221	5			
Spanish-American	6	40	1	485	62	4	2	13		7		1	2	2	168			30	
Syrian		2	1	5	31	2		57		1		33	14	4	165			90	9
Turkish					1								2			1		9	3
Welsh	1		2	46	34	3	4	13	2	1		1	6	1	45			2	
West Indian (other than Cuban)													14		253				
Other peoples		51		75				34				20	10		129			108	
Total	423	655	1,146	17,070	7,529	2,933	41	3,386	955	695	402	1,622	12,401	246	83,608	80	229	13,238	235

Race or people.	Oreg.	Pa.	P.I.	P.R.	R.I.	S.C.	S.Dak	Tenn.	Tex.	Utah	Vt.	Va.	Wash.	W.Va.	Wis.	Wyo.	Not specified.	Total.[1]
African (black)	1	13		59	97				2		2		1				20	1,671
Armenian		12			111				7		1				12		2	676
Bohemian and Moravian (Czech)	2	64			1				74	24			4		29		36	871
Bulgarian, Servian, and Montenegrin	218	1,081			7		2	14	143	6	9	2	431	4	156	87	267	13,525
Chinese	60	67		29	3		36	2	16	72	1	5	70	101	10	4	2	2,250
Croatian and Slovenian	70	2,897			1		5	2	16		1	4	175	320	316	63	904	10,209
Cuban		29		7		6	6					8					6	1,264
Dalmatian, Bosnian, and Herzegovinian	15				11			3	54	3	9	2	32	39	3			849
Dutch and Flemish	8	169		10	153	3	1	12	8	49	14		21	4	32	19	773	2,148
East Indian	15	44			2	21	4	1	107	16	6	1	107	55		26	1,127	213
English	45	701	2		33		7		45	3	1	3	82	15	37	6	4,133	10,794
Finnish	26	50		2	98			2	16		3	20	3	19	572	132	664	3,053
French	5	141		29	33		19	31	5	811	20		49	168	885	1	2,366	4,019
German	30	1,509		10	98		23	3	34		3		685	5	23	4	180	11,871
Greek	573	1,044			51				62	10	173		13	154	2	40	1,337	31,556
Hebrew	3	326			55		1	22	8	177			205	1,597	88	9	1,378	6,697
Irish	4	605		4	1,356	5	1	31		119	16		241		501		461	4,458
Italian (north)	44	1,386		18		2	1			17	36		95	18	1	46	909	10,995
Italian (south)	87	15,937			11									256		40	7	79,057
Japanese	16	10											7			9		733
Korean	3												3					44
Lithuanian	7	497			226			1	49		98	49	55	194	40	11	237	3,276
Magyar	2	2,764			211		6		2			5	4		252		4	11,496
Mexican		11		1					12	5		11	96	91	442			910
Pacific Islander									42	4			6	155	1	17		4
Polish	10	4,925			3	3	1	1			31	1	334	47	25		772	24,107
Portuguese	2	8			8				30	10	4		28	16	140	1	3	1,583
Roumanian	19	406			19				7	5			11	139	2	5	67	3,156
Russian	1	1,386			17	4	64	2	27	4	32	4	15	31	193	12	1,946	10,548
Ruthenian (Russniak)		1,733			19	1	1	1		7	17	13			33	6	2,140	5,327
Scandinavian (Norwegians, Danes, and Swedes)	74	152		5	17	4		2	1		7	5		10	160	3	4,800	9,291
Scotch	12	260		4	19	1	1	1	6	10		6	12	1			1,780	4,118
Slovak	5	5,155			1		7		6	5	3	1		1		11		9,851
Spanish	9	34		417	3	3		1	5				18	9	4	1	47	3,181
Spanish-American		23		76			4	1									5	457
Syrian	4	143		19	65			2			7	6				1	43	797
Turkish		46															22	1,297
Welsh		40									3						118	298
West Indian (other than Cuban)	15	17		51	1			1				1	12	1		1	109	584
Other peoples		139			3		7	1		5			18	1	4		143	1,118
Not specified							4	2						9			19,838	19,838
Total	1,385	43,836	2	741	2,593	53	106	134	806	1,349	557	407	2,827	3,492	4,037	505	46,646	308,190

[1] Last United States residence unknown.   Departed via Canadian border.   Reported by Canadian Government.

TABLE X.—IMMIGRANT ALIENS ADMITTED, FISCAL YEAR ENDED JUNE 30, 1913, BY OCCUPATIONS AND RACES OR PEOPLES.

Occupation.	Korean.	Japanese.	Italian (South).	Italian (North).	Irish.	Hebrew.	Greek.	German.	French.	Finnish.	English.	East Indian.	Dutch and Flemish.	Dalmatian, Bosnian, and Herzegovinian.	Cuban.	Croatian and Slovenian.	Chinese.	Bulgarian, Servian, and Montenegrin.	Bohemian and Moravian (Czech).	Armenian.	African (black).
PROFESSIONAL.																					
Actors	-	6	29	55	36	15	1	111	56	-	452	-	12	-	3	2	-	-	1	-	-
Architects	-	4	3	9	5	12	-	66	22	1	83	-	10	-	3	-	-	-	-	1	-
Clergy	1	36	61	28	127	31	12	117	69	1	206	1	24	1	6	6	3	1	5	11	15
Editors	-	8	4	7	10	11	2	23	7	1	66	-	5	-	6	5	2	2	9	3	-
Electricians (professional)	-	3	44	23	56	91	8	137	36	6	212	-	24	-	5	1	-	2	1	5	3
Engineers (professional)	-	24	27	36	44	48	-	350	163	14	540	-	69	-	28	-	-	3	13	-	6
Lawyers	-	1	20	7	4	14	10	23	14	-	53	2	8	2	43	6	-	6	14	4	1
Literary and scientific persons	-	4	13	15	23	53	5	115	23	3	104	1	12	-	14	-	-	-	3	3	5
Musicians	-	1	173	127	12	203	-	198	47	2	160	-	35	-	4	1	-	-	20	-	13
Officials (government)	-	30	10	8	6	1	6	49	33	1	53	1	6	-	15	3	10	-	-	-	2
Physicians	-	20	38	6	26	20	9	45	25	5	77	1	12	1	51	1	9	1	1	5	3
Sculptors and artists	-	9	55	72	13	50	6	131	64	2	115	-	38	-	2	5	-	-	10	3	1
Teachers	2	61	30	39	205	295	26	384	300	14	416	4	28	-	19	10	31	3	9	50	54
Other professional	5	108	14	16	227	128	6	268	64	10	616	4	30	-	11	3	25	1	14	6	43
Total	8	315	521	447	794	972	98	2,017	923	60	3,152	14	309	4	210	43	80	19	100	91	146
SKILLED.																					
Bakers	-	1	391	204	61	1,090	132	827	94	23	184	-	180	4	2	23	-	27	146	55	18
Barbers and hairdressers	-	6	1,470	56	34	517	121	318	53	3	116	-	18	-	16	13	1	14	23	91	9
Blacksmiths	-	7	697	199	138	772	54	579	65	37	223	-	111	9	3	80	-	22	133	109	36
Bookbinders	-	-	3	7	5	366	3	40	2	6	30	-	6	-	-	3	-	-	17	2	1
Brewers	-	1	2	3	4	10	-	140	2	-	11	-	12	-	-	4	-	-	18	-	-
Butchers	-	-	217	48	70	1,317	31	716	55	2	240	-	104	-	-	38	-	11	217	26	5
Cabinetmakers	-	-	25	6	17	162	1	72	7	1	48	-	9	1	-	6	-	3	12	1	6
Carpenters and joiners	-	14	1,843	525	391	2,971	249	1,257	331	170	935	3	418	7	15	141	-	42	322	222	182

Occupation													
Cigarette makers													64
Cigarmakers	1		1			2 5 4		1 1	4 11 5		4 2	8 7 1	2	137 209
Cigar packers	1		1		6 1	329 163	54 13				38 99 24			30
Clerks and accountants	60 18		162 37	26 5	46 39	40	5	2 946 2 240	306 20	1 978 349	2 273 360		165 31	7 1
Dressmakers	23		17	1	7	7 38 3	1 1 1	42	25 11 11 3	176	537	1	26	7 4
Engineers (locomotive, marine, and stationary)	2 12	3 3	4 33 5	5 13 1	3 3 3	42 28	16	474 33 649	40 3	24 181 23	6 352 20		3 127 2	16 125 34
Furriers and fur workers	75 23 10 5 22	1	50	2	10 1 22 108 68	8 132 22 56	21 142 15	43 162 79 175 56 188	13 282 99	157 31 734 370 212 513	414 47 708 190 550	1	25 3 3 35 35 104	27
Gardeners	16		17		4	87	9	107	8	289	259		48	6
Hat and cap makers	35 1 2 5 18	1 20 3	9 35 4 251 62	1 17 1 281 10	1 7 1	21 12 27 454 78 5	9 1 1 196 40	227 173 796 39 1 423	22 1 6 19 14	82 120 55 763 366 3	130 31 96 177 444 38	1	23 13 8 90 149	7 7 29
Iron and steel workers	6	1	3		2	11 3 19 13	5	3 134 13 193 327	3 1 2 19	20 21 59 124	58 146 215 164		7 18 19 27	2 1 10 15
Jewelers	8 71 613	4 1 2 7	23 249 17 18 307 11	10 13 87	9 95 8	7 49 78 33 26 62 4	2 77 32 10 11 109 4	252 5 042 2 569 14 17 15 408 234	3 49 314 39 5 244 17	85 301 472 119 48 695 25	30 96 159 177 74 238 17		3 69 58 13 10 54 5	6 367 46 12
Tailors	435 22		307 11		9 95 8									100 1
Tanners and curriers	2 19 3 5		7 18	1 6	9	42 9	12 4	34 459 17 132	7 2 8	34 89 3 36	666 36 4 21		3 8	5
Textile workers (not specified)	6 143	2	4 43	2	1 9	31 664	10 12	364 328	1 13	37 369	30 947	3	5 211	100 1

TABLE X.—IMMIGRANT ALIENS ADMITTED, FISCAL YEAR ENDED JUNE 30, 1913, BY OCCUPATIONS AND RACES OR PEOPLES—Continued.

Occupation.	Korean.	Japanese.	Italian (South).	Italian (North).	Irish.	Hebrew.	Greek.	German.	French.	Finnish.	English.	East Indian.	Dutch and Flemish.	Dalmatian, Bosnian, and Herzegovinian.	Cuban.	Croatian and Slovenian.	Chinese.	Bulgarian, Servian, and Montenegrin.	Bohemian and Moravian (Czech).	Armenian.	African (black).
SKILLED—continued.																					
Wheelwrights			4	1	5	45		93	4	1	24		7			10		2	21		3
Woodworkers (not specified)			18	2	24	74	1	49	15	3	70		3			4			20	4	2
Other skilled	1	33	294	186	349	1,040	53	679	323	30	1,277	2	138	3	11	34	12	7	78	62	56
Total	3	192	20,978	5,914	5,225	44,617	2,265	13,788	3,567	1,108	14,845	18	2,616	160	760	1,241	22	392	2,849	2,209	1,593
MISCELLANEOUS.																					
Agents		5	10	21	110	129	12	94	57	3	425		32		7	4			5	10	2
Bankers		9	6	2	11	9	1	19	37		114	1	24	1	14	1			3		
Draymen, hackmen, and teamsters		2	296	61	74	86	2	47	29	5	132		8		5	6			8	2	11
Farm laborers	15	3,483	85,922	4,115	3,049	2,159	8,158	11,624	862	522	1,116	3	2,391	2,769	34	12,257		3,012	1,045	2,152	1,248
Farmers		256	601	309	1,070	126	1,334	1,667	608	136	1,296	2	763	98		896		57	85	249	37
Fishermen		12	460	6	102	6	11	9	16	5	87		8	12	3	7	3		2		5
Hotel keepers		25	6	14	19	19	59	56	26		34	1	5			3			5	3	
Laborers	1	158	52,439	18,524	7,201	4,116	21,429	5,777	2,729	5,978	3,123	40	1,399	799	22	15,579	107	4,004	1,077	2,370	597
Manufacturers	4	1	6	14	22	28	4	72	40	1	148		18						1	1	
Merchants and dealers	2	202	2,003	406	228	3,842	371	1,975	361	24	969	30	259	8	213	23	605	25	62	114	39
Servants		125	14,841	3,331	11,753	6,009	1,768	11,110	1,913	3,008	5,133	7	760	298	38	5,005	5	247	2,086	494	1,342
Other miscellaneous		590	944	346	1,117	1,554	222	1,464	614	80	2,771	42	233	11	79	59	748	22	119	71	320
Total	22	4,868	157,534	27,149	24,756	18,083	33,371	33,914	7,292	9,762	15,348	126	5,900	3,996	412	33,840	1,468	7,367	4,498	5,466	3,601
No occupation (including women and children)	31	2,927	52,580	9,024	6,248	37,658	2,910	31,176	8,870	1,826	22,177	30	5,682	360	1,717	7,375	452	1,309	3,844	1,527	1,294
Grand total	64	8,302	231,613	42,534	37,023	101,330	38,644	80,865	20,652	12,756	55,522	188	14,507	4,520	3,099	42,499	2,022	9,087	11,091	9,353	6,634

Occupation.	Lithuanian.	Magyar.	Mexican.	Pacific Islander.	Polish.	Portuguese.	Roumanian.	Russian.	Ruthenian (Russniak).	Scandinavian (Norwegian, Danes, and Swedes).	Scotch.	Slovak.	Spanish.	Spanish-American.	Syrian.	Turkish.	Welsh.	West Indian (other than Cuban).	Other peoples.	Total.	Admitted in Philippine Islands.
PROFESSIONAL.																					
Actors		4	8		2	1	3	4		9	35		29	3			5	3	27	911	8
Architects	5	4	2		9	7	1	3		11	35	1	2	3	20		1	1	5	299	
Clergy	2	11	14		20	1	3	2		34	54	2	48	4	1	3	24	8	2	1,031	86
Editors		1	9		3	5	1	9	9	9	7		4	26	1		10		3	207	
Electricians	3	2	23		28	6	3	21	2	107	76	1	12	15	1	3	12			941	3
Engineers (professional)	2	13	23		16			7		156	215	1	13	3	1	1	25	1	2	1,917	3
Lawyers		22			5	1	1	8	2	9	9	1	20	52	5			13	4	290	1
Literary and scientific persons	3	6	25		13	3		9		18	27	1	11	14	4	3	1		4	493	1
Musicians		4	3		86	2	3	13		28	15	1	20	5	22	1	13		3	1,284	1
Officials (government)	1	25	25			4	1	16		19	11		17	14	3	2				365	8
Physicians		2	3		3	4	2	13		24	43	1	15	10			28	10	2	508	3
Sculptors and artists	4	6	17		10	5	5	10		69	15		24	24			20	12	4	676	1
Teachers	4	7	4		37	8		16	3	93	142	1	19	19	22		18		4	2,399	44
Other professional		16	12	1	14		5	10	2	93	313	1			3	2			3	2,168	32
Total	24	129	188	1	244	51	23	129	23	599	997	8	234	168	62	9	134	69	54	13,469	191
SKILLED.																					
Bakers	5	33	19		289	27	4	23	12	154	138	12	47		10	6	10	3	8	4,256	6
Barbers and hairdressers	6	47	18		60	9	13	10	12	42	33	12	16	2	35	11	9		8	3,213	7
Blacksmiths	67	98	21		979	5	23	197	40	449	111	55	32		49	1	26		1	6,431	4
Bookbinders	1	5			11	1			6	14	4	4		1	1				1	543	
Brewers	4	1	6		12			17	7	95	92	34	8	5	16		57	11		240	2
Butchers	3	69			284		12	6	7	25	21	1	4		206			1	1	3,748	
Cabinetmakers	8	13	12		35		37	367	1	567	444	93	217		1			7	28	501	
Carpenters and joiners	138	198	152		1,389	67		2		13	2	1	106	1			110		17	15,035	169
Cigarette makers		5	12			2				13	1	1	9	5		11	18		3	64	
Cigarmakers	1	99			7	90	20	61	20	856	1,038	23	471	44	80	1			17	899	50
Cigar packers		185			216	6	15	28	24	199	198		17	2	40				3	86	2
Clerks and accountants	34	13	1		390		20	14		141	228	3	13	6	5	7	110	114	1	14,025	
Dressmakers	27	11			42		15	7	8	4	4	2	17		1	3	18	33	2	6,411	33
Engineers (locomotive, marine, and stationary)	9	13			19		1													1,594	
Furriers and fur workers	2	11					1										31	3		607	

TABLE X.—IMMIGRANT ALIENS ADMITTED, FISCAL YEAR ENDED JUNE 30, 1913, BY OCCUPATIONS AND RACES OR PEOPLES—Continued.

Occupation	Lithuanian	Magyar	Mexican	Pacific Islander	Polish	Portuguese	Roumanian	Russian	Ruthenian (Russniak)	Scandinavian (Norwegians, Danes, and Swedes)	Scotch	Slovak	Spanish	Spanish-American	Syrian	Turkish	Welsh	West Indian (other than Cuban)	Other peoples	Total	Admitted in Philippine Islands
SKILLED—continued.																					
Gardeners	3	14			93	1	1	11		118	137	5	5		2	6	5	1		1,516	1
Hat and cap makers	23	6	1		20		1	3	1	5	4	1	3		12	1		1	7	805	
Iron and steel workers	2	29	6		98	2	6	5	8	102	223	10	19		8	6	14		1	1,728	2
Jewelers	42	4		1	7		5	6		14	4	1	6	1	2	1	1	3	1	404	
Locksmiths	11	93	47		637	2	1	124	29	194	303	52	1	6	6		14	83	3	2,811	3
Machinists	4	30	6		92	9	1	38	5	1,060	84	7	33	8	5	1	13	2	9	2,725	24
Mariners	18	1	15		19	78	1	39	3	224	137	2	525	14	76	4	26	3	1	4,979	2
Masons	2	68	36		411	18	10	46	21	82	79	38	64		8	5	12	2		7,377	13
Mechanics (not specified)		22	1		54	3	7	14		45	37	2	5	1	7	5	9		1	1,853	
Metal workers (other than iron, steel, and tin)	2	6	1		17	1	1	1	3	37	6	11	2	1	1		1	1		793	9
Millers	2	28	198		150	2	1	4	6	44	40	1	229	3	7	2	4	2	8	804	
Milliners	2	2	12		14			7		254	771	93	13	4	8		500	2	5	1,193	2
Miners	162	67			396	7	13	36	52	353	189	13	2	1	4		20	1	2	9,510	
Painters and glaziers	9	37	4		177		3	41	7	1	47	1	1		4	2	1	4	1	3,888	
Patternmakers			3				1	1		32	16	3	4				2	1	1	106	
Photographers	2	4	4		14			2	1	14	94	2	8		4		10	1		369	1
Plasterers		1	5		1					22	123	4	2				4	1		418	
Plumbers	3	4			13	3	2	3		53	74	6	6		4		5	3	2	778	3
Printers	50	12	3		28	20	2	6	2	19	7	12	20	1	188	1	2	2	89	1,104	11
Saddlers and harnessmakers	69	10	16		74	94	6	27	18	138	59	103	137	2	190	27	1	57	18	616	
Seamstresses	8	49	12		704	1	26	153	78	131	46	5	18		5	17	8	10	1	8,723	
Shoemakers	1	183	3		904	16	9	10	3	126	63	6	19	6	15	3	12	1		11,578	2
Stokers		4			28	3		1	1	145	180	64			169	3	5	1		1,112	
Stonecutters	227	4	20		22		41	311	92	170	108	20			8	24	5	12	40	1,111	
Tailors		168			885	1	2	2	4	4	6	15		1	1	3	4			22,934	
Tanners and curriers	1	5			29	16				29	163		1		14	2	13			487	
Textile workers (not specified)	2		1			3	2			29	13		2	1	1	1			2	1,179	3
Tinners		7	1		19	14	2	2	1	1			2							879	11
Tobacco workers					26	1	1	4	2				7			1				52	

Upholsterers	1	1						2		6	6				1				262	
Watch and clock makers	3	8	1				1	6	2	29	12				1	4			611	
Weavers and spinners	2	4	1				1	11	11	50	268	1		103	7	2	1	16	3,909	1
Wheelwrights	6	19					2	2	9	8	7		1		1	38	7		380	
Woodworkers (not specified)		3					5	5		11	29					2	1	2	358	8
Other skilled	30	61	34			9	29	29	16	326	501	44	4	22	7	38	7	19	6,083	27
Total	995	1,731	755	1	9,240	495	302	1,699	569	7,486	6,161	2,200	119	1,316	168	1,011	376	303	160,108	383
MISCELLANEOUS.																				
Agents	2	6	2		4	1	1	1	3	39	117	14	10	7	2	10	5		1,148	18
Bankers		3	3							4	16	6	3	1		2	1	1	293	5
Draymen, hackmen, and teamsters	13,233	4	1		20	4		1	2	42	74	7	9	1		1	1		933	737
Farm laborers	54	6,540	144		82,130	2,898	6,467	26,090	15,096	5,308	529	1,473	32	1,771	882	73	27	661	320,105	103
Farmers	1	116	90		404	135	45	648	173	978	449	95		102	38	87	22	47	13,180	33
Fishermen		1			10	120			1	239	13	31				3	3	1	1,174	2
Hotel keepers	1,856	5,323	3,021		3	2		2		5	15	3				123	1	2	315	
Laborers		1			19,286	3,666	3,011	16,287	2,631	8,548	1,123	2,024	5	1,855	663	5	44	1,436	220,992	99
Manufacturers	8	102	222		3		16	75	9	10	58	9	154	3	1	43	57	44	454	1
Merchants and dealers	4,961	5,115	259	2	130	40	906	2,595	6,965	159	246	489	66	310	36	262	130	94	13,919	527
Servants	31	96	98	1	254	1,922	23	92	28	8,680	2,500	417	40	937	35	103	28		140,218	55
Other miscellaneous					280	29				669	1,196	140		73	9				14,396	207
Total	20,146	17,309	3,843	7	132,524	8,817	10,470	45,798	24,908	24,681	6,336	4,708	319	5,062	1,086	715	318	2,305	727,127	1,787
No occupation (including women and children)	3,482	11,441	6,168	2	32,357	4,203	2,656	3,846	5,088	5,971	7,799	1,900	737	2,770	152	960	408	376	297,188	2,047
Grand total	24,647	30,610	10,954	11	174,365	3,566	13,451	51,472	30,588	38,737	21,293	27,234	9,042	1,363	9,210	2,015	2,820	1,171	3,038	1,197,892	4,408

TABLE X A.—EMIGRANT ALIENS DEPARTED, FISCAL YEAR ENDED JUNE 30, 1913, BY OCCUPATIONS AND RACES OR PEOPLES.

Occupation.	African (black).	Armenian.	Bohemian and Moravian (Czech).	Bulgarian, Servian, and Montenegrin.	Chinese.	Croatian and Slovenian.	Cuban.	Dalmatian, Bosnian, and Herzegovinian.	Dutch and Flemish.	East Indian.	English.	Finnish.	French.	German.	Greek.	Hebrew.	Irish.	Italian (North).	Italian (South).	Japanese.	Korean.
PROFESSIONAL.																					
Actors	4			1	1		4		2		137		28	38	1	3	3	19	9	2	
Architects	6					1			4		19		6	21		16		4	6	2	
Clergy	2	2	2	2	3	1	2		6	5	36		70	19	3		16	6	11	7	
Editors			1				1				6		1	2	5		1		2	2	
Electricians	2								4		19		1	13	10		7	1	8		
Engineers (professional)	1						6		10	3	114		37	75		9			6		
Lawyers	1		4		1		3		1		10	1	2	14	2	2	11	8		5	
Literary and scientific persons									12		18	1	8	15		2	2			2	1
Musicians	2	2	2	1	3	2	2				18		13	9	1	10	2	11	39	1	
Officials (Government)	3	1		1	4	3	1		5	1	12		11	20	1	3	1	6	1	6	
Physicians			1	1		2	5		5		23		7	19		3	1	2	13	3	
Sculptors and artists							7	1	1		22		30				1	16	15	1	
Teachers	4	3	1	1	9	1	2		4	1	54	4	169	107	4	28	11	5	14	4	
Other professional	6				6		2		4		102	1	15	47	1	5	52	3	8	6	
Total	29	8	11	6	27	10	35	1	58	10	590	7	398	499	28	83	108	81	132	41	1
SKILLED.																					
Bakers	1	3	6	9	1	4	1		10		18	1	12	111	19	52	6	25	102	1	
Barbers and hairdressers	1		4	5		2	10		2		12	3	5	27	22	21	5	13	354	1	
Blacksmiths	2		2	5		13	1		3		21	1	2	29	1	25	12	9	54	1	
Bookbinders			1				1				3			4		7			2		
Brewers			1								15	1		23	1				1		
Butchers	1	1	13			8			8		7	1	8	71	6	34	5	5	37		
Cabinetmakers		1	2		1		4		1				1	10	3	4	1	1	3	2	
Carpenters and joiners	9		13	13		26			41		131	60	8	111	2	112	36	44	196		
Cigarette makers											1										
Cigarmakers	12		5	1		1	345		11		3			21		4		6	44		
Cigar packers											2			6							
Clerks and accountants	7	3	7	6	5	11	65	1	25	1	321	4	67	331	78	157	117	41	104	11	

Dressmakers	13		3	1					3		22	1	40	36	2	68	24	18	101		
Engineers (locomotive, marine, and stationary)	3					1	1		4		48	2	6	11	1		1	2	5	1	
Furriers and fur workers			1			2			2					7	19	37		1			
Gardeners				2	4	1			13		36		7	24	6		23	34	7	2	
Hat and cap makers							1				2		1	1	3	10		6	10		
Iron and steel workers		2	1	1		4			1		30	1	1	16	4	11	18	5	43		
Jewelers		2			1				1		3		26	9	2	16		2	11		
Locksmiths			2	1							2			10		3			1		
Machinists		1	9	14		7	8		12		158	7	11	138	7	15	30	14	36	1	
Mariners	66			1	7	15		3	8	2	64	9		15	14	16	8	11	69	1	
Masons	3		4	3		52	1		6		63	2	1	43	2	16	9	81	203		
Mechanics (not specified)	6		4	2		25	16		93		1,078	80	87	304	19	80	211	71	131		
Metal workers (other than iron, steel, and tin)						2			1		6			4		3		2	7		
Millers														3					1		
Milliners			2						1		7		16	7		17	5		2		
Miners		5	12	261	6	1,075		42	45		517	280	35	83	42	10	76	1,352	955	3	
Painters and glaziers		1	2	3		3			8		40	5	9	41	16	74	4	3	32		
Patternmakers			1								16			5			1				
Photographers						1			1		16		1	3	4	6	1	1	5	1	
Plasterers							1		4		20		1	3	1	3	7	4	12		
Plumbers				1		2			2		13			8		7	3	1	4		
Printers	1		1	2		1	1		5		32			14	4	12	5	2	9		
Saddlers and harness makers			1								2		1	5	2	4	1	1	1		
Seamstresses	48		3	2		1					10	2	8	7	1	13	16	2	19		
Shoemakers		3	9	3	1	3		1	4		12	1	3	33	56	87	11	24	441		
Stokers	1	1	1	3	1	2	1		2		14	2		13	5		18	4	24		
Stonecutters			2			1		2	1		6	15		4	2		5	31	95		
Tailors	4	7	32	10	5	12	2	2	6		15	14	11	56	25	843	7	21	437	5	
Tanners and curriers		5	1	1		2		1			3	1		1				2	1		
Textile workers (not specified)		3							1		97	9		7	29	2	22	4	262		
Tinners			1						3		6	1	1	13		18		2	6		
Tobacco workers							1											1	2		
Upholsterers			1								4			3		2			3		
Watch and clock makers				1					1		2	2	3	4	1	12	1	3	3		
Weavers and spinners	1	1	1						16		85	21	43	32	12	6	16	56	55		
Wheelwrights													1	8							
Woodworkers (not specified)			1								4	1		7		2	1	7	1		
Other skilled	7	14	9	3	55	33	1		28		130	11	25	100	28	104	40	41	107	5	
Total	186	54	157	354	87	1,310	461	52	373	3	3,099	537	441	1,822	439	1,913	746	1,953	3,998	35	

TABLE X A.—EMIGRANT ALIENS DEPARTED, FISCAL YEAR ENDED JUNE 30, 1913, BY OCCUPATIONS AND RACES OR PEOPLES—Continued.

Occupation.	African (black).	Armenian.	Bohemian and Moravian (Czech).	Bulgarian, Servian, and Montenegrin.	Chinese.	Croatian and Slovenian.	Cuban.	Dalmatian, Bosnian, and Herzegovinian.	Dutch and Flemish.	East Indian.	English.	Finnish.	French.	German.	Greek.	Hebrew.	Irish.	Italian (North).	Italian (South).	Japanese.	Korean.
MISCELLANEOUS.																					
Agents				2		1	1		7	1	37		10	20	2	8	4	6	3		
Bankers						1	1		3		22		3	13		1	2	1	1	6	
Draymen, hackmen, and teamsters			1		12						11			15		18	13	10	24		
Farm laborers	406	2	7	8	40	28	8	1	73	9	274	2	44	257	4	21	85	23	257	74	2
Farmers	4	10	48	427		470		40	149	14	380	36	100	554	6	24	145	89	122	99	4
Fishermen	16			1		5			1		1	50		2	26		1	2	102	1	
Hotel keepers												5	8	13	45	2		7	4	11	
Laborers	405	548	287	12,282	1,591	7,129	32	721	745	158	1,185	1,463	580	3,470	29,433	2,194	1,132	6,032	64,118	194	28
Manufacturers							5		1		9		8	12	1	7	2		2		
Merchants and dealers		7	3	28	346	7	44	1	27	6	403	10	809	420	493	727	75	179	443	78	2
Servants	180	9	141	81	8	398	18	10	89		678	403	411	1,311	378	400	1,192	521	2,204	17	1
Other miscellaneous	167	5	19	75	76	68	23	2	52	6	311	43	154	237	300	200	148	149	313	45	3
Total	1,185	581	506	12,904	2,075	8,108	132	776	1,151	194	3,316	2,032	2,127	6,324	30,688	3,602	2,799	7,019	67,593	525	40
No occupation (including women and children)	486	95	365	621	175	2,101	1,132	73	997	19	7,478	1,021	1,892	5,547	868	3,095	1,659	3,976	11,464	208	4
Grand total	1,671	676	871	13,525	2,250	10,209	1,264	849	2,148	213	10,794	3,053	4,019	11,871	31,556	6,697	4,458	10,995	79,057	733	44

Occupation.	Lithuanian.	Magyar.	Mexican.	Pacific Islander.	Polish.	Portuguese.	Roumanian.	Russian.	Ruthenian (Russniak).	Scandinavian (Norwegian, Danes, and Swedes).	Scotch.	Slovak.	Spanish.	Spanish-American.	Syrian.	Turkish.	Welsh.	West Indian (other than Cuban).	Other peoples.	Not specified.	Total.	Departed from Philippine Islands.
PROFESSIONAL																						
Actors	4	2	4		2			1		1	10	2	57	4			1	2	1		333	4
Architects		5	2		1			1		13	5	1	21	4		9	3	2	6		97	38
Clergy		2			13	4	1	17	1	25	8		3	3		1	3	3			335	
Editors		2	2		1	2		2		7	5		12	10				1	2		28	2
Electricians		6	4		1	1		6		46	32		5	5			3	3			103	
Engineers (professional)		1	2		1		1			1	1	4	2	2		1		1	1		408	3
Lawyers		1				2		2		5	6		2	1	1			1			42	4
Literary and scientific persons		14	1					2		8	2		5	11	1		8	3			73	
Musicians		2	3			1		5		5	1		12	12				1	1		284	4
Officials (Government)		1	2					4		1	5	4	11	2				5			98	11
Physicians		3	4		1	2		4		4	2		15	6		1	1	10			137	
Sculptors and artists		4	2		2	1	1	5	1	13	16		8								139	
Teachers										26	33			10					2		494	4
Other professional	1																				364	11
Total	6	41	28		35	12	3	49	3	155	126	7	154	70	2	11	19	28	13		2,925	66
SKILLED																						
Bakers	3	10	2		26			9	1	13	12	7	5		1	2		1	2		475	1
Barbers and hairdressers	1	14	1		5	6		1		8	3	7	3		2			1	2		537	1
Blacksmiths	10	13	1		35	1	3	4	2	16	12	4	2			1		1	2		292	
Bookbinders		2								3	3	6									25	
Brewers		30			27		3	9		7	4	4									29	
Butchers		7	5		9			1	8	6	5	3				2	2	9	1		298	43
Cabinetmakers	6	57			117	5	7	52	4	255	77	24	38		1			1	7		62	
Carpenters and joiners	47	52			11	1		1				12	223				4				1,529	
Cigarette makers																					4	
Cigarmakers	3	34	18		11	9	4	20	1	69	89	4	108	20	16	9	4	19	7		760	39
Cigar packers																					0	
Clerks and accountants	1	24			31	2		11	2	35	6	11	1		1	1	2	22	4		1,804	
Dressmakers																					482	

TABLE X A.—EMIGRANT ALIENS DEPARTED, FISCAL YEAR ENDED JUNE 30, 1913, BY OCCUPATIONS AND RACES OR PEOPLES.—Continued.

Occupation.	Lithuanian.	Magyar.	Mexican.	Pacific Islander.	Polish.	Portuguese.	Roumanian.	Russian.	Ruthenian (Russian).	Scandinavian (Norwegians, Danes, and Swedes).	Scotch.	Slovak.	Spanish.	Spanish-American.	Syrian.	Turkish.	Welsh.	West Indian (other than Cuban).	Other peoples.	Not specified.	Total.	Departed from Philippine Islands.
SKILLED—contd.																						
Engineers (locomotive, marine, and stationary)	1	1			6			3		32	12	1	8	1			2	1	4		158	6
Furriers and fur workers		7			1			3		16	9							1			80	
Gardeners	1	2			4					1		2							1		196	
Hat and cap makers		4							2			2	1					1	1		45	
Iron and steel workers	4	19	2		27		12	5		22	24	8	3	1			2	1			263	1
Jewelers	1	2	2	1	4	1		3	4	6	1	1	5		2			2	3		80	1
Locksmiths	38	2			62		6	26		66	71	16	70		3	2	3	18			817	1
Machinists	4	46			4	20	1	2		237	9	7	4	1			3				696	1
Mariners	1	5			18	6		4	1	15	42	10	14	4				26	35		616	3
Masons		19																				
Mechanics (not specified)	8	26		1	162		7	162	52	660	529	6	14	4	3	1	25	26	35	2,829	6,758	3
Metal workers (other than iron, steel, and tin)					7		1			5	4	2	2	1		2	1				47	
Millers	1	1	5		1	7	1	13		1	1	2	2	1	5	1	62	2	11		11	1
Milliners		3	1		2		31	186	381	155	103	1114	53				1	1	1	142	71	
Miners	69	526			574		1	6		42	40	3	1	1		1		7	11		8,280	
Painters and glaziers	5	9			13		1	1	1	2	1	1	2	1				1	1		366	
Patternmakers										1											33	
Photographers												2									48	
Plasterers						1		2	4		22	2	2				1	1	1		85	
Plumbers		1			1			16	3	7	17	5					2		2		76	
Printers		2			1			1		1	7	17	1	1							114	
Saddlers and harness makers	1	1			1	7	1	1	4	9	1	18	1	1	11	1	1	7	5		24	
Seamstresses	5	7	3		46	7	4	2	3	9	17	1	386		1	1	1	1	1		217	1
Shoemakers	3	22			26	43	5	16		16	8	15	12					1	1		838	
Stokers		12			14	2		4		15	53		4						5		605	
Stonecutters		3			1	9		70		23	7										254	
Tailors	43	50			107			2		1		1					4				1,850	1
Tanners and curriers					5							4									40	

Occupation	Total
Textile workers (not specified)	711
Tinners	72
Tobacco workers	12
Upholsterers	14
Watch and clock makers	51
Weavers and spinners	457
Wheelwrights	15
Woodworkers (not specified)	50
Other skilled	1,169
Total	**31,563**
MISCELLANEOUS.	
Agents	136
Bankers	72
Draymen, hackmen, and teamsters	140
Farm laborers	3,948
Farmers	6,120
Fishermen	261
Hotel keepers	106
Laborers	191,604
Manufacturers	66
Merchants and dealers	5,979
Servants	16,220
Other miscellaneous	3,654
Total	**228,306**
No occupation (including women and children)	45,396
Grand total	**308,190**

¹ Departed via Canadian border.   Reported by Canadian Government as Canadians.

TABLE XI.—IMMIGRANT ALIENS ADMITTED, FISCAL YEAR ENDED JUNE 30, 1913, BY STATES OF INTENDED FUTURE RESIDENCE AND OCCUPATIONS.[1]

Occupation.	Ala.	Alaska.	Ariz.	Ark.	Cal.	Colo.	Conn.	Del.	D. C.	Fla.	Ga.	Hawaii.	Idaho.
PROFESSIONAL.													
Actors	1				44	2	8		2	15	3	4	
Architects	1		1		27	1	4		1	1			
Clergy	3	3	2		58	9	10		15	4	3	17	2
Editors	1		1		18	1	2		2	1		3	1
Electricians	2		1	1	51	3	12	4	3	3	1	1	
Engineers (professional)	3		7		109	16	32	1	13	6	1	3	1
Lawyers			7		17	1	6		4	2	1	2	2
Literary and scientific persons					30	1	5		5	2			2
Musicians	3		9		44	1	14		2	5	3	2	1
Officials (Government)					32	1			83	2	1	3	
Physicians		1		1	39	1	3		16	1	1	11	1
Sculptors and artists			3		34		9	2		2		1	
Teachers	4	5	3	3	132	19	40	3	37	11	8	40	6
Other professional	5		6	2	128	11	27		19	4	13	135	2
Total	23	9	38	8	763	69	172	10	201	59	35	231	17
SKILLED.													
Bakers	2	1	12	4	143	16	78	5	8	17	4	2	6
Barbers and hairdressers	3	5	10	1	48	5	90	2	8	25	2	9	2
Blacksmiths	4		22	2	109	25	132	6	2	15			19
Bookbinders			1	1	13		7	1	1				2
Brewers					3		6						1
Butchers	2	3	8	1	59	1	62		5	6	4	1	7
Cabinetmakers					16	14	10		1		2	22	2
Carpenters and joiners	10	28	55	8	474	44	374	19	22	172	8		30
Cigarette makers	1						1						
Cigarmakers					5		7						
Cigar packers					5				2	491			
Clerks and accountants	24	4	34	4	660	49	207	9	46	7	25	23	15
Dressmakers	6	4	4	1	163	18	150	5	9	213	3	1	6
Engineers (locomotive, marine, and stationary)	2	4	6		95	10	23		5	11	1	9	6
Furriers and fur workers	1	1	2		2		6	2	3	1		1	
Gardeners	1	1		2	102	3	36		3	1	2	1	5
Hat and cap makers					4		12			12		1	
Iron and steel workers	2		5		25	5	44	1	2	3	2	2	1
Jewelers			2		17		7	3	4	3	1	1	4
Locksmiths		3			26	2	53	6	3	1	1		
Machinists	3	3	30	2	126	7	62	2	4	18	11	1	5
Mariners	2	3	3	1	224	7	53	1	7	310	3	1	6
Masons	37	2	16		302	5	294	9	5	17	3	2	6
Mechanics (not specified)	5	2	7	1	61	32	68	1	5	21	3	2	10
Metal workers (other than iron, steel, and tin)	2	1	7	1	16	6	26	1	2	2			

Occupation																		Total
Millers	1									2		1		15		1		1
Milliners	1									1			1	21		1		1
Miners	31	179	402	14			161	254	9	16		82	14	254	402	14		98
Painters and glaziers	1		5	1			2	121	16	4		70	1	121	5	1		5
Pasternmakers								2				7		2				
Photographers	1		1		3	1	1	22				9		22	1		1	
Plasterers	1		2		1		2	28			2	21		28	2		3	
Plumbers	1		2		3		2	30		2	2	21	6	30	2		1	1
Printers	2		2					27	52		1	16	8	27	2		3	
Saddlers and harnessmakers	3		4	1	6	12	12	12	13	1	1	227	2	12	4			4
Seamstresses	11		2	4	8	25	25	61	6	1	11	369	1	61	2			5
Shoemakers			1		2	5	5	115		37		15	17	115	1			5
Stokers					1	4	4	39	31			30	2	39				2
Stonecutters	9		1	7	17	31	31	41	1	39	39	411		41	1			
Tailors					2	1	1	169	3			14	3	169			23	
Tanners and curriers								7				32		7				
Textile workers (not specified)								15		1		13		15				
Tinners	3		1			2	2	14				4		14	1		2	6
Tobacco workers			1		1			2				13	4	2	1		6	
Upholsterers			1		5			5	1	4	4	167	1	5	1			
Watch and clock makers			1		1	1	1	37		1	1	5		37	1			
Weavers and spinners					1			1				2	1	1				
Wheelwrights					1			1	2			10		1				
Woodworkers (not specified)	10	2	19	1	16	16	16	12	21	7	9	9	7	12	19	1	6	12
Other skilled		8						304				109		304				
Total	182	247	667	58	522	4,057	522	4,057	1,544	271	157	3,560	131	4,057	667	58	131	273
MISCELLANEOUS.																		
Agents	3				2	121		121	10	2	1	11						1
Bankers		1	1	2	1	21		21	1									
Draymen, hackmen, and teamsters	165	11	166	42	3	34	1,092	4,014	4	181	751	26	3	4,043	166	42	3	260
Farm laborers	31	4	46	9	137	4,014	137	1,013	932	5	7	11,377	58	9	46	9	84	84
Farmers	2	8				1,013		36	131			213	14	8			9	8
Fishermen		2			2	36	2	42	12			7		1			1	
Hotel keepers				2		42		5,881	1	2		4		1		2	3	
Laborers	270	221	1,221	54	980	5,881	980	29	504	155	174	6,227	114	25	1,221	54		436
Manufacturers	24	8	23	11	4	29		980	7	2		6	1	1	23	11	9	9
Merchants and dealers	74	20	88	22	38	980	38	2,682	135	39	190	190	35	49	88	22	49	122
Servants	21	23	47	12	440	2,682	440	1,508	191	282	281	5,172	67	106	47	12	106	37
Other miscellaneous					41	1,508			318	44	16	239	18	32			32	
Total	591	299	1,593	155	2,740	16,361	2,740	16,361	2,240	712	1,240	23,472	313	4,277	1,593	155	313	958
No occupation (including women and children)	374	63	1,647	132	2,342	11,096	2,342	11,096	1,509	533	403	7,934	307	1,198	1,647	132	307	434
Grand total	1,170	618	3,945	353	5,673	32,277	5,673	32,277	5,352	1,717	1,810	35,138	787	6,837	3,945	353	787	1,682

1 For intended future permanent residence of immigrant aliens admitted in the Philippine Islands, see Table X.

For intended future permanent residence of immigrant aliens admitted in the Philippine Islands, see Table IX; for occupations of immigrant aliens admitted in the Philippine Islands, see Table X.

TABLE XI.—IMMIGRANT ALIENS ADMITTED, FISCAL YEAR ENDED JUNE 30, 1913, BY STATES OF INTENDED FUTURE RESIDENCE AND OCCUPATIONS—Continued.

Occupation.	Ill.	Ind.	Iowa.	Kans.	Ky.	La.	Me.	Md.	Mass.	Mich.	Minn.	Miss.
PROFESSIONAL.												
Actors	69	2			1	2		1	45	12	1	
Architects	16	4	2			3	1		18	12	2	
Clergy	58	13	11	7	9	26	12	10	68	41	30	1
Editors	5								7	1		
Electricians	83	8	9	2		2	2	7	60	77	26	1
Engineers (professional)	90	16	7	1		6	4	6	56	71	14	1
Lawyers	12	2		2	1	4	5	1	10	3	3	
Literary and scientific persons	29	2				4		1	16	10	5	
Musicians	98	4	5	1	1	3	4	9	57	29	9	1
Officials (Government)	9	1				4	1	3	17	3	1	
Physicians	29		1	2		7	1		24	10	9	
Sculptors and artists	38	15	22			4	19	3	38	11	2	1
Teachers	143	12	15	11	6	8	11	24	207	76	31	1
Other professional	133			6	4	5		24	117	118	27	2
Total	812	79	73	32	22	76	61	99	751	474	160	6
SKILLED.												
Bakers	351	22	50	10	3	10	9	53	276	204	54	2
Barbers and hairdressers	198	18	18	4		7	13	29	290	499	18	4
Blacksmiths	587	64	47	11	2	2	28	42	322	367	112	
Bookbinders	50	2	6				1	10	26	11	3	
Brewers	33	3	5					9	10	8		2
Butchers	443	25	48	7	2	1	13	55	215	160	52	
Cabinetmakers	57	5	2		6	5		7	31	42	11	
Carpenters and joiners	1,430	87	127	33	9	24	89	102	1,221	857	335	3
Cigarette makers	3							2	4	1		1
Cigarmakers	22	3	2		1	1	1		127	9	1	2
Cigar packers	6	1						1	26	8		
Clerks and accountants	1,000	78	116	42	14	53	64	119	982	677	246	3
Dressmakers	474	34	34	8	5	9	18	70	554	188	66	1
Engineers (locomotive, marine, and stationary)	106	16	9	1		14	14	7	160	142	24	2
Furriers and fur workers	33		2	1	2			5	19	6	10	
Gardeners	112	11	18	1	2	7	6	7	146	99	31	
Hat and cap makers	44	1	1	5	6	1	1	13	48	7	5	1
Iron and steel workers	156	18	21				14	10	193	154	31	1
Jewelers	24	1	2	5	1	1	1		29	6	2	
Locksmiths	382	22	12	6		1	4	30	99	142	30	
Machinists	222	19	26	5		5	22	13	233	380	44	1
Masons	153	8	11	4		55	13	27	345	108	53	1
Mariners	702	65	55	18	4	7	21	45	527	404	95	
Mechanics (not specified)	98	11	8	5	1	4	2	9	114	85	26	28

Metal workers (other than iron, steel, and tin)	49	6	8	2		2	3	2	61	48	14	
Millers	103	9	6	2	1	1	3	11	33	54	17	
Milliners	107	4	8	3	9	1	1	12	99	46	4	
Miners	1,384	240	101	158	6	6	18	26	214	728	152	4
Painters and glaziers	367	22	40	13		3	16	24	27	237	92	
Patternmakers	24	2	1			2			17	21	1	
Photographers	39	1			1		1	3	28	16	8	
Plasterers	52	1	8	3	1		1	1	38	40	6	
Plumbers	75	4	4	2	7	2	5	5	64	86	12	1
Printers	69	5	37	4	3	7	4	66	80	59	21	6
Saddlers and harnessmakers	630	22	73	18		27	22	102	38	15	12	
Seamstresses	861	53	73		1	9	43	19	749	201	62	5
Shoemakers	56	6	8	2	26		28	4	1,235	343	94	
Stokers	49	11	6	13		36	41	375	78	86	29	1
Stonecutters	1,819	56	4				1	7	120	23	16	
Tailors	51	1	5		1	1	28	6	1,632	418	146	
Tanners and curriers	36	5	5	2		3	3	5	56	8	10	1
Textile workers (not specified)	66	1	0					14	513	19	1	
Tinners	4	4	3	1	2			3	45	46	5	
Tobacco workers	13		4	1	1		1	5	7	16	1	
Upholsterers	45	3	25	1		3	74	9	14	18	2	1
Watch and clock makers	161	33	3	1		1		2	26	126	10	
Weavers and spinners	53	8	2	2		2		9	1,079	27	26	
Wheelwrights	28		3	12	4		8	2	10	35	6	
Woodworkers (not specified)	444	28	35		26	11	47	44	41	398	4	1
Other skilled									430		116	
Total	**13,271**	**1,044**	**1,086**	**408**	**115**	**325**	**692**	**1,419**	**12,976**	**7,278**	**2,116**	**66**
MISCELLANEOUS.												
Agents	68	6	3	1	3	6	5	6	52	80	16	
Bankers	10	1		1		2		1	16	2		
Draymen, hackmen, and teamsters	73	8	7					7	98	46		50
Farm laborers	30,789	4,477	2,056	697	155	140	964	2,715	26,283	15,833	3,547	6
Farmers	1,010	135	273	77	14	20	113	38	703	782	443	1
Fishermen	38		12		1	20	7	7	177	71	24	
Hotel keepers	26	2	3	1		1			12	4		
Laborers	18,757	2,845	1,739	515	114	292	1,851	956	20,093	13,024	5,805	62
Manufacturers	19		1		3	2		1	23	13		14
Merchants and dealers	687	54	74	12	10	65	23	102	628	292	81	27
Servants	13,990	1,164	956	326	52	110	646	847	15,205	5,169	2,290	10
Other miscellaneous	1,023	88	115	27	19	52	90	56	790	825	228	
Total	**66,490**	**8,780**	**5,239**	**1,657**	**371**	**710**	**3,706**	**4,736**	**64,140**	**36,141**	**12,439**	**100**
No occupation (including women and children)	**26,487**	**3,102**	**2,268**	**1,566**	**253**	**663**	**2,165**	**1,914**	**23,807**	**15,299**	**3,978**	**183**
Grand total	**107,060**	**13,005**	**8,666**	**3,663**	**761**	**1,774**	**6,624**	**8,168**	**101,674**	**59,192**	**18,693**	**415**

TABLE XI.—IMMIGRANT ALIENS ADMITTED, FISCAL YEAR ENDED JUNE 30, 1913, BY STATES OF INTENDED FUTURE RESIDENCE AND OCCUPATIONS—Continued.

Occupation.	Mo.	Mont.	Nebr.	Nev.	N.H.	N.J.	N.M.	N.Y.	N.C.	N. Dak.	Ohio.	Okla.	Oreg.	Pa.
PROFESSIONAL.														
Actors	13		1		2	5		594		3	3		5	26
Architects	2	2				18		141			3		1	23
Clergy	13	9	14			28	4	287	1	24	26	1	12	83
Editors	1					6	1	139						8
Electricians	7	3	3	1	5	42		308		2	23		6	80
Engineers (professional)	14	10	1		1	87	4	1,010	6		55	7	12	150
Lawyers	1		2			8		177			2		1	7
Literary and scientific persons	3	2	2		1	19		285	1		9		2	34
Musicians	8		6	1	1	49	1	657		3	32			121
Officials (Government)	3	3			1	2		163			2		2	7
Physicians	6		1	1	1	9	1	257		3	4		3	19
Sculptors and artists	4		5		2	17		411		1	27		3	35
Teachers	23	7	4	1	10	88	1	946	7	9	60		12	170
Other professional	18	12		1	10	90	1	814	2	7	40	3	20	144
Total	116	48	42	8	34	468	13	6,199	17	52	298	11	79	907
SKILLED.														
Bakers	57	15	26	3	24	239	2	1,739	2	7	124	6	13	371
Barbers and hairdressers	35	6	9		12	188	1	1,495	1	5	92	1	8	310
Blacksmiths	55	23	48	5	19	303	2	1,571		20	275	4	24	640
Bookbinders	9	2	4		2	14		298			12			54
Brewers	6					13		75			13		1	22
Butchers	59	13	22	4	10	192	1	1,437	1	8	142	2	14	388
Cabinetmakers	6	3		7		19		171	2	1	25		1	49
Carpenters and joiners	112	78	94		86	764	5	4,786		104	567	5	102	1,390
Cigarette makers	1		1	1		1		34			3		1	7
Cigarmakers	1		1		15	25		154						15
Cigar packers		1		1	4	1		12		1	1			5
Clerks and accountants	121	67	79		43	612		5,895	9	2	377	11	99	956
Dressmakers	74	13	56	3	17	350	1	2,927	2	46	198		12	647
Engineers (locomotive, marine, and stationary)	7	20	3		4	63	5	432		12	54	3	28	114
Furriers and fur workers	2	1	1		1	23		427	4		11	1		43
Gardeners	16	7	8		2	85	1	441		8	56		19	118
Hat and cap makers	6	1	3			29		469			20	2	2	107
Iron and steel workers	15	8	7	1	10	77	1	408	2	4	104		7	224
Jewelers	1		2		1	16		215		1	8		2	30
Locksmiths	41	3	19		3	190		987	1	6	160	6	4	388
Machinists	16	8	10	1	17	118	7	2,293	3	5	128	3	20	209
Mariners	27	6	6	1	5	201	3	658	3	16	75		43	159
Masons	62	29	48	11	29	350	3	2,338		15	322	9	20	926

Occupation	1	2	3	4	5	6	7	8	9	10	11	12	13	14
Mechanics (not specified)	173	5	4	69	2		784	2	100		2	6	7	13
Metal workers (other than iron, steel, and tin)	53			28	1		363		47	3		1		4
Millers	99	2	2	41	5	1	253		38	2		11	2	7
Milliners	135	5	88	28	2	1	555		59	7	35	21	342	14
Miners	1,689	26	1	387	35		704	1	153	8	3	19	14	82
Painters and glaziers	270	22		113	15		1,638	42	186	8		1	1	35
Patternmakers	11	1	1	7		1	26		5			3	2	2
Photographers	30	10		3	1	1	186		16	2	1	4		3
Plasterers	18	9		9	4		127	1	20	1		6		9
Plumbers	56	5	3	31	2	3	267	1	40	4	2	18		10
Printers	86	5	1	33	3	2	508	1	56	2	1	47		6
Saddlers and harnessmakers	56	8	7	30	9		244		25	19		4		60
Seamstresses	569	12	1	208	11	4	4,912		436	73	3	4		137
Shoemakers	1,445	5		441	8	7	4,678	4	627	26		67	1	9
Stokers	67	7	2	36	4		432		40	45		2	5	221
Stonecutters	58			24	9		324	1	53	1	1	3		10
Tailors	2,370	45	11	645		1	12,491	1	920	22		1	5	3
Tanners and curriers	49		1	17			173		32					15
Textile workers (not specified)	106			16	2	3	103	1	48	1		1	2	5
Tinners	91	1	2	39	3		405		35	178		2		9
Tobacco workers	3						11		16			20		19
Upholsterers	18	1		10	1		135	2	44	2		7		19
Watch and clock makers	54	6		13	5		304		335	53	3			9
Weavers and spinners	332			64	1		672	3	18					5
Wheelwrights	58	3		35	13	1	89		7				28	51
Woodworkers (not specified)	37	28		15			104				4	22		
Other skilled	483			228		8	2,134		326	53				
Total	**15,588**	**626**	**186**	**5,340**	**415**	**62**	**61,884**	**90**	**7,555**	**764**	**91**	**723**	**771**	**1,474**

MISCELLANEOUS.

Category	1	2	3	4	5	6	7	8	9	10	11	12	13	14
Agents	45	17	2	24		3	485		44	1			6	
Bankers	8	1		2			200		5				2	
Draymen, hackmen, and teamsters	67	3		41			289		32		5	5	19	
Farm laborers	71,089	614	160	19,873	1,087	36	73,577	232	18,609	1,736	229	1,343	722	
Farmers	978	301	25	531	264	11	2,096		300	170	32	131	1,097	
Fishermen	30	19		8	16		274		14					
Hotel keepers	22	6		16	1		116		4			2	3	
Laborers	32,751	1,005	128	12,859	678	66	54,251		8,266	2,274	310	848	817	
Manufacturers	18	1		9	17		275		18					
Merchants and dealers	802	69	5	285		12	7,513	9	545	16	13	64	27	
Servants	19,278	398	67	6,726	462	33	41,992	47	10,312	933	90	681	356	
Other miscellaneous	1,195	173	10	416	48	15	4,433	10	646	48	14	68	71	
Total	**126,373**	**2,607**	**397**	**40,790**	**2,583**	**178**	**185,501**	**456**	**38,795**	**5,183**	**691**	**3,143**	**3,120**	**6,586**
No occupation (including women and children)	**39,876**	**1,682**	**424**	**16,579**	**1,235**	**172**	**76,947**	**199**	**14,540**	**2,249**	**210**	**2,358**	**1,857**	**3,328**
Grand total	**182,744**	**4,994**	**1,018**	**63,007**	**4,285**	**429**	**330,531**	**758**	**61,358**	**8,230**	**1,000**	**6,266**	**5,796**	**11,504**

Table XI.—Immigrant Aliens Admitted, Fiscal Year Ended June 30, 1913, by States of Intended Future Residence and Occupations—Continued.

Occupation.	P.I.	P.R.	R.I.	S.C.	S.Dak.	Tenn.	Tex.	Utah	Vt.	Va.	Wash.	W.Va.	Wis.	Wyo.	Total.
PROFESSIONAL.															
Actors		12	1				9	1		1	12		11	1	911
Architects			1			1					8		4		290
Clergy		19	5		7	3	23	5	9	4	30	5	30	2	1,051
Editors			1	1			1				2		2		207
Electricians		4	9			1	7	4	2	2	41	2	14	2	941
Engineers (professional)		6	12			2	1	4	1	5	24	1	13	1	1,917
Lawyers		1				1	1	1		1	4	1	2		290
Literary and scientific persons		5	4		1		4	1		1	3		2		493
Musicians		1	7			2	3	1	3	8	14		11		1,254
Officials (Government)		10	1			2	1			1	6		1		305
Physicians		2	4	1		1	1	2	4	3	5		1		508
Sculptors and artists		1		2	3		3	8	7	2	4		2		676
Teachers		19	26			4	29	3	3	5	39	3	22	2	2,389
Other professional		1	15		2	2	44			12	56	4	33		2,168
Total		81	88	4	19	19	158	30	29	45	248	16	153	9	13,469
SKILLED.															
Bakers		5	37	1	3	6	45	15	6	13	65	18	72	4	4,256
Barbers and hairdressers		4	40		2	2	14	4	8	6	39	11	28		3,213
Blacksmiths		6	47	2	17	8	38	7	14	8	164	32	155	4	5,431
Bookbinders			4			2	2		2				6		543
Brewers			3				2				3		12		240
Butchers		1	22		8	3	44	3	3	13	58	1	84	3	3,748
Cabinetmakers		3	4				4	2			16		5		501
Carpenters and joiners		15	136	2	25	12	150	28	44	24	515	53	338	6	15,035
Cigarette makers		1	1	7		1	1					2			64
Cigarmakers		1	2		1	1			1	1	2		2		899
Cigar packers			2												86
Clerks and accountants	1	86	117	1	26	16	196	32	22		204	29	157	8	14,025
Dressmakers		5	60	6	6	3	28	15	10	35	38	7	68	4	6,411
Engineers (locomotive, marine, and stationary)		6	16	1			11	6	8	13	98	2	25	2	1,594
Furriers and fur workers			2				2			3	1		3		607
Gardeners			13	1	3	2	15	4	5	1	40	5	35	1	1,516
Hat and cap makers			5				5		3	10	1	1	10		805
Iron and steel workers			47		4		13	5	3	1	41	1	36	2	1,728
Jewelers		3	7	2			27	2	2	3	1		2		404
Locksmiths			6				36	1	8	1	11	8	103		2,811
Machinists		28	60		4		51	9	8	6	118	8	44	2	2,725
Mariners		10	49	3	7	9	57		44	7	334	100	79	1	4,970
Masons		8	67		5	2	57	40	4	22	95	94	130	7	7,377
Mechanics (not specified)			29		2		35			9	25	3	27		1,853

Occupation	Total
Metal workers (other than iron, steel, and tin)	793
Millers	804
Milliners	193
Miners	9,510
Painters and glaziers	3,888
Patternmakers	108
Photographers	389
Plasterers	418
Plumbers	778
Printers	1,104
Saddlers and harnessmakers	616
Seamstresses	8,723
Shoemakers	11,578
Stokers	1,112
Stonecutters	1,111
Tailors	22,984
Tanners and curriers	487
Textile workers (not specified)	1,179
Tinners	879
Tobacco workers	52
Upholsterers	282
Watch and clock makers	611
Weavers and spinners	3,909
Wheelwrights	380
Woodworkers (not specified)	358
Other skilled	6,063
Total	**160,108**
MISCELLANEOUS.	
Agents	1,148
Bankers	293
Draymen, hackmen, and teamsters	933
Farm laborers	320,105
Farmers	13,180
Fishermen	1,174
Hotel keepers	315
Laborers	220,992
Manufacturers	454
Merchants and dealers	13,919
Servants	140,218
Other miscellaneous	14,396
Total	**727,127**
No occupation (including women and children)	297,188
Grand total	**1,197,892**

TABLE XI a.—EMIGRANT ALIENS DEPARTED, FISCAL YEAR ENDED JUNE 30, 1913, BY STATES OF LAST PERMANENT RESIDENCE AND OCCUPATIONS.[1]

Occupation.	Ala.	Alaska.	Ariz.	Ark.	Cal.	Colo.	Conn.	Del.	D. C.	Fla.	Ga.	Hawaii.	Idaho.
PROFESSIONAL.													
Actors					29		2			7		2	
Architects					3		4				1		
Clergy					17				1	1	1	6	1
Editors					3					1		1	
Electricians	1				8	1	1		2	1		1	1
Engineers (professional)			1		26	1	4	1				1	1
Lawyers					4	1					1	1	
Literary and scientific persons	1				8	1			1	1	1	1	
Musicians					10				20			2	
Officials (Government)	1				8		1		2	3		2	
Physicians					9				2	1			
Sculptors and artists					10		2		4	3		6	3
Teachers			1		17		15	1				6	
Other professional					24	1	7		4	3	3	6	
Total	3	1	2		176	9	36	2	36	19	7	27	4
SKILLED.													
Bakers					25	3	9	1	2	5			
Barbers and hairdressers		1	1		8	2	12		2	11		2	1
Blacksmiths	1		1		10		3	1		1			
Butchers					11	2	2	1	2	1			3
Cabinetmakers	2	1	4		4		1	2	4	42	2	6	2
Carpenters and joiners					57	8	36			596			
Cigarette makers	7		1		3	1	1			61			
Cigarmakers					88	6	28		5	6	7	16	
Clerks and accountants			1		7	3	10		3	6			
Dressmakers	5		1		19	2	3	2	2	1	1	1	
Engineers (locomotive, marine, and stationary)	1				46		7	4		1			
Gardeners					1	1	9	3	1	2	1		
Hat and cap makers					3		10						
Iron and steel workers				1	1								
Jewelers					3		2			2		1	
Locksmiths		1			32		32	2	1	69		1	
Machinists	4		1		37	3	5	4		2	1	1	
Mariners	1				21		20	3		6	1		
Masons					18		30					3	
Mechanics (not specified)							3						
Metal workers (other than iron, steel, and tin)													

Millers	35						1							
Milliners							19							
Miners			76	3	94	207	7	2		2	1		1	39
Painters and glaziers					14		2							
Patternmakers	1						1			1			1	
Photographers					4	1	2							
Plasterers					5		1							
Plumbers					3		3	1			1			
Printers					6	2	1							
Saddlers and harness makers					2	1	21				34			
Seamstresses					11	1	22				2		1	
Shoemakers					6		4			5	4		2	
Stokers					9	5	30			2			2	
Stonecutters					23		1			2		1		
Tailors					3		9			1				
Tanners and curriers					3									
Textile workers (not specified)					2						4			
Tinners													1
Tobacco workers				4			3						4	
Watch and clock makers					3	1	32	1						
Weavers and spinners					2		2	3						
Woodworkers (not specified)		2			1		38	1	5	7	1	1	2	1
Other skilled					91	4								
Total	57	34	90	4	680	249	427	27	43	858	22	38	47

MISCELLANEOUS.

Agents	11	3	1	2	9	1	1	1		1			2	
Bankers					3		2							14
Draymen, hackmen, and teamsters					10		12		2					9
Farm laborers			12		135	3	32			409	2	56		
Farmers					346	33				13		3		
Fishermen					25					3				
Hotel keepers				1	18				1					
Laborers	246	59	453	26	5,157	1,176	4,135	143	137	355	93	371	266
Manufacturers						1	1			5				
Merchants and dealers	8	1	8	2	331	11	23	3	27	48	10	16	8
Servants	5	1	8		222	47	531	13	26	29	5	14	2
Other miscellaneous	7	5	4	2	161	7	107	3	9	175	1	22	15
Total	277	69	486	33	6,419	1,282	4,844	163	202	1,039	114	484	313
No occupation (including women and children)	38	2	35	19	845	124	952	50	73	604	15	133	21
Grand total	375	106	613	56	8,120	1,664	6,259	242	354	2,520	158	682	385

¹ For last permanent residence of emigrant aliens departed from the Philippine Islands, see Table X A.

¹ For last permanent residence of emigrant aliens departed from the Philippine Islands, see Table IX A; for occupations of emigrant aliens departed from the Philippine Islands, see Table X A.

TABLE XI a.—EMIGRANT ALIENS DEPARTED, FISCAL YEAR ENDED JUNE 30, 1913, BY STATES OF LAST PERMANENT RESIDENCE AND OCCUPATIONS—Continued.

Occupation.	Ill.	Ind.	Iowa	Kans	Ky.	La	Me.	Md.	Mass.	Mich.	Minn.	Miss.
PROFESSIONAL.												
Actors	6							1	23		1	
Architects	5	2				4		2	8	4	5	
Clergy	30	1			1	4	1		26	7		
Editors	3		5					1	1	1		
Electricians	10	2		1	1	3			4	1		
Engineers (professional)	21							1	25	2		
Lawyers	1				1				3	7	1	
Literary and scientific persons	8	2							4		2	
Musicians	25		1			1	1	2	8	1		
Officials (Government)	3	2				6			2	2		
Physicians	15					3		1	8	2		1
Sculptors and artists	14			1				2	6	6		
Teachers	34	1	4		2	2	1	2	34		4	1
Other professional	22	1	2			3		3	13		1	
Total	197	11	12	4	4	34	3	13	165	32	17	2
SKILLED.												
Bakers	34	4	3			1	6	2	46	13	3	
Barbers and hairdressers	32	3	3				2	3	126	8	1	
Blacksmiths	38	6	1					2	33	10	2	
Bookbinders	2								1			
Brewers	3											
Butchers	45	7	3	2		2		4	17	7	1	
Cabinetmakers	13				1	2	2	2	3	8	2	
Carpenters and joiners	215	28	13	1	1	2	1	11	85	80	25	
Cigarette makers	2											
Cigarmakers			1		4				15	1		
Cigar packers									1			
Clerks and accountants	163	10	9	1	4	18	4	4	101	16	20	
Dressmakers	34		4	1		1	3	2	38	3	4	
Engineers (locomotive, marine, and stationary)	7		3	1		3	1	5	14	6	2	
Furriers and fur workers	1	1						1	1	1		
Gardeners	11			1		2			8	5		
Hat and cap makers	1											
Iron and steel workers	21	3	2	1		1	2	2	20	1		
Jewelers	11							1	2	12		
Locksmiths	3			1				2	1	2		
Machinists	102	17	5	1		2	2	6	44	67	8	
Mariners	11	3	1	2	1	6	1	5	50	2	3	
Masons	52	16	2	3			3	5	85	12	5	
Mechanics (not specified)	26					4	1	1	23	15	2	

	Total
Metal workers (other than iron, steel, and tin)	4
Millers	1
Milliners	2
Miners	413
Painters and glaziers	47
Patternmakers	3
Photographers	6
Plasterers	11
Plumbers	3
Printers	16
Saddlers and harness makers	3
Seamstresses	5
Shoemakers	29
Stokers	9
Stonecutters	7
Tailors	204
Tanners and curriers	2
Textile workers (not specified)	3
Tinners	5
Watch and clock makers	2
Weavers and spinners	2
Wheelwrights	10
Woodworkers (not specified)	107
Other skilled	
Total	**1,727**
MISCELLANEOUS.	
Agents	18
Bankers	4
Draymen, hackmen, and teamsters	13
Farm laborers	31
Farmers	255
Fishermen	1
Hotel keepers	20
Laborers	17,797
Manufacturers	5
Merchants and dealers	288
Servants	1,048
Other miscellaneous	246
Total	**19,726**
No occupation (including women and children)	2,528
Grand total	**24,178**

Table XI a.—Emigrant Aliens Departed Fiscal Year Ended June 30, 1913, by States of Last Permanent Residence and Occupations—Continued.

Occupation.	Mo.	Mont.	Nebr.	Nev.	N.H.	N.J.	N.Mex.	N.Y.	N.C.	N.Dak.	Ohio.	Okla.	Oreg.	Pa.
PROFESSIONAL.													
Actors	1					4		226			1			3
Architects			1		1	8		42			4			6
Clergy		1	3			8		134		3	2	1		28
Editors						1		14						1
Electricians						9		47			3			9
Engineers (professional)	2	1	1	3	1	29		205			10		2	31
Lawyers								23						1
Literary and scientific persons						2		30						9
Musicians	1		1			20		150			6			36
Officials (Government)								43			1		1	1
Physicians	1					3	2	48			5		1	19
Sculptors and artists	1				2	3		75		1	1			9
Teachers	4	1	2		2	13		259	3		4		2	28
Other professional	2				1	21		163		1	5			52
Total	12	3	8	3	7	121	2	1,459	3	4	42	1	6	223
SKILLED.													
Bakers	10	2	1		3	38		178		1	9	1		46
Barbers and hairdressers	9	1			3	25		193	1		12	1	1	41
Blacksmiths	6					15		74			18		1	38
Bookbinders								17			1			2
Brewers								11			2			6
Butchers	5	2	5		6	22		107		2	6		2	29
Cabinetmakers						2		12		1	3			10
Carpenters and joiners	10		14	1		114	1	471	1	2	57	2	9	107
Cigarette makers								2						
Cigar makers						14		50						70
Cigar packers						1								5
Clerks and accountants	16	2	4	1		51	1	832	3	1	35	3	11	132
Dressmakers	2		3		1	19		281			8		3	32
Engineers (locomotive, marine, and stationary)														6
Furriers and fur workers	3	1	2	1		8	1	43		1	7			1
Gardeners			2	1	1	18		74			5		1	22
Hat and cap makers	3	1				5		44						6
Iron and steel workers	4				1	15		17			36		1	57
Jewelers						1		55			1			8
Locksmiths						3		51			2			4
Machinists	7		3			108		175		1	54		3	105
Mariners	6		3	1		12		331			6		4	41
Masons	51	1	1		6	25		148			22		3	81
Mechanics (not specified)	1	2ª				15		105			6		1	39

Occupation	1	2	3	4	5	6	7	8	9	10	11	12	13	14
Metal workers (other than iron, steel, and tin)	4					1		17			3			7
Millers						18		1			2			3
Milliners	44					22		45			1			7
Miners	6	90		181		4		140			181			4,077
Painters and glaziers						3		149			17			29
Pattern makers						4		6			3			4
Photographers						8		16						6
Plasterers						9		35			1			3
Plumbers						2		28			3			2
Printers						2		47			1			5
Saddlers and harness makers						40		10			1			1
Seamstresses						18		79			3			14
Shoemakers						5		277			26			65
Stokers						34		470			5			37
Stonecutters						1		22			43			22
Tailors						9		1,113			1			140
Tanners and curriers						4		4			1			1
Textile workers (not specified)								14			6			34
Tinners						3		24						8
Tobacco workers						99		7			1			
Upholsterers								9			3			3
Watch and clock makers						3		17			1			7
Weavers and spinners								32			1			49
Wheelwrights								8						1
Woodworkers (not specified)														6
Other skilled						85		372			48			137
Total	249	107	48	56	106	887	79	6,224	8	11	646	67	67	5,555
MISCELLANEOUS.														
Agents	5					3		55						9
Bankers						2		51			8			1
Draymen, hackmen, and teamsters	8					11		58			256			19
Farm laborers	239					14		72						46
Farmers	2					42		286			10,315			580
Fishermen						6		35			1			
Hotel keepers								32			46			5
Laborers	2,359					7,558		54,081			557			29,567
Manufacturers	31					3		41			77			1
Merchants and dealers	124					91		2,488						243
Servants	41					1,152		6,017						2,163
Other miscellaneous						302		1,114						471
Total	2,811	804	576	325	1,396	9,188	147	64,310	43	172	11,263	140	1,245	33,105
No occupation (including women and children)	314	41	63	18	113	2,205	18	11,615	26	42	1,287	27	67	4,943
Grand total	3,386	955	695	402	1,622	12,401	246	83,608	80	229	13,238	235	1,385	43,836

TABLE XI A.—EMIGRANT ALIENS DEPARTED FISCAL YEAR ENDED JUNE 30, 1913, BY STATES OF LAST PERMANENT RESIDENCE AND OCCUPATIONS—Continued.

Occupation.	P.I.	P.R.	R.I.	S.C.	S. Dak.	Tenn.	Tex.	Utah.	Vt.	Va.	Wash.	W. Va.	Wis.	Wyo.	Unknown.[1]	Total.
PROFESSIONAL.																
Actors		18	1								2	2	8			333
Architects											2	1	1			97
Clergy		17		1	1	1			1		4	3	10			335
Editors							2									28
Electricians				1	1		1						2			103
Engineers (professional)		5		1	3		1			2	2	1	7	1		408
Lawyers		4		1								1	1			42
Literary and scientific persons		3		1		2	2			1	1	1				73
Musicians		5	1					2		1	3		1			284
Officials (Government)		2									3					98
Physicians		6			1		1			2	1	1	1			137
Sculptors and artists		14					1	2		2	2	2	2			139
Teachers		7	4	1	1	1	4		1		2	1	2			494
Other professional			1						3							364
Total		81	7	4	6	4	13	5	5	10	23	10	36	1		2,925
SKILLED.																
Bakers			12			1	4		1	2	5	1	8			475
Barbers and hairdressers			26				1			1	1	1	7			537
Blacksmiths		1	2				1	1			4		14			292
Bookbinders													2			25
Brewers					1								5			29
Butchers							1			1	1	1	7			298
Cabinetmakers			10										1			62
Carpenters and joiners		7			3		4	2		2	36	2	35	2		1,529
Cigar makers			1							1		1				4
Cigarette makers																760
Cigar packers		1														9
Clerks and accountants		50	10			6	21	4	2	6	23	6	12	1		1,804
Dressmakers			1								3		1			462
Engineers (locomotive, marine, and stationary)		1	1	1		1	4	1		2	5					158
Furriers and fur workers			3				3	1			3		2			80
Gardeners		1					1	2			4		1			196
Hat and cap makers			5													45
Iron and steel workers			6					3				2				263
Jewelers							3	1		2	3		1			89
Locksmiths							12		1	1	16		15			28
Machinists		14	8	1			1		1		6	1	6			817
Mariners		2	38										11			696
Masons		9	13										2			616
Mechanics (not specified)			6									5			6,439	6,758

	Total
Metal workers (other than iron, steel, and tin)	47
Millers	11
Milliners	71
Miners	8,280
Painters and glaziers	366
Pattern makers	33
Photographers	48
Plasterers	85
Plumbers	76
Printers	114
Saddlers and harness makers	24
Seamstresses	217
Shoemakers	838
Stokers	606
Stonecutters	254
Tailors	1,850
Tanners and curriers	40
Textile workers (not specified)	711
Tinners	72
Tobacco workers	12
Upholsterers	14
Watch and clock makers	51
Weavers and spinners	457
Wheelwrights	15
Woodworkers (not specified)	60
Other skilled	1,169
Total	**31,563**
MISCELLANEOUS.	
Agents	136
Bankers	72
Draymen, hackmen, and teamsters	140
Farm laborers	3,948
Farmers	6,120
Fishermen	261
Hotel keepers	106
Laborers	191,604
Manufacturers	66
Merchants and dealers	5,979
Servants	16,220
Other miscellaneous	3,654
Total	**228,306**
No occupation (including women and children)	45,396
Grand total	**308,190**

1 Last United States residence unknown. Departed via Canadian border. Reported by Canadian Government.

TABLE XII.—IMMIGRANT ALIENS ADMITTED DURING SPECIFIED PERIODS, JAN. 1, 1912, TO JUNE 30, 1913, BY RACES OR PEOPLES AND SEX.

Race or people.	Year ended June 30, 1913.			6 months ended June 30, 1913.			6 months ended Dec. 31, 1912.			Year ended Dec. 31, 1912.		
	Males.	Females.	Total.	Males.	Females.	Total.	Males.	Females.	Total.	Males.	Females.	Total.
African (black)	3,691	2,943	6,634	2,154	1,490	3,644	1,537	1,453	2,990	3,714	2,877	6,591
Armenian	7,893	1,460	9,353	4,002	469	4,471	3,891	991	4,882	6,428	1,295	7,723
Bohemian and Moravian (Czech)	6,328	4,763	11,091	3,532	2,344	5,876	2,796	2,419	5,215	5,303	4,277	9,580
Bulgarian, Servian, and Montenegrin	7,834	1,253	9,087	2,999	507	3,506	4,835	746	5,581	12,525	1,317	13,842
Chinese	1,692	330	2,022	744	131	875	948	199	1,147	1,340	301	1,641
Croatian and Slovenian	31,590	10,909	42,499	17,666	5,679	23,345	13,924	5,230	19,154	26,501	9,125	35,626
Cuban	2,126	973	3,099	681	338	1,019	1,445	635	2,080	2,183	1,062	3,245
Dalmatian, Bosnian, and Herzegovinian	3,938	582	4,520	2,284	242	2,526	1,654	340	1,994	3,968	593	4,561
Dutch and Flemish	9,471	5,036	14,507	6,749	3,135	9,884	2,722	1,901	4,623	7,137	4,375	11,512
East Indian	184	4	188	73	1	74	111	3	114	182	7	189
English	31,320	24,202	55,522	16,098	11,065	27,163	15,222	13,137	28,359	28,510	23,202	51,712
Finnish	8,219	4,537	12,756	5,670	2,203	7,873	2,549	2,334	4,883	4,466	3,714	8,180
French	11,620	9,032	20,652	5,316	3,809	9,125	6,304	5,223	11,527	11,251	8,818	20,069
German	45,974	34,891	80,865	24,303	16,311	40,614	21,671	18,580	40,251	41,471	32,341	73,812
Greek	35,143	3,501	38,644	8,483	818	9,301	26,660	2,683	29,343	45,321	4,126	49,447
Hebrew	57,148	44,182	101,330	29,634	19,295	48,929	27,514	24,887	52,401	46,226	39,513	85,739
Irish	19,072	17,951	37,023	10,953	8,770	19,723	8,119	9,181	17,300	17,453	17,335	34,788
Italian (North)	32,428	10,106	42,534	21,233	5,164	26,397	11,195	4,942	16,137	22,054	8,703	30,757
Italian (South)	176,472	55,141	231,613	113,409	25,653	139,062	63,063	29,488	92,551	132,413	52,350	184,763
Japanese	3,157	5,145	8,302	1,409	2,156	3,565	1,748	2,989	4,737	2,880	5,286	8,166
Korean	15	49	64	5	19	24	10	30	40	14	36	50
Lithuanian	16,069	8,578	24,647	9,596	4,027	13,623	6,473	4,551	11,024	10,843	7,269	18,112
Magyar	16,637	13,973	30,610	5,976	6,498	12,474	10,661	7,475	18,136	19,717	12,584	32,301
Mexican	6,359	4,595	10,954	2,869	2,134	5,003	3,490	2,461	5,951	10,063	5,067	15,130
Pacific Islander	8	3	11	1	2	3	7	1	8	4	1	5
Polish	115,772	58,593	174,365	75,615	34,370	109,985	40,157	24,223	64,380	75,491	44,803	120,294
Portuguese	8,696	4,870	13,566	5,731	2,608	8,339	2,965	2,262	5,227	7,181	4,553	11,734
Roumanian	10,373	3,078	13,451	4,573	1,497	6,070	5,800	1,581	7,381	11,150	2,630	13,780
Russian	45,633	5,839	51,472	30,731	3,471	34,202	14,902	2,368	17,270	29,385	4,151	33,536
Ruthenian (Russniak)	18,980	11,608	30,588	10,557	6,552	17,109	8,423	5,056	13,479	17,103	10,169	27,272
Scandinavian	25,243	13,494	38,737	15,764	5,970	21,734	9,479	7,524	17,003	20,374	12,637	33,011
Scotch	11,545	9,748	21,293	6,275	4,476	10,751	5,270	5,272	10,542	10,825	9,777	20,602
Slovak	16,242	10,992	27,234	6,689	5,592	12,281	9,553	5,400	14,953	19,320	10,295	29,525
Spanish	7,240	1,802	9,042	4,539	1,144	5,683	2,701	658	3,359	7,237	2,092	9,329
Spanish-American	978	385	1,363	432	185	617	546	200	746	992	398	1,390
Syrian	6,177	3,033	9,210	2,753	1,177	3,930	3,424	1,856	5,280	5,048	2,653	7,701
Turkish	1,866	1,149	3,015	662	38	700	1,204	111	1,315	2,084	153	2,237
Welsh	1,771	1,049	2,820	960	528	1,488	811	521	1,332	1,536	876	2,412
West Indian (other than Cuban)	1,655	516	2,171	314	257	571	341	259	600	640	526	1,166
Other peoples	2,585	453	3,038	777	109	886	1,808	344	2,152	4,312	518	4,830
Total	808,144	389,748	1,197,892	462,215	190,234	652,449	345,929	199,514	545,443	674,555	351,805	1,026,360

TABLE XII A.—EMIGRANT ALIENS DEPARTED DURING SPECIFIED PERIODS, JAN. 1, 1912, TO JUNE 30, 1913, BY RACES OR PEOPLES AND SEX.

Race or people.	Year ended June 30, 1913.			6 months ended June 30, 1913.			6 months ended Dec. 31, 1912.			Year ended Dec. 31, 1912.		
	Males.	Females.	Total.	Males.	Females.	Total.	Males.	Females.	Total.	Males.	Females.	Total.
African (black)	1,127	544	1,671	402	263	665	725	281	1,006	1,142	481	1,623
Armenian	640	36	676	209	6	215	431	30	461	687	41	728
Bohemian and Moravian (Czech)	545	326	871	264	185	449	281	141	422	641	316	957
Bulgarian, Servian, and Montenegrin	13,222	303	13,525	3,475	116	3,591	9,747	187	9,934	11,432	262	11,694
Chinese	2,204	46	2,250	827	18	845	1,377	28	1,405	2,156	53	2,209
Croatian and Slovenian	9,098	1,111	10,209	3,799	541	4,340	5,299	570	5,869	9,634	1,156	10,790
Cuban	835	429	1,264	488	224	712	347	205	552	748	383	1,131
Dalmatian, Bosnian, and Herzegovinian	824	25	849	420	11	431	404	14	418	618	31	649
Dutch and Flemish	1,600	548	2,148	592	270	862	1,008	278	1,286	1,505	509	2,014
East Indian	212	1	213	39		39	173	1	174	192	3	195
English	6,797	3,997	10,794	3,131	1,796	4,927	3,666	2,201	5,867	6,391	3,731	10,122
Finnish	2,221	832	3,053	874	435	1,309	1,347	397	1,744	2,302	705	3,007
French	2,550	1,469	4,019	1,183	801	1,984	1,367	668	2,035	3,073	1,626	4,699
German	7,613	4,258	11,871	3,220	1,989	5,209	4,393	2,269	6,662	7,891	4,387	12,278
Greek	31,115	441	31,556	12,286	161	12,447	18,829	280	19,109	22,006	411	22,417
Hebrew	5,215	1,482	6,697	2,094	631	2,725	3,121	851	3,972	5,844	1,641	7,485
Irish	2,439	2,019	4,458	991	952	1,943	1,448	1,067	2,515	2,300	1,888	4,188
Italian (North)	9,378	1,617	10,995	4,145	761	4,906	5,233	856	6,089	8,977	1,435	10,412
Italian (South)	70,619	8,438	79,057	19,241	2,802	22,043	51,378	5,636	57,014	68,251	8,028	76,279
Japanese	561	172	733	215	61	276	346	111	457	661	183	844
Korean	38	6	44	11	1	12	27	5	32	37	7	44
Lithuanian	2,412	864	3,276	1,219	425	1,644	1,193	439	1,632	2,776	864	3,640
Magyar	8,225	3,271	11,496	4,045	1,481	5,526	4,180	1,790	5,970	9,163	3,569	12,732
Mexican	773	137	910	448	72	520	325	65	390	473	111	584
Pacific Islander	3	1	4				3	1	4	3	2	5
Polish	18,886	5,221	24,107	8,194	1,975	10,169	10,692	3,246	13,938	23,983	6,194	30,177
Portuguese	1,128	455	1,583	321	174	495	807	281	1,088	1,139	442	1,581
Roumanian	2,811	345	3,156	1,247	137	1,384	1,564	208	1,772	3,149	382	3,531
Russian	9,040	1,508	10,548	4,753	789	5,542	4,287	719	5,006	8,134	1,214	9,348
Ruthenian (Russniak)	4,643	684	5,327	1,689	325	2,014	2,954	359	3,313	5,383	740	6,123
Scandinavian	6,989	2,302	9,291	2,744	1,048	3,792	4,245	1,254	5,499	7,195	2,346	9,541
Scotch	2,706	1,412	4,118	1,156	595	1,751	1,550	817	2,367	2,499	1,320	3,819
Slovak	7,678	2,173	9,851	4,321	1,048	5,369	3,357	1,125	4,482	8,298	2,241	10,539
Spanish	2,692	489	3,181	1,302	283	1,585	1,390	206	1,596	2,358	367	2,725
Spanish-American	310	147	457	200	79	279	110	68	178	239	87	326
Syrian	616	181	797	200	58	258	416	123	539	669	172	841
Turkish	1,266	31	1,297	560	13	573	706	18	724	1,132	28	1,160
Welsh	231	67	298	122	33	155	109	34	143	190	60	250
West Indian (other than Cuban)	299	285	584	141	129	270	158	156	314	263	250	513
Other peoples	1,050	68	1,118	618	34	652	432	34	466	634	40	674
Not specified¹	11,197	8,641	19,838	4,956	3,555	8,511	6,241	5,086	11,327	9,794	7,679	17,473
Total	251,808	56,382	308,190	96,125	24,294	120,419	155,683	32,088	187,771	244,000	55,385	299,385

¹ Departed via Canadian border. Reported by Canadian Government as Canadians.

TABLE XIII.—SEX, AGE, LITERACY, FINANCIAL CONDITION, ETC., OF NONIMMIGRANT

Race or people.	Number admitted.	Sex.		Age.			Literacy, 14 years and over.				Total.
		Male.	Female.	Under 14 years.	14 to 44.	45 and over.	Can read but can not write.		Can neither read nor write.		
							Male.	Female.	Male.	Female.	
African (black)...	3,100	2,157	943	171	2,674	255	10	12	529	98	649
Armenian........	201	166	35	15	167	19			16	11	27
Bohemian and Moravian (Czech)........	761	416	345	64	630	67	1		10	7	18
Bulgarian, Servian, and Montenegrin.......	996	898	98	34	910	52			178	22	200
Chinese...........	1,465	1,437	28	41	776	648	1		169	7	177
Croatian and Slovenian...........	2,255	1,802	453	154	1,955	146	1		326	74	401
Cuban............	3,022	2,060	962	300	2,191	531	1	1	20	28	50
Dalmatian, Bosnian, and Herzegovinian.....	255	226	29	9	228	18			104	7	111
Dutch and Flemish...........	4,239	3,038	1,201	434	3,382	423			34	11	45
East Indian......	45	42	3	1	35	9			8	1	9
English..........	44,540	28,992	15,548	4,136	33,363	7,041	5	3	93	93	194
Finnish..........	2,164	1,448	716	115	1,979	70			6	5	11
French..........	5,857	3,426	2,431	361	4,477	1,019		1	28	14	43
German..........	20,899	12,462	8,437	2,437	15,423	3,039	3	5	289	275	572
Greek..........	2,289	2,165	124	56	2,147	86	1		277	43	321
Hebrew..........	4,496	2,923	1,573	617	3,405	474	5	1	158	181	345
Irish..........	11,080	4,697	6,383	404	9,391	1,285	1	2	29	37	69
Italian (North)...	11,637	10,087	1,550	529	10,463	645	3	2	560	68	633
Italian (South)...	32,735	29,235	3,500	1,474	28,581	2,680	13		12,519	1,382	13,914
Japanese.........	3,370	3,031	339	13	3,022	335			198	99	297
Korean..........	10	8	2		9	1					
Lithuanian......	882	628	254	109	742	31	13	5	177	89	284
Magyar.........	2,951	1,627	1,324	433	2,232	286			106	97	203
Mexican........	4,541	2,621	1,920	614	3,170	757	6	7	530	670	1,213
Pacific Islander...	16	7	9	2	14				1		1
Polish...........	10,842	8,011	2,831	1,119	9,204	519	124	61	2,243	732	3,160
Portuguese.......	1,065	766	299	40	867	158		1	338	131	470
Roumanian.......	1,329	1,040	289	94	1,096	139			321	96	417
Russian..........	6,908	6,290	618	349	6,282	277	7	2	1,832	110	1,951
Ruthenian (Russniak).....	8,817	6,624	2,193	960	7,321	536	12	3	2,340	844	3,208
Scandinavian.....	12,913	7,303	5,610	610	11,322	981		1	8	5	14
Scotch...........	10,141	6,252	3,889	759	7,660	1,722	1	1	4	11	17
Slovak...........	1,860	1,279	581	187	1,572	101			164	61	225
Spanish..........	5,975	4,710	1,265	402	4,690	883		1	839	29	869
Spanish-American	2,046	1,356	690	256	1,441	349	1		5	6	13
Syrian..........	809	607	202	140	592	77		1	94	75	170
Turkish..........	117	100	17	10	102	5			20	2	22
Welsh..........	1,102	774	328	70	879	153	2	1	4	4	11
West Indian (other than Cuban)........	1,131	687	444	110	859	162		2	13	13	28
Other peoples.....	474	373	101	22	396	56			80	3	83
Total......	229,335	161,771	67,564	17,651	185,649	26,035	211	114	24,679	5,441	30,445
Admitted in Philippine Islands..	8,238	7,797	441	205	5,947	2,086			1,486	57	1,543

ALIENS ADMITTED, FISCAL YEAR ENDED JUNE 30, 1913, BY RACES OR PEOPLES.

Money.			By whom passage was paid.			Going to join—			Admitted in Philippine Islands.
Aliens bringing—		Total. amount of money shown.	Self.	Relative.	Other than self or relative.	Relative.	Friend.	Neither relative nor friend.	
$50 or over.	Less than $50.								
739	1,762	$88,435	2,458	486	156	1,093	343	1,664	....
68	117	10,266	166	34	1	125	40	36	1
301	320	75,298	583	161	17	461	161	139	1
250	701	54,109	830	100	66	397	340	259	....
352	833	94,444	1,327	105	33	352	708	405	6,634
389	1,617	90,225	1,909	337	9	1,377	744	134	....
1,370	624	160,513	2,025	971	26	1,174	121	1,727	....
47	173	24,537	231	22	2	132	81	42	....
1,862	1,213	312,793	3,052	1,078	109	1,899	1,101	1,239	23
47	4	6,773	39	4	2	4	13	28	74
23,789	10,300	2,987,822	31,369	10,844	2,327	16,469	5,528	22,543	451
484	1,407	92,873	1,764	337	63	961	1,015	188	....
4,048	762	579,149	4,075	1,185	597	1,395	525	3,937	53
10,560	4,868	1,990,796	14,328	5,736	835	9,434	3,587	7,878	172
785	1,452	159,661	2,118	130	41	1,302	639	348	4
1,427	1,646	318,006	2,668	1,781	47	3,265	488	743	2
4,745	4,929	751,483	8,978	1,572	530	6,340	1,088	3,652	18
3,569	6,787	621,222	10,200	1,249	188	6,690	3,686	1,261	21
6,833	21,773	1,428,894	28,583	3,926	226	27,227	3,362	2,146	....
2,463	712	281,193	2,990	340	40	822	692	1,856	228
5	3	950	8	2	....	4	1	5	11
187	454	48,787	584	284	14	750	105	27	1
636	1,633	130,759	1,958	966	27	2,182	510	259	6
959	1,989	121,757	3,065	1,416	60	2,236	116	2,189	4
10	....	4,135	6	6	4	6	....	10	1
1,759	7,275	411,788	7,977	2,699	166	8,741	1,640	461	3
311	469	51,533	779	275	11	742	182	141	101
165	981	40,995	991	316	22	922	305	102	4
891	5,278	223,958	5,639	1,164	105	3,758	2,386	764	12
472	6,559	205,087	6,006	2,607	204	6,572	1,934	311	....
4,259	6,751	723,569	10,456	1,636	821	5,808	3,180	3,925	13
5,751	2,514	737,696	7,305	2,220	616	3,987	1,438	4,716	55
294	1,312	68,307	1,504	347	9	1,529	287	44	....
2,966	1,690	579,864	4,750	1,065	160	1,146	545	4,284	311
1,586	62	198,932	1,270	640	136	266	214	1,566	3
363	185	203,453	538	267	4	408	77	324	5
61	115	12,298	96	20	1	37	21	59	10
550	323	88,073	865	187	50	421	202	479	....
674	213	88,076	820	284	• 27	370	145	616	....
218	149	28,056	373	79	22	138	101	235	16
86,245	99,955	14,096,570	174,683	46,878	7,774	120,942	37,651	70,742	8,238
2,904	5,342	42,614	7,727	354	157	712	862	6,664	....

TABLE XIII A.—SEX, AGE, AND LENGTH OF RESIDENCE IN UNITED STATES OF NONEMIGRANT ALIENS DEPARTED, FISCAL YEAR ENDED JUNE 30, 1913, BY RACES OR PEOPLES.

Race or people.	Number departed.	Sex.		Age.			Continuous residence in the United States.					Residence outside U. S.	Departed from P. I.
		Male.	Female.	Under 14 years.	14 to 44.	45 and over.	Not over 5 years.	5 to 10 years.	10 to 15 years.	15 to 20 years.	Over 20 years.		
African (black)	2,385	1,689	696	149	2,018	218	178	95	21	4	5	2,082	
Armenian	357	326	31	13	303	41	113	55	10	1	5	173	
Bohemian and Moravian	757	475	282	51	608	98	223	165	28	6	17	318	
Bulgarian, Servian, Montenegrin	5,359	5,180	179	43	5,024	292	1,887	620	37	2	2	2,811	
Chinese	3,499	3,428	71	45	2,216	1,238	493	509	310	248	774	1,165	7,463
Croatian and Slovenian	3,726	3,235	491	95	3,261	370	1,572	815	150	16	10	1,103	
Cuban	6,128	4,065	2,063	843	4,453	832	1,364	135	55	5	7	4,562	1
Dalmatian, Bosnian, Herzegovinian	521	498	23	5	478	38	162	97	5			255	
Dutch and Flemish	5,619	4,103	1,516	494	4,480	645	1,317	538	106	16	43	3,599	26
East Indian	122	118	4	1	113	8	32					58	85
English	61,168	39,590	21,578	5,180	45,987	10,001	6,736	2,663	566	206	350	50,647	485
Finnish	3,071	2,123	948	77	2,862	132	1,270	687	202	21	22	869	
French	6,218	3,726	2,492	350	4,834	1,034	1,090	467	128	33	49	4,461	
German	23,160	14,169	8,991	2,121	17,694	3,345	5,353	3,062	707	147	386	13,515	58
Greek	19,321	18,928	395	120	18,507	694	7,293	5,634	664	33	17	5,680	145
Hebrew	4,841	3,348	1,493	563	3,644	614	879	423	86	20	24	3,409	
Irish	13,256	5,872	7,384	336	11,559	1,361	3,484	3,718	1,077	319	361	4,297	5
Italian (North)	14,335	12,624	1,711	465	12,905	965	2,986	2,049	457	53	60	8,730	13
Italian (South)	40,075	35,789	4,286	1,478	35,290	3,307	12,100	5,859	1,300	243	164	20,409	26
Japanese	7,707	6,495	1,212	49	6,705	953	1,306	4,253	1,349	277	117	405	286
Korean	19	16	3		16	3	2	11	5			1	
Lithuanian	1,343	1,036	307	87	1,133	123	382	137	36	4	5	779	4
Magyar	4,596	3,143	1,453	287	3,761	548	1,664	937	123	11	16	1,845	2
Mexican	1,883	1,293	590	194	1,418	271	147	39	38	5	6	1,648	
Pacific Islander	16	10	6	3	9	4	6					10	
Polish	11,705	9,195	2,510	605	10,298	802	3,522	1,151	207	19	22	6,784	120
Portuguese	1,916	1,385	531	92	1,572	252	641	679	119	40	47	390	3
Roumanian	2,022	1,688	334	108	1,706	208	697	225	10	2	1	1,087	15
Russian	8,910	8,039	871	345	8,069	496	1,419	324	60	6	8	7,093	
Ruthenian (Russniak)	7,038	5,375	1,663	685	5,937	416	505	108	21	1	4	6,399	
Scandinavian	14,211	8,765	5,446	428	12,588	1,195	5,367	3,822	1,039	158	269	3,556	28
Scotch	12,302	7,678	4,624	877	9,388	2,037	2,553	945	171	45	77	8,511	57
Slovak	3,237	2,448	789	117	2,785	335	1,766	639	114	18	16	684	
Spanish	5,503	4,597	906	245	4,586	672	715	245	142	20	11	4,370	288
Spanish-American	1,980	1,324	656	211	1,455	314	69	22	4	2	4	1,879	3
Syrian	1,335	1,044	291	121	1,069	145	376	283	73	13	6	584	

[Continuation of preceding table]

Peoples	France, incl. Corsica	German Empire	Greece	Italy, incl. Sicily and Sardinia	Portugal/Norway	Roumania	Russian Empire	Spain, incl. Canary and Balearic Islands	Switzerland	United Kingdom	Other Europe	Total Europe
Turkish	649	32	10	630	41	306	148	11	6	18	216	4
Welsh	789	294	66	864	143	177	62	6	2	1	804	1
West Indian (except Cuban)	860	652	124	1,081	177	100	60	26	2	2	1,193	
Other peoples	845	112	20	838	99	268	105	11			569	18
Total	225,961	77,773	17,123	252,144	34,467	70,510	41,808	9,474	2,004	2,928	177,010	9,138
Departed from Philippine Islands	8,643	495	378	6,749	2,011	6,145	1,132	321	84	60		

Left-hand column totals: 303,734 — 9,138

TABLE XIV.—NONIMMIGRANT ALIENS ADMITTED, FISCAL YEAR ENDED JUNE 30, 1913, BY COUNTRIES.

Countries of intended future residence.

Countries of last permanent residence	Austria	Hungary	Belgium	Bulgaria, Servia, and Montenegro	Denmark	France, incl. Corsica	German Empire	Greece	Italy, incl. Sicily and Sardinia	Netherlands	Norway	Portugal, incl. Cape de Verde and Azore Islands	Roumania	Russian Empire	Spain, incl. Canary and Balearic Islands	Sweden	Switzerland	Turkey in Europe	United Kingdom	Other Europe	Total Europe
Austria	535						4		1										1		541
Hungary		137																	1		138
Belgium			228			3	2												1		236
Bulgaria, Servia, and Montenegro	2			24				2													24
Denmark					116		2,514	24											1		117
France, including Corsica						710	2,514	2	4										6		730
German Empire			5		2														7		2,526
Greece							2														24
Italy, including Sicily and Sardinia	1						2	1	538										49		596
Netherlands							1			226									2		230
Norway											939								1		940
Portugal, including Cape de Verde and Azore Islands							1					35									35
Roumania							4	1	3				28								30
Russian Empire	1		1		7		1		2					555					1		565
Spain, including Canary and Balearic Islands						1	2								221				2	2	236
Sweden							2									101	1				105
Switzerland							2										152		3		159

Table XIV.—Nonimmigrant Aliens Admitted, Fiscal Year Ended June 30, 1913, by Countries—Continued.

Countries of intended future residence—Continued.

Countries of last permanent residence.	Austria.	Hungary.	Belgium.	Bulgaria, Servia, and Montenegro.	Denmark.	France, including Corsica.	German Empire.	Greece.	Italy, including Sicily and Sardinia.	Netherlands.	Norway.	Portugal, including Cape de Verde and Azore Islands.	Roumania.	Russian Empire.	Spain, including Canary and Baleric Islands.	Sweden.	Switzerland.	Turkey in Europe.	United Kingdom.	Other Europe.	Total Europe.
Turkey in Europe	2	2				5	3	2	5									21			23
United Kingdom			1		1												1		4,702	18	4,721
Other Europe																			3		22
Total Europe	540	139	237	24	117	733	2,538	29	553	228	939	35	28	556	221	103	155	21	4,782	20	11,998
China	1					4	18				1	1		2	1				81		112
Japan						10	16			4									68		98
India						1	2					1							51		55
Turkey in Asia						1						3									1
Other Asia	1				3	5	15					5							50		80
Total Asia	2				3	21	51		2	4	1			2	1		1		250		346
Africa	85	1	54	112	13	1	1	141	402	1	4		1	128	9	22	1	26	15	2	17
Australia, Tasmania, and New Zealand	3	12	11		7	10	4	9	44	36	7	4		3	37	8	3		322	16	342
Pacific Islands, not specified	4	1	6			59	18		78	2		4		29	353	2	13		17	2	98
British North America	12	4	12		1	74	68		45	4	2			4	22		25		834		2,053
Central America	2		16		6	166	153	2	91	10	13			48	467	2	7		140		611
Mexico	1		2		1	196	95	2	5	23	1			2	2		7	4	315		1,093
South America						277	231	1									5		343		972
West Indies						383	92										2		526		1,683
United States						9	12												139		176
Other countries						2															2
Grand total	649	157	339	136	148	1,931	3,263	182	1,221	308	967	49	29	772	1,112	137	218	51	7,683	40	19,391
Male	464	115	245	134	105	1,299	2,513	169	984	260	909	34	20	602	730	111	149	45	4,907	35	13,830
Female	185	42	94	2	43	632	750	13	237	48	58	14	9	170	382	26	69	6	2,776	5	5,561
Admitted in Philippine Islands	18		2		1	9	37	4	10	3			1	5	3	2	3		125		223

Countries of intended future residence—Continued.

Countries of last permanent residence.	Admitted in Philippine Islands.	Female.	Male.	Grand total.	Other countries.	United States.	West Indies.	South America.	Mexico.	Central America.	British North America.	Pacific Islands not specified.	Australia, Tasmania, and New Zealand.	Africa.	Total Asia.	Other Asia.	Turkey in Asia.	India.	Japan.	China.
Austria	18	2,959	8,444	11,403			9	11	7	1	10,833		1		1				1	
Hungary	1	408	825	1,233					1		1,091				3					3
Belgium		392	990	1,382			31	13	15	12	1,072		2							
Bulgaria, Servia, and Montenegro	15	35	170	205							180									
Denmark	35	106	263	369							240									
France, including Corsica	8	820	1,664	2,484			8		287	1	753				6				5	1
German Empire	6	1,253	3,531	4,784			298	120	88	146	1,837	110	2		20				17	3
Greece	7	58	470	528			102	90		97	504	19	6		1					1
Italy, including Sicily and Sardinia	1	2,223	19,932	22,155	29		475	25	89	29	20,939	1		1	4			1	2	1
Netherlands	5	260	664	924			22	1	14	5	652				2					2
Norway	6	161	1,207	1,368			4		11		409									
Portugal, including Cape de Verde and Azore Islands	2	18	38	56			21				151									
Roumania		70	113	183																
Russian Empire	7	2,824	11,296	14,120			19	1	9	1	13,517		1		7				5	2
Spain, including Canary and Balearic Islands		361	1,699	2,060			478	18	297	59	970				2					2
Sweden		137	588	725			6		3	1	609		2		1					1
Switzerland		116	290	406			17	10	20	19	179									
Turkey in Europe		22	195	217			2		3	9	180									
United Kingdom	123	9,128	19,581	28,709			513	117	395	129	22,535	31	134	1	134	2		3	81	48
Other Europe		10	199	209			1		1		185									
Total Europe	302	21,361	72,159	93,520	29		2,006	407	1,241	510	76,836	162	148	2	181	2		4	111	64
China	330	81	228	309			71	8	14	1	19	1	2	2	83				1	82
Japan	62	50	323	373			9	1	2	1	39	2			224			1	221	1
India	64	45	106	151			1		18		47				42			42		
Turkey in Asia		82	183	265			5				198				39		39			
Other Asia	12	27	91	118			6				21				10	10				
Total Asia	468	285	931	1,216			92	11	34	5	324	3	2	1	398	10	39	42	224	83
Africa	1	87	247	334			19		29		145	1	5	110						
Australia, Tasmania, and New Zealand	80	557	1,039	1,596			1	2	4	4	165	2	1,075		2				1	1

TABLE XIV—NONIMMIGRANT ALIENS ADMITTED, FISCAL YEAR ENDED JUNE 30, 1913, BY COUNTRIES—Continued.

Countries of last permanent residence.	China	Japan	India	Turkey in Asia	Other Asia	Total Asia	Africa	Australia, Tasmania, and New Zealand	Pacific Islands, not specified	British North America	Central America	Mexico	South America	West Indies	United States	Other countries	Grand total	Male	Female	Admitted in Philippine Islands
										Countries of intended future residence—Continued.										
Pacific Islands, not specified	4	2				6		3	72	9		1	2				191	125	66	10
British North America	1	1				3	4	33	4	11,906	6	8	26	62			14,165	10,070	4,089	23
Central America	106			13		120	3	1	1	99	1,033	19	7	33			1,926	1,379	547	1
Mexico	3			1		3	2	6	3	78	5	852	88	12			2,134	1,469	665	3
South America							1			433	12	39	909	117		4	2,502	1,756	746	3
West Indies		10		2		13	2	7	1	1,259	20	62	126	5,061			8,591	6,835	2,756	4
United States	332	2	1	37		371	2			272	19	25	16	29	102,604		103,150	66,747	36,403	7,303
Other countries						1										8	10	8	2	40
Grand total	598	351	47	92	13	1,101	127	1,280	249	91,586	1,614	2,314	1,596	7,432	102,604	41	229,335	161,771	67,564	8,238
Male	538	314	36	67	13	968	96	819	164	70,464	1,104	1,634	1,135	5,233	66,295	29	161,771			7,797
Female	60	37	11	25		133	31	461	85	21,122	510	680	461	2,199	36,309	12	67,564			441
Admitted in Philippine Islands	377	54	64		14	499	2	76	3	23		3	2	7,370	4	33	8,238			

TABLE XIV a.—NONEMIGRANT ALIENS DEPARTED, FISCAL YEAR ENDED JUNE 30, 1913, BY COUNTRIES.

Countries of intended future residence.

Countries of last permanent residence.	Austria	Hungary	Belgium	Bulgaria, Servia, and Montenegro	Denmark	France, including Corsica	German Empire	Greece	Italy, including Sicily and Sardinia	Netherlands	Norway	Portugal, including Cape de Verde and Azore Islands	Roumania	Russian Empire	Spain, including Canary and Balearic Islands	Sweden	Switzerland	Turkey in Europe	United Kingdom	Other Europe	Total Europe
Austria	2,499	2		1		8	10		2					2			1		7	1	2,532
Hungary	4	2,726		5		3	5										2		1		2,743
Belgium			535			5	3														546
Bulgaria, Servia, and Montenegro				1,445																	1,445
Denmark					326		1														330
France, including Corsica	3		7			1,726	12		8	1	1			1	4	1	11		38		1,803
German Empire	6	3	5			19	4,721		5					1	3		1		32		4,813
Greece						2	3	3,937										1	4		3,944
Italy, including Sicily and Sardinia	2		1		3	34	1	1	5,807	3		2		4					11		5,858
Netherlands			1			1				769	1								1		774
Norway						1	6			1	570			1		1			1		575
Portugal, including Cape de Verde and Azore Islands												222									227
Roumania						3							76								82
Russian Empire	3		1			4	1		2					4,108	1		1		2		4,151
Spain, including Canary and Balearic Islands					1				1						555				1		605
Sweden							7		1		1					424		1	15		428
Switzerland	1	2	3	3		47	37		1	2				1			317	3	2		344
Turkey in Europe						9		9	10	2			1	3	1		3	360	1		377
United Kingdom						42		2			1								15,669	15	15,777
Other Europe																					15
Total Europe	2,516	2,733	553	1,454	330	1,916	4,807	3,949	5,837	779	574	224	77	4,121	564	426	334	363	15,796	16	47,309
China	1		1		3	2	8		3	1	2			2	1		1		80		98
Japan							4		2										40		53
India					1	3	1												27		29
Turkey in Asia																			1		4
Other Asia																			1		1
Total Asia	1		1		4	5	13		5	1	2			2	1		1		149		185

TABLE XIV A.—NONEMIGRANT ALIENS DEPARTED, FISCAL YEAR ENDED JUNE 30, 1913, BY COUNTRIES—Continued.

Countries of intended future residence.

Countries of last permanent residence.	Austria.	Hungary.	Belgium.	Bulgaria, Servia, and Montenegro.	Denmark.	France, including Corsica.	German Empire.	Greece.	Italy, including Sicily and Sardinia.	Netherlands.	Norway.	Portugal, including Azore and Cape de Verde Islands.	Roumania.	Russian Empire.	Spain, including Canary and Balearic Islands.	Sweden.	Switzerland.	Turkey in Europe.	United Kingdom.	Other Europe.	Total Europe.
Africa	1		1			2	1			1	1			1		1			6		12
Australia, Tasmania, and New Zealand			1			1	2			1	1						1	183	114		121
Pacific Islands, not specified						4	1												2	1	9
British North America	528	116	104	302	15	120	99	338	2,305	40	48	2		280	54	42	20		2,470		7,076
Central America	1	2	5		4	63	48	2	7	2	1	2		2	21	5	13		45		203
Mexico	15		9			100	76		36	1	1			4	57		5		261		569
South America	2		7		1	104	99		14	1	9				45		2	1	149		432
West Indies			8	1	2	101	63		38	24		13			183		5		209		655
Grand total	3,064	2,851	688	1,757	356	2,406	5,209	4,289	8,242	859	637	241	77	4,410	925	474	381	547	19,201	17	56,681
Male	2,465	2,103	493	1,737	217	1,582	3,576	4,220	7,234	654	485	161	64	3,692	732	334	248	529	12,489	13	43,028
Female	599	748	195	20	139	824	1,633	60	1,008	205	152	80	13	718	193	140	133	18	6,712	4	13,603
Departed from Philippine Islands	5		2	2	5	33	52		7	7		1		6	52	11	5		144		330

Countries of intended future residence.

Countries of last permanent residence.	China.	Japan.	India.	Turkey in Asia.	Other Asia.	Total Asia.	Africa.	Australia, Tasmania, and New Zealand.	Pacific Islands, not specified.	British North America.	Central America.	Mexico.	South America.	West Indies.	United States.	Other countries.	Grand total.	Male.	Female.	Departed from Philippine Islands.
Austria										8,778				14	128		11,465	8,605	2,860	3
Hungary						1				979	1			2	138		3,808	2,790	1,078	3
Belgium		1						2		1,018	1		5	8	65		1,652	1,179	473	
Bulgaria, Servia, and Montenegro										160	1	1	6		92		1,608	1,646	52	

																					Total	Male	Female
Denmark	1																				211	377	588
France, including Corsica					1																1,091	2,086	3,177
German Empire	8																				2,251	5,017	7,278
Greece																					107	4,624	4,731
Italy, including Sicily and Sardinia				1																	2,765	22,495	25,260
Netherlands																					407	1,087	1,494
Norway																					249	745	994
Portugal, including Cape de Verde and Azore Islands																					78	198	276
Roumania																					83	175	258
Russian Empire	4																				2,892	13,235	16,127
Spain, including Canary and Balearic Islands																					253	1,778	2,031
Sweden																					262	764	1,026
Switzerland																					198	415	613
Turkey in Europe																					33	572	605
United Kingdom	10			1																	11,955	25,511	37,496
Other Europe																					11	83	94
Total Europe	15			2																	27,349	93,382	120,731
China	213																				70	897	976
Japan																					49	370	419
India																					46	100	146
Turkey in Asia																					118	364	482
Other Asia																					10	31	41
Total Asia	213			2																	302	1,762	2,064
Africa																					86	244	330
Australia, Tasmania, and New Zealand																					511	1,009	1,520
Pacific Islands, not specified																					59	145	204
British North America	10																				9,316	23,871	33,187
Central America																					510	1,112	1,622
Mexico																					822	1,905	2,727
South America	3																				678	1,834	2,512
West Indies	164																				3,783	8,327	12,110
United States																					34,356	92,368	126,724
Other countries																					1	2	3
Grand total	407																				77,773	225,961	303,734
Male	324																						
Female	83																						
Departed from Philippine Islands	613																				495	8,643	9,138

TABLE XV.—IMMIGRATION, FISCAL YEARS ENDED JUNE 30, 1900–1913, BY RACES OR PEOPLES.

Race or people.	1900	1901	1902	1903	1904	1905	1906	1907	1908	1909	1910	1911	1912	1913
African (black)	714	594	832	2,174	2,386	3,598	3,786	5,235	4,626	4,307	4,966	6,721	6,759	6,634
Armenian	982	1,855	1,151	1,759	1,745	1,878	1,895	2,644	3,299	3,108	5,508	3,092	5,222	9,353
Bohemian and Moravian (Czech)	3,060	3,766	5,590	9,591	11,911	11,757	12,958	13,554	10,164	6,850	8,462	9,223	8,439	11,091
Bulgarian, Servian, and Montenegrin	204	611	1,291	6,479	4,577	5,823	11,548	27,174	18,246	6,214	15,130	10,222	10,057	9,087
Chinese	1,250	2,452	1,631	2,192	4,327	1,971	1,485	770	1,263	1,841	1,770	1,307	1,608	2,022
Croatian and Slovenian	17,184	17,928	30,233	32,907	21,242	35,104	44,272	47,826	20,472	20,181	39,562	18,982	24,366	42,499
Cuban	2,678	1,622	2,423	2,944	4,811	7,259	5,591	5,475	3,323	3,380	3,331	3,914	3,155	3,099
Dalmatian, Bosnian, and Herzegovinian	675	732	1,004	1,736	2,036	2,639	4,508	7,303	3,747	1,888	4,911	4,400	3,672	4,520
Dutch and Flemish	2,702	3,299	4,117	6,495	7,832	8,498	9,735	12,467	9,526	8,114	13,012	13,862	10,935	14,507
East Indian	9	20	84	83	258	145	271	1,072	1,710	337	1,782	517	165	188
English	12,012	13,488	14,842	28,451	41,479	50,865	45,070	51,126	49,056	39,021	53,498	57,258	49,689	55,522
Finnish	12,095	9,999	13,308	18,864	10,157	17,012	14,136	14,800	6,746	11,687	15,730	9,779	6,641	12,756
French	2,095	4,030	4,122	7,165	11,557	11,347	10,379	9,392	12,881	19,423	21,107	18,432	18,382	20,652
German	29,682	34,742	51,066	71,782	74,790	92,360	86,813	92,936	73,038	59,534	71,380	66,471	65,343	80,865
Greek	3,773	5,919	8,115	14,376	12,625	12,144	23,127	46,283	28,808	20,262	39,135	37,021	31,506	38,644
Hebrew	60,764	58,098	57,688	76,203	106,236	129,910	153,748	149,182	103,387	57,551	84,260	91,223	80,595	101,330
Irish	35,607	30,404	29,001	35,363	37,076	54,206	40,930	39,705	36,427	31,185	38,382	40,246	33,922	37,023
Italian (north)	17,316	22,103	27,020	37,423	36,099	39,030	45,285	51,564	24,700	25,150	30,780	30,312	26,443	42,534
Italian (south)	84,346	115,704	152,915	196,117	159,322	186,390	240,528	242,497	110,547	165,248	192,673	159,038	135,830	231,613
Japanese	12,028	5,249	14,455	20,041	14,382	11,021	14,243	30,824	16,418	3,275	2,798	4,575	6,172	8,302
Korean	71	47	28	564	1,907	4,923	127	39	26	11	19	8	33	64
Lithuanian	10,311	8,815	11,029	14,432	12,780	18,004	14,257	25,884	13,720	15,254	22,714	17,027	14,078	24,647
Magyar	13,777	13,311	23,610	27,124	23,883	46,030	44,261	60,071	24,378	28,704	27,302	19,996	23,599	30,610
Mexican	261	350	715	486	447	227	141	91	5,682	15,591	17,700	18,784	22,001	10,954
Pacific Islander	188	167		185	41		13	3				61	3	11
Polish	46,938	43,617	69,620	82,343	67,757	102,437	95,835	138,033	68,105	77,565	128,348	71,446	85,163	174,365
Portuguese	4,241	4,176	5,309	8,433	6,338	4,855	8,729	9,648	6,809	4,006	7,657	7,409	9,403	13,586
Roumanian	398	761	2,033	4,740	4,364	7,818	11,425	19,200	9,629	8,041	14,199	5,311	8,329	13,451
Russian	1,200	672	1,551	3,608	3,961	3,746	5,814	16,807	17,111	10,038	17,294	18,721	22,558	51,472
Ruthenian (Russniak)	2,832	5,288	7,533	9,843	9,592	14,473	16,257	24,081	12,361	15,843	27,907	17,724	21,965	30,588
Scandinavian (Norwegians, Danes, and Swedes)	32,952	40,277	55,780	79,347	61,029	62,284	58,141	53,425	32,789	34,996	52,037	45,859	31,601	38,737
Scotch	1,757	2,004	2,432	6,219	11,483	16,144	16,463	20,516	17,014	16,440	24,612	25,625	20,293	21,293
Slovak	29,243	29,343	36,934	34,427	27,940	52,308	38,221	42,041	16,170	22,586	32,416	21,415	25,281	27,234
Spanish	1,111	1,202	1,954	3,297	4,662	5,590	5,332	9,495	6,636	4,939	5,837	8,008	9,070	9,042
Spanish-American	97	276	496	978	1,666	1,658	1,585	1,060	1,063	890	900	1,153	1,342	1,363
Syrian	2,920	4,064	4,982	5,551	3,653	4,822	5,824	5,880	5,520	3,958	6,317	5,444	6,525	9,210
Turkish	184	136	165	449	1,482	2,145	2,033	1,902	2,337	820	1,253	918	1,336	2,015
Welsh	762	674	760	1,278	1,820	2,531	2,367	2,754	2,504	1,699	2,244	2,248	2,239	2,820
West Indian (except Cuban)	78	82	137	1,497	1,942	1,548	1,476	1,381	1,110	1,024	1,150	2,141	2,132	1,171
Other peoples	73	35	147	89	668	351	1,027	2,058	1,530	1,537	3,330	3,323	3,660	3,038
Total	448,572	487,918	648,743	857,046	812,870	1,026,499	1,100,735	1,285,349	782,870	751,786	1,041,570	878,587	838,172	1,197,892

TABLE XVI.—TOTAL IMMIGRATION EACH YEAR, 1820–1913.

Period.	Number.	Period.	Number.
Year ended Sept. 30—		Year ended June 30—	
1820	8,385	1866	332,577
1821	9,127	1867	303,104
1822	6,911	1868	282,189
1823	6,354	1869	352,768
1824	7,912	1870	387,203
1825	10,199	1871	321,350
1826	10,837	1872	404,806
1827	18,875	1873	459,803
1828	27,382	1874	313,339
1829	22,520	1875	227,498
1830	23,322	1876	169,986
1831	22,633	1877	141,857
Oct. 1, 1831, to Dec. 31, 1832	60,482	1878	138,469
Year ended Dec. 31—		1879	177,826
1833	58,640	1880	457,257
1834	65,365	1881	669,431
1835	45,374	1882	788,992
1836	76,242	1883	603,322
1837	79,340	1884	518,592
1838	38,914	1885	395,346
1839	68,069	1886	334,203
1840	84,066	1887	490,109
1841	80,289	1888	546,889
1842	104,565	1889	444,427
Jan. 1 to Sept. 30, 1843	52,496	1890	455,302
Year ended Sept. 30—		1891	560,319
1844	78,615	1892	579,663
1845	114,371	1893	439,730
1846	154,416	1894	285,631
1847	234,968	1895	258,536
1848	226,527	1896	343,267
1849	297,024	1897	230,832
1850	310,004	1898	229,299
Oct. 1 to Dec. 31, 1850	59,976	1899	311,715
Year ended Dec. 31—		1900	448,572
1851	379,466	1901	487,918
1852	371,603	1902	648,743
1853	368,645	1903	857,046
1854	427,833	1904	812,870
1855	200,877	1905	1,026,499
1856	195,857	1906	1,100,735
Jan. 1 to June 30, 1857	112,123	1907	1,285,349
Year ended June 30—		1908	782,870
1858	191,942	1909	751,786
1859	129,571	1910	1,041,570
1860	133,143	1911	878,587
1861	142,877	1912	838,172
1862	72,183	1913	1,197,892
1863	132,925		
1864	191,114	Grand total	30,808,944
1865	180,339		

TABLE XVII.—ALIENS DEBARRED FROM ENTERING THE UNITED STATES,

Race or people.	Idiots.	Imbeciles.	Feeble-minded.	Epileptics.	Insane, have been insane within five years, or have had two attacks of insanity.	Tuberculosis (noncontagious).	Loathsome or dangerous contagious diseases.				Professional beggars.	Paupers.	Likely to become a public charge.
							Tuberculosis (contagious).	Trachoma.	Favus.	Others.			
African (black)			2		2		2	10		14			162
Armenian		1	2		1			50		5			85
Bohemian and Moravian	1	1			5			8		2			37
Bulgarian, Servian, Montenegrin			3		1		2	40		5			121
Chinese							1	50		6			12
Croatian and Slovenian		3	9	1	3		2	88	2	5		1	144
Cuban					1		1			1			6
Dalmatian, Bosnian, Herzegovinian			4		1			1					21
Dutch and Flemish			3				1	5	3	3			63
East Indian					3			18		20			159
English	4	1	19	3	25	1	10	12		10			752
Finnish			2		2			9		1			72
French	2	3	5	2	3		10	8		2	2	1	334
German		3	11		16		5	106	2	12	1		403
Greek			14				7	45	2	17			343
Hebrew		5	39		9		5	132	19	38	1		447
Irish		1	16	5	28	1	10	9		5	1	2	358
Italian (North)	2	4	12	1	3		3	41	1	8			131
Italian (South)	4	18	181	3	24		13	283	14	54		1	1,139
Japanese					1			171		15			33
Korean								1					
Lithuanian			10		2			73	2	3			68
Magyar		1	3				1	19		4			105
Mexican	4	1	6	3	5		2	149		58	5		743
Pacific Islander													
Polish		8	61	1	8		4	349	4	19			503
Portuguese			2		2			6		1			82
Roumanian		1	1				1	16	2	2			101
Russian			11		4		1	63	4	6			276
Ruthenian (Russniak)		1	39		2		1	22		2			161
Scandinavian			6	2	9		6	10	1	12			153
Scotch	1	1	2	1	6			9		4			241
Slovak			7	1	3			28		1			47
Spanish			5		2		1	29	1	2			93
Spanish-American					2					1			14
Syrian		1	5		1			156		6			337
Turkish			1		1			14	1	1			50
Welsh					1		1	1		1			19
West Indian (except Cuban)					2		1			2			5
Other peoples			2				2	16	3	1			61
Total	18	54	483	23	175	2	105	2,047	61	349	10	5	7,941
Debarred from Philippine Islands					1			72		16			33

FISCAL YEAR ENDED JUNE 30, 1913, BY RACES OR PEOPLES AND CAUSES.

Surgeon's certificate of defect mentally or physically which may affect alien's ability to earn a living.[1]	Contract laborers.	Accompanying aliens (under section 11).	Under 16 years of age unaccompanied by parent.	Assisted aliens.	Criminals.	Polygamists.	Anarchists.	Prostitutes and females coming for immoral purpose.	Aliens who are supported by or receive proceeds of prostitution.	Aliens who procure or attempt to bring in prostitutes or females for any immoral purpose.	Under passport provision, section[1].	Under provisions Chinese-exclusion act.	Total debarred.	Debarred from Philippine Islands.
10	5	6	10	3	8			2	1	5			242	
48	135	5	9	4	2			1		3			348	
16		1	2		4			3		3			83	
68	44	1	8	1	4	1		2		1			302	
												333	402	73
176	13	4	9		26			4		4			494	
3		1	2					2					17	
14		2	4		3			1					51	
12	38	2	2	6	8			8		8			162	
8	23		1		1	3							236	58
51	56	24	46	22	58	1		55		39			1,189	2
7	13		2		7			1		1			117	
37	32	5	29	8	34			35		11			563	
114	20	17	20	13	66			31		28			868	
732	32	12	25	3	16	1		1		1			1,251	
401	6	33	23	9	32			18		7			1,224	
38	27	8	8	10	25			10		13			575	
140	95	5	15	3	23			4		1			492	
1,186	302	62	65	13	246		1	27		21			3,657	
			1								47		268	58
											1		2	
34	13	2	5	2	1		1			2			216	
96		2	3	1	24			6		2			269	
3	71	87	56	1				90	1	64			1,349	
428	124	22	24	7	89			16		14			1,741	
12	34	2	16	1	5								163	
117	8	3	3	1	16			3		2			277	
91	176	2	9	1	36		1	4		6			691	
128	12	7	14	2	30			4		2			427	
17	8	5	4	2	8			9		7			259	
23	36	4	14	8	15			18	1	7			400	
67	2	4	3		13			2					178	
22	268	4	10	1				2		3			441	1
3			2		1			2					25	
51	8	21	36	4	3	21							650	1
8	4	1	5	1		9			1				97	
7	4	2	2		2					1			41	1
1			1		1			1					14	
39	15	1	4	2		3		5		2			157	
4,208	1,624	357	492	129	808	40	2	367	4	253	48	333	19,938	1
				1				3		4		64		

[1] Include hereunder only cases not comprehended in causes 1 to 13.

TABLE XVII A.—ALIENS DEBARRED AND ALIENS DEPORTED AFTER ENTERING, 1892–1913, BY CAUSES.

Year ended June 30—	Immigration.	Idiots.	Imbeciles.	Feeble-minded.	Epileptics.	Insane persons.	Tuberculosis (noncontagious).	Loathsome or dangerous contagious diseases.	Professional beggars.	Paupers, or likely to become public charges.	Surgeon's certificate of defect, mentally or physically which may affect alien's ability to earn a living.	Contract laborers.
1892	579,663	4				17		80		1,002		932
1893	439,730	3				8		81		431		518
1894	285,631	4				5		15		802		553
1895	258,536	6								1,714		694
1896	343,267	1				10		2		2,010		776
1897	230,832	1				6		1		1,277		328
1898	229,299	1				12		258		2,261		417
1899	311,715	1				19		348		2,599		741
1900	448,572	1				32		393		2,974		833
1901	487,918	6				16		309		2,798		327
1902	648,743	7				27		709		3,944		275
1903	857,046	1				23		1,773		5,812		1,086
1904	812,870	16				33		1,560		4,798		1,501
1905	1,026,499	38				92		2,198		7,898		1,164
1906	1,100,735	92				139		2,273		7,069		2,314
1907	1,285,349	29				180		3,822		6,866		1,434
1908	782,870	20	45	121	25	159	6	2,900	31	3,710	870	1,932
1909	751,786	18	42	121	26	141	8	2,382	56	4,402	370	1,172
1910	1,041,570	16	40	125	29	169	5	3,123	9	15,918	312	1,786
1911	878,587	12	26	126	33	111	15	2,831	9	12,039	3,055	1,336
1912	838,172	10	44	110	28	105	15	1,733	22	8,160	2,288	1,333
1913	1,197,892	18	54	483	23	175	2	2,562	10	7,946	4,208	1,624

Debarred from entering—Continued.

Year ended June 30—	Accompanying aliens (under sec. 11).	Under 16 years of age unaccompanied by parent.	Assisted aliens.	Criminals.	Polygamists.	Anarchists.	Prostitutes and females coming for any immoral purpose.	Aliens who procure or attempt to bring in prostitutes and females for any immoral purpose.	Supported by proceeds of prostitution.	Under passport provision, sec. 1.	Under provisions of Chinese-exclusion act.	Total debarred.	Deported after entry.
1892			23	26			80					2,164	637
1893				12								1,053	577
1894			1	8			2					1,389	417
1895				4								2,419	177
1896			3	1								2,799	238
1897												1,617	263
1898			79	2								3,030	199
1899			82	8								3,798	263
1900			2	4			7					4,246	356
1901			50	7			3					3,516	363
1902				9			3					4,974	465
1903			9	51	1		13					8,769	547
1904			38	35		1	9	3				7,994	779
1905			19	44	3	1	24	4				11,879	845
1906	180			205	5	1	30	2			122	12,432	676
1907	134			341	10		18	1		60	160	13,064	995
1908	168	88	54	136	6	2	124	43		272	190	10,902	2,069
1909	206	138	34	273	24		323	181		81	413	10,411	2,124
1910	315	206	34	580	134	5	316	179	1	59	819	24,270	2,095
1911	359	549	116	644	57		253	141	5	27	605	22,349	2,788
1912	226	395	94	592	38	2	263	192	7	50	350	16,057	2,456
1913	357	492	129	808	40	2	367	253	4	48	333	19,938	3,461

TABLE XVII B.—PERMANENT RESIDENTS OF FOREIGN CONTIGUOUS TERRITORY APPLYING FOR TEMPORARY SOJOURN IN THE UNITED STATES REFUSED ADMISSION, FISCAL YEAR ENDED JUNE 30, 1913, BY CAUSES.

Cause.	Canadian border.	Mexican border.	Boston, Mass.	Total.
Idiots..	1	3	....	4
Imbeciles..	5	3	....	8
Feeble-minded.......................................	5	3	....	8
Epileptics...	2	2	....	4
Insane persons.......................................	9	....	....	9
Tuberculosis (noncontagious).........................	1	....	....	1
Loathsome or dangerous contagious diseases...........	91	184	....	275
Professional beggars.................................	....	4	....	4
Paupers, or likely to become public charge...........	247	872	5	1,124
Surgeons' certificates...............................	10	1	....	11
Contract laborers....................................	1	160	1	162
Accompanying aliens (under sec. 11)..................	12	106	....	118
Under 16 years of age and unaccompanied by parent...	15	103	....	118
Assisted aliens......................................	8	....	....	8
Criminals...	29	3	1	33
Anarchists..	1	....	....	1
Prostitutes and females coming for any immoral purpose......	35	92	....	127
Aliens who are supported by or receive proceeds of prostitution.	26	6	....	32
Aliens who procure or attempt to bring in prostitutes and females for any immoral purpose............................	1	65	....	66
Under passport provision, sec. 1.....................	....	5	....	5
Total...	499	1,612	7	2,118

TABLE XVIII.—ALIENS DEPORTED TO COUNTRIES WHENCE THEY CAME AFTER ENTERING THE UNITED STATES, FISCAL YEAR ENDED JUNE 30, 1913, BY RACES OR PEOPLES AND CAUSES.

Race or people.	Imbeciles.	Feeble-minded.	Epileptics.	Insane, have been insane within 5 years or have had 2 attacks of insanity.	Tuberculosis (contagious).	Trachoma.	Favus.	Others.	Professional beggars.	Paupers.	Likely to become a public charge.	Contract laborers.	Under 16 years of age at time of entry, unaccompanied by parent.	Criminals.	Polygamists.	Anarchists.	Prostitutes and females coming for any immoral purpose.	Aliens who procure or attempt to bring in prostitutes or females for any immoral purpose.	Under passport provision, section 1.	Other causes.	Total members of excluded classes at time of entry.
African (black)				2	1			1			14		1				2				20
Armenian											5	3								1	9
Bohemian and Moravian			1	2							14		1	1			5	4			27
Bulgarian, Servian, Montenegrin		2									9	14		2			3				29
Chinese						1					28	3		2			3	1			32
Croatian and Slovenian				2	2			1			20	3	3				6				40
Cuban											4						2				8
Dalmatian, Bosnian, Herzegovinian	1	1	4	2				4			4			1		1	4	4			4
Dutch and Flemish	1	2	1	10							15	2	1	22			19	1			28
East Indian				4				3			21	1	5	5							23
English	1	1	3	3	2			1	1		134		2	14		1	16	12			216
Finnish			1	12				3			6		8	3			24				13
French		1		3	2	1					54		2	8			4	9			88
German				18				4	1		138	10		4			5	22			225
Greek				11	1						33			4			1	3			62
Hebrew				3	1	1		3			100			25				7			150
Irish			1	14	1			4			53		4				12				73
Italian (North)	1	3		1				1			31			1			2	1			42
Italian (South)		1			5						159	13		13			1	7			234
Japanese				2							8	6	5	2				1			12
Lithuanian				4							9										11
Magyar	1			5	1			14			30					1	31	20			43
Mexican	1				2	1					64						15	10			170
Polish					2						93			2							133

	Total
Portuguese	10
Roumanian	25
Russian	30
Ruthenian (Russniak)	39
Scandinavian	68
Scotch	36
Slovak	25
Spanish	25
Spanish-American	1
Syrian	57
Turkish	1
Welsh	2
West Indian (except Cuban)	3
Other peoples	5
Total	2,019
Deported from Philippine Islands	2

TABLE XVIII.—ALIENS DEPORTED TO COUNTRIES WHENCE THEY CAME AFTER ENTERING THE UNITED STATES, FISCAL YEAR ENDED JUNE 30, 1913, BY RACES OR PEOPLES AND CAUSES—Continued.

| Race or people | Deportation compulsory within 3 years—Continued. Public charges from following causes existing prior to entry— | | | | | | | | Prostitutes after entry. | Aliens who are supported by or receive the proceeds of prostitution. | Entered without inspection. | Total mandatory within 3 years. | Deportation compulsory without time limit. | | | | Public charges within 1 year after entry, from subsequent causes. | | | | | | Grand total returned. | Under act 1741, Philippine Commission, violation of Philippine opium law. | Deported from Philippine Islands. |
	Insanity.	Other mental conditions.	Loathsome or dangerous contagious diseases. Tuberculosis (contagious).	Others.	Pregnancy.	Physical conditions.	Other causes.	Total public charges from prior causes.					Prostitutes and females coming for any immoral purpose.	Aliens who procure or attempt to bring in prostitutes or females for any immoral purpose.	Aliens who are supported by or receive the proceeds of prostitution.	Total without time limit.	Insanity.	Loathsome or dangerous contagious diseases.	Dependent members of family.	Physical conditions.	Other causes.	Total public charges from subsequent causes.			
African (black)	8		2	2		2	1	13	2			33											33		
Armenian	2	1	1	1			1	5	6			14	1			1							14		
Bohemian and Moravian	3	1	3			1		6	4	1		33	1			2							33		
Bulgarian, Servian, Montenegrin	3					1		3	1			35	1			1							35		
Chinese	1			4		1		1	1		366	407				2							409	67	182
Croatian and Slovenian	10							16	1		1	62											63		
Cuban			2						1			9				1							9		
Dalmatian, Bosnian, Herzegovinian	4		2					6	1			10											10		
Dutch and Flemish	3		2	2		2		4				34	1			1	1					2	34		
East Indian										7		32											32		
English	26	3	10			4	1	36	11	2	9	282	3		6	6			1		1	2	285		
Finnish	16		7			5		20	12	8	12	33	6		2								33		
French	16	1	8	7		5		18	22	6	5	140	1	1	6	14				1	1	1	150		
German	71	3	7	8	2	5	1	89	8	2	7	335	5		3	1					1	3	345		
Greek	16		2	7	1	1		29	3		5	101			1	9							116		
Hebrew	67	3	22	2		8		82	9	6	7	247	3		6	15			1		1	3	253		
Irish	39	2	1	8		1		51	5			132	1		1	11						1	132		
Italian (North)	19		1	7		8		24	1		1	71											73		
Italian (South)	49	5	22	2		8		85	6		3	334	5		2	9					3	3	346		
Japanese	3		1			2	2	4				53			6	8							61		
Lithuanian	7	1	1			2		10	1		1	21									1	1	22		
Magyar	9		1	1				13	6	8	34	70				11							81		2

Mexican	1					1			10	2			5	10	2			203
Polish	40	1	7			10	2		3	60	10	2		3				201
Portuguese	5					1				6	1				1			16
Roumanian	1		2	1		1	1		1	2	1	1				1		28
Russian	11		3	1		1	1		1	14	1	1			1			46
Ruthenian (Russniak)	10	1	5	1		2	4	1		16	2	1						55
Scandinavian	44		2	1		2	2			53	2	3	1					126
Scotch	7		1			1	2			11	1	5			1			51
Slovak	13					3	1			17	1	2		1	1			45
Spanish	4									6	1	1						33
Spanish-American																		1
Syrian	5		2			1	1			7								70
Turkish			2	1						3		2						4
Welsh			1	1						1					1			3
West Indian (except Cuban)	1						1			1								4
Other peoples																		6
Total	514	19	99	12	5	63	2	714	116	61	464	3,374	36	4	39	79		3,461
Deported from Philippine Islands										96	19	115						67

TABLE XIX.—APPEALS FROM DECISIONS UNDER IMMIGRATION LAWS, AND APPLICATIONS FOR ADMISSION UNDER BOND, FISCAL YEAR ENDED JUNE 30, 1913, BY CAUSES.

Action taken.	Total.	Under passport provision, sec. 1.	Aliens who procure or attempt to bring in prostitutes or females for any immoral purpose.	Proceeds of prostitution.	Prostitutes and females coming for any immoral purposes.	Anarchists.	Polygamists.	Criminals.	Assisted aliens.	Under 16 years of age unaccompanied by parent.	Accompanying aliens (under sec. 11).	Contract laborers.	Paupers, or likely to become public charges, and professional beggars.	Loathsome or dangerous contagious diseases.	Mentally defective.
APPEALS FROM EXCLUDING DECISIONS.															
Number of appeals	6,947	9	43	2	120	2	13	221	14	435	334	988	4,641	80	45
Disposition on appeal:															
Admitted without bond	2,130		6		19		5	64	5	97	224	332	1,308	50	20
Admitted on bond	678				2	1	1	1	3	159	20	1	485		5
Debarred	4,139	9	37	2	99	1	7	156	6	179	90	655	2,848	30	20
APPEALS FROM ADMITTING DECISIONS.															
Number of appeals	55	1			2			4		1	1	11	33	2	
Disposition on appeal:															
Admitted without bond	34	1			1			2		1	1	6	21	1	
Admitted on bond	2												2		
Debarred	19				1			2				5	10	1	
APPLICATIONS FOR ADMISSION ON BOND WITHOUT APPEAL.															
Admitted	68														
Refused	33														

TABLE XIX A.—APPEALS FROM DECISIONS UNDER IMMIGRATION LAWS, AND APPLICATIONS FOR ADMISSION UNDER BOND, FISCAL YEAR ENDED JUNE 30, 1913, BY PORTS.

Action taken.	New York, N.Y.	Boston, Mass.	Philadelphia, Pa.	Baltimore, Md.	Montreal, Canada.	San Francisco, Cal.	Galveston, Tex.	Mexican border.	Honolulu, Hawaii.	San Juan, P. R.	New Orleans, La.	Seattle, Wash.	Jacksonville, Fla.	New Bedford, Mass.	Providence, R. I.	Total.
APPEALS FROM EXCLUDING DECISIONS.																
Number of appeals	4,309	352	450	194	1,064	51	117	300	45	18	16	4	22	1	4	6,947
Disposition on appeal:																
Admitted without bond	1,413	139	178	86	192	17	12	63	22	3	2	1	2			2,130
Admitted on bond	381	43	110	41	80	6	6	1		7		3				678
Debarred	2,515	170	162	67	792	28	99	236	23	8	14		20	1	4	4,139
APPEALS FROM ADMITTING DECISIONS.																
Number of appeals	9		3	3	17		10	10	4		2					55
Disposition on appeal:																
Admitted without bond	7		3		9		8	2	3		2					34
Admitted on bond					1		1									2
Debarred	2				7		1	8	1							19
APPLICATIONS FOR ADMISSION ON BOND WITHOUT APPEAL.																
Admitted	21	9	5	3	12	1	12			1						68
Refused	1	6	3		9	1	12	1							4	33

TABLE XX.—DESERTING ALIEN SEAMEN, FISCAL YEAR ENDED JUNE 30, 1913, BY PORTS.

New York, N. Y.	2,272	Portland, Oreg.	336
Boston, Mass.	614	Seattle, Wash.	249
Philadelphia, Pa.	1,471	Gulfport, Miss.	412
Baltimore, Md.	328	Charleston, S. C.	92
Portland, Me.	40	Pascagoula, Miss.	29
New Bedford, Mass		Newport News, Va.	177
Providence, R. I.		Los Angeles, Cal.	15
Norfolk, Va.	130	Port Arthur, Tex.	110
Savannah, Ga.	138	Brunswick, Ga.	17
Key West, Fla.	4	Wilmington, N. C.	
Tampa, Fla.	104	Jacksonville, Fla.	47
Pensacola, Fla.	237	Fernandina, Fla.	25
Mobile, Ala.	348	Honolulu, Hawaii.	28
New Orleans, La.	673	San Juan, Porto Rico.	16
Galveston, Tex.	318	Boca Grande.	2
San Diego, Cal.	25		
San Francisco, Cal.	879	Total.	9,136

TABLE XXI.—ALIEN STOWAWAYS FOUND ON BOARD VESSELS ARRIVING AT PORTS OF THE UNITED STATES, FISCAL YEAR ENDED JUNE 30, 1913, BY PORTS.

New York, N. Y.	367	Galveston, Tex.	6
Boston, Mass.	21	San Diego, Cal.	10
Baltimore, Md.	37	San Francisco, Cal.	56
Philadelphia, Pa.	41	Seattle, Wash.	40
Portland, Me.	5	Gulfport, Miss.	9
New Bedford, Mass.		Charleston, S. C.	2
Norfolk, Va.	7	Newport News, Va.	8
Savannah, Ga.	5	Los Angeles, Cal.	
Miami, Fla.		Port Arthur, Tex.	1
Key West, Fla.	1	Jacksonville, Fla.	
Tampa, Fla.	4	Fernandina, Fla.	
Pensacola, Fla.		Honolulu, Hawaii.	2
Mobile, Ala.	19		
New Orleans, La.	19	Total.	660

TABLE XXII.—AGREEMENT BETWEEN ALIEN ARRIVALS AND HEAD-TAX SETTLE-
MENTS, FISCAL YEAR ENDED JUNE 30, 1913.

```
Immigrant aliens admitted....................................  1, 197, 892
Nonimmigrant aliens admitted.............................      229, 335
Aliens debarred..........................................       19, 938
Aliens from Porto Rico, Hawaii, and Guam.................          381
Died.....................................................          340
Erroneous head-tax collections...........................        2, 421
Head-tax payments pending from previous year.............       86, 351
                                                                         1,536,658
Exempt from head-tax payment, as follows:
  In transit.............................................       91, 877
  One-year residents of Cuba.............................        7, 599
  One-year residents of British North America............       55, 644
  One-year residents of Mexico...........................       13, 936
  Domiciled citizens of British North America, Mexico, and
    Cuba (Rule 1, sub. 3c)...............................       16, 821
  Government officials...................................        1, 419
  Arrivals in Hawaii.....................................        7, 675
  Arrivals in Porto Rico.................................        2, 129
  Exemptions on account of aliens debarred...............       17, 225

    Total exempt ........................................      214, 325
Head-tax payments pending at close of year...............      138, 585
                                                                          352,910

Aliens on whom head tax was paid.........................              1,183,748

Amount of head tax collected during year.................              $4,734,992
```

TABLE XXIII.—PASSENGERS DEPARTED FROM THE

[In the absence of law requiring masters of vessels departing from the United States for foreign countries to deliver to collectors of customs returns of all passengers embarking on such vessels, reliance is had upon the courtesy of the agents of steamship and packet lines for information on the outward passenger movement. It is probable, however, that the departures given embrace the entire passenger movement from the United States to foreign countries.]

Line of vessels.	Ports of departure and destination.	Aliens.						
		Number.	Sex.		Age.		Class.	
			Male.	Female.	Under 14 years.	14 years and over.	Cabin.	Steerage.
	From Baltimore, Md., to—							
North German Lloyd...	Bremen	1,883	1,310	573	94	1,789	270	1,613
United Fruit Co.......	British West Indies..	1	1	......	......	1	1	......
	Total Baltimore....	1,884	1,311	573	94	1,790	271	1,613
	From Boston, Mass., to—							
Allan...	Glasgow	1,264	637	627	120	1,144	463	801
Cunard...	Boulogne	7	1	6	......	7	7	......
	Fishguard	55	32	23	2	53	47	8
	Liverpool	5,515	3,122	2,393	289	5,226	1,669	3,846
	Queenstown	1,685	466	1,219	11	1,674	235	1,450
Hamburg-American....	Hamburg	112	62	50	1	111	53	59
	Plymouth	10	3	7	3	7	10	......
Leyland...	Gibraltar	2	2	......	......	2	2	......
	Liverpool	446	210	236	33	413	443	3
	Madeira	17	15	2	2	15	......	17
Lloyd Sabaudo...	Naples	725	649	76	26	699	53	672
United Fruit Co...	British West Indies..	28	12	16	1	27	......	28
	Costa Rica	32	18	14	1	31	32	......
	Panama	1	1	......	......	1	1	......
White Star...	Genoa	389	259	130	26	363	172	217
	Gibraltar	26	24	2	1	25	14	12
	Liverpool	1,988	1,235	753	116	1,872	681	1,307
	Naples	7,524	6,329	1,195	223	7,301	440	7,084
	Queenstown	651	250	401	7	644	100	551
	Algiers	1	1	......	......	1	1	......
	Azores	1,608	1,020	588	98	1,510	111	1,497
	Madeira	133	113	20	3	130	41	92
	Total Boston	22,219	14,461	7,758	963	21,256	4,574	17,645
Sailing vessel...	**From Brunswick, Ga., to—** British West Indies...	1	......	1	......	1	1	......
Allan...	**From Canada (Atlantic seaports) to—** Glasgow	638	503	135	40	598	153	485
	Havre	324	303	21	2	322	22	302
	Liverpool	1,687	1,341	346	78	1,609	194	1,493
	London	105	75	30	5	100	48	57
Canadian Northern.....	Bristol	713	593	120	45	668	77	636
Canadian Pacific......	Antwerp	16	16	......	......	16	......	16
	Bristol	93	76	17	12	81	6	87
	Liverpool	1,765	1,385	380	80	1,685	333	1,432
	London	31	31	......	......	31	......	31
	Naples	2	......	2	1	......	2	......
	Trieste	7	7	......	......	7	7	......
Cunard...	London	79	45	34	3	76	33	46
	Southampton	146	83	63	9	137	73	73
Donaldson...	Glasgow	877	711	166	41	836	164	713
Compagnie Generale Transatlantique.	Havre	3	1	2	......	3	3	......
White Star Dominion...	Liverpool	1,381	1,007	374	117	1,264	309	1,072
	Total Atlantic seaports of Canada.	7,867	6,177	1,690	433	7,434	1,417	6,450
By land...	**Via Canadian border stations to—** Canada	129,862	97,250	32,612	13,692	116,170	129,862	......

UNITED STATES, FISCAL YEAR ENDED JUNE 30, 1913.

[In the absence of law requiring masters of vessels departing from the United States for foreign countries to deliver to colletors of customs returns of all passengers embarking on such vessels, reliance is had upon the courtesy of the agents of steamship and packet lines for information on the outward passenger movement. It is probable, however, that the departures given embrace the entire passenger movement from the United States to foreign countries.]

	Citizens.						Total.					
	Sex.		Age.		Class.			Sex.		Age.		Class.
Number.	Male.	Female.	Under 14 years.	14 years and over.	Cabin.	Steerage.	Number.	Male.	Female.	Under 14 years.	14 years and over.	Cabin.	Steerage.
1,855	867	988	425	1,430	1,303	552	3,738	2,177	1,561	519	3,219	1,573	2,165
							1	1			1	1	
1,855	867	988	425	1,430	1,303	552	3,739	2,178	1,561	519	3,220	1,574	2,165
595	275	320	160	435	380	215	1,859	912	947	280	1,579	843	1,016
55	21	34	5	50	55		62	22	40	5	57	62	
106	63	43	7	99	90	16	161	95	66	9	152	137	24
4,292	2,568	1,724	837	3,455	2,693	1,599	9,807	5,690	4,117	1,126	8,681	4,362	5,445
873	542	331	175	698	291	582	2,558	1,008	1,550	186	2,372	526	2,032
382	197	185	65	317	208	174	494	259	235	66	428	261	233
38	20	18	1	37	38		48	23	25	4	44	48	
5	2	3		5	5		7	4	3		7	7	
1,106	411	695	70	1,036	1,106		1,552	621	931	103	1,449	1,549	3
4		4		4		4	21	19	2	2	19		21
135	71	64	67	68	108	27	860	720	140	93	767	161	699
75	45	30	8	67	74	1	103	57	46	9	94	74	29
36	27	9	1	35	36		68	45	23	2	66	68	
71	61	10		71	71		72	62	10		72	72	
506	200	306	77	429	433	73	895	459	436	103	792	605	290
60	23	37	3	57	57	3	86	47	39	4	82	71	15
1,433	714	719	333	1,100	1,075	358	3,421	1,949	1,472	449	2,972	1,756	1,665
3,111	1,435	1,676	745	2,366	1,615	1,496	10,635	7,764	2,871	968	9,667	2,055	8,580
413	217	196	121	292	135	278	1,064	467	597	128	936	235	829
3		3		3	3		4	3		4	4	3	1
515	311	204	329	186	74	441	2,123	1,331	792	427	1,096	185	1,938
25	16	9	14	11	4	21	158	129	29	17	141	45	113
13,839	7,223	6,616	3,019	10,821	8,551	5,288	36,058	21,684	14,374	3,981	32,077	13,125	22,933
3	3			3	3		4	3	1		4	4	
638	262	376	82	556	557	81	1,276	765	511	122	1,154	710	566
63	30	33	8	55	42	21	387	333	54	10	377	64	323
912	623	289	146	766	641	271	2,599	1,964	635	224	2,375	835	1,764
181	68	113	20	161	157	24	286	143	143	25	261	205	81
96	44	52	31	65	69	27	809	637	172	76	733	146	663
							16	16			16		16
11	8	3	6	5	2	9	104	84	20	18	86	8	96
375	183	192	133	242	257	118	2,140	1,568	572	213	1,927	590	1,550
2	2			2		2	33	33			33		33
							2		2	1	1	2	
							7	7			7		7
50	20	30	10	40	39	11	129	65	64	13	116	72	57
190	89	101	34	156	131	59	336	172	164	43	293	204	132
374	121	253	66	308	348	26	1,251	832	419	107	1,144	512	739
							3	1	2		3		3
1,046	456	590	109	937	760	286	2,427	1,463	964	226	2,201	1,069	1,358
3,938	1,906	2,032	645	3,293	3,003	935	11,805	8,083	3,722	1,078	10,727	4,420	7,385
90,129	63,836	26,293	16,763	73,366	90,129		219,991	161,086	58,905	30,455	189,536	219,991	

TABLE XXIII.—PASSENGERS DEPARTED FROM THE UNITED

Line of vessels.	Ports of departure and destination.	Aliens.						
		Number.	Sex.		Age.		Class.	
			Male.	Female.	Under 14 years.	14 years and over.	Cabin.	Steerage.
Canadian Australian Royal Mail.	From Canada (Pacific seaports) to—							
	Australia	402	265	137	27	375	323	79
	New Zealand	90	64	26	2	88	74	16
	Pacific Islands	14	11	3	.....	14	13	1
Canadian Pacific......	Hongkong	864	839	25	9	855	84	780
	Kobe	1	1	.....	.....	1	1	.....
	Nagasaki	1	.....	1	.....	1	1	.....
	Shanghai	24	17	7	2	22	24	.....
	Yokohama	18	15	3	.....	18	15	3
	Australia	160	109	51	11	149	138	22
	Total Canadian Pacific.	1,574	1,321	253	51	1,523	673	901
Booth..................	From Galveston, Tex., to—							
	Liverpool	32	20	12	4	28	32	.....
Hogan..................	....do	9	6	3	2	7	9	.....
North German Lloyd...	Bremen	840	675	165	30	810	114	726
	Spain	7	6	1	.....	7	.....	7
	Cuba							
Norway Mexico Gulf....	Christiania	16	12	4	.....	16	10	6
United Fruit Co........	Costa Rica							
	Guatemala							
	Panama	1	1	.....	.....	1	1	.....
United Steamship Co...	Cuba	2	2	.....	.....	2	2	.....
	Total Galveston.....	907	722	185	36	871	168	739
Canadian Australian Royal Mail.	From Honolulu, Hawaii, to—							
	Australia	109	61	48	13	96	87	22
	New Zealand	26	12	14	2	24	21	5
	Pacific Islands	10	8	2	.....	10	7	3
	British North America	170	91	79	10	160	149	21
Oceanic.................	Australia	41	30	11	1	40	33	8
	Pacific Islands	2	2	.....	.....	2	2	.....
Pacific Mail............	Hongkong	480	457	23	.....	480	24	456
	Kobe	432	329	103	9	423	12	420
	Shanghai	2	2	.....	.....	2	2	.....
	Yokohama	525	367	158	35	490	64	461
Toyo Kisen Kaisha.....	Hongkong	147	133	14	.....	147	32	115
	Kobe	795	568	227	3	792	3	792
	Nagasaki	1	1	.....	.....	1	.....	1
	Shanghai	9	6	3	.....	9	3	6
Sailing vessels.........	Yokohama	1,280	872	408	22	1,258	100	1,180
	British West Indies...	3	2	1	1	2	3	.....
	Total Honolulu.....	4,032	2,941	1,091	96	3,936	542	3,490
Not stated..............	From Jacksonville, Fla—							
	Not stated............	3	.....	3	.....	3	3	.....
Peninsular & Occidental.	From Key West to—							
	British West Indies...	78	47	31	3	75	57	21
	Cuba..................	7,180	5,105	2,075	863	6,317	2,618	4,562
	Panama...............	3	1	2	2	1	3	.....
Sailing vessels.........	British West Indies...	109	85	24	2	107	38	71
	Total Key West....	7,370	5,238	2,132	870	6,500	2,716	4,654
Compania Naviera del Pacifico.	Via Mexican border stations to—							
	Mexico................	1,631	1,310	321	115	1,516	947	684
Ensenada Transportation Co.	.....do	72	53	19	11	61	72	.....
Pacific Mail............	....do	7	2	5	.....	7	7	.....
	Panama...............	7	4	3	.....	7	7	.....
Motor Boat Co........	Mexico................	324	230	94	21	303	324	.....
	Total Mexican border.	2,041	1,599	442	147	1,894	1,357	684

STATES, FISCAL YEAR ENDED JUNE 30, 1913—Continued.

	Citizens.							Total.						
		Sex.		Age.		Class.			Sex.		Age.		Class.	
Number.	Male.	Female.	Under 14 years.	14 years and over.	Cabin.	Steerage.	Number.	Male.	Female.	Under 14 years.	14 years and over.	Cabin.	Steerage.
164	101	63	21	143	132	32	566	366	200	48	518	455	111
47	36	11	1	46	41	6	137	100	37	3	134	115	22
20	11	9	1	19	16	4	34	22	12	1	33	29	5
190	153	37	20	170	84	106	1,054	992	62	29	1,025	168	886
10	6	4	5	5	10	......	11	7	4	5	6	11	......
					1		1		1			1	
44	22	22	12	32	44	......	68	39	29	14	54	68	......
15	12	3	......	15	15	......	33	27	6	......	33	30	3
51	26	25	17	34	31	20	211	135	76	28	183	169	42
541	367	174	77	464	373	168	2,115	1,688	427	128	1,987	1,046	1,069
22	9	13	6	16	22	......	54	29	25	10	44	54	......
2	......	2	......	2	2	......	11	6	5	2	9	11	......
749	403	346	129	620	497	252	1,589	1,078	511	159	1,430	611	978
1	......	1	1	......	......	1	8	6	2	1	7	......	8
2	......	2	......	2	2	......	2	......	2	......	2	2	......
19	6	13	10	9	19	......	35	18	17	10	25	29	6
2	2	......	......	2	2	......	2	2	......	......	2	2	......
15	14	1	......	15	15	......	15	14	1	......	15	15	......
1	1	......	......	1	1	......	2	2	......	......	2	2	......
14	11	3	3	11	14	......	16	13	3	3	13	16	......
827	446	381	149	678	574	253	1,734	1,168	566	185	1,549	742	992
50	32	18	3	47	47	3	159	93	66	16	143	134	25
17	11	6	1	16	17	......	43	23	20	3	40	38	5
2	1	1	......	2	2	......	12	9	3	......	12	9	3
252	124	128	42	210	208	44	422	215	207	52	370	357	65
73	51	22	3	70	66	7	114	81	33	4	110	99	15
4	3	1	2	2	4	......	6	5	1	2	4	6	......
197	129	68	59	138	96	101	677	586	91	59	618	120	557
117	65	52	116	1	......	117	549	394	155	125	424	12	537
23	17	6	......	23	15	8	25	19	6	......	25	17	8
336	161	175	162	174	176	160	861	528	333	197	664	240	621
135	72	63	29	106	113	22	282	205	77	29	253	145	137
319	159	160	303	16	6	313	1,114	727	387	306	808	9	1,105
1	......	1	......	1	1	......	2	1	1	......	2	1	1
26	21	5	3	23	7	19	35	27	8	3	32	10	25
555	272	283	441	114	131	424	1,835	1,144	691	463	1,372	231	1,604
3	2	1	1	2	3	......	6	4	2	2	4	6	......
2,110	1,120	990	1,165	945	892	1,218	6,142	4,061	2,081	1,261	4,881	1,434	4,708
......	......	......	......	......	......	......	3	......	3	......	3	3	......
196	89	107	17	179	188	8	274	136	138	20	254	245	29
12,961	7,926	5,035	711	12,250	12,223	738	20,141	13,031	7,110	1,574	18,567	14,841	5,300
1,494	892	602	14	1,480	1,489	5	1,497	893	604	16	1,481	1,492	5
22	16	6	4	18	1	21	131	101	30	6	125	39	92
14,673	8,923	5,750	746	13,927	13,901	772	22,043	14,161	7,882	1,616	20,427	16,617	5,426
697	573	124	51	646	681	16	2,328	1,883	445	166	2,162	1,628	700
17	14	3	2	15	17	......	89	67	22	13	76	89	......
80	58	22	5	75	80	......	87	60	27	5	82	87	......
38	31	7	......	38	38	......	45	35	10	......	45	45	......
374	289	85	15	359	374	......	698	519	179	36	662	698	......
1,206	965	241	73	1,133	1,190	16	3,247	2,564	683	220	3,027	2,547	700

TABLE XXIII.—PASSENGERS DEPARTED FROM THE UNITED

Line of vessels.	Ports of departure and destination.	Aliens.						
			Sex.		Age.		Class.	
		Number.	Male.	Female.	Under 14 years.	14 years and over.	Cabin.	Steerage.
From Miami, Fla., to—								
Peninsular & Occidental.	British West Indies...	65	38	27	5	60	31	34
Saunders..............	....do	949	778	171	47	902	63	886
Sailing vessels.........	....do	1,035	724	311	97	938	387	648
	Total Miami........	2,049	1,540	509	149	1,900	481	1,568
From Mobile, Ala., to—								
Hubbard Zemurray....	Honduras.............	30	20	10	2	28	30	......
Orr Laubenheimer.....	....do	33	17	16	7	26	33	......
	Guatemala...........	3	1	2	......	3	3	......
Seeberg................	British West Indies...	15	9	6	1	14	15	......
United Fruit Co........	Honduras.............	10	4	6	4	6	10	......
	Total Mobile........	91	51	40	14	77	91	......
From New Bedford, Mass., to—								
Fabre...................	Cape Verde Islands...	221	186	35	14	207	......	221
Tramp.................	....do	282	267	15	7	275	......	282
	Total New Bedford.	503	453	50	21	482	......	503
From New Orleans, La., to—								
Bluefields.............	Nicaragua............	128	92	36	7	121	113	15
Compagnie Generale Transatlantique.	Havre................	153	112	41	9	144	35	118
Hamburg-American....	Mexico...............							
	West Indies..........	15	8	7	2	13	15	......
Leyland...............	Bremen..............	1	1	......	......	1	1	......
	Liverpool............	21	10	11	4	17	21	......
	London..............	19	8	11	3	16	19	......
	Rotterdam...........	4	2	2	......	4	4	......
Norway-Mexico Gulf...	Christiania	19	14	5	4	15	10	9
	Copenhagen..........	1	1	......	......	1	......	1
Rio Grande S. S. Co....	Nicaragua............	5	4	......	......	5	5	......
Southern Pacific Co....	Cuba................	569	458	111	30	539	344	225
Texas Transport & Terminal Co.	Havre................	49	35	14	4	45	9	40
United Fruit Co........	British Honduras.....	167	120	47	12	155	167	......
	Costa Rica..........	76	51	25	6	70	76	......
	Guatemala...........	595	409	186	55	540	595	......
	Honduras............	137	97	40	20	117	137	......
	Nicaragua...........	20	19	1	......	20	20	......
	Panama.............	277	227	50	24	253	277	......
Vaccaro...............	Honduras............	192	134	58	21	171	192	......
Vogeman..............	Christiania	2	2	......	......	2	......	2
Not stated............	Not specified.........	3	2	1	1	2	1	2
	Total New Orleans..	2,453	1,806	647	202	2,251	2,041	412
From Newport News, Va., to—								
Norway-Mexico Gulf...	Mexico...............	3	2	1	1	2	3	......
From New York, N. Y., to—								
American..............	Cherbourg...........	7,182	6,672	510	82	7,100	369	6,813
	Plymouth............	302	200	102	22	280	184	118
	Southampton........	5,086	4,219	867	155	4,931	991	4,095
Anchor................	Genoa	9	8	1	......	9	......	9
	Glasgow.............	10,912	7,863	3,049	511	10,401	3,708	7,204
	Londonderry.........	3,156	1,297	1,859	89	3,067	953	2,203
	Messina.............	255	232	23	9	246	......	255
	Naples..............	3,682	3,384	298	91	3,591	22	3,660
	Palermo.............	458	352	106	37	421	1	457
Atlantic Fruit Co......	British West Indies...	8	7	1	......	8	8	......
Atlantic Transport.....	London..............	814	397	417	55	759	814	......
Austro-American.......	Lisbon..............	4	3	1	......	4	......	4
	Naples..............	2,880	2,594	286	72	2,808	158	2,722
	Patras..............	16,767	16,409	358	85	16,682	1,311	15,456

STATES, FISCAL YEAR ENDED JUNE 30, 1913—Continued.

	Citizens.							Total.						
		Sex.		Age.		Class.			Sex.		Age.		Class.	
Number.	Male.	Female.	Under 14 years.	14 years and over.	Cabin.	Steerage.	Number.	Male.	Female.	Under 14 years.	14 years and over.	Cabin.	Steerage.	
177	90	87	8	169	168	9	242	128	114	13	229	199	43	
80	56	24	27	53	5	75	1,029	834	195	74	955	68	961	
33	23	10	19	14	21	12	1,068	747	321	116	952	408	660	
290	169	121	54	236	194	96	2,339	1,709	630	203	2,136	675	1,664	
107	82	25	7	100	107	......	137	102	35	9	128	137	......	
48	30	18	......	48	48	......	81	47	34	7	74	81	......	
4	3	1	......	4	4	......	7	4	3	......	7	7	......	
9	3	6	1	8	9	......	24	12	12	2	22	24	......	
16	12	4	2	14	16	......	26	16	10	6	20	26	......	
184	130	54	10	174	184	......	275	181	94	24	251	275	......	
5	4	1	4	1	......	5	226	190	36	18	208	......	226	
3	1	2	1	2	......	3	285	268	17	8	277	......	285	
8	5	3	5	3	......	8	511	458	53	26	485	......	511	
200	147	53	14	186	196	4	328	239	89	21	307	309	19	
48	22	26	21	27	18	30	201	134	67	30	171	53	148	
1	1	......	......	1	1	......	1	1	......	......	1	1	......	
444	264	180	8	436	444	......	459	272	187	10	449	459	......	
......	......	......	......	......	......	......	1	1	......	......	1	1	......	
22	7	15	2	20	22	......	43	17	26	6	37	43	......	
38	16	22	6	32	38	......	57	24	33	9	48	57	......	
13	5	8	2	11	13	......	17	7	10	2	15	17	......	
2	1	1	1	1	2	......	21	15	6	5	16	12	9	
2	1	1	......	2	2	......	3	2	1	......	3	2	1	
12	8	4	1	11	12	......	17	12	5	......	16	17	......	
1,392	912	480	110	1,282	1,242	150	1,961	1,370	591	140	1,821	1,586	375	
14	10	4	4	10	3	11	63	45	18	8	55	12	51	
224	160	64	20	204	224	......	391	280	111	32	359	391	......	
238	160	78	15	223	238	......	314	211	103	21	293	314	......	
518	380	138	31	487	518	......	1,113	789	324	86	1,027	1,113	......	
369	291	78	19	350	369	......	506	388	118	39	467	506	......	
45	41	4	2	43	45	......	65	60	5	2	63	65	......	
5,055	3,349	1,706	288	4,767	5,055	......	5,332	3,576	1,756	312	5,020	5,332	......	
313	236	77	28	285	313	......	505	370	135	49	456	505	......	
......	......	......	......	......	......	......	2	2	......	......	2	......	2	
5	5	......	......	5	5	......	8	7	1	......	7	6	2	
8,955	6,016	2,939	572	8,383	8,760	195	11,408	7,822	3,586	774	10,634	10,801	607	
1	......	1	......	1	1	......	4	2	2	1	3	4	......	
1,279	762	517	415	864	660	619	8,461	7,434	1,027	497	7,964	1,029	7,432	
294	187	107	37	257	255	39	596	387	209	59	537	439	157	
1,710	1,018	692	393	1,317	1,197	513	6,796	5,237	1,559	548	6,248	2,188	4,608	
......	......	......	......	......	......	......	9	8	1	......	9	......	9	
4,344	2,057	2,287	1,033	3,311	3,257	1,087	15,256	9,920	5,336	1,544	13,712	6,965	8,291	
1,933	979	954	563	1,370	1,026	907	5,089	2,276	2,813	652	4,437	1,979	3,110	
19	11	8	14	5	......	19	274	243	31	23	251	......	274	
391	249	142	276	115	10	381	4,073	3,633	440	367	3,706	32	4,041	
89	56	33	77	12	4	85	547	408	139	114	433	5	542	
2	......	2	......	2	2	......	10	7	3	......	10	2	8	
1,499	617	882	107	1,392	1,499	......	2,313	1,014	1,299	162	2,151	2,313	......	
1	1	......	......	1	1	......	5	3	2	......	5	......	5	
547	251	296	210	337	317	230	3,427	2,845	582	282	3,145	475	2,952	
571	362	209	230	341	374	197	17,338	16,771	567	315	17,023	1,685	15,653	

TABLE XXIII.—PASSENGERS DEPARTED FROM THE UNITED

| Line of vessels. | Ports of departure and destination· | Number. | Aliens. | | | | | |
| | | | Sex. | | Age. | | Class. | |
			Male.	Female.	Under 14 years.	14 years and over.	Cabin.	Steerage.
	From New York, N. Y., to—Continued.							
Austro-American—Con.	Trieste	5,830	4,592	1,238	167	5,663	553	5,277
	Algiers	26	23	3	......	26	3	23
	Azores	17	15	2	......	17	5	12
Booth	Brazil	160	119	41	11	149	109	51
	British West Indies	364	179	185	22	342	95	269
Clyde	....do	22	12	10	......	22	22	......
	Santo Domingo	419	298	121	37	382	419	......
Compagnie Generale Transatlantique.	Havre	31,187	27,550	3,637	466	30,721	5,396	25,791
Cunard	Fishguard	4,586	3,170	1,416	135	4,451	3,892	694
	Fiume	4,935	3,300	1,635	355	4,580	138	4,797
	Genoa	406	279	127	21	385	88	318
	Gibraltar	78	66	12	1	77	32	46
	Liverpool	22,821	17,003	5,818	810	22,011	6,572	16,249
	Madeira	145	122	23	6	139	33	112
	Messina	3	......	3	1	2	3	......
	Naples	10,938	9,785	1,153	229	10,709	774	10,164
	Patras	2,592	2,570	22	4	2,588	162	2,430
	Queenstown	1,675	605	1,070	20	1,655	343	1,332
	Trieste	639	559	80	9	630	69	570
	Alexandria	77	34	43	1	76	65	12
	Algiers	5	4	1	......	5	5	......
	Miscellaneous	85	34	51	4	81	85	......
Fabre	Lisbon	204	185	19	3	201	40	164
	Marseille	5,855	5,735	120	19	5,836	273	5,582
	Naples	9,606	8,434	1,172	303	9,303	797	8,809
	Patras	3,721	3,684	37	9	3,712	310	3,411
	Spain	6	4	2	......	6	6	......
	Villefranche	13	6	7	3	10	13	......
	Algiers	4	3	1	......	4	4	......
	Azores	127	101	26	4	123	35	92
Hamburg-American	Boulogne	26	14	12	3	23	26	......
	Cherbourg	564	317	247	27	537	559	5
	Genoa	250	152	98	10	240	235	15
	Gibraltar	33	20	13	6	27	28	5
	Hamburg	22,422	15,011	7,411	910	21,512	4,507	17,915
	Naples	7,547	6,726	821	217	7,330	266	7,281
	Plymouth	366	238	128	10	356	366	......
	Southampton	129	75	54	7	122	129	......
	Villefranche	8	5	3	......	8	8	......
	Madeira	5	4	1	......	5	5	......
	British West Indies	364	207	157	30	334	352	12
	Colombia	73	55	18	4	69	73	......
	Costa Rica	89	55	34	14	75	89	......
	Cuba	229	152	77	17	212	229	......
	Haiti	227	161	66	14	213	227	......
	Panama	245	191	54	22	223	245	......
	Santo Domingo	10	5	5	3	7	10	......
	Miscellaneous	15	13	2	2	13	3	12
Hellenic	Calamata	6	5	1	......	6	......	6
	Patras	16	15	1	1	15	2	14
	Piræus	786	748	38	10	776	46	740
Holland America	Boulogne	685	368	317	29	656	581	104
	Plymouth	143	82	61	6	137	143	......
	Rotterdam	11,506	8,671	2,835	465	11,041	2,136	9,370
Italia	Genoa	598	426	172	25	573	158	440
	Messina	254	218	36	13	241	22	232
	Naples	4,728	4,353	375	83	4,645	258	4,470
	Palermo	494	429	65	12	482	49	445
Lamport & Holt	Argentina	958	737	221	55	903	354	604
	Brazil	770	573	197	80	690	320	450
	British West Indies	18	10	8	......	18	7	11
	Uruguay	64	51	13	5	59	26	38
La Veloce	Genoa	554	386	168	15	539	160	394
	Messina	199	177	22	7	192	7	192
	Naples	4,225	3,816	409	84	4,141	194	4,031
	Palermo	446	359	87	20	426	36	410
Lloyd Italiano	Genoa	628	446	182	30	598	172	456
	Messina	442	388	54	14	428	6	436
	Naples	5,664	5,157	507	135	5,529	293	5,371
	Palermo	805	633	172	28	777	60	745
	Piraeus	26	26	......	......	26	......	26
Lloyd Sabaudo	Genoa	448	340	108	22	426	75	373

STATES, FISCAL YEAR ENDED JUNE 30, 1913—Continued.

	Citizens.							Total.						
	Sex.		Age.		Class.			Sex.		Age.		Class.		
Number.	Male.	Female.	Under 14 years.	14 years and over.	Cabin.	Steerage.	Number.	Male.	Female.	Under 14 years.	14 years and over.	Cabin.	Steerage.	
1,483	766	717	869	614	695	788	7,313	5,358	1,955	1,036	6,277	1,248	6,065	
3	1	2	......	3	3	......	29	24	5	......	29	6	23	
14	10	4	4	10	10	4	31	25	6	4	27	15	16	
193	163	30	6	187	185	8	353	282	71	17	336	294	59	
137	81	56	65	72	75	62	501	260	241	87	414	170	331	
5	3	2	......	5	5	......	27	15	12	......	27	27	......	
395	311	84	36	359	395	......	814	609	205	73	741	814	......	
11,631	6,807	4,824	2,936	8,695	6,710	4,921	42,818	34,357	8,461	3,402	39,416	12,106	30,712	
5,429	3,255	2,174	388	5,041	5,042	387	10,015	6,425	3,590	523	9,492	8,934	1,081	
990	497	493	818	172	121	869	5,925	3,797	2,128	1,173	4,752	259	5,666	
410	192	218	101	309	298	112	816	471	345	122	694	386	430	
145	51	94	7	138	135	10	223	117	106	8	215	167	56	
10,060	6,283	4,377	2,065	8,595	5,522	5,138	23,481	13,286	10,195	2,875	30,606	12,094	21,387	
46	22	24	11	35	39	7	191	144	47	17	174	72	119	
2	1	1	......	2	2	......	5	1	4	3	2	5	......	
4,303	1,769	2,534	872	3,431	3,390	913	15,241	11,554	3,687	1,101	14,140	4,104	11.077	
35	28	7	11	24	25	10	2,627	2,598	29	15	2,612	187	2,440	
1,470	758	712	336	1,134	543	927	3,145	1,363	1,782	356	2,789	886	2,259	
143	68	75	43	100	103	40	782	627	155	52	730	172	610	
314	138	176	8	306	314	......	391	172	219	9	382	379	12	
33	7	26	2	31	33	......	38	11	27	2	36	38	......	
203	87	116	12	191	203	......	288	121	167	16	272	288	......	
32	20	12	12	20	19	13	236	205	31	15	221	59	177	
488	241	247	73	415	419	69	6,343	5,976	367	92	6,251	692	5,651	
1,839	927	912	1,153	686	791	1,048	11,445	9,361	2,084	1,456	9,989	1,588	9,857	
43	26	17	23	20	30	13	3,764	3,710	54	32	3,732	340	3,424	
9	4	5	2	7	5	4	15	8	7	2	13	11	4	
44	21	23	1	43	44	......	57	27	30	4	53	57	......	
11	4	7	......	11	11	......	15	7	8	......	15	15	......	
48	34	14	19	29	25	23	175	135	40	23	152	60	115	
61	24	37	5	56	61	......	87	38	49	8	79	87	......	
2,084	897	1,187	131	1,953	2,082	2	2,648	1,214	1,434	158	2,490	2,641	7	
819	338	481	67	752	807	12	1,069	490	579	77	992	1,042	27	
40	19	21	......	40	40	......	73	39	34	6	67	68	5	
14,786	7,387	7,399	3,881	10,905	9,441	5,345	37,208	22,398	14,810	4,791	32,417	13,948	23,260	
1,980	948	1,032	821	1,159	1,125	855	9,527	7,674	1,853	1,038	8,489	1,391	8,136	
1,203	623	580	70	1,133	1,203	......	1,569	861	708	80	1,489	1,569	......	
350	179	171	13	337	350	......	479	254	225	20	459	479	......	
18	7	11	......	18	18	......	26	12	14	......	26	18	8	
11	7	4	1	10	11	......	16	11	5	1	15	16	......	
472	271	201	32	440	472	......	836	478	358	62	774	824	12	
36	31	5	2	34	36	......	109	86	23	6	103	109	......	
215	135	80	7	208	215	......	304	190	114	21	283	304	......	
358	232	126	45	313	358	......	587	384	203	62	525	587	......	
178	153	25	17	161	178	......	405	314	91	31	374	405	......	
644	435	209	19	625	644	......	889	626	263	41	848	889	......	
......	......	......	......	......	......	......	10	5	5	......	10	10	......	
12	8	4	2	10	9	3	27	21	6	4	23	12	15	
1	1	......	......	1	1	......	7	6	1	1	6	......	7	
1	......	1	1	......	......	1	17	15	2	1	16	2	15	
29	17	12	24	5	5	24	815	765	50	34	781	51	764	
1,376	495	881	138	1,238	1,349	27	2,061	863	1,198	167	1,894	1,930	131	
509	234	275	37	472	509	......	652	316	336	43	609	652	......	
5,719	2,979	2,740	1,783	3,936	4,094	1,625	17,225	11,650	5,575	2,248	14,977	6,230	10,995	
273	157	116	129	144	154	119	871	583	288	154	717	312	559	
19	11	8	13	6	7	12	273	229	44	26	247	29	244	
551	309	242	339	212	240	311	5,279	4,662	617	422	4,857	498	4,781	
77	50	27	54	23	44	33	571	479	92	66	505	93	478	
886	610	276	121	765	739	147	1,844	1,347	497	176	1,668	1,093	751	
829	559	270	178	651	676	153	1,599	1,132	467	258	1,341	996	603	
12	7	5	1	11	11	1	30	17	13	1	29	18	12	
43	35	8	2	41	39	4	107	86	21	7	100	65	42	
240	128	112	126	114	146	94	794	514	280	141	653	306	488	
19	15	4	10	9	7	12	218	192	26	17	201	14	204	
658	363	295	394	264	258	400	4,883	4,179	704	478	4,405	452	4,431	
103	55	48	79	24	48	55	549	414	135	99	450	84	465	
150	68	82	105	45	82	68	778	514	264	135	643	254	524	
73	37	36	54	1s	b	6s	515	425	90	73	442	11	504	
615	352	263	437	178	167	448	6,279	5,509	770	572	5,707	460	5,819	
179	108	71	124	55	17	162	984	741	243	152	832	77	907	
......	......	......	......	......	......	......	26	26	......	......	26	......	26	
195	92	103	111	84	95	100	643	432	211	133	510	170	473	

TABLE XXIII.—PASSENGERS DEPARTED FROM THE UNITED

Line of vessels.	Ports of departure and destination.	Aliens.						
		Num-ber.	Sex.		Age.		Class.	
			Male.	Fe-male.	Under 14 years.	14 years and over.	Cabin.	Steer-age.
	From New York, N. Y., to—Continued.							
Lloyd Sabaudo—Con.	Messina	212	139	23	1	211	......	215
	Naples	3,526	3,119	407	138	3,388	61	3,462
	Palermo	584	467	117	36	548	10	574
Munson	Cuba	175	112	63	26	149	175	......
National Steam Navigation Co.	Ghython	25	25	......	......	25	2	23
	Kalamata	26	26	......	......	26	......	26
	Naples	1,515	1,190	325	85	1,430	33	1,482
	Patras	71	71	......	......	71	2	69
	Piraeus	7,676	7,444	232	56	7,620	824	6,852
	Miscellaneous	3	2	1	1	2	1	2
Navigazione Generale Italiana	Genoa	1,114	797	317	51	1,063	301	813
	Messina	561	507	54	11	550	18	543
	Naples	9,541	8,705	836	175	9,366	422	9,119
	Palermo	1,017	888	129	16	1,001	77	940
	Piraeus	599	599	......	......	599	......	599
New York & Cuba Mail.	British West Indies	314	174	140	30	284	293	21
	Cuba	3,955	2,972	983	284	3,671	2,830	1,125
	Mexico	1,185	837	348	103	1,082	1,073	112
North German Lloyd...	Bremen	34,626	25,423	9,203	1,216	33,410	5,322	29,304
	Cherbourg	1,121	720	401	45	1,076	1,110	11
	Genoa	921	631	290	35	886	508	413
	Gibralter	77	55	22	4	73	59	18
	Messina	348	313	35	10	338	20	328
	Naples	9,869	8,946	923	195	9,674	678	9,191
	Palermo	1,149	993	156	34	1,115	63	1,086
	Plymouth	1,079	780	299	20	1,059	1,079	......
	Algiers	15	9	6	......	15	14	1
Panama R. R. Co	Panama	283	209	74	19	264	170	113
Quebec Steamship Co...	Bermuda	1,652	813	839	143	1,509	1,652	......
	British Guana	50	39	11	5	45	21	29
	British West Indies	549	286	263	25	524	222	327
	Canada	28	11	17	2	26	28	......
	Danish West Indies	122	54	68	5	117	58	64
	French West Indies	50	18	32	2	48	21	29
Red Cross	Canada	469	286	183	21	448	469	......
	Miscellaneous	1	1	......	......	1	1	......
Red D	Dutch West Indies	84	58	26	9	75	84	......
	Venezuela	238	170	68	15	223	238	......
Red Star	Antwerp	14,106	10,173	3,933	552	13,554	2,063	12,043
	Dover	172	97	75	7	165	172	......
	Plymouth	30	25	5	1	29	30	......
Royal Dutch West Indian Mail.	British Guiana	19	10	9	......	19	19	......
	British West Indies	203	129	74	11	192	202	1
	Dutch Guiana	16	13	3	......	16	16	......
	Dutch West Indies	16	11	5	......	16	16	......
	Haiti	50	36	14	5	45	50	......
	Santo Domingo	8	6	2	1	7	8	......
	Venezuela	11	5	6	1	10	11	......
Royal Mail Steam Packet Co.	Southampton	56	31	25	7	49	56	......
	Bermuda	673	379	294	30	643	673	......
	British West Indies	340	181	159	20	320	329	11
	Colombia	103	69	34	6	97	99	4
	Cuba	88	58	30	5	83	85	3
	Panama	127	97	30	4	123	124	3
Russia-American	Libau	7,766	6,135	1,631	381	7,385	934	6,832
	Rotterdam	4,069	3,421	648	118	3,951	272	3,797
Scandinavian-American	Christiana	3,198	1,634	1,564	110	3,088	661	2,537
	Christiansand	1,602	927	675	50	1,552	97	1,505
	Copenhagen	3,053	1,561	1,492	109	2,944	718	2,335
Sicula-Americana	Genoa	67	54	13	1	66	10	57
	Messina	476	399	77	13	463	26	450
	Naples	3,946	3,502	444	149	3,797	120	3,826
	Palermo	1,614	1,255	359	59	1,555	141	1,473
	Patras	18	18	......	......	18	......	18
	Piraeus	216	216	......	......	216	......	216
Spanish	Spain	999	912	87	20	979	173	826
	Cuba	196	141	55	31	165	153	43
	Mexico	38	29	9	2	36	33	5
Trinidad	British West Indies	205	121	84	17	188	203	2
	British Guiana	8	2	6	6	2	8	......
United Fruit Co	British West Indies	380	233	147	19	361	379	1

STATES, FISCAL YEAR ENDED JUNE 30, 1913—Continued.

Citizens.							Total.						
Number.	Sex.		Age.		Class.		Number.	Sex.		Age.		Class.	
	Male.	Female	Under 14 years	14 years and over.	Cabin.	Steerage.		Male.	Female.	Under 14 years.	14 years and over	Cabin.	Steerage
26	11	15	25	1		26	238	200	38	26	212		238
405	236	169	342	63	55	350	3,931	3,355	576	480	3,451	116	3,815
106	57	49	92	14	10	96	690	524	166	128	562	20	670
335	201	134	60	275	335		510	313	197	86	424	510	
2	1	1	2			1	27	26	1	2	25	3	24
26						26	26				26		26
306	177	129	283	23	14	292	1,821	1,367	454	368	1,453	47	1,774
71						71	71				71	2	69
242	159	83	164	78	142	100	7,918	7,603	315	220	7,698	966	6,952
3	3		3			3	6	5	1	4	2	1	5
466	245	221	228	238	273	193	1,580	1,042	538	279	1,301	574	1,006
41	30	11	31	10	13	28	602	537	65	42	560	31	571
1,260	732	528	770	490	449	811	10,801	9,437	1,364	945	9,856	871	9,930
135	75	60	91	44	45	90	1,152	963	189	107	1,045	122	1,030
							599	599			599		599
1,049	560	489	47	1,002	992	57	1,363	734	629	77	1,286	1,285	78
5,675	3,725	1,950	300	5,375	5,403	272	9,630	6,697	2,933	584	9,046	8,233	1,397
1,370	915	455	116	1,254	1,315	55	2,555	1,752	803	219	2,336	2,388	167
17,440	9,203	8,237	5,644	11,796	10,928	6,512	52,066	34,626	17,440	6,860	45,206	16,250	35,816
3,236	1,666	1,570	163	3,073	3,227	9	4,357	2,386	1,971	208	4,149	4,337	20
1,223	556	667	208	1,015	1,135	88	2,144	1,187	957	243	1,901	1,643	501
124	55	69	7	117	122	2	201	110	91	11	190	181	20
38	21	17	30	8	7	31	386	334	52	40	346	27	359
3,038	1,454	1,584	976	2,062	1,972	1,066	12,907	10,400	2,507	1,171	11,736	2,650	10,257
179	109	70	135	44	29	150	1,328	1,102	226	169	1,159	92	1,236
2,106	1,289	837	102	2,004	2,106		3,185	2,049	1,136	122	3,063	3,185	
34	14	20	7	27	34		49	23	26	7	42	48	1
7,176	4,817	2,359	849	6,327	6,838	338	7,459	5,026	2,433	868	6,591	7,008	451
7,929	3,576	4,353	319	7,610	7,929		9,581	4,389	5,192	462	9,119	9,581	
56	33	23	3	53	55	1	106	72	34	8	98	76	30
275	147	128	97	178	185	90	824	433	391	122	702	407	417
514	225	289	18	496	514		542	236	306	20	522	542	
82	54	28	19	63	60	22	204	108	96	24	180	118	86
14	10	4		14	12	2	64	28	36	2	62	33	31
1,666	861	805	113	1,553	1,666		2,135	1,147	988	134	2,001	2,135	
5	4	1		5	5		6	6			6	6	
45	36	9	6	39	45		129	94	35	15	114	129	
112	87	25	9	103	112		350	257	93	24	326	350	
6,135	3,028	3,107	2,151	3,984	3,925	2,210	20,241	13,201	7,040	2,703	17,538	5,988	14,253
418	182	236	32	386	418		590	279	311	39	551	590	
22	12	10		22	22		52	37	15	1	51	52	
13	10	3	1	12	13		32	20	12	1	31	32	
114	74	40	21	93	114		317	203	114	32	285	316	1
21	17	4		21	21		37	30	7		37	37	
5	3	2	1	4	5		21	14	7	1	20	21	
12	11	1	1	11	12		62	47	15	6	56	62	
1	1			1	1		9	7	2	1	8	9	
3	3			3	3		14	8	6	1	13	14	
156	82	74	3	153	156		212	113	99	10	202	212	
9,289	4,122	5,167	289	9,000	9,289		9,962	4,501	5,461	319	9,643	9,962	
422	234	188	41	381	417	5	762	415	347	61	701	746	16
70	44	26	1	69	70		173	113	60	7	166	169	4
242	149	93	31	211	242		330	207	123	36	294	327	3
443	297	146	33	410	435	8	570	394	176	37	533	559	11
1,059	525	534	905	154	331	728	8,825	6,660	2,165	1,286	7,539	1,265	7,560
669	321	348	473	196	256	413	4,738	3,742	996	591	4,147	528	4,210
2,243	1,122	1,121	832	1,411	683	1,560	2,526	1,452	1,074	460	2,066	194	2,332
924	525	399	410	514	97	827	5,880	3,041	2,839	958	4,922	1,821	4,059
2,827	1,480	1,347	849	1,978	1,103	1,724	81	62	19	13	68	13	68
14	8	6	12	2	3	11	4,432	3,777	655	577	3,855	172	4,260
74	40	34	63	11	11	63	1,979	1,460	519	373	1,606	209	1,770
486	275	211	428	58	52	434	18	18			18		18
365	205	160	314	51	68	297	216	216			216		216
133	77	56	60	73	104	29	1,132	989	143	80	1,052	277	855
20	7	13	3	17	20		216	148	68	34	182	173	43
3	2	1		3	3		41	31	10	2	39	36	5
186	146	40	17	169	186		391	267	124	34	357	389	2
772	429	343	36	736	772		1,152	662	490	55	1,097	1,151	1

TABLE XXIII.—PASSENGERS DEPARTED FROM THE UNITED

Line of vessels.	Ports of departure and destination.	Number.	Sex.		Age.		Class.	
			Male.	Female.	Under 14 years.	14 years and over.	Cabin.	Steerage.
	From New York, N. Y., to—Continued.							
United Fruit Co.—Con.	Colombia	187	141	46	11	176	187	......
	Costa Rica	88	48	40	1	87	88	......
	Honduras							
	Panama	626	438	188	50	576	624	2
Uranium	Rotterdam	6,998	5,890	1,108	238	6,760	297	6,701
White Star	Cherbourg	5,055	4,425	630	88	4,967	878	4,177
	Genoa	176	139	37	4	172	29	147
	Gibraltar	8	7	1	......	8	4	
	Liverpool	15,155	11,487	3,668	672	14,483	5,261	9,894
	Naples	4,955	4,522	433	68	4,887	346	4,609
	Plymouth	1,044	796	248	35	1,009	638	406
	Queenstown	3,350	1,207	2,143	48	3,302	560	2,790
	Southampton	6,775	5,153	1,622	230	6,545	2,469	4,306
	Alexandria	102	61	41	2	100	65	37
	Algiers	16	7	9	1	15	13	3
	Miscellaneous	20	18	2	......	20	6	14
Miscellaneous	Miscellaneous	62	30	32	9	53	58	4
	Total New York	398,442	318,111	80,331	12,293	386,149	78,649	319,793
	From Norfolk, Va., to—							
Norway-Mexico Gulf...	Miscellaneous	23	16	7	2	21	......	23
Miscellaneous	....do	2	2			2	......	2
	Total Norfolk	25	18	7	2	23	......	25
	From Philadelphia, Pa., to—							
Allan	British North America.	31	15	16	......	31	17	14
	Glasgow	36	11	25	9	27	28	8
American	Liverpool	2,040	1,205	835	156	1,884	615	1,425
	Queenstown	305	86	219	2	303	57	248
Atlantic Fruit	British West Indies...	7	2	5	1	6	7	......
Hamburg-American....	Boulogne	64	50	14	8	56	7	57
	Hamburg	1,074	578	496	53	1,021	268	806
Italia	Genoa	39	30	9	1	38	2	37
	Messina	124	112	12	3	121	......	124
	Naples	1,944	1,776	168	54	1,890	32	1,912
	Palermo	79	66	13	4	75	......	79
La Veloce	Genoa	11	8	3	......	11	1	10
	Messina	36	31	5	2	34	1	35
	Naples	967	916	51	14	953	12	955
	Palermo	24	21	3	......	24	1	23
Lloyd Italiano	Genoa	17	14	3	1	16	4	13
	Messina	85	70	15	5	80	......	85
	Naples	869	794	75	21	848	6	863
	Palermo	41	31	10	1	40	......	41
Navigazione Generale Italiana.	Genoa	39	31	8	1	38	14	25
	Messina	128	112	16	7	121	......	128
	Naples	1,543	1,390	153	47	1,496	30	1,513
	Palermo	86	66	20	5	81	9	77
Red Star	Antwerp	112	37	75	11	101	112	......
United Fruit	British West Indies...	92	63	29	4	88	92	......
Miscellaneous	Miscellaneous	5	4	1	......	5	......	5
	Total Philadelphia..	9,798	7,519	2,279	410	9,388	1,315	8,483
	From Portland, Me., to—							
Allan	Glasgow	768	547	221	78	690	232	536
Austro-American	Trieste	8	6	2	......	8	2	6
Canada	Liverpool	338	239	99	43	295	159	179
	London	737	570	167	51	686	207	530
White Star Dominion..	Liverpool	3,312	2,646	666	227	3,085	890	2,422
Sailing vessel	Not stated	1	1			1	1	
	Total Portland, Me..	5,164	4,009	1,155	399	4,765	1,491	3,673
	From Portland, Oreg.—							
Sailing vessel	Not stated	1	1	......	......	1	1	......

STATES, FISCAL YEAR ENDED JUNE 30, 1913—Continued.

	Citizens.						Total.						
	Sex.		Age.		Class.			Sex		Age		Class	
Number.	Male.	Female.	Undr 14 years.	14 years and over.	Cabin.	Steerage.	Number.	Male.	Female.	Under 14 years.	14 years and over.	Cabin.	Steerage.
288	183	105	19	269	288	......	475	324	151	30	445	475	......
291	162	129	14	277	291	......	379	210	169	15	364	379	......
3	3	......	......	3	3	......	3	3	......	......	3	3	......
1,585	1,083	502	81	1,504	1,584	1	2,211	1,521	690	131	2,080	2,208	3
995	518	477	716	279	341	654	7,993	6,408	1,585	954	7,039	638	7,355
2,055	1,157	898	405	1,650	1,532	523	7,110	5,582	1,528	493	6,617	2,410	4,700
148	71	77	35	113	107	41	324	210	114	39	285	136	188
29	16	13	3	26	24	5	37	23	14	3	34	28	9
7,213	4,084	3,129	1,089	6,124	5,308	1,905	22,368	15,571	6,797	1,761	20,607	10,569	11,799
1,297	563	734	268	1,029	993	304	6,252	5,085	1,167	336	5,916	1,339	4,913
999	602	397	117	882	859	140	2,043	1,398	645	152	1,891	1,497	546
2,736	1,472	1,264	663	2,073	1,107	1,629	6,086	2,679	3,407	711	5,375	1,667	4,419
4,004	2,412	1,592	603	3,401	2,761	1,243	10,779	7,565	3,214	833	9,946	5,230	5,549
335	134	201	23	312	321	14	437	195	242	25	412	386	51
76	31	45	7	69	76	......	92	38	54	8	84	89	3
36	19	17	3	33	35	1	56	37	19	3	53	41	15
89	37	52	7	82	89	......	151	67	84	16	135	147	4
195,094	104,802	90,292	44,927	150,167	140,114	54,980	593,536	422,913	170,623	57,220	536,316	218,763	374,773
4	4	......	4	......	......	4	27	20	7	6	21	......	27
1	1	......	......	1	1	......	3	3	......	......	3	1	2
5	5	......	4	1	1	4	30	23	7	6	24	1	29
23	9	14	4	19	19	4	54	24	30	4	50	36	18
15	9	6	7	8	10	5	51	20	31	16	35	38	13
1,474	569	905	293	1,181	1,144	330	3,514	1,774	1,740	449	3,065	1,759	1,755
199	89	110	45	154	114	85	504	175	329	47	457	171	333
15	4	11	......	15	15	......	22	6	16	1	21	22	......
35	12	23	5	30	34	1	99	62	37	13	86	41	58
1,560	668	892	260	1,300	1,290	270	2,634	1,246	1,388	313	2,321	1,558	1,076
10	3	7	4	6	3	7	49	33	16	5	44	5	44
17	11	6	15	2	......	17	141	123	18	18	123	......	141
192	99	93	150	42	25	167	2,136	1,875	261	204	1,932	57	2,079
12	12	......	10	2	1	11	91	78	13	14	77	1	90
12	6	6	6	6	2	10	23	14	9	6	17	3	20
11	7	4	10	1	1	10	47	38	9	12	35	2	45
50	33	17	43	7	6	44	1,017	949	68	57	960	18	999
3	2	1	3	......	......	3	27	23	4	3	24	1	26
8	7	1	6	2	8	......	25	21	4	7	18	12	13
15	4	11	14	1	......	15	100	74	26	19	81	......	100
88	45	43	77	11	3	85	957	839	118	98	859	9	948
14	4	10	14	......	......	14	55	35	20	15	40	......	55
17	15	2	5	12	11	6	56	46	10	6	50	25	31
19	10	9	19	......	......	19	147	122	25	26	121	......	147
196	105	91	134	62	53	143	1,739	1,495	244	181	1,558	83	1,656
13	7	6	13	......	......	13	99	73	26	18	81	9	90
535	174	361	44	491	535	......	647	211	436	55	592	647	......
304	194	110	7	297	304	......	396	257	139	11	385	396	......
							5	4	1	......	5	......	5
4,837	2,098	2,739	1,188	3,649	3,578	1,259	14,635	9,617	5,018	1,598	13,037	4,893	9,742
25	21	4	2	23	14	11	793	568	225	80	713	246	547
2	2	......	......	2	......	2	10	8	2	......	10	2	8
47	29	18	4	43	38	9	385	268	117	47	338	197	188
30	19	11	1	29	20	10	767	589	178	52	715	227	540
128	88	40	21	107	42	86	3,440	2,734	706	248	3,192	932	2,508
							1	......	1	......	......	......	1	......
232	159	73	28	204	114	118	5,396	4,168	1,228	427	4,969	1,605	3,791
							1	1	......	......	1	1	......

TABLE XXIII.—PASSENGERS DEPARTED FROM THE UNITED

Line of vessels.	Ports of departure and destination.	Number.	Aliens.						
			Sex.		Age.		Class.		
			Male.	Female.	Under 14 years.	14 years and over.	Cabin.	Steerage.	
Compagnie Generale Transatlantique.	From Porto Rico to— France	14	8	6	3	11	13	1	
	Cuba								
	Danish West Indies	11	6	5	......	11	9	2	
	French West Indies	4	2	2	......	4	2	2	
	Haiti	4	3	1	......	4	2	2	
	Santo Domingo	131	79	52	19	112	55	76	
Compagnie Generale Transatlantique de Barcelona.	France	45	30	15	7	38	16	29	
	Italy	35	29	6	3	32	19	16	
	Spain	464	334	130	36	428	350	114	
	Cuba	104	77	27	5	99	41	63	
	Mexico	12	10	2	5	7	9	3	
	Panama								
Hamburg American	Santo Domingo	6	6	......	......	6	1	5	
	Hamburg	17	8	9	6	11	17	......	
	British West Indies	3	3	......	......	3	3	......	
	Danish West Indies	122	67	55	16	106	77	45	
	Haiti	5	3	2	......	5	5	......	
Herrera	Santo Domingo	143	96	47	20	123	85	58	
	Cuba	153	100	53	18	135	106	47	
	Santo Domingo	133	96	37	13	120	64	69	
New York & Porto Rico.	Santo Domingo	2	2	......	......	2	2	......	
Pinillos Red D	Spain	156	110	46	5	151	133	23	
	Dutch West Indies	65	51	14	6	59	65	......	
Sailing vessels	Venezuela	128	90	38	8	120	128	......	
	British West Indies	3	2	1	......	3	3	......	
	Danish West Indies	20	12	8	1	19	9	11	
	Dutch West Indies	44	26	18	......	44	44	......	
	Total Porto Rico	1,824	1,250	574	171	1,653	1,258	566	
Fabre	From Providence, R. I., to— Lisbon	281	219	62	11	270	12	269	
	Marseille	274	254	20	3	271	36	238	
	Naples	1,174	1,055	119	26	1,148	4	1,170	
	Azores	520	319	201	27	493	58	462	
	Total Providence	2,249	1,847	402	67	2,182	110	2,139	
Atlantic & Pacific	From San Francisco to— Chile	3	2	1	1	2	3	......	
Oceanic	Peru								
	Australia	403	297	106	32	371	274	129	
	New Zealand	22	16	6	......	22	11	11	
Pacific Mail	Samoa	15	12	3	......	15	15	......	
	Hongkong	1,952	1,867	85	13	1,939	191	1,761	
	Kobe	106	90	16	1	105	30	76	
	Nagasaki	44	32	12	3	41	19	25	
	Shanghai	93	58	35	17	76	89	4	
	Yokohama	928	819	109	9	919	329	599	
	Costa Rica	3	2	1	......	3	......	3	
	Guatemala	33	22	11	2	31	28	5	
	Honduras	9	9	......	1	8	7	2	
	Mexico	195	111	84	27	168	117	78	
	Nicaragua	16	10	6	2	14	15	1	
	Panama	91	77	14	5	86	39	52	
	Peru	3	2	1	......	3	2	1	
Toyo Kisen Kaisha	San Salvador	49	34	15	3	46	42	7	
	Hongkong	846	784	62	8	838	164	682	
	Kobe	151	126	25	1	150	19	132	
	Nagasaki	81	70	11	......	81	11	70	
	Shanghai	62	45	17	5	57	58	4	
Union	Yokohama	2,575	2,267	308	18	2,557	1,017	1,558	
	Australia	681	499	182	59	622	420	261	
	New Zealand	280	200	80	25	255	168	112	
	Total San Francisco	8,641	7,451	1,190	232	8,409	3,068	5,573	

STATES, FISCAL YEAR ENDED JUNE 30, 1913—Continued.

| | Citizens. | | | | | | | Total. | | | | | |
| | Sex. | | Age. | | Class. | | | Sex. | | Age. | | Class. | |
Number.	Male.	Female.	Under 14 years.	14 years and over.	Cabin.	Steerage.	Number.	Male.	Female.	Under 14 years.	14 years and over.	Cabin.	Steerage.
6	4	2	2	4	5	1	20	12	8	5	15	18	2
6	2	4	3	3		6	6	2	4	3	3		6
6	2	4	4	2	6		17	8	9	4	13	15	2
							4	2	2		4	2	2
1	1			1	1		5	4	1		5	3	2
281	166	115	59	222	97	184	412	245	167	78	334	152	260
8	3	5	2	6	7	1	53	33	20	9	44	23	30
16	10	6	7	9	15	1	51	39	12	10	41	34	17
273	119	154	102	171	250	23	737	453	204	138	599	600	137
90	59	31	10	80	61	29	194	136	58	15	179	102	92
2	2			2	2		14	12	2	5	9	11	3
3	3			3	3		3	3			3	3	
4	4			4	3	1	10	10			10	4	6
							17	8	9	6	11	17	
26	22	4		26	26		29	25	4		29	29	
37	22	15	13	24	33	4	159	89	70	29	130	110	49
5	5			5	5		10	8	2		10	10	
195	137	58	21	174	76	119	338	233	105	41	297	161	177
342	222	120	59	283	119	223	495	322	173	77	418	225	270
408	252	156	71	337	55	353	541	348	193	84	457	119	422
4	4			4	4		6	6			6	6	
92	47	45	58	34	86	6	248	157	91	63	185	219	29
30	19	11	3	27	30		95	70	25	9	86	95	
170	107	63	29	141	168	2	298	197	101	37	261	296	2
3	3			3	3		6	5	1		6	6	
39	33	6	1	38	38	1	59	45	14	2	57	47	12
2	1	1		2	2		46	27	19		46	46	
2,049	1,249	800	444	1,605	1,095	954	3,873	2,499	1,374	615	3,258	2,353	1,520
31	15	16	20	11	4	27	312	234	78	31	281	16	296
62	27	35	28	34	42	20	336	281	55	31	305	78	258
132	68	64	93	39	19	113	1,306	1,123	183	119	1,187	23	1,283
219	130	89	107	112	66	153	739	449	290	134	605	124	615
444	240	204	248	196	131	313	2,693	2,087	606	315	2,378	241	2,452
							3	2	1	1	2	3	
18	11	7	4	14	18		18	11	7	4	14	18	
405	263	142	36	369	367	38	808	560	248	68	740	641	167
11	7	4		11	10	1	33	23	10		33	21	12
40	34	6	2	38	40		55	46	9	2	53	55	
1,339	920	419	78	1,261	741	598	3,291	2,787	504	91	3,200	932	2,359
167	81	86	43	124	163	4	273	171	102	44	229	193	80
30	13	17	10	20	21	9	74	45	29	13	61	40	34
348	154	194	48	300	348		441	212	229	65	376	437	4
435	229	206	78	357	407	28	1,363	1,048	315	87	1,276	736	627
2	2			2	2		5	4	1		5	2	3
37	22	15	2	35	33	4	70	44	26	4	66	61	9
21	18	3		21	19	2	30	27	3	1	29	26	4
214	153	61	25	189	177	37	409	264	145	52	357	294	115
20	15	5	1	19	18	2	36	25	11	3	33	33	3
306	227	79	15	291	237	69	397	304	93	20	377	276	121
23	18	5		23	16	7	26	20	6		26	18	8
16	12	4	1	15	16		65	46	19	4	61	58	7
792	500	292	63	729	542	250	1,638	1,284	354	71	1,567	706	932
97	51	46	35	62	86	11	248	177	71	36	212	105	143
33	17	16	15	18	20	13	114	87	27	15	99	31	83
159	80	79	29	130	159		221	125	96	34	187	217	4
555	281	274	334	221	421	134	3,130	2,548	582	352	2,778	1,438	1,692
539	346	193	69	470	423	116	1,220	845	375	128	1,092	843	377
92	61	31	13	79	57	35	372	261	111	38	334	225	147
5,699	3,515	2,184	901	4,798	4,341	1,358	14,340	10,966	3,374	1,133	13,207	7,409	6,931

TABLE XXIII.—PASSENGERS DEPARTED FROM THE UNITED

Line of vessels.	Ports of departure and destination.	Aliens.						
		Num-ber.	Sex.		Age.		Class.	
			Male.	Fe-male.	Under 14 years.	14 years and over.	Cabin.	Steer-age.
Bank	From Seattle, Wash., to— Hongkong							
Great Northern	Do	102	94	8		102	14	88
	Kobe	29	23	6		29	2	27
	Nagasaki							
	Yokohama	4	4			4	1	3
Nippon Yusen Kaisha	Hongkong	149	136	13	2	147	40	109
	Kobe	561	486	75	4	557	30	531
	Moji	17	12	5		17	5	12
	Shanghai	39	24	15	9	30	36	3
	Nagasaki	8	6	2		8		8
	Yokohama	586	530	56	5	581	234	352
Ocean	Hongkong	739	738	1	1	738		739
Osaka Shosen Kaisha	Do	49	49			49	5	44
	Kobe	291	265	26	4	287	8	283
	Moji	11	9	2		11		11
	Nagasaki	4	3	1		4		4
	Shanghai	7	2	5		7	7	
	Yokohama	317	303	14		317	17	300
	Total Seattle	2,913	2,684	229	25	2,888	399	2,514
Sailing vessels	From Tampa, Fla., to— British West Indies	7	6	1		7	5	2
	Honduras	1	1			1		1
	Mexico							
	Total Tampa	8	7	1		8	5	3

RECAPITULATION.

Baltimore, Md		1,884	1,311	573	94	1,790	271	1,613
Boston, Mass		22,219	14,461	7,758	963	21,256	4,574	17,645
Brunswick, Ga		1		1		1		1
Canada (Atlantic seaports)		7,867	6,177	1,690	433	7,434	1,417	6,450
Canadian border stations		129,862	97,250	32,612	13,692	116,170	129,862	
Canada (Pacific seaports)		1,574	1,321	253	51	1,523	673	901
Galveston, Tex		907	722	185	36	871	168	739
Honolulu, Hawaii		4,032	2,941	1,091	96	3,936	542	3,490
Jacksonville, Fla		3		3		3	3	
Key West, Fla		7,370	5,238	2,132	870	6,500	2,716	4,654
Mexican border stations		2,041	1,599	442	147	1,894	1,357	684
Miami, Fla		2,049	1,540	509	149	1,900	481	1,568
Mobile, Ala		91	51	40	14	77	91	
New Bedford, Mass		503	453	50	21	482		503
New Orleans, La		2,453	1,806	647	202	2,251	2,041	412
Newport News, Va		3	2	1	1	2	3	
New York, N. Y		398,442	318,111	80,331	12,293	386,149	78,649	319,793
Norfolk, Va		25	18	7	2	23		25
Philadelphia, Pa		9,798	7,519	2,279	410	9,388	1,315	8,483
Portland, Me		5,164	4,009	1,155	399	4,765	1,491	3,673
Portland, Oreg		1	1			1		
Porto Rico		1,824	1,250	574	171	1,653	1,258	566
Providence, R. I		2,249	1,847	402	67	2,182	110	2,139
San Francisco, Cal		8,641	7,451	1,190	232	8,409	3,068	5,573
Seattle, Wash		2,913	2,684	229	25	2,888	399	2,514
Tampa, Fla		8	7	1		8	5	3
Total		611,924	477,769	134,155	30,368	581,556	230,496	381,428
Steamships		480,902	379,698	101,204	16,576	464,326	100,195	380,707
Sailing vessels		1,160	821	339	100	1,060	439	721
By land		129,862	97,250	32,612	13,692	116,170	129,862	

BY YEARS.

1910		380,418	279,896	100,522	22,942	357,476	141,789	238,629
1911		518,215	400,294	117,921	27,175	491,040	172,485	345,730
1912		615,292	480,732	134,560	28,593	586,699	188,550	426,742
1913		611,924	477,769	134,155	30,368	581,556	230,496	381,428

STATES, FISCAL YEAR ENDED JUNE 30, 1913—Continued.

	Citizens.						Total.					
Num- ber.	Sex.		Age.		Class.		Num- ber.	Sex.		Age.		Class.
	Male.	Fe- male.	Under 14 years.	14 years and over.	Cabin.	Steer- age.		Male.	Fe- male.	Under 14 years.	14 years and over.	Cabin.	Steer- age.
1	1			1		1	1	1			1		1
82	49	33	11	71	45	37	184	143	41	11	173	59	125
7	1	6	6	1	3	4	36	24	12	6	30	5	31
38	17	21	12	26	38		38	17	21	12	26	38	
6	3	3	1	5	6		10	7	3	1	9	7	3
132	79	53	13	119	100	32	281	215	66	15	266	140	141
78	40	38	56	22	31	47	639	526	113	60	579	61	578
6	3	3	5	1	1	5	23	15	8	5	18	6	17
46	25	21	15	31	34	12	85	49	36	24	61	70	15
							8	6	2		8		8
100	58	42	41	59	63	37	686	588	98	46	640	297	389
205	204	1	1	204		205	944	942	2	2	942		944
7	6	1	3	4		7	56	55	1	3	53	5	51
33	16	17	22	11	9	24	324	281	43	26	298	17	307
4	2	2	2	2	3	1	15	11	4	2	13	3	12
							4	3	1		4		4
6	2	4	4	2	6		13	4	9	4	9	13	
25	12	13	12	13	5	20	342	315	27	12	330	22	320
776	518	258	204	572	344	432	3,689	3,202	487	229	3,460	743	2,946
3	2	1		3	2	1	10	8	2		10	7	3
3	3			3	3		4	4			4	3	1
1	1			1	1		1	1			1	1	
7	6	1		7	6	1	15	13	2		15	11	4

RECAPITULATION.

1,855	867	988	425	1,430	1,303	552	3,739	2,178	1,561	519	3,220	1,574	2,165
13,839	7,223	6,616	3,018	10,821	8,551	5,288	36,058	21,684	14,374	3,981	32,077	13,125	22,933
3		3		3	3		4	3	1		4	4	
3,938	1,906	2,032	645	3,293	3,003	935	11,805	8,083	3,722	1,078	10,727	4,420	7,385
90,129	63,836	26,293	16,763	73,366	90,129		219,991	161,086	58,905	30,455	189,536	219,991	
541	367	174	77	464	373	168	2,115	1,688	427	128	1,987	1,046	1,069
827	446	381	149	678	574	253	1,734	1,168	566	185	1,549	742	992
2,110	1,120	990	1,165	945	892	1,218	6,142	4,061	2,081	1,261	4,881	1,434	4,708
							3		3		3	3	
14,673	8,923	5,750	746	13,927	13,901	772	22,043	14,161	7,882	1,616	20,427	16,617	5,426
1,206	965	241	73	1,133	1,190	16	3,247	2,564	683	220	3,027	2,547	700
290	169	121	54	236	194	96	2,339	1,709	630	203	2,136	675	1,664
184	130	54	10	174	184		275	181	94	24	251	275	
8	5	3	5	3		8	511	458	53	26	485		511
8,955	6,016	2,939	572	8,383	8,760	195	11,408	7,822	3,586	774	10,634	10,801	607
1		1		1	1		4	2	2	1	3	4	
195,094	104,802	90,292	44,927	150,167	140,114	54,980	593,536	422,913	170,623	57,220	536,316	218,763	374,773
5	5			4	1	4	30	23	7	6	24	1	29
4,837	2,098	2,739	1,188	3,649	3,578	1,259	14,635	9,617	5,018	1,598	13,037	4,893	9,742
232	159	73	28	204	114	118	5,356	4,168	1,228	427	4,969	1,605	3,791
							1	1			1		
2,049	1,249	800	444	1,605	1,095	954	3,873	2,499	1,374	615	3,258	2,353	1,520
444	240	204	248	196	131	313	2,693	2,087	606	315	2,378	241	2,452
5,699	3,515	2,184	901	4,798	4,341	1,358	14,340	10,966	3,374	1,133	13,207	7,409	6,931
776	518	258	204	572	344	432	3,689	3,202	487	229	3,460	743	2,946
7	6	1		7	6	1	15	13	2		15	11	4
347,702	204,568	143,134	71,646	276,056	278,782	68,920	959,626	682,337	277,289	102,014	857,612	509,278	450,348
257,506	140,683	116,823	54,859	202,647	188,620	68,886	738,408	520,381	218,027	71,435	666,973	288,815	449,593
67	49	18	24	43	33	34	1,227	870	357	124	1,103	472	755
90,129	63,836	26,293	16,763	73,366	90,129		219,991	161,086	58,905	30,455	189,536	219,991	
342,600	201,950	140,650	57,847	284,753	254,251	88,349	723,018	481,846	241,172	80,789	642,229	396,040	326,978
349,471	211,644	137,827	69,717	279,754	263,585	85,886	867,686	611,938	255,748	96,892	770,794	436,070	431,616
353,890	208,666	145,224	74,117	279,773	275,149	78,741	969,182	689,398	279,784	102,710	866,472	463,699	505,483
347,702	204,568	143,134	71,646	276,056	278,782	68,920	959,626	682,337	277,289	102,014	857,612	509,278	450,348

TABLE XIII.—PASSENGERS DEPARTED FROM THE UNITED

TOTAL PASSENGERS DEPARTED, 1890-1909.

Year ended June 30—	Cabin passengers.						Total cabin.
	Under 12 years of age.			12 years of age and over.			
	Males.	Females.	Total.	Males.	Females.	Total.	
1890	5,297	4,099	9,396	66,130	30,359	96,489	105,885
1891	5,604	3,756	9,360	65,056	32,692	97,748	107,108
1892	5,717	3,706	9,423	61,763	33,966	95,729	105,152
1893	5,503	3,727	9,230	57,904	27,995	85,899	95,129
1894	7,622	4,834	12,456	70,864	38,611	109,475	121,931
1895	5,828	3,812	9,640	64,887	38,366	103,253	112,893
1898[1]	5,111	3,780	8,891	54,533	31,130	85,663	94,554
1899	6,418	4,624	11,042	76,106	41,099	117,205	128,247
1900	10,315	7,443	17,758	87,041	51,096	138,137	155,895
1901	7,646	6,326	13,972	84,853	49,739	134,592	148,564
1902	7,757	5,277	13,034	91,308	53,770	145,078	158,112
1903	6,965	4,994	11,959	99,432	57,293	156,725	168,684
1904	8,235	6,112	14,347	109,469	60,797	170,266	184,613
1905	8,544	6,231	14,775	119,287	67,146	186,433	201,208
1906	8,798	6,060	14,858	125,340	74,471	199,811	214,669
1907	13,008	8,336	21,344	130,276	73,273	203,549	224,893
1908	13,489	8,181	21,670	136,981	78,130	215,111	236,781
1909	11,200	7,581	18,781	136,781	89,238	226,019	244,800

[1] For 1896 and 1897 no figures are available.

STATES, FISCAL YEAR ENDED JUNE 30, 1913—Continued.

TOTAL PASSENGERS DEPARTED, 1890-1909.

Passengers other than cabin.						Total other than cabin.	Total passengers departed.
Under 12 years of age.			12 years of age and over.				
Males.	Females.	Total.	Males.	Females.	Total.		
8,698	7,532	16,230	83,110	32,914	116,024	132,254	238,139
9,268	6,004	15,272	89,034	35,092	124,126	139,398	246,506
9,999	5,969	15,968	96,834	38,602	135,436	151,404	256,556
8,352	5,444	13,796	88,315	33,384	121,699	135,495	230,624
15,798	9,307	25,105	112,941	52,794	165,735	190,840	312,771
17,257	10,612	27,869	123,845	64,951	188,796	216,665	329,558
10,001	5,789	15,790	78,621	36,446	115,067	130,857	225,411
8,836	6,447	15,283	78,061	34,417	112,478	127,761	256,008
13,906	9,095	23,001	78,230	36,268	114,498	137,499	293,394
10,968	8,042	19,010	96,797	42,353	139,150	158,160	306,724
12,067	8,256	20,323	99,966	48,359	148,325	168,648	326,760
13,395	9,082	22,477	132,894	51,206	184,100	206,577	375,261
18,249	13,086	31,335	209,191	83,065	292,256	323,591	508,204
22,104	15,335	37,439	210,270	87,234	297,504	334,943	536,151
16,591	11,144	27,735	179,869	74,464	254,333	282,068	496,737
25,704	16,203	41,907	214,997	88,085	303,082	344,989	569,882
63,751	27,430	91,181	378,246	168,478	546,724	637,905	874,686
30,249	17,400	47,649	199,851	94,152	294,003	341,652	586,452

TABLE A.—JAPANESE APPLIED FOR ADMISSION, ADMITTED, DEBARRED, DEPORTED. AND DEPARTED, FISCAL YEARS ENDED JUNE 30, 1912 AND 1913.

	1912		1913	
	Continental U. S.	Hawaii.	Continental U. S.	Hawaii.
Applications for admission	5,461	3,294	6,859	5,081
Admitted	5,358	3,231	6,771	4,901
Debarred from entry	103	63	88	180
Deported after entry	35			
Departures	5,437	2,593	5,647	2,793

TABLE B.—INCREASE OR DECREASE OF JAPANESE POPULATION BY IMMIGRATION AND EMIGRATION, FISCAL YEARS ENDED JUNE 30, 1912 AND 1913, BY MONTHS.

Month.	Continental United States.			Hawaii.		
	Admitted.	Departed.	Increase(+) or decrease (−).	Admitted.	Departed.	Increase(+) or decrease (−).
1911–12.						
July	354	269	+ 85	181	158	+ 23
August	509	397	+ 112	327	282	+ 45
September	466	471	− 5	240	352	− 112
October	319	621	− 302	228	395	− 167
November	370	1,037	− 667	210	79	+ 131
December	287	782	− 495	244	146	+ 98
January	399	405	− 6	280	73	+ 207
February	329	348	− 19	187	109	+ 78
March	367	373	− 6	336	126	+ 210
April	561	136	+ 425	331	378	− 47
May	538	256	+ 282	349	58	+ 291
June	859	342	+ 517	318	437	− 119
Total	5,358	5,437	− 79	3,231	2,593	+ 638
1912–13.						
July	650	273	+ 377	328	437	− 109
August	646	256	+ 390	410	259	+ 151
September	380	532	− 152	385	246	+ 139
October	624	718	− 94	466	259	+ 207
November	580	919	− 339	565	226	+ 339
December	626	764	− 138	612	332	+ 280
January	332	513	− 181	411	136	+ 275
February	385	387	− 2	399	76	+ 323
March	497	280	+ 217	367	137	+ 230
April	663	400	+ 263	283	137	+ 146
May	654	396	+ 258	337	215	+ 122
June	734	209	+ 525	338	333	+ 5
Total	6,771	5,647	+1,124	4,901	2,793	+2,108

TABLE C.—OCCUPATIONS OF JAPANESE ADMITTED AND DEPARTED, FISCAL YEAR ENDED JUNE 30, 1913.

Occupation.	Continental U. S. Admitted.	Departed.	Hawaii. Admitted.	Departed.
PROFESSIONAL.				
Actors	6	7	15	8
Architects	9	4		
Clergy	30	19	13	9
Editors	20	21	4	
Electricians	5	5		
Engineers (professional)	73	68	2	
Lawyers	3	2		
Literary and scientific persons	9	5		1
Musicians		1	3	
Officials (Government)	56	50	1	1
Physicians	19	16	14	6
Sculptors and artists	11	6		
Teachers	53	40	47	13
Other professional	15	15	110	8
Total professional	309	259	209	46
SKILLED.				
Bakers	6	6		
Barbers and hairdressers	33	39	4	7
Blacksmiths		1	12	6
Cabinetmakers	1			
Carpenters and joiners	14	17	26	18
Clerks and accountants	78	75	16	14
Dressmakers	2	2		1
Engineers (locomotive, marine, and stationary)	9	8	5	7
Gardeners	20	37	1	2
Hat and cap makers		1	1	
Iron and steel workers	3			
Jewelers	3	2		
Machinists	5	3		
Mariners	2	5		1
Masons			3	
Mechanics (not specified)				1
Metal workers (other than iron, steel, and tin)	1			1

Occupation.	Continental U. S. Admitted.	Departed.	Hawaii. Admitted.	Departed.
SKILLED—continued.				
Millers	1			
Miners	3	10		
Painters and glaziers	2	4		1
Photographers	8	10	4	3
Plasterers				1
Plumbers		1	1	
Printers	11	6	3	1
Seamstresses	13	1	6	
Shoemakers	7	15		2
Tailors	23	29	30	23
Tinners				1
Watch and clock makers	1	2	3	2
Weavers and spinners			7	
Other skilled	55	83	3	1
Total skilled	301	357	126	93
MISCELLANEOUS.				
Agents	17	12	1	1
Bankers	23	25		
Draymen, hackmen, and teamsters	2		5	4
Farm laborers	472	227	3,725	572
Farmers	927	1,886	7	2
Fishermen	23	35	14	8
Hotel keepers	118	140	4	5
Laborers	542	1,211	29	1,520
Manufacturers	5	6	2	
Merchants and dealers	483	492	101	117
Servants	82	78	118	46
Other miscellaneous	783	365	56	44
Total miscellaneous	3,477	4,477	4,062	2,319
No occupation (including women and children)	2,684	554	504	335
Grand total	6,771	5,647	4,901	2,793

TABLE D.—STATISTICS OF IMMIGRATION AND EMIGRATION OF JAPANESE, COLLECTED BY THE UNITED STATES GOVERNMENT, COMPARED WITH THOSE REPORTED BY THE JAPANESE GOVERNMENT, FISCAL YEAR ENDED JUNE 30, 1913.

From Japan.	Reported by Japan.	Reported by U. S.	To Japan.	Reported by Japan.	Reported by U. S.
To Hawaii	5,358	4,925	From Hawaii	4,410	2,782
To continental U. S.	6,465	6,400	From continental U. S.	6,682	5,378
Total	11,823[1]	11,325[1]	Total	11,092[2]	8,160[1]

[1] Embarked within the year. [2] Debarked within the year.

TABLE E.—JAPANESE ARRIVALS IN CONTINENTAL UNITED STATES, FISCAL
JAPANESE

| | Came from— | | | | | | In possession of proper passports. | | |
| | | | | | | | Entitled to passports under Japanese agreement: Former residents. | | |
	Japan.	Hawaii.	Canada.	Mexico.	Europe.	Other countries.	Nonlaborers.	Laborers.	Total.
Total applications	6,381	87	46	76	232	37	1,661	1,176	2,837
Admitted:									
Male	3,608	66	29	59	221	29	1,506	1,154	2,660
Female	2,721	14	3	3	10	8	153	21	174
Total	6,329	80	32	62	231	37	1,659	1,175	2,834
Debarred:									
Male	42	6	13	13	1	.....	2	1	3
Female	10	1	1	1	.....	.....	.....	.....	.....
Total	52	7	14	14	· 1	.....	2	1	3
Housewives without other occupation	2,425	8	.....	2	7	3	146	....	146
Children under 14 without occupation	160	2	.....	.....	1	.....	5	....	5
Came from—									
Japan	6,381	.....	.....	.....	.....	.....	1,561	1,161	2,722
Hawaii	.....	87	.....	.....	.....	.....	14	2	16
Canada	.....	.....	46	.....	.....	.....	6	5	11
Mexico	.....	.....	.....	76	.....	.....	16	8	24
Europe	.....	.....	.....	.....	232	.....	56	....	56
Other countries	.....	.....	.....	.....	.....	37	8	....	8
Resided in continental United States:									
After Jan. 1, 1907	2,712	16	10	11	50	11	1,621	1,165	2,786
Prior to Jan. 1, 1907	11	.....	7	22	22	1	40	11	51
Total former residents	2,723	16	17	33	72	12	1,661	1,176	2,837
How related to resident:									
Parents	44	.....	.....	.....	.....	.....	.....	.....	.....
Wives	2,387	6	1	1	.....	3	.....	.....	.....
Children	614	28	.....	.....	.....	.....	.....	.....	.....
Total parents, wives, and children of residents	3,045	34	1	1	.....	3	.....	.....	.....
Kind of passport:									
Limited to United States	6,142	75	20	27	37	14	1,616	1,176	2,792
Limited to other countries	1	.....	1	.....	47	6	13	....	13
Limited to United States and other countries	154	1	5	.....	119	7	28	....	28
Unlimited	44	2	.....	1	9	3	4	....	4
Passports dated during—									
Month covered by this report	2,312	72	.....	.....	14	12	694	515	1,209
First month preceding	2,602	6	.....	.....	26	4	563	544	1,107
Second month preceding	742	.....	1	1	7	1	184	57	241
Third month preceding	345	.....	.....	.....	22	1	87	24	111
Fourth month preceding	150	.....	.....	1	19	.....	43	11	54
Fifth month preceding	87	.....	1	1	11	.....	22	8	30
Sixth month preceding	56	.....	.....	1	8	.....	18	1	19
Prior to sixth month, but not before Mar. 14, 1907	47	.....	11	11	95	7	29	7	36
Prior to Mar. 14, 1907	.....	.....	13	13	10	5	21	9	30
Occupations mentioned in passports:									
Nonlaboring occupations	956	41	8	2	167	18	463	33	496
Laboring occupations	166	2	7	1	.....	8	17	131	148
Occupations not mentioned in passports	5,219	35	11	25	45	4	1,181	1,012	2,193

[1] 18 nonlaborers and 25 laborers held passports limited to Hawaii, Canada, or Mexico; 2 laborers held passports not their own; 25 nonlaborers and 13 laborers claimed to have lost or left passports held at time of departure from Japan; 10 nonlaborers and 41 laborers were not in possession of any kind of passport at

YEAR ENDED JUNE 30, 1913, SHOWING VARIOUS DETAILS BEARING ON THE AGREEMENT.

In possession of proper passports—Continued.										Without proper passport.			With and without proper passport.		
Entitled to passports under Japanese agreement—Continued.					Total with proper passports.										
Parents, wives, and children of residents.			Settled agriculturists—nonlaborers.	Not former residents, parents, wives, or children of residents, nor settled agriculturists—nonlaborers.	Total entitled to passports.	Not entitled to passport: former residents, parents, wives, or children of residents, nor agriculturists—laborers.									
Nonlaborers.	Laborers.	Total.					Nonlaborers.	Laborers.	Total.	Nonlaborers.	Laborers.	Total.	Nonlaborers.	Laborers.	Grand total.
2,905	178	3,083	14	739	6,673	42	5,319	1,396	6,715	63	81	¹144	5,382	1,477	6,859
468	76	544	14	697	3,915	26	2,685	1,256	3,941	60	11	71	2,745	1,267	4,012
2,423	102	2,525	...	41	2,740	15	2,617	138	2,755	2	2	4	2,619	140	2,759
2,891	178	3,069	14	738	6,655	41	5,302	1,394	6,696	62	13	75	5,364	1,407	6,771
4		4	...	1	8	1	7	2	9	1	65	66	8	67	75
10		10	...		10		10		10	...	3	3	10	3	13
14		14	...	1	18	1	17	2	19	1	68	69	18	70	88
2,288		2,288	...	10	2,444		2,444		2,444	1		1	2,445		2,445
156		156	...	2	163		163		163				163		163
2,868	178	3,046	14	533	6,315	26	4,976	1,365	6,341	3	37	40	4,979	1,402	6,381
32		32	...	29	77	1	75	3	78	...	9	9	75	12	87
1		1	...	8	20	6	15	11	26	9	11	20	24	22	46
1		1	...	3	28		20	8	28	25	23	48	45	31	76
			...	156	212		212		212	20		20	232		232
3		3	...	10	21	9	21	9	30	6	1	7	27	10	37
					2,786		1,621	1,165	2,786	21	3	24	1,642	1,168	2,810
					51		40	11	51	5	7	12	45	18	63
					2,837		1,661	1,176	2,837	26	10	36	1,687	1,186	2,873
33	11	44			44		33	11	44				33	11	44
2,294	103	2,397			2,397		2,294	103	2,397	1		1	2,295	103	2,398
578	64	642			642		578	64	642				578	64	642
2,905	178	3,083	...		3,083		2,905	178	3,083	1		1	2,906	178	3,084
2,904	178	3,082	14	395	6,283	32	4,929	1,386	6,315						
				42	55		55		55						
				249	277	9	277	9	286						
1		1		53	58	1	58	1	59						
973	65	1,038	9	135	2,391	19	1,811	599	2,410						
1,207	80	1,287	4	232	2,630	8	2,006	632	2,638						
382	19	401	1	106	749	3	673	79	752						
185	5	190	...	65	366	2	337	31	368						
77	2	79	...	36	169	1	156	14	170						
32	2	34	...	34	98	2	88	12	100						
27	2	29	...	16	64	1	62	3	65						
22	3	25	...	107	168	3	157	14	171						
				8	38	3	29	12	41						
272		272	12	406	1,186	6	1,153	39	1,192						
6	5	11	...	1	160	24	24	160	184						
2,627	173	2,800	2	332	5,327	12	4,142	1,197	5,339						

time of leaving Japan; 3 nonlaborers were diplomats holding no passport and 1 nonlaborer holding no passport was a resident of the United States, and as to 6 nonlaborers the reason for not being in possession of proper passports are not known.

TABLE F.—JAPANESE ARRIVALS IN HAWAII, FISCAL YEAR ENDED JUNE 30, 1913, SHOWING VARIOUS DETAILS BEARING ON THE JAPANESE AGREEMENT.

	Came from—		In possession of passports.															Without passport.			With and without passport.		
			Entitled to passports under Japanese agreement.									Not entitled to passport.			Total with passports.								
	Japan.	Other countries.	Former residents of Hawaii.			Parents, wives, and children of Hawaiian residents.			Total entitled to passports.			Not former residents nor parents, wives, or children of residents.											
			Non-laborers.	Laborers.	Total.	Non-laborers.	Laborers.	Total.	Non-laborers.	Laborers.	Total.	Non-laborers.	Laborers.	Total.	Non-laborers.	Laborers.	Total.	Non-laborers.	Laborers.	Total.	Non-laborers.	Laborers.	Grand total.
Total applications	5,076	3	304	977	1,281	439	3,182	3,621	743	4,159	4,902	147	20	167	880	4,179	5,069	4	8	12	894	4,187	5,081
Admitted:																							
Male	2,173	3	177	760	937	229	879	1,108	406	1,639	2,045	109	16	125	515	1,655	2,170	3	3	6	518	1,658	2,176
Female	2,725		124	214	338	196	2,150	2,346	320	2,364	2,684	35	4	39	355	2,368	2,723		2	2	355	2,370	2,725
Total	4,898	3	301	974	1,275	425	3,029	3,454	726	4,003	4,729	144	20	164	870	4,023	4,893	3	5	8	873	4,028	4,901
Debarred:																							
Male	57		2	3	5	9	38	47	11	41	52	2		2	13	41	54	1	2	3	14	43	57
Female	123		1		1	5	115	120	6	115	121	1		1	7	115	122		1	1	7	116	123
Total	180		3	3	6	14	153	167	17	156	173	3		3	20	156	176	1	3	4	21	159	180
Housewives without other occupation	79		35		35	42		42	77		77	2		2	79		79				79		79
Children under 14 without occupation	208		17		17	189		189	206		206	2		2	208		208				208		208
Resided in Hawaii:																							
After Jan. 1, 1907	1,069		232	837	1,069				232	837	1,069				232	837	1,069				232	837	1,069
Prior to Jan. 1, 1907	212		72	140	212				72	140	212				72	140	212				72	140	212
Total former residents	1,281		304	977	1,281				304	977	1,281				304	977	1,281				304	977	1,281

How related to resident:																							
Parents	308					7	301	308	7	301	308				7	301	308				7	301	308
Wives	2,198					95	2,103	2,198	95	2,103	2,198				95	2,103	2,198				95	2,103	2,198
Children	1,115					337	778	1,115	337	778	1,115				337	778	1,115				337	778	1,115
Total parents, wives, and children of residents	3,621					439	3,182	3,621	439	3,182	3,621				439	3,182	3,621				439	3,182	3,621
Kind of passport:																							
Limited to Hawaii	5,052		295	977	1,272	439	3,182	3,621	734	4,159	4,893	139	20	159	873	4,179	5,052						
Limited to United States	13		8		8				8		8	5		5	13		13						
Limited to other countries	4		1		1				1		1	3		3	4		4						
Passports dated during:																							
Month covered by this report	2,304		139	517	656	180	1,395	1,575	319	1,912	2,231	59	14	73	378	1,926	2,304						
First month preceding	2,513		100	423	523	228	1,697	1,925	328	2,120	2,448	60	5	65	388	2,125	2,513						
Second month preceding	146		39	22	61	20	56	76	59	78	137	8	1	9	67	79	146						
Third month preceding	49		15	2	17	5	18	23	20	20	40	9		9	29	20	49						
Fourth month preceding	30		6	7	13	5	5	10	11	12	23	7		7	18	12	30						
Fifth month preceding	22		5	5	10	1	9	10	6	14	20	2		2	8	14	22						
Sixth month preceding	5			1	1		2	2		3	3	2		2	2	3	5						
Occupations mentioned in passports:																							
Nonlaboring occupations	84		46		46	2		2	48		48	35	1	36	83	1	84						
Laboring occupations	1												1	1		1	1						
Occupations not mentioned in passports	4,984		258	977	1,235	437	3,182	3,619	695	4,159	4,854	112	18	130	807	4,177	4,984						

[1] 4 nonlaborers and 3 laborers claimed to have lost or left passports held at time of departure from Japan, and 5 laborers were not in possession of any kind of passport at time of leaving Japan.

TABLE 1.—SUMMARY OF CHINESE SEEKING ADMISSION TO THE UNITED STATES, FISCAL YEARS ENDED JUNE 30, 1908–1913, BY CLASSES.

Class alleged.	1908		1909			1910			1911		1912			1913		
	Admitted.	Deported.	Admitted.	Deported.	Escaped.	Admitted.	Deported.	Escaped.	Admitted.	Deported.	Admitted.	Deported.	Died.	Admitted.	Deported.	Escaped.
United States citizens	1,609	127	2,530	254	16	2,109	490	5	1,639	284	1,756	170	1	2,171	121	....
Wives of United States citizens	37	2	98	2	....	110	14	....	80	5	88	5	....	126	9	....
Returning laborers	883	36	950	3	....	1,037	12	....	1,113	19	1,103	1	....	1,036	5	....
Returning merchants	773	55	947	20	5	869	31	....	1,092	33	1,093	18	1	986	13	1
Other merchants	216	11	292	19	....	228	29	....	199	28	170	8	....	105	16	....
Members of merchants' families	806	128	1,242	237	10	1,029	332	....	559	259	558	133	....	738	92	....
Students	157	3	161	6	....	268	31	....	213	25	413	20	....	370	11	....
Travelers	13	....	27	....	....	83	3	....	52	....	80	7	....	19	....	....
Teachers	23	....	14	....	....	24	1	....	32	....	33	1	....	33	1	....
Officials	83	....	82	....	....	145	....	1	87	....	47	1	....	38	....	....
Miscellaneous	24	2	52	23	....	48	26	....	41	39	33	36	....	40	116	....
Total	4,624	364	6,395	564	31	5,950	969	6	5,107	692	5,374	400	2	5,662	384	1

TABLE 2.—CHINESE SEEKING ADMISSION TO THE UNITED STATES, FISCAL YEAR ENDED JUNE 30, 1913, BY CLASSES AND PORTS.

Class or port	Applications: New applications	Applications: Pending July 1, 1912	Applications: Total	Preliminary — Rejected: By inspectors	Preliminary — Rejected: Appeals dismissed by department	Preliminary — Rejected: Writs dismissed by courts	Final — Admitted: By inspectors	Final — Admitted: By department	Final — Admitted: By court	Final — Admitted: Male	Final — Admitted: Female	Final — Admitted: Total	Deported: Male	Deported: Female	Deported: Total	Escaped	Pending June 30, 1913: Before inspectors	Pending June 30, 1913: Before department	Pending June 30, 1913: Before courts	Pending June 30, 1913: Total	Total cases
By classes:																					
U. S. citizens	2,382	74	2,456	166	62		2,149	21	1	2,076	95	2,171	121		121		127	35	2	164	2,456
Wives of U. S. citizens	153	5	158	10	3		123	3			126	126		9	9		16	7		23	158
Returning laborers	1,047	4	1,051	7			1,033	3		1,035	1	1,036	5		5		10			10	1,051
Returning merchants	1,011	14	1,025	17	7		980	6		984	2	986	13		13		20	5	1	26	1,025
Other merchants	122	9	131	19	17		98	7		105		105	16		16		2	8		10	131
Merchants' wives	176	3	179	7	4		153	2			155	155		6	6		15	3		18	179
Merchants' children	723	69	792	104	43		563	20		555	28	583	85	1	86	1	96	12		110	792
Students	345	53	398	12	5		366	4		351	19	370	10	1	11		10	19		29	398
Travelers	19		19				19			17	2	19								1	19
Teachers	33	2	35				32			32	1	33	1		1			1		2	35
Officials	40		40				38			36	2	38						2			40
Miscellaneous	199	9	208	100	37		40	1		29	11	40	107	9	116		15	37	2	52	208
Total	6,250	242	6,492	442	178		5,594	67	1	5,220	442	5,662	358	26	384	1	311	129	5	445	6,492
By ports:																					
San Francisco, Cal.	3,696	200	3,896	220	93		3,340	43	1	3,145	239	3,384	162	8	170		235	103	4	342	3,896
Seattle, Wash.	1,204	22	1,286	67	26		1,171	5		1,128	48	1,176	56	5	61	1	38	9	1	48	1,286
Honolulu, Hawaii	797		797	81	35		694	4		578	120	698	72	9	81		18			18	797
Baltimore, Md.	11		11	1	1		7			3	4	7	4		4						11
New York, N. Y.	46	2	48	12	18		33			31	2	33	13		13		1	1		2	48
Vancouver, B. C.	391	16	407	50	2		328	15		316	27	343	31	3	34		18	12		30	407
Montreal, Canada	23	2	25	6	2		10			9	1	10	9	1	10		1	4		5	25
Philadelphia, Pa.	2		2	2									2		2						2
New Orleans, La.	6		6	1									6		6						6
Mexican border stations	14		14	2			11			10	1	11	3		3						14
Total	6,250	242	6,492	442	178		5,594	67	1	5,220	442	5,662	358	26	384	1	311	129	5	445	6,492
Section 6 cases	489	83	572	31	22		494	11		489	16	505	25	1	26		12	29		41	572

TABLE 3.—CHINESE CLAIMING AMERICAN CITIZENSHIP ADMITTED, FISCAL YEAR ENDED JUNE 30, 1913, BY PORTS.

Port.	Foreign-born children of natives.	Native born.				Total.
		No record of departure (known as "raw natives").	Record of departure (known as "returning natives").			
			Status as native born determined by U. S. Government previous to present application for admission.	Status not previously determined.		
San Francisco, Cal.	435	75	578	184		1,272
Seattle, Wash.	19	2	291	6		318
Baltimore, Md.			6			6
New York, N. Y.			1			1
Vancouver, B. C.	28	1	139	3		171
Montreal, Can.		1	2			3
Mexican border.	2			1		3
Total continental United States	484	79	1,017	194		1,774
Honolulu, Hawaii.	11	162	63	38		274
Grand total	495	241	1,080	232		2,048
BY WHOM ADMITTED.						
Inspection officers.	479	240	1,078	230		2,027
Department.	16	1	2	2		21

TABLE 4.—APPEALS TO DEPARTMENT FROM EXCLUDING DECISIONS UNDER CHINESE-EXCLUSION LAWS, FISCAL YEAR ENDED JUNE 30, 1913, BY PORTS.

Action taken.	San Francisco, Cal.	Seattle, Wash.	Honolulu, Hawaii.	Mexican border.	New York, N. Y.	Vancouver, B. C.	Montreal, Canada.	Total.
Number of appeals	136	31	39	3	1	33	2	245
Disposition:								
Sustained (admitted)	43	5	4			15		67
Dismissed (rejected)	93	26	35	3	1	18	2	178

TABLE 5.—DISPOSITION OF CASES OF RESIDENT CHINESE APPLYING FOR RETURN CERTIFICATES, FISCAL YEAR ENDED JUNE 30, 1913.

Class.	Applications submitted.	Primary disposition.		Disposition on appeal.		Total number of certificates granted.	Total number of certificates finally refused.
		Granted.	Denied.	Sustained.	Dismissed.		
Native born	1,261	1,180	81	6	28	1,186	75
Exempt classes	1,055	990	65	3	10	993	62
Laborers	847	826	21	1	7	827	20
Total	3,163	2,996	167	10	45	3,006	157

TABLE 6.—ACTION TAKEN IN THE CASES OF CHINESE PERSONS ARRESTED ON THE CHARGE OF BEING IN THE UNITED STATES IN VIOLATION OF LAW, FISCAL YEAR ENDED JUNE 30, 1913.

CASES BEFORE UNITED STATES COMMISSIONERS.

Until order of deportation or discharge:
Arrests.. 191
Pending before hearing at close of previous year......................... 163

Total... 354

Disposition:
Discharged... 71
Pending before hearing at close of present year...... 120
Ordered deported.. 163

After order of deportation:
Ordered deported.. 163
Awaiting deportation or appeal at close of previous year................. 35

Total... 198

Disposition:
Deported.. 103
Awaiting deportation or appeal to United States district courts at close
of present year.. 14
Appealed to United States district courts........................... 81

CASES BEFORE UNITED STATES DISTRICT COURTS.

Until order of deportation or discharge:
Appealed to United States district courts................................ 81
Pending before trial at close of previous year.......................... 139

Total... 220

Disposition:
Forfeited bail.. 11
Discharged.. 45
Pending before trial at close of present year.......................... 85
Ordered deported.............. :..................................... 79

After order of deportation:
Ordered deported.. 79
Awaiting deportation or appeal to higher courts at close of previous year.... 5

Total... 84

Disposition:
Deported.. 47
Awaiting deportation or appeal at close of present year................ 19
Appealed to higher courts... 18

CASES BEFORE HIGHER UNITED STATES COURTS.

Until order of deportation or discharge:
Appealed to higher United States courts................................. 18
Pending before trial at close of previous year.......................... 6

Total... 24

Disposition:
Discharged.. 1
Pending before trial at close of present year.......................... 17
Ordered deported.. 6

7686°—14——10

After order of deportation:
Ordered deported... 6
Awaiting deportation at close of previous year............................ 23

Total... 29

Disposition:
Escaped... 1
Deported.. 15
Awaiting deportation at close of present year........................... 13

RECAPITULATION OF ALL CASES.

Arrests.. 191
Pending at close of previous year, including those waiting deportation or appeal.. 371

Total... 562

Disposition:
Died, escaped, and forfeited bail....................................... 12
Discharged.. 117
Deported.. 165
Pending at close of present year, including those awaiting deportation
or appeal... 268

SUMMARY OF ACTION TAKEN IN THE CASES OF CHINESE ARRESTED, FISCAL YEAR
ENDED JUNE 30, 1913, BY MONTHS.

	July.	Aug.	Sept.	Oct.	Nov.	Dec.	Jan.	Feb.	Mar.	Apr.	May.	June.	Total.
Arrests made.................................	12	10	13	19	20	19	15	10	26	17	14	16	191
Died, escaped, and forfeited bail..............	1	1	1						1		3	5	12
Discharged..................................	13	5	2	6	15	17	8	17	12	3	7	12	117
Deported...................................	34	3	6	8	22	3	16	3	18	17	27	8	165

TABLE 7.—CHINESE ARRESTED AND DEPORTED, FISCAL YEARS ENDED JUNE 30, 1909–1913, BY JUDICIAL DISTRICTS.

Judicial district.	1910		1911		1912		1913	
	Arrests.	Deportations.	Arrests.	Deportations.	Arrests.	Deportations.	Arrests.	Deportations.
Vermont		1			4			
New Hampshire								
Massachusetts	1		4	1	6		2	
Connecticut			1					
Northern New York	36	15	58	12	13	24	2	5
Southern New York	5	3	20	5	27	17	18	12
Western New York		6	3	1	6	4	2	1
Eastern New York	4		5	1	10	7	8	
Eastern Pennsylvania	1				5			
Western Pennsylvania	2	1					3	
Middle Pennsylvania	1							
New Jersey	1				2	1	6	2
Maryland	8	3	2		1	1	1	1
District of Columbia	4	2					1	
South Carolina	6	2						
Eastern Virginia	1				3			
Northern Georgia	2	1						
Southern Florida					1			
Middle Alabama								
Northern Mississippi					1			
Southern Mississippi			1	1	1			1
Eastern Louisiana	8	6	4				1	
Western Louisiana					1	1	1	2
Western Tennessee			2		2			
Middle Tennessee							1	
Northern Ohio	1		1		2		3	2
Southern Ohio			1		1		1	
Indiana					2		1	
Northern Illinois	22	1	27	13	43	7	10	22
Southern Illinois			1	1	2			
Eastern Michigan	3	2	2		7	5	1	
Western Michigan	21	6	1			1	1	
Minnesota	7				6		5	
Western Wisconsin	1							
Eastern Wisconsin	1							
North Dakota			1					
South Dakota			1					
Eastern Missouri	7	7	1				3	1
Nebraska			8	4				
Idaho	13	7	3		1		2	
Montana			1	1			1	
Wyoming								
Kansas							1	
Eastern Washington	5	1	1					
Western Washington	8	4	5	7	7	8	5	2
Oregon	8	2	1	2	5	4		1
Nevada								
Utah	1						6	3
Northern California	29	13	23	13	49	25	42	27
Southern California	19	20	172	135	170	120	33	57
Colorado	1		1	1				
Arizona	302	349	85	74	52	49	10	11
New Mexico	93	73	56	65	23	27	3	6
Northern Texas	32	29	8	9	19	20	4	3
Southern Texas	18	18	4	3				
Eastern Texas					6	6		
Western Texas	272	226	157	168	137	69	10	6
Oklahoma		1						
Eastern Arkansas	3	1						
Hawaii	30	25	8	5	2		1	
First Alaska							2	
Total	977	825	669	522	616	397	191	165

TABLE 8.—MISCELLANEOUS CHINESE TRANSACTIONS, BY PORTS, FISCAL YEAR ENDED JUNE 30, 1913.

Class.	San Francisco, Cal.	Seattle, Wash.	Honolulu, Hawaii.	Montreal, Canada.	Vancouver, B.C.	New York, N.Y.	Mexican border.	New Orleans, La.	Baltimore, Md.	Philadelphia, Pa.	Total.
United States citizens (Chinese) admitted	1,372	318	296	3	172	2	6		7		2,176
Alien Chinese admitted	2,012	859	402	7	171	31	5				3,487
Alien Chinese debarred	170	61	81	9	34	14	3	6	4	2	384
Chinese granted the privilege of transit in bond across land territory of the United States	966	2		587			373	216	124		2,268
Chinese denied the privilege of transit in bond across land territory of the United States	128			23			7		30		188
Chinese granted the privilege of transit by water	620	2					22	2	30		676
Chinese denied the privilege of transit by water	81						1				82
Chinese laborers with return certificates departing	346	349	271		98						1,064
Chinese merchants with return certificates departing	723	250	56	1	49		1				1,080
Chinese students with return certificates departing	11	10	1	3	4	2					31
Chinese teachers with return certificates departing	1	2	5								8
Native-born Chinese with return certificates departing	875	267	44	1	134	1	1				1,323

ANNUAL REPORT OF THE CHIEF OF THE DIVISION OF INFORMATION

FOR THE

FISCAL YEAR ENDED JUNE 30, 1913

REPORT

OF THE

CHIEF OF THE DIVISION OF INFORMATION.

DEPARTMENT OF LABOR,
BUREAU OF IMMIGRATION,
DIVISION OF INFORMATION,
Washington, July 1, 1913.

Herewith is submitted the annual report of the Division of Information for the year ended June 30, 1913.

As in former years, tables are presented showing a part of the activities of the division. They give the number applying in person for information, the number directed to opportunities, the callings of those applying, together with their races and the States to which they were directed.

Table I deals with those applying directly at the branches of the division. As in former years many applicants stated that they represented groups all the members of which could not find it convenient to call in person.

While these tables do not deal with those applying by mail for information concerning the purchase, rental, or character of lands, the number so applying is considerable and constantly increasing. Such correspondence is turned over to the State, or group of States, concerning which inquiry is made and the writers so informed. They are also supplied with the division's bulletin of Agricultural Opportunities which relates to the locality indicated by the correspondent.

In this connection it is worthy of mention, and consideration also, that correspondence received from residents of Euporean countries indicate a growing desire to know more about the opportunities for the agriculturist in the United States. Those who write for themselves and in behalf of groups of their fellow countrymen are, apparently, of an exceptionally industrious class. In nearly every instance they are men who own their farms, but wish to dispose of them, migrate to and invest in farm lands in the United States. As a rule the writers express a preference for some particular State, group of States, or locality near good markets. They also indicate what kind of crops they have been accustomed to growing. They state explicitly that they wish to migrate to the United States to engage in agriculture, the amount of capital they possess, and how well equipped they are to prosecute the work in this country. Under existing law no encouragement can be extended to those residing abroad to come to the United States for the purpose indicated, but their letters are referred to the officials of the States most likely to offer the inducements they seek. These inquiries come principally from Germans, Hollanders, Poles, and Belgians. The writers possess means, the fruit of agriculture, and should prove desirable

151

acquisitions to the rural population of this country.   In all probability such people will migrate anyway, and it would be far better to direct them to the place and the kind of land they desire than have them waste time and means in seeking the proper locality after landing here.   The following is a translation of a letter received in May from Piotrowska, Russia Poland:

We take the liberty of writing to you for information in regard to farm lands which we wish to purchase for cash in the United States of America.   There will be about 207 prospective settlers who would be ready to start to emigrate to America, North or South, in next fall.   We would like to know the laws governing settlers of foreign birth.   Also we would like to get information as to the kind of land there is for sale, where, price per acre, whether for cash or installment plans.   Please give us the prices in dollars and rubles.   We would also like to know whether the section of the country where the land is for sale is inhabited.   The majority of us would like to buy land and own it.   * * *   We would also like to know whether there is any difficulty of hiring farm hands and what the current wages are.

If the officials of the various States have given the required information as suggested by the division, it is probable this country will be the gainer, for those who are far-seeing enough to settle the question of where the right kind of land may be had before migrating will undoubtedly make good farmers and citizens.

Others writing from foreign countries state, among other things, what capital they possess.   A resident of Bavaria writes that he has 8,000 marks ($1,904) with which to buy land here.

It appears that the bulletins of the division, which dwell briefly on the agricultural opportunities of the United States, have found their way to agriculturists in Europe, and as a result the advantages of farm life in the United States are being considered abroad.

Reference to Table I will show that among foreigners the Germans lead all others in applying for information, 2,411 having applied in person.   The Poles come next, with 2,268 applicants.   Spain furnishes 1,125, while Swedish applicants number 1,306.   Information was given to 2,552 native-born citizens of the United States.   Many of these, as in former years, represented groups of men who could not apply in person.   The number of naturalized citizens applying was 534, making a total of 3,086 citizens who sought the aid of the division in obtaining information concerning agricultural or common-labor opportunities.

Among those who went direct to places indicated by the division, the Polish and German are in the lead among foreigners, but American citizens furnish the largest number of those directly benefited.   See Table III.

It is gratifying to be able to say that the number of complaints received from those directed by the division was less than in former years, and in each case the cause was traced and a satisfactory remedy applied.

Table I.—Applications for Information, Fiscal Year Ended June 30, 1913, by Races or Peoples and by Occupations.

Race or people.	Bakers.	Barbers.	Blacksmiths.	Bookbinders.	Butchers.	Carpenters.	Clerks.	Domestics.	Drivers.	Electricians.	Engineers (civil).	Engineers (mechanical).	Engravers.	Factory hands.	Farmers.	Farm laborers.	Firemen.	Fishermen.	Furriers.	Gardeners.	Hat and cap makers.	Hotel porters.	Interpreters.	Iron and steel workers.	Jewelers and watchmakers.	Laborers.
Arabian (Morocco)																4	1					2				65
Armenian	1		3			1	1	3	1					10		26	5			2				6		38
Bohemian		1																								6
Bosnian								2						2		1	2					4				1
Bulgarian	3	2							5					3		40	8							2		18
Canadian	6		1				1	3	2	5		1		3	3	10	89			2		2				38
Croatian	1				1			33		3				62		237	15	11		6		49		5		17
Cuban				2	2		2	17						23	1	82	16			7		15	1			52
Dalmatian																										100
Danish			6		2	25	18	13	5	1		1		10	4	53	39			5	2	8		1		44
Dutch				1	1	10	10	11	2	2		1		28	10	117	8			3	1	9		30		1
Egyptian							1									14	7			1				1		58
English	1	1	19	1	1	333	8	70	81	26	3	2		8		47	118		1	3	1	3	1	8	1	255
Finnish			3		2	1	1	11	12	2				208		642	161			63	1	172		32		8
Flemish								17						45		38	2					5		20		48
French			18	2	17	64	2	8	72	15		2		171	4	76	29			18	10	34		1	1	389
German	26		6	1	2	23	64	40	14	8		4		58		13	35			30	4	2		23	3	212
Greek	5	1	4		4	10	9	17	1	16			1	73		245	8					91		30		63
Hebrew		2			1	27	19	8	2	3				12	1	142	21			4		37		2		5
Herzegovinian						7	3		4					27		4	3							1		
Irish	3	4	14	3	5	1	25	24	15	1				3		62	151			10		1				316
Italian			1		9	3	1	76	18	7	1			59	1	74	74					11				296
Lettish																5										4
Lithuanian	1					2	6	6						188	2	208	3		1			13		101		72
Magyar	1					55	6	76	1					13		550	151			10		125				87
Mexican						41		6						6		6	74			34		3				35
Montenegrin							2	1								34	3									4
Norwegian	7					2				7	1						75							1		144
Persian																										
Polish																										765
Porto Rican																										27
Portuguese			1																							127

TABLE I.—APPLICATIONS FOR INFORMATION, FISCAL YEAR ENDED JUNE 30, 1913, BY RACES OR PEOPLES AND BY OCCUPATIONS—Continued.

Race or people.	Bakers.	Barbers.	Blacksmiths.	Bookbinders.	Butchers.	Carpenters.	Clerks.	Domestics.	Drivers.	Electricians.	Engineers (civil).	Engineers (mechanical).	Engravers.	Factory hands.	Farmers.	Farm laborers.	Firemen.	Fishermen.	Furriers.	Gardeners.	Hat and cap makers.	Hotel porters.	Interpreters.	Iron and steel workers.	Jewelers and watchmakers.	Laborers.
Roumanian	1		2			7		11	4	1				1	1	12	4			10	3	32		8		35
Russian	1		1			1	1	2	2	2				55		302	34			1				46		468
Ruthenian										1				1		55	3									89
Scotch								1						3		19	3							2		20
Servian																5	2									17
Slovak	1	1	6											12		44	6							9		81
Slovenian		1	11												2		1			1		1				13
Spanish	2		2		2	21	29	7	1	7		2		40	1	94	417					2		38		256
South American							6					1		2		8	6					6				7
Swedish			1		3	81	11	28	10	14	1	3		90		298	130			45		22	1	29		235
Swiss				1		2	5	3	2	3		1		1		46	1			2		4	1	1		16
Syrian					2	3	3							8		11								5		57
Turkish	11		2		1		1							3		1										7
United States born (negroes)					2	55	54	81	152	17		5		300	12	607	62			35	1	160		79		571
United States born			1					3	1					2		25	10					3				31
United States naturalized citizens			2			5	8	14	24	1				46	2	206	13			17		27		7		146
Total	70	9	101	9	55	786	299	515	432	135	5	23	1	1,601	42	4,465	1,564	11	1	300	23	833	2	488	4	6,344

TABLE I.—APPLICATIONS FOR INFORMATION, FISCAL YEAR ENDED JUNE 30, 1913, BY RACES OR PEOPLES AND BY OCCUPATIONS—Continued.

Race or people.	Literary and scientific persons.	Locksmiths.	Machinists.	Mariners.	Masons.	Merchants.	Metal workers (other than iron and steel).	Millers.	Miners.	Painters.	Plasterers.	Plumbers and pipe fitters.	Printers.	Saddlers and harness makers.	Shipwrights and joiners.	Shoemakers.	Stonecutters and drillers.	Tailors.	Tanners and curriers.	Tinners.	Tobacco workers.	Upholsterers.	Weavers.	Wheelwrights.	Woodworkers, turners, etc.	Total.
Arabian (Morocco)			4						1					2				2		1			1			1
Armenian			7		2																					74
Bohemian				2																						110
Bosnian				1																						6
Bulgarian			3	4												1		1								4
Canadian			1	11						1																74
Croatian				117																						58
Cuban				28																						41
Dalmatian			28	18																						90
Danish			18	64				3		7		4			4	1					7		3	2	1	824
Dutch				3				2		13	1		3		72									4		300
Egyptian					1					6																2
English		4	7	103	1	6	3		10	3	1	13	12	2	9	2		1		6	3	1	9	2	2	217
Finnish		3	16	28	1	4	16	7		2	1	5	10			1				1		3	1	4		1,009
Flemish			2		2			1	2	20	1	1		1			1			1			4			41
French			11		16		3	3	18											1						173
German		8	131	16	8	2	36	1	32		2						6	3			3	3				2,411
Greek			11	33	24		2	3	7	22								8					5			588
Hebrew				3			2					1				3		7		1			3			471
Herzegovinian					4		5		2	4	2							1		1						44
Irish		1	15	16	4		46		65			1						10			12		1		8	961
Italian		1	60	33	1		1																			1,024
Lettish			1	3																						14
Lithuanian			9		4																					170
Magyar			6	2	15					4			3		3											284
Mexican				2	1					4																65
Montenegrin																										8
Norwegian		1	45	158				1				1														925
Persian		1	1		15																					2
Polish			35	41																						2,288
Porto Rican		2	1	5	1											8					12				8	76
Portuguese			1	3																						256

TABLE I.—APPLICATIONS FOR INFORMATION, FISCAL YEAR ENDED JUNE 30, 1913, BY RACES OR PEOPLES AND BY OCCUPATIONS—Continued.

Race or people.	Literary and scientific persons.	Locksmiths.	Machinists.	Mariners.	Masons.	Merchants.	Metal workers (other than iron and steel).	Millers.	Miners.	Painters.	Plasterers.	Plumbers and pipe fitters.	Printers.	Saddlers and harness makers.	Shipwrights and joiners.	Shoemakers.	Stonecutters and drillers.	Tailors.	Tanners and curriers.	Tinners.	Tobacco workers.	Upholsterers.	Weavers.	Wheelwrights.	Woodworkers, turners, etc.	Total.
Roumanian			4	15					28	2			1					3								61
Russian			1		2		2		2	1																1,030
Ruthenian																										159
Scotch			3	2					3																	57
Servian			2	2																						25
Slovak		1	38	46	9		15	3	68	8		4				1										161
Slovenian			1	8	1		4			1	1						1									22
Spanish		1	82	156		1	1		7	18		8	6		6		3		2						2	1,125
South American			4				2																		1	42
Swedish			4																							1,306
Swiss			6	2	5							2						2	1							96
Syrian			2	32	1																1					120
Turkish																										20
United States born (negroes)	3	1	100	10			27		10	36	3	19	18	1	3	1		3		7		3	18		2	2,475
United States born																							1			77
United States naturalized citizens			4																							534
Total	3	23	663	926	97	13	165	15	258	146	11	61	53	6	97	27	14	44	3	16	23	7	54	6	42	19,891

TABLE II.—DISTRIBUTION OF ALIENS AND OTHERS APPLYING TO DIVISION OF INFORMATION, FISCAL YEAR 1913, BY STATES AND BY OCCUPATIONS.

State	Bakers	Bakers, assistant	Blacksmiths	Blacksmith helpers	Boarding-house keepers	Cabinetmakers	Carpenters	Carpenters' apprentices	Children (unemployed)	Deck hands	Domestics	Factory workers	Farmers	Farm workers	Firemen	Foremen	Fisherman	Gardeners	Garden workers	Harness makers	Hostlers	Hotel workers	Interpreters	Janitors, assistant	Laborers (common)	Machinists	Miscellaneous	Painters	Porters	Seamen	Seeking employment	Shoemakers	Stable hands	Tailors	Teamsters	Upholsterers	Waiters	Watchmen	Wives (employed)	Wives (unemployed)	Woodsman	Total
Alabama									4					1											2															1		7
California						4	2		5		4			120			1								78		2												7	1		220
Connecticut														12											89		1															101
Illinois									3		2						4										1															3
Indiana														15													1				2									1		22
Iowa	2										2			7				3									1			2										1		7
Kansas									2					10			8								157						1								1	1		199
Louisiana														5											17		1															6
Maine									1					1											66														16			18
Maryland														44								3			51														22			112
Massachusetts														24											17								4		5		3	1	4			75
Michigan														15						1					10		1	3	6		1	1			5				1			20
Minnesota																									8				75				1	1	5		1					25
Mississippi																																									38	52
Missouri									2			41		2											3		6															8
Montana														2																												2
Nebraska																																										10
New Hampshire																			17																							
New Jersey							1		13	25	15	6		773				9			2			6	251	4	6	3	6			1							16	5		1,114
New York			3				50	2	13		63			815				1					3		530	1	16		75										8	3		1,707
North Dakota														5																												5
Ohio														8	1										124		1	1											4			134
Pennsylvania					1				1		1	1		9		2									941	1	1				2								1			978
Rhode Island														3																												4
South Dakota														1																												1
Tennessee							1		1					16											21														4			23
Texas									7		5	1		8	2										5		1												1			27
Vermont														2											90																	99
Virginia																																										4
Washington																																										1
West Virginia							1																		22																	22
Wisconsin	2	2	1	1								1	1	16													1															18
Total	2	2	4	1	2	6	56	2	49	25	90	49	1	1,920	13	3	13	12	17	1	2	3	3	6	2,482	5	31	4	81	2	8	1	4	1	10	1	4	1	53	17	38	5,025

TABLE III.—DISTRIBUTION OF ALIENS AND OTHERS APPLYING TO THE DIVISION OF INFORMATION, FISCAL YEAR ENDED JUNE 30, 1913, BY STATES AND BY RACES OR PEOPLES.

State	Arabian	Argentinian	Armenian	Australian	Austrian	Belgian	Bohemian	Bosnian	British West Indian	Brazilian	Canadian	Chilean	Costa Rican	Croatian	Cuban	Dalmatian	Danish	Dutch	Egyptian	English	Esthonian	Finnish	Flemish	French	German	Greek	Hebrew	Hindoo
California							1		1								6	2			1	31		6	1	1	1	
Connecticut					1												7					1		4	29	1		
Illinois																	3			3		1			12			
Iowa													1												7			1
Kansas																												
Louisiana				3	50												1	1		2					1	1		
Maine																	2	1		1		13		16	16			
Maryland																	8					9						
Massachusetts																	1								1			
Michigan					8												1											
Minnesota																												
Mississippi																												
Missouri							2									1												
Montana																	1											
New Hampshire			1				2		3											5					9			
New Jersey			6		1	2	9		8		8														7			
New York		3				1	9	1		1	7			4		4								2	5	5	1	
North Dakota																												
Ohio						2	8			2	1			1	7	6			2						2			
Pennsylvania	2		7				5							1			50	8		8	1	41	1	5	185	9	12	
Rhode Island																	63	18		27	5	88		11	286	11	17	
Tennessee																									3			
Texas			4		5											1	6	3		2	1	23	1	8	37	119		
Vermont																	4	1		3				3	4	7		
Virginia																									2			
Washington																	2	1							1		1	
West Virginia														1						1		1			7			
Wisconsin																	2								11			
Total	2	3	18	3	65	5	36	1	12	3	16	....	1	7	7	12	157	35	2	52	8	212	2	55	638	154	32	1

State	Irish	Italian	Lettish	Lithuanian	Magyar	Maltese	Mexican	Montenegrin	Norwegian	Persian	Polish	Portuguese	Porto Rican	Roumanian	Russian	Ruthenian	Scotch	Servian	Siamese	Slovenian	Slovak	Spanish	Swede	Swiss	Syrian	Turkish	U.S. Citizen	Total
Alabama	7																	1										7
California	1	14		4	3		2		10	1	29	4			15	5	1				3	22	28	5	1		29	1
Connecticut		2							2						1								5				20	220
Illinois				1			1			1	4		3		2								1				3	101
Indiana	2										1				7	1							1				3	3
Iowa	5																										2	22
Kansas											2																1	7
Louisiana	2								3																		16	199
Maine	1			1																							3	6
Maryland		24		1							31																1	18
Massachusetts		3							1		21					8						1	6				2	112
Michigan											1					5	1						5				4	75
Minnesota																							5					20
Mississippi																			1	1			1					25
Missouri											1												1					62
Montana									1		2																2	8
Nebraska																												2
New Hampshire																												10
New Jersey	64	26	4	15	1				23		132	1	5	4	86	16	3	4			6	6	35	1			325	1,114
New York	76	69		13	3				42		213	8	2	3	112	22	9	5			9	35	63	12	2	2	439	1,707
North Dakota											1												1				10	5
Ohio	3	4		2	10		3	3	1		12			3	19		2				1		4	14			18	134
Pennsylvania		5		9	10	1			5		1	72	8	3	104	15		1		2	9	349	5		27	2	2	978
Rhode Island											135	10																4
South Dakota																												
Tennessee																											20	23
Texas	2										2				1		1				2		5	1			1	27
Vermont		19		1							18				15							1	1	2	2			99
Virginia															2													4
Washington											1																7	1
West Virginia											2																	22
Wisconsin		4													4		1						2				5	18
Total	163	171	4	47	27	1	6	3	91	2	644	95	18	13	416	72	18	11	1	3	30	442	170	38	32	4	964	5,025

It is the opinion of the Division of Information that on July 1, the date of this report, no man, able and willing to work, need be out of employment in the United States, for the demand for farm laborers, common laborers, and other kinds of workers was much more in evidence than the supply.

It happens every year, however, and at various times during the year, that men of a given calling are idle in one locality while workmen of that calling are needed elsewhere. This is due to two causes: Lack of information among the idle workingmen and the employers who need them, and lack of means to defray transportation expenses in getting from the place of idleness to a place of employment.

One of the best means of "promoting a beneficial distribution of admitted aliens" would be to keep American workingmen constantly and profitably employed. By promptly notifying men who are thrown out of work where it may be had, the opportunities for the alien are increased and his presence in this country need not be regarded as a menace to American workingmen.

In 1882, when what is now called the new immigration was on its initial move to the United States, the statement was made that the unemployed in this country numbered 2,000,000. Each year since then that same number of unemployed is given as current. These figures tell little and explain nothing. They are unreliable and at best only guesswork.

No real, intelligent effort has ever been made to ascertain the number out of work and the causes of unemployment. This can and should be done. It can be made possible for the Division of Information to state at any time the number of unemployed, and where they are unemployed; also the number that may obtain employment, and where it may be had throughout the United States.

The Government does excellent work in indicating to manufacturers where they may find markets for the finished product. The Government has not as yet undertaken the much easier and equally as important task of providing the manufacturers' partner in production—the workman—with information which may keep him steadily employed.

The promotion of a beneficial "distribution of admitted aliens" is not, as many believe, solely in the interest of the aliens. It would not be beneficial to the United States to have any considerable number of the aliens who are admitted remain in idleness or sell their labor in ruinous competition with American workingmen. The Division of Information is in no way responsible for the presence of the alien in this country, for, up to the hour of landing, the division can have no dealings with him; but after he lands he should not be permitted to wrong himself and others through ignorance of opportunities about which he can know nothing, but which could be made known to him on landing and afterwards, when he will be in a more receptive mood than when, anxious and worried, he is passing examination for admission.

Thousands of immigrants go at once, on being admitted, to localities where their labor is not in demand and have to remain indefinitely awaiting employment. Even if not educated in our language or their own, they are surely intelligent, and it would be a reflection on that intelligence to attribute their remaining idle in one place to being at work in another to choice or a previous knowledge of existing conditions. It came under the personal observation of the chief of this division that a number of aliens passing through Ellis Island were destined to a certain locality in Pennsylvania where they could not obtain employment without displacing others. Such as these furnish a supply for the labor agent, the employment agent, and the padrone to direct later on, and it is a well-known fact that many of these, through collusion with corporation foremen, practically sell the same workmen over and over again for a fee of $1 or $2 a head. This can not be other than detrimental to American labor.

EMPLOYMENT AGENCIES.

The Division of Information believes that every private employment agency, every agent for a corporation, and every other person directing men to employment across State lines, should be subject to the supervision of this division.

A Federal Weather Bureau, receiving its information from many sources throughout the world, is enabled to inform the inhabitants of the United States of coming storms and other changes in the weather. The work of the Weather Bureau was not deemed necessary at first and not appreciated until long after that bureau was in operation. It is just as important to all the people of the United States, and more especially the working people, that changes or coming changes in industrial life should be speedily and accurately recorded.

BRANCHES OF THE DIVISION.

The division wishes to commend the New York branch for the effective and practical manner in which not only admitted aliens and other residents are directed to opportunities for employment, but also for the assistance it thus renders employers of agricultural and common laborers in obtaining necessary additional help. Before this report goes to press the New, York branch of the division will have moved to quarters in the new United States Barge Office, Battery Park, near South Ferry, New York City, and it is believed that the facilities afforded by the new location will increase the usefulness and efficiency of that office.

There should be a branch of the Division of Information in every industrial center in the United States. Through cooperation with the Post Office Department this can be successfully done and without great expense.

The Division of Information can at the present time, through the assistance rendered by the Post Office Department, state the labor requirements of the farmers of the United States. A system of postal-card inquiry, inaugurated some years ago, enables the division to keep in touch with agriculturists, and details of their wants may be made known to applicants for positions on farms.

CITIES AND TOWNS.

In each city and town of sufficient population to maintain a post office a daily registration of those out of work should be made without expense to the unemployed. Registration should consist of such detail as to enable an employer to make selection. Employers in need of workmen could register their needs at the same place. By this means and part of the time of a single clerk in the post offices, the tide of the unemployed could be turned toward places of employment.

A classified list of names of unemployed workmen, giving occupations and such other details as might be necessary, exhibited for public inspection at the post office, would enable the employer to secure help and also give employed workmen an opportunity of notifying idle men of opportunities for employment. The unemployed could in this way first advertise his need in his own locality, then have a record sent on to a State information bureau and also to the Division of Information of the Bureau of Immigration.

Through the cooperation of labor unions and brotherhoods the danger of directing men to points where strikes or lockouts might be in progress or contemplation would be obviated, and these organizations could materially assist in furnishing accurate information concerning unemployment of others as well as of their own members.

NEW INDUSTRIES.

At present when a new industry or enterprise is about to begin operations advertisements appear in the papers of different cities stating the number and kind of workmen required. It frequently happens, and this division has had abundant evidence of it, that more than double the number of men advertised for apply. Many of these give up employment and at much expense travel to the place indicated, only to be disappointed in not securing work and to find themselves financially embarrassed as well. All this can be avoided by a proper system of registration and notification.

The details of the plan above referred to can be worked out in a short time and, when perfected, it will be possible to prevent any considerable number of men remaining idle for any great length of time in any part of the United States.

Employers throughout the United States are supplied through labor agencies with information concerning the laying off or dismissal of workmen in their lines of business. Business foresight appears to require this. Those in need of workmen know from day to day where men of the class they require are out of work. Workingmen who lose their positions through dull times in one locality have no ready means of ascertaining, without loss of time and money, just where they may be needed. The plan herein suggested will change this.

PREPAID TICKETS.

The sending of money abroad to defray the expenses of aliens emigrating from Europe and the prepaid ticket are responsible for much of the crowding of already overpopulated industrial centers.

Though difficult of proof, the charge has been made that labor agents enlist the aid of aliens in this country to induce the coming of relatives, or alleged relatives, to the United States, and in this way endeavor to evade the immigration laws.

The sending of money and prepaid tickets should be subject to Federal supervision. Where the end in view is legitimate no harm may follow the sending of money or prepaid tickets. Where a doubt exists, the sender may prove to be a violator of the immigration laws.

REPORT OF COMMISSIONER GENERAL OF IMMIGRATION. 163

With the record of money advanced and prepaid tickets filed with the Bureau of Immigration, and the destination of intending immigrants known, it will be an easy matter for the Division of Information to tell what conditions exist in the place designated, and the attention of the aliens directed to other points if deemed best.

BULLETINS OF THE DIVISION.

The work of translating the bulletins into foreign languages progresses slowly, owing to lack of sufficient appropriation to pay for the work. These bulletins are growing in favor, but the demand for their publication in many languages can not readily be complied with for the reason stated. The Polish edition is nearly ready. Inquiries for it are numerous and becoming more so. When these bulletins in foreign languages are ready for distribution they should be read to immigrants aboard ship en route to the United States. They may be the means of turning many agriculturists toward the land and away from crowded centers.

It is a well-authenticated fact that hundreds of thousands of immigrants were farmers in Europe; it is natural to suppose that they would prefer following agriculture in the United States. Two causes combine to prevent this. One is lack of funds, the other lack of information concerning the agricultural possibilities of this country. That immigrants come here with their pockets bursting with money is a fallacy. They are driven here, in the main, by economic necessity, and their capital is a combination of ambition, muscle, and hope. All three are good, but not sufficient to make a farm productive. To educate them as quickly as possible in the ways of this country and as to its superiority over others in its agricultural opportunities would seem to be the part of wisdom, if not of necessity. The work of reclaiming our immigration and turning its attention to the land can not be done in a day or a year, but it can and should be done. One great cause of the high cost of living, so much complained of, is the drift from farm to city. To increase the number of producers of foodstuffs and keep the stream of idle city workers at low ebb by properly directing them to employment is the sanest and best way of solving the high-priced food problem.

Men who were farmers in Europe and save their earnings with which to buy land would more willingly buy cheap, productive land in the United States than high-priced land elsewhere, and to the end that they may invest their savings in land here they should be fully and frequently informed of what the various States have to offer to one in earnest in his desire to till the soil for a livelihood. With a branch of the division in each industrial center, always open and ready to impart information, it is probable that the greater part of the vast amount of money taken abroad each year by aliens returning to Europe would be invested in land in the United States.

The port of entry is not the only place to tell the alien about the United States. Every industrial center should have its representative of this division prepared to tell alien and citizen the things they do not know about farm life in this country.

Many men who came to the United States with but little money and who were directed to the land as farm laborers by this division have invested their savings in American land and now own or are paying for farms of their own. The man who lacks capital, but who knows how, will often succeed where the man who has plenty of money to invest may fail because he does not know how.

FARM TESTING STATIONS.

The tendency of American life is away from the farm. The first object the immigrant's eyes focus on is the skyscraper, the many-storied factory, or the coal mine. Nothing to indicate that agriculture is carried on here is disclosed to the immigrant on landing. The Chief of the Division of Information has for years entertained the opinion that no immigrant whose occupation is shown by the manifest to be a farmer or farm laborer should be allowed to pass final examination inside of a week after arrival and that during his stay he should be required to demonstrate his ability to work on a trial farm to be stationed near the immigrant station. Such a plan, fully worked out in detail, would serve a double purpose—test the immigrant's industrial fitness and enable him to learn something about the United States, for each evening should be devoted to giving lantern-slide lectures on subjects which would educate the new arrival and stimulate the desire to become the owner of "a piece of land." The information gathered by this division pertaining to agricultural opportunities could be given these probationers at our gates.

A DIVISION OF GENERAL INFORMATION.

Inquiries come to the Division of Information on every conceivable subject. They come from all parts of the country and are of such importance to the writers, who are entitled to the information they seek, that they should receive full consideration and prompt attention.

People residing away from Washington are unfamiliar with the official titles of the many divisions, bureaus, offices, and departments, and the respective scope and duties of each, and do not know therefore just which one should act upon the matters submitted by them. Owing to its title, they naturally infer that ours is a division of general information. Knowing where each inquiry may obtain proper attention and reply, this division forwards the letter to the place where the citizen may secure the information he seeks. The division performs this service now as a matter of necessity because the work is forced on it, due to its designation as a division of information. It is therefore suggested that the title of this division be changed to Division of General Information, its scope and duties enlarged as suggested in the foregoing, and publicity given to the fact that inquiries may be addressed to it on general matters as well as on the subjects with which it deals at present.

Respectfully,   T. V. Powderly,
                                                      Chief of Division.
Hon. A. Caminetti,
     Commissioner General of Immigration.

REPORTS OF COMMISSIONERS AND INSPECTORS IN CHARGE OF DISTRICTS

REPORTS OF COMMISSIONERS AND INSPECTORS IN CHARGE OF DISTRICTS.

REPORT OF UNITED STATES COMMISSIONER OF IMMIGRATION FOR CANADA, IN CHARGE OF DISTRICT NO. 1, COMPRISING ALL CANADIAN SEAPORTS AND THE ENTIRE CANADIAN BORDER.

As in previous reports of like character, the aliens examined have been so classified as to show at a glance the character of immigration being received via Canada.

Class A. Aliens manifested on board steamships and examined at ports of arrival under the immigration laws of the United States:

Number examined at Canadian Atlantic seaports	47,647
Number examined at Canadian Pacific seaports	916
Total	48,563

Percentage debarred at Atlantic seaports, 0.70.
Percentage debarred at Pacific seaports, 0.00.

Causes for exclusion:

Feeble-minded	6
Insane	2
Tuberculosis	1
Trachoma	18
Favus	1
Other dangerous contagious diseases	6
Likely to become public charges	105
Surgeon's certificate	60
Contract laborers	62
Accompanying aliens	8
Under 16 years	29
Assisted aliens	0
Criminals	17
Prostitutes	10
Procurers	8
Total	333

Class B. Aliens coming originally to Canada and who sought entry to the United States within 1 year from date of arrival:

Total number examined	14,132
Total number debarred	895

Percentage debarred, 6.33.

Class C. Aliens who entered Canada via United States ports and aliens from the United States who sought reentry thereto within 1 year:

Total number examined	16,304
Total number debarred	878

Percentage debarred, 5.37.

Class CC. Aliens claiming residence of more than 1 year in Canada, but who were unable to give satisfactory proof thereof:

Total number examined	2,666
Total number debarred	209

Percentage debarred, 7.84.

167

Class D. Aliens who applied for admission to the United States after a residence of more than 1 year in Canada, the transportation companies being exempt from payment of head tax as to this class:

Total number examined... 11,311
Total number debarred..................................... 804

Percentage debarred, 7.11.

Class E. Citizens of Canada entering the United States for permanent residence:

Total number examined.. 44,701
Total number debarred................................... 1,936

Percentage debarred, 4.33.

Aliens debarred at border stations, but not included in above figures, who applied for admission to the United States for a temporary sojourn........ 499

Total number examined at border stations........................... 89,613

Causes for exclusion:

Idiots......	8
Imbeciles...	13
Feeble-minded...	35
Epileptics...	12
Insane...	53
Tuberculosis...	80
Trachoma...	440
Favus...	3
Other dangerous contagious diseases...	65
Professional beggars...	5
Paupers...	5
Likely to become public charges...	3,035
Surgeon's certificate...	127
Contract laborers...	405
Accompanying aliens (sec. 11)...	63
Under 16 years...	169
Assisted aliens...	121
Criminals...	228
Polygamists...	5
Anarchists...	2
Prostitutes, etc...	186
Procurers, etc...	144
Receiving proceeds of prostitution...	6
Passport provision, section 1...	11
Total...	5,221

Chinese examined.. 838
Number debarred... 58 ,

Percentage debarred, 6.92.

For the year covered by this report 2,008 aliens were refused examination owing to nonreceipt of guaranty of payment of head tax. There were also 1,161 returned from the border for board of special inquiry hearing who failed to present themselves for such examination, and these two classes may very properly be added to the number debarred.

Grand total of border class debarred......................... 8,448

Percentage debarred, 9.02.

Grand total examined.. 142,183
Grand total debarred.. 8,781

Percentage of grand total debarred, 6.17.

Number of United States citizens returning after residence in Canada...... 54,497

For handy comparison of immigration to Canada with the records of immigration to our own country, the following table is appended through the courtesy of Hon. W. D. Scott, superintendent of immigration, Ottawa, Canada:

TOTAL IMMIGRATION TO CANADA FROM ALL SOURCES, FISCAL YEAR ENDED JUNE 30, 1913, BY MONTHS.

Year and month.	British.	Conti-nental, etc.	From United States.	Total.
1912.				
July	13,399	8,340	12,557	34,296
August	11,824	7,734	13,309	32,867
September	13,189	7,501	10,450	31,140
October	10,166	6,545	10,481	27,192
November	6,316	6,006	7,895	20,217
December	3,062	4,200	5,763	13,025
1913.				
January	2,634	3,238	5,028	10,900
February	3,202	3,574	5,572	12,348
March	16,831	13,659	14,611	45,101
April	25,566	28,459	19,260	73,285
May	31,374	27,517	14,247	73,138
June	37,365	24,927	11,491	63,783
Total	164,928	141,700	130,664	437,292

OCCUPATIONS OF IMMIGRANTS ADMITTED INTO CANADA FROM THE UNITED STATES, FISCAL YEAR ENDED JUNE 30, 1913, BY MONTHS.

Year and month.	Farming class.	Common laborers.	Skilled laborers.	Female servants.	Not classified.	Total.
1912.						
July	3,271	3,566	3,376	387	1,957	12,557
August	3,694	4,528	3,799	183	1,105	13,309
September	2,483	3,936	2,027	274	1,730	10,450
October	2,297	3,750	2,430	323	1,681	10,481
November	2,138	2,491	1,479	295	1,492	7,895
December	1,621	1,184	1,687	136	1,135	5,763
1913.						
January	1,130	1,044	1,713	202	939	5,028
February	1,607	1,672	1,221	194	878	5,572
March	6,763	2,918	3,166	162	1,602	14,611
April	7,481	3,798	4,780	299	2,902	19,260
May	3,860	3,095	4,225	328	2,739	14,247
June	3,296	2,263	3,195	· 346	2,391	11,491
Total	39,641	34,245	33,098	3,129	20,551	130,664

The following table shows the immigration movement from the United States to Canada, and from Canada to the United States, for the last two fiscal years:

1912.

Month.	Canada to the United States.				United States to Canada.			
	United States citizens.	Canadian citizens.	Other aliens.	Total.	United States citizens.	Canadian citizens.	Other aliens.	Total.
Pending from previous year..........		13	21	34				
1911.								
July..................	2,752	3,126	2,055	7,933	7,055	1,656	2,301	11,012
August..............	2,633	3,705	2,968	9,306	11,719	1,954	3,346	17,019
September...........	3,176	3,609	2,256	9,041	7,921	1,447	2,116	11,484
October.............	4,058	4,164	2,452	10,674	7,414	1,396	1,446	10,256
November...........	5,994	4,039	3,160	13,193	5,476	1,322	1,315	8,113
December...........	3,680	2,867	2,335	8,882	3,689	1,280	710	5,679
1912.								
January.............	2,249	2,842	1,574	6,665	2,830	964	547	4,341
February............	1,956	2,723	1,527	6,206	3,884	1,179	689	5,752
March...............	2,486	3,290	1,619	7,395	12,555	1,820	1,877	16,252
April................	3,202	2,993	2,164	10,359	15,779	2,183	3,532	21,494
May.................	2,667	4,236	2,280	9,183	11,317	2,894	3,890	18,101
June.................	3,464	3,042	2,566	9,072	8,312	19,991	3,445	13,748
Total..........	38,317	42,649	26,977	107,943	97,951	38,086	25,214	143,251

1913.

Month.	United States citizens.	Canadian citizens.	Other aliens.	Total.	United States citizens.	Canadian citizens.	Other aliens.	Total.
Pending from previous year..........		13	20	33				
1912.								
July..................	3,735	3,042	2,880	9,657	7,553	1,902	3,102	12,557
August..............	3,384	3,073	3,564	10,021	8,603	1,753	2,953	13,309
September...........	4,235	4,118	3,727	12,080	6,894	1,276	2,280	10,450
October.............	5,619	4,641	4,041	14,301	6,886	1,511	2,084	10,481
November...........	7,273	4,674	4,420	16,367	5,166	1,323	1,406	7,895
December...........	6,139	3,761	3,678	13,578	3,739	1,252	772	5,763
1913.								
January.............	3,139	2,975	2,629	8,743	3,235	890	903	5,028
February............	3,493	2,628	2,452	8,573	3,726	926	920	5,572
March...............	3,538	3,146	2,726	9,410	10,851	1,690	2,070	14,611
April................	4,496	4,903	3,926	13,325	13,847	2,430	2,983	19,260
May.................	4,452	4,055	4,990	13,497	9,345	2,494	2,408	14,247
June.................	4,994	3,672	5,360	14,026	7,815	1,832	1,844	11,491
Total..........	54,497	44,701	44,413	143,611	87,660	19,279	23,725	130,664

NOTE.—Above figures show applications for admission to the United States, but do not include aliens arriving at Canadian seaports having United States destinations.

It will be observed from the foregoing that a total of 142,183 aliens sought entry to the United States through and from Canada during the past year, an increase of 98 per cent at the seaports, of 27 per cent at border ports of entry, and of 42 per cent in citizens of the United States who, after residence in Canada, have returned to resume residence in their own country. Heavy immigration to North America generally, augmented steamship service to Canadian ports by the regular lines, and the introduction of a steamship service by the Canadian Pacific and Austro-Americana Lines from Mediterranean ports direct to Quebec and Montreal are the principal causes for the unusual increase in immigration to the United States via Canadian seaports.

The increase in the number shown to have entered the United States after residence in Canada, however, is not so easily accounted for. Reference to the Dominion records shows that during our last fiscal year transoceanic immigration to Canada totaled 306,628. There has been the suggestion of immigrants coming to Canada in unassimilable numbers and of a money stringency in that country retarding development enterprises, thus lessening demand for workmen, but to what extent these alleged conditions have stimulated migration to the United States of aliens previously resident in Canada must be left to conjecture. The movement has been neither spasmodic nor sectional in character, but has been general throughout the year and quite evenly distributed as regards border ports of entry to the United States, and it would therefore seem that at least a portion of such influx must be attributed to the steady enlargement of steamship service to Canada, bringing, as such service no doubt does, many aliens of the roving, prospecting class, who are never satisfied to remain in one country until they have tried conditions in the other.

As to the fitness of aliens arriving at Canadian seaports destined to the United States, exclusions for medical reasons amount to but one-fifth of 1 per cent of the number examined, while exclusions for other causes represent one-half of 1 per cent of such number. From this satisfactory showing it will be seen that the various Canadian steamship lines with which our department is in agreement have exercised care with regard to the class of immigrants allowed to embark on their steamers. * * *

The agreement under which we are working (and the ends of good administration as well) contemplate that our Government shall at all times supply sufficient help to render possible the prompt examination of arriving aliens having United States destinations, but the fact is that for many months our staff of help at the seaports has been inadequate to meet the needs of the situation, and as a consequence at times our service has all but broken down. Long hours of duty have almost invariably characterized the inspection at Quebec and Halifax, the officers at these ports on numerous occasions having been compelled to work 36 consecutive hours with no period for rest, and on account of the mental and physical exhaustion which must result from such a strain it is obvious that it has been simply impossible to enforce that careful inspection of aliens which the immigration laws and regulations and the interests of our country demand.

From this inadequacy of force still another unfortunate situation has arisen against which the steamship lines, arriving aliens, and finally the Dominion Government have entered vigorous protest, viz, our inability to examine immigrants promptly on arrival. During recent months, owing to the congestion at Quebec, aliens held for board of special inquiry hearing have been compelled to undergo detention in the crowded hospital for periods of from six to eight days before their cases could be heard, and thus for the prompt inspection that should have been accorded arriving aliens was substituted what amounted to annoying hardships, which were keenly felt, particularly in the cases of women and children, who, wearied from weeks of travel from their foreign homes, were anything but prepared cheerfully to endure such vexatious delay.

By the vote of a substantial majority of its Members and with no little enthusiasm, the last Congress passed a new immigration bill, which failed to become law only by reason of Executive veto. The debates attending passage of the new law left no room for doubt that the support given the measure was due almost entirely to new features calculated to restrict immigration. When we consider the fact that, owing to lack of help and funds, the restrictive features of the present immigration act have not been fully taken advantage of for several recent years, present enthusiasm for greater restriction is difficult to comprehend, and as to the desire of Congress further to restrict immigration, the futility of such legislation to that end is obvious unless such laws are enforced, a condition simply unattainable under the present limited-funds program.

In this connection, alluding to the district under my own control, owing to the constant and ever-annoying drawback of inadequate help, it has been an impossibility to enforce the immigration and Chinese-exclusion laws and regulations as I believe Congress intended they should be enforced. As a result of immigration, Canada is now adding to its population (less the number outgoing) at the rate of 450,000 souls per year, approximately two-thirds of this influx being from transoceanic countries. As our records will show, there are thousands of such aliens constantly seeking access to the United States, despite any advantages Canada may have to offer. For the purpose of our immigration laws, aliens of this class are immigrants precisely as if they were landing at New York, and their examination should be as carefully conducted as at any other point of ingress; but to illustrate how insufficient help and lack of funds operate in the inspection of aliens entering the United States along the Canadian border, I may state that during the eight months subsequent to August, 1912, no less than 54,000 passengers entered the United States at one point by ferry, shortage of help rendering it impossible to question even one of these aliens as to his status under the immigration laws.

It seems needless to dwell upon the inefficiency of an inspection system whereby the Government expends no inconsiderable amount of money to enforce the immigration laws at one point and at the same time maintains a wide-open door but a short distance away. An analogous situation would be presented by the enforcement of proper inspection at the port of New York, leaving the port of Philadelphia an unguarded gateway for all the aliens who might care to enter.

As to the importance of strengthening and protecting our border inspection, one has but to consult the tables herewith transmitted, which show that practically 9 per cent of all aliens seeking entry at the boundary are debarred, whereas at the four principal Atlantic seaports of the United States, according to the bureau's records for recent years, the number debarred has represented but 1½ per cent of the total arrivals.

Adverting to conditions above described existing at Canadian ocean ports, so far as our own service is concerned, it may also be said that there is scarcely an important substation on the border where employees are not required to observe hours of duty never contemplated in present-day Government service. The department already having been the recipient of numerous petitions looking to a termination of such practice, and in view of the situation portrayed, it is earnestly hoped that steps may be taken to provide such additional help as the constantly growing importance of the Canadian border branch of the bureau's service may demand.

It is gratifying to know that it is the purpose of the new department to contend for an Immigration Service that will be efficient throughout, and in this connection it is my personal belief that nothing would be more conducive to the strengthening and betterment of our inspection work than a radical change in the present policy relating to promotions, so that officers of ability who are doing conscientious work might be assured that promotions will be made on the basis of merit and length of service, and that advancements would not be left to the uncertainties of change in the service caused by death, dismissal, resignation, or transfer. It is generally conceded that the matter of selecting prospective citizens of the United States at the gateways of the Nation is a serious and important work, and that our inspection system should aim at the highest possible standard. It would involve no great task, however, to show that the present policy with regard to promotions has operated to retard rather than to stimulate efficiency; hence my earnest conviction that a change should be urged.

There are at present employed in this district 182 inspectors. As a large majority of the inspectors employed are now in the lower-salaried grades, and as the changes from those grades must be decidedly more numerous than from the higher grades (this condition also holding good as regards interpreters and clerks), it will be seen that promotion prospects for those employed in the lower grades are anything but encouraging, and it would seem that no further comment is necessary to support my contention that the present policy pertaining to promotions does not make for efficiency in the service. In most instances appointees enter the Immigration Service having in view permanency in such employment, and in justice to such employees, and as an incentive to intelligent and conscientious endeavor, it would seem of the greatest importance that some plan be devised as to promotions that will eliminate the element of doubt and uncertainty, and that will place faithful officers of the bureau in a position to determine without longer delay whether or not it is for the interests of themselves and the families dependent upon them for support that they continue their connection with the Immigration Service.

The border inspectors have earned special commendation for the important work done in the way of preventing violations of the immigration, Chinese, and white-slave acts by, in many instances, accomplishing the arrest and prosecution of the offenders. The following table gives the number of arrests made, cause for arrest, and termination of each case:

CIVIL ACTIONS AND PROSECUTIONS CONCLUDED DURING THE FISCAL YEAR ENDED JUNE 30, 1913 (OTHER THAN THOSE RELATING TO CHINESE CASES).

[Table only includes those where the Government was sustained.]

NORTHERN DISTRICT OF NEW YORK.

Name of defendant.	Section violated.	Result.
George McDonald	3, immigration act	Pleaded guilty; sentence suspended and defendant turned over to military authorities for prosecution for desertion.
George Saunders	do	Pleaded guilty; sentence suspended.
Giuseppe Zackeo	8, immigration act	Pleaded guilty; fined $50.
William Francis Ronen	do	Pleaded guilty; fined $500.

CIVIL ACTIONS AND PROSECUTIONS CONCLUDED DURING THE FISCAL YEAR ENDED JUNE 30, 1913 (OTHER THAN THOSE RELATING TO CHINESE CASES)—Contd.

WESTERN DISTRICT OF NEW YORK.

Name of defendant.	Section violated.	Result.
Harry Patterson	3, immigration act	Pleaded guilty; 9 months Erie County Penitentiary.
Tomasso Giannacono	....do	Forfeited $1,000 bond.
Bernardo Giannacono	....do	Do.
Elmer E. Smith	8, immigration act	Pleaded guilty; fined $25.
George Smith	3, immigration act	Do.
Charles Lemontchek	79. Federal Penal Code.	Pleaded guilty; fined $50.
Juzefla Derusz	3, immigration act	Pleaded guilty; sentence suspended.
Frank Charles Ter Reace	....do	Pleaded guilty; fined $1 and sentenced to 6 months Erie County Penitentiary.
Nicola Pantaleo	8, immigration act	Pleaded guilty; fined $50.
Jan Spinalski	3 and 8, immigration act.	Pleaded guilty; sentence suspended.
John Mates	....do	Do.

EASTERN DISTRICT OF MICHIGAN.

Emma Foubert	3, immigration act	Pleaded guilty; 2 years Detroit House of Correction.
Edward Hill	White-slave traffic act.	Pleaded guilty; 2 years Federal Prison, Leavenworth, Kans.
Chas. S. Phillips	3, immigration act	Pleaded guilty; 9 months Detroit House of Correction.
Herbert L. Newcomb	....do	Convicted; 16 months Federal Prison, Leavenworth, Kans.
Ignate Van Middel	....do	Pleaded guilty; 6 months Detroit House of Correction.
J. L. Grant	....do	Pleaded guilty; 2 years Federal Prison, Leavenworth, Kans.
Stojan Boric	....do	Pleaded guilty; 6 months Detroit House of Correction.
Gaston Cardinal	....do	Pleaded guilty; 60 days Detroit House of Correction.
Maxim Motylinska	....do	Pleaded guilty; 3 months Detroit House of Correction.
Emil Neiriucx	....do	Do.
Chas. H. A. Anderson	....do	Convicted; 4 years Detroit House of Correction.
William Menary	....do	Pleaded guilty; 4 months Detroit House of Correction.
Sadie Nall or Mall	....do	Pleaded guilty; 3 months Detroit House of Correction.

WESTERN DISTRICT OF MICHIGAN.

George Sullivan	3, immigration act	Convicted; 1 year and 6 months Federal Prison, Leavenworth, Kans.

DISTRICT OF MINNESOTA.

Marc Autun Raus	White-slave traffic act.	Convicted; 2 years and 6 months Federal Prison, Leavenworth, Kans.

DISTRICT OF VERMONT.

Charles Anderson	3, immigration act	Pleaded guilty; 7 months Chittenden County Jail, Burlington, Vt.

WESTERN DISTRICT OF WASHINGTON.

Ercole del Grande	79, Federal Penal Code.	Pleaded guilty; fined $100.

PROSECUTIONS CONCLUDED DURING THE FISCAL YEAR ENDED JUNE 30, 1913, FOR CHINESE SMUGGLING, IN VIOLATION OF SECTION 8 OF THE IMMIGRATION ACT AND SECTION 11 OF THE CHINESE EXCLUSION ACT, HANDLED BY OFFICERS IN THE MONTREAL JURISDICTION.

DISTRICT OF VERMONT.

Name.	Result.
Charles Buffa	Pleaded guilty; sentenced to 2 months in jail. Judge Martin.
Yeolande R. Brown (alias Q. R. Maggie).	Convicted on two offenses; sentenced to 2 years' imprisonment in Atlanta Penitentiary. Judge Martin.
Bert Smith	Convicted; sentenced to 3 months in jail. Judge Martin.

EASTERN DISTRICT OF MICHIGAN.

George Copp	Convicted; sentenced to pay a fine of $1,000. Judge Sessions.
Fred O'Neill	Convicted; sentenced to pay a fine of $100; in jail 3 months awaiting trial. Judge Sessions.
Ovla Latour, alias "Bay City" Latour.	Do.
John Geiser	Convicted; sentence suspended. Judge Sessions.
Harry Freeman	Convicted; sentenced to 6 months in jail. Judge Sessions.
William Anderson	Do.
Jack Clydesdale	Convicted; sentenced to 6 months' imprisonment with hard labor. Judge Sessions.
Franklin T. Hargrave	Convicted; sentenced to 13 months' imprisonment at Leavenworth Penitentiary. Judge Tuttle.
John Humphrey	Convicted on 2 offences; sentenced to 4 years' imprisonment in Detroit House of Correction and to pay fine of $2,000. Judge Tuttle.
Robert Haskins	Convicted; sentence suspended. Judge Tuttle.
Charles Rose	Do.
Jack McGraw, alias Bertrand	Convicted; sentenced to 5 months' imprisonment in Detroit House of Correction. Judge Tuttle.
Edward Dunford	Convicted; sentenced to 6 months' imprisonment in Detroit House of Correction. Judge Tuttle.
Percy (alias Philip) Deneau	Convicted; sentenced to 2 years' imprisonment in Detroit House of Correction and to pay $1,000 fine. Judge Tuttle.
Ray McLean, alias Lounsbury.	Do.
Lee Ah Hoon	Convicted; sentenced to 1 year's imprisonment and to pay $1,000 fine; jail sentence suspended upon payment of fine. Judge Tuttle.
Roy Beckerson	Convicted; sentence suspended. Judge Tuttle.

PROSECUTIONS FOR CHINESE SMUGGLING PENDING AT CLOSE OF FISCAL YEAR, JUNE 30, 1913.

Northern New York... 7
Eastern Michigan... 6

The foregoing table is not, of course, intended to represent all the smuggling with which our officers have had to contend, for in many instances aliens who set out to effect unlawful entry to the United States proceeded upon their own initiative and without leaders, in which event, when arrests were made, deportation, not prosecution, was the result.

In this connection, along practically the entire northern border officers of the bureau meet with much trouble in arranging for the temporary detention of aliens who surreptitiously enter the country pending receipt of department warrant authorizing arrest. The only aid at all available is derived from local police officers, who * * * arrange for the temporary commitment of such aliens to local jails. It may be said, however, that in most instances such assistance to our service is rendered with reluctance through fear of legal complications, and as the matter is one of a strictly Federal character, it would seem that our department's officers should be relieved of the necessity of constantly calling upon sheriffs and police officers to assist in the detention of aliens whose examination by immigration officials is surely contemplated under the present immigration law, and for whose temporary detention pending receipt of warrant the authority should be made clear and unequivocal in any new immigration legislation that may be enacted. The heavier the immigration to Canada, the greater need for an amendment to our law such as is suggested in the foregoing, and it is earnestly hoped that the bureau may be pleased to urge adoption of the change recommended.

Of the warrants of arrest issued by the department during the past fiscal year, officers in this district served no less than 848, and the aliens involved were disposed of as follows:

Pending July 1, 1912	178
Reported during year	966
Total	1,144

Deported from United States ports	285
Deported from Canadian ports	78
Deported to Canada	208
Warrants canceled	235
Pending June 30, 1913	220
Deported by other districts to Canada	118
Total	1,144

Of the foregoing, 253 male and 110 female aliens were deported to trans-Atlantic countries for the following causes:

Insane	84
Public charges	134
Criminals	49
Entered without inspection	20
Prostitutes	51
Procurers	25
Total	363

Divided as to occupations, our records show the following:

Laborers	217
Domestics	75
Mechanics	8
Professional	10
Not given	41
Clerks	8
Prostitutes	4
Total	363

LITERACY.

Can read and write	250
Can not read or write	105
No record	8
Total	363

These figures indicate but meagerly the Government funds expended and the time spent by our officers in investigations, travel, and handling of clerical work which execution of the above-mentioned warrants involved, all of such expense and labor, to my mind, constituting unassailable support of the contention that our inspection of aliens at time of entry to the country is not what it should be. Economically, it seems far from good management to * * * admit aliens at the ports only later to expel them at heavy expense and with increased hardship. * * *

During the past year 433 citizens of the United States residing in Canada were found to be deportable under Dominion laws, and the following are the causes prompting expulsion of these citizens from Canada:

Criminals	277
Procurers	7
Prostitutes	16
Insane	42
Public charges	85
Illegal entry	2
"Industrial Workers of the World"	4
Total	433

Regarding citizens of our own country who are ordered deported from Canada, and who are helpless because of physical or mental defects, and arranging for their proper care in the United States constitutes one of the most difficult problems that this office has to deal with. Frequently cases are presented where the dependent has been absent for many years from the State of which once a citizen, affording basis for the claim by the particular State that citizenship has been relinquished, no settled residence in any State having subsequently been acquired. As a citizen of the United States, deportation within the period prescribed by the Canadian act must be assented to, and a suitable institution to which to return such dependent must be found, in which quest it may be taken for granted no encouragement or aid is received from any State in the United States, the practice being, regardless of how many different States the dependent may have resided in before crossing into Canada, for each State to vie with the other in disclaiming or shirking all responsibility with regard to any such dependent.

The question may be asked, Is this really an immigration matter? Possibly not, but it devolves upon immigration officers to pass upon the question of citizenship, and in cases of insanity, illness, and infancy, protection to helpless citizens precludes desertion of such dependents immediately upon their reaching United States territory, hence necessity for an investigation in each instance which will show the actual State and county to which the dependent should be delivered.

From previous figures it will be observed that 326 citizens of Canada were deported from the United States during the fiscal year just past, our deportation orders being enforced only after the Canadian authorities, as the result of investigation, had assented thereto. The following shows the causes for deportation and the occupations of those deported:

Criminals	58
Procurers	25
Prostitutes	81
Insane	49
Public charges	92
Entered without inspection	21
Total	**326**

Laborers	132
Domestics	90
Mechanics	2
Professional	10
Not given	68
Clerks	15
Prostitutes	9
Total	**326**

LITERACY.

Can read and write	247
Can not read or write	44
No record	35
Total	**326**

THE ENFORCEMENT OF THE CHINESE-EXCLUSION LAWS.

As to the conditions outlined in the foregoing with regard to regular immigration, their counterpart is found in connection with our efforts to enforce the Chinese exclusion laws along the northern border.

During the twelve months ending June 30, 1913, 8,122 Chinese entered Canada. Of this number 7,760 were admitted upon payment of the $500 capitation tax; the remainder entered as members of the exempt classes named in the Dominion act relating to Chinese. The Dominion census of 1911 shows a Chinese population of 27,000. In the past three years 23,866 Chinese have been admitted to Canada, 18,809 being taxable, and yielding a revenue of more than nine millions to the Dominion Government. No one familiar with the line of employment followed by the Chinese would be likely to maintain that this large number of Chinese found ready and profitable employment in Canada. The fact is, in their determination to get into the United States in defiance of law, Canada is but a vantage ground for the Chinese; and, as thousands effect entry to Canada yearly, it is obvious that in its efforts to enforce the exclusion laws along the Canadian border, the bureau has on its hands a task of gigantic proportions, demanding very serious consideration.

Referring to Chinese who are admitted to Canada, it has often been facetiously remarked that "Canada gets the head tax and the United States gets the Chinese." At the present rate of admissions to Canada and on account of inadequate help in our service to check the operations of the smugglers, I feel we may reasonably expect a more disquieting verification of the above-quoted saying than has ever manifested itself in the past. The operations of the smugglers now involve the use of fast motor boats, high-power automobiles, and bonded freight cars, to cope with which means of smuggling, officers especially fitted for the work should be provided, for, while the bureau is already maintaining quite a numerous force of help in this district, it is of course well known that there are less than a half-dozen officers whose entire time is devoted to enforcement of the Chinese exclusion laws, the efforts of other inspectors being necessarily devoted to the inspection of aliens coming within the terms of our immigration laws who seek entry to the United States in a lawful manner.

Until the Dominion Government regulates the introduction of Chinese into Canada by the adoption of laws more restrictive in character than those now in use, the above described will be the conditions with which our Government will have to deal along our northern border, and, if it be the intention of the department to render thoroughly effective our Chinese-exclusion laws, then additional inspectors and a more generous allotment of funds for this work are a necessity.

EXAMINATION OF CHINESE AT VANCOUVER.

June 30, 1913, ended the second statistical year of enforcement of the exclusion laws under an agreement entered into between the Canadian Pacific Railway Co. and the United States Government, whereby all Chinese from the Orient destined to the United States via Canadian border ports arriving on said transportation company's steamers are inspected by United States officers at Vancouver, British Columbia, instead of, as formerly, at the eastern border ports and later at Boston, Mass.

As conditions at Vancouver have continued very much the same (except for a slight decrease in the number of applicants) as during the previous year, and as the practical working of the law was covered in the report of last year, it is not deemed necessary to enter now into a further discussion thereof. The methods employed in handling Chinese applicants at Vancouver differ very little, if any, from those employed at Chinese ports of entry in the United States, and all rights and privileges there accorded them can be taken advantage of at the former port. As during the previous year, no Chinese found inadmissible to the United States by our officers at Vancouver have been allowed by the Canadian Government to resort to payment of the $500 head tax and thereby secure admission to Canada, from which country surreptitious entry could later be made into the United States; neither have the requirements of the law as to deportation failed of enforcement in respect of Chinese who, after exhausting their rights before the department, were of the class to be returned to the country whence they came.

While there has been a small decrease in the number of Chinese applying for admission at Vancouver during the last year, when compared with the previous year, a large proportion of the same appears in the so-called "son cases." In my previous report comment was made upon the large number of "sons" applying for admission, it being felt at that time that this condition was due to the fact that Vancouver was a newly organized port and interested parties were taking advantage of that fact. The decrease in this class of cases has tended to prove that our suspicions were correct, as it would now seem that no special effort is being made to divert this class of immigration to the above port, it having been found that the inspection there is no less rigid than at the ports in the United States.

Somewhat of an increase will be noted in the number of Chinese women applying for admission. However, after a very careful examination in each case, we were satisfied that the claim set forth was bona fide, except in a very few instances when denial was entered, but in each case, upon appeal to the department, the applicant was allowed to land. There have, though, been several Chinese women deported from Vancouver under the immigration law during the past year for the reason that they were certified by the medical examiner as being afflicted with a dangerous contagious disease. No "raw natives" have been admitted during the past year, and but few section 6 applicants have applied. Those of the latter class have all been promptly admitted.

In the handling of Chinese business at Vancouver our officers come into close contact with those of the Dominion immigration service, and their assistance in consulting old Canadian records of prior landings of Chinese has on many occasions been found of material value to this office, and we have thus been able to furnish officials of our service in the United States with information which they would otherwise find it difficult to secure.

The Canadian Pacific Railway Co.'s officials have continued to carry out the terms of the agreement made with the Government in all its details, and our relations with this company have been most pleasant. This company has recently added to their trans-Pacific service two vessels of considerably greater carrying capacity than the three now in operation, and there is no doubt that the number of Chinese applicants at Vancouver will thereby be increased in the near future.

    *   *   *   †   *   *   *

The second year of the existence of Vancouver as a United States port of entry for Chinese has only tended further to demonstrate the wisdom of the plan from an administrative standpoint and appears to have fully justified the arrangement.

    *   *   *   *   *   *

JOHN H. CLARK,
Commissioner.

REPORT OF COMMISSIONER OF IMMIGRATION AT BOSTON, IN CHARGE OF DISTRICT NO. 2, COMPRISING THE NEW ENGLAND STATES.

The annual report of the New England district for the fiscal year ended June 30, 1913, is the record of a district containing, in respect to volume of immigration, the second, fifth, and sixth ports of the United States. The total inward passenger movement, aggregating 119,811, represents an increase of 45 per cent over the preceding year, while an increase of 50 per cent is denoted by the total of 106,585 in relation to alien passengers. Appended to this report, also, are the usual statistical statements showing, among other matters, the year's record of penalties incurred by steamship companies under section 9 and an account of aliens landed under the provisions of sections 19 and 37 for hospital treatment. The report of the Chinese division follows in due course.

IMMIGRATION STATIONS.

The problem of conducting the business of the port of Boston in the quarters which have been rented during the past 10 years becomes increasingly difficult. These quarters form part of the second or top story of a wooden building (sheathed on the outside with tin) used for the purposes of a steamship dock. The administrative offices, detention rooms, and dormitories, which were prepared for occupancy at considerable expense to the Government, are mainly of wooden construction. An attempt was made to protect the detention quarters by reinforcing the floors and stairways with concrete, which, it is believed, might delay materially the progress of a fire.

The task of keeping the premises in a sanitary condition becomes harder as the building ages. With a demand for accommodations which the detention quarters were never intended to meet the problem grows complex. We are unprovided with conveniences comparable to those afforded second-class passengers on trans-Atlantic liners.

In spite of the fact that the Boston immigration station long since proved inadequate to meet local demands, we are constantly under the necessity of caring for detained aliens arriving at the subport of Providence. This is only an additional reason for regret, however, that no appreciable progress has been made toward erecting a new immigration station on the site purchased at East Boston several years ago

A modern steamship dock is in process of construction at Providence, which is intended to provide suitable facilities for inspection purposes. At present, however, the inspection of immigrants is conducted aboard ship under conditions which are conducive neither to comfort nor efficiency.

An earnest attempt was made last winter by the Board of Trade at Portland, Me., to secure adequate quarters for detained aliens. It seemed impossible, however, to obtain a suitable building for use during the comparatively limited season of immigration at that subport. Better success is hoped for next year.

ILLEGAL IMMIGRATION.

The subject of illegal immigration, with special reference to stowaways and deserting seamen, was treated at some length last year. The abuses to which reference was made continue and doubtless will continue until stopped through effective legislation by Congress.

The number of stowaways discovered this year, totaling 28, is the smallest on record. Of these, 7 were Americans and 21 aliens. There is no reason to suppose that the number of alien seamen, 636, reported by masters of vessels as deserting during the year, actually represents the total desertions. A total of 137 seamen presented themselves at this office for inspection, 15 of whom declared their intention to remain ashore.

DETENTIONS.

Cases brought before the boards of special inquiry at Boston numbered 9,266, or about 19 per cent of the total alien arrivals. The number of aliens actually deported, 397, represents seven-tenths of 1 per cent of the immigrant alien arrivals or six-tenths of 1 per cent of the total aliens.

The nightly average number of occupants in the detention quarters at Boston was 67, an increase of nearly 50 per cent over the preceding year. The highest average for any one month occurred this year, as last, in June. But the average for June, 1912, was only 88 as compared with 121 for 1913. The month of January shows the lowest average in 1913 as well as 1912.

PUBLIC CHARGES.

A very important part of our duties consists of the investigation of violations of the immigration laws and the expulsion of such aliens as are found, any time within three years after landing, to be illegally in the United States. It is clear, however, that a proper observance of those sections of the law concerning public charges implies a reasonable degree of cooperation among Federal, State, and local authorities. The common interests of the community obviously demand the removal of alien criminals and public charges to the countries of which they are citizens. But the initial steps in the removal process must usually be taken by the local authorities; and it is a careless public, indeed, which permits the continuance of the prevailing indifference among local officials charged with the care of the delinquent and defective classes. The results now achieved in ridding the country of "undesirables" are only a suggestion of what might be accomplished by efficient coordination of the various governmental agencies. But even the highest degree of efficiency will be unavailing fairly to meet the issue under the handicaps presented by the existing law. The problem can never be satisfactorily solved until the law is amended to provide for the expulsion of aliens who demonstrate their "undesirability" at any time within five years after arrival.

BOND CASES.

Enforcement of the provisions of the so-called school bonds, which are sometimes accepted to permit the landing of children under 16 years of age unaccompanied by parents, is attended with constant friction. Among the provisions of the school bond is one specifying the submission of quarterly reports of school attendance until the alien reaches the age of 16. Seldom, however, are the reports furnished voluntarily. It often becomes necessary to enter into a protracted correspondence with the bondsmen or persons responsible for the alien's care. Sometimes an officer is specially detailed to investigate the conditions under which the child is living and to ascertain whether or not it has been placed at work unsuited to its years. On several occasions there has been no alternative to enforcing the conditions of the bond but by deporting the alien involved.

Occasionally a child under 16 years of age unaccompanied by either parent, but going to a close relative who satisfies the immigration officers of his trustworthiness, is deemed a "meritorious case" and allowed to land without bond. A recent investigation in a New England mill city, however, of a group of five such cases, demonstrates the need of great care in dealing with alien children. In only one of the five cases were the conditions found to be satisfactory. Two of the aliens, both girls, were at work in the mills; one was serving as a domestic in the home of her relatives, one had disappeared altogether and, as was subsequently learned, had proceeded to California with relatives shortly after arrival—the New England address being fictitious; the fifth alien was attending school according to agreement.

It would not be difficult to point out abuses in connection with ordinary public-charge bonds which are accepted by the Government to permit landing in certain cases of aliens who are decrepit or diseased. It is believed that the new form of bond recently adopted, which provides for a limited degree of surveillance in the case of a bonded alien during a period of one year after landing, will prove of advantage.

FIELD INVESTIGATIONS.

According to the existing method of inspecting arriving immigrants, it is often desirable to make a second inspection at the proposed destination. This is particularly the case in reference to young women, children, and groups of men going to a single address. Practical experience demonstrates the need of this second inspection also to cover affiants from whom are received affidavits in behalf of immigrants destined to remote sections of the country. New England has a large Canadian population and at some seasons the demand for investigations of cases of aliens entering the United States from Canada is most insistent. Under existing conditions the burden of proof in doubtful matters too often is placed upon the Government. Cases of suspected contract labor, immorality or other delinquencies, concerning which direct evidence is lacking, are perforce landed and, owing to pressure of routine business, may be lost to sight. It is believed that a considerable proportion of such aliens are actually in the country in violation of law.

The solution of the problems suggested in the foregoing paragraph may be met by the creation of a permanent field force for continuous investigation. The regular or routine work of the port must take precedence over outside matters; and during busy seasons of immigration it is entirely impracticable to spare men for special details, no matter how great the need.

CHINESE.

Investigations of Chinese have been made in 376 cases. Of these 204 were applications for return certificates, 71 were applications for entry (on which reports were made to other officers in charge), and 101 were miscellaneous investigations. Moreover, it was necessary during the year to keep watch over 1,459 Chinese laborers who came into the ports of the district as employees of vessels. Four of these "seamen" escaped, bonds given on account of three of them being forfeited.[1]

PERSONNEL.

The difficulties of supervising several widely separated ports of entry with the limited force at my command were mentioned in last year's report. Great praise is due the personnel in this district for the spirit in which it has met the extraordinary demands of the year 1913. In spite of a remarkable expansion of business there has been no corresponding increase in the number of employees. Under the circumstances our force has resembled a small army overwhelmed by superior numbers, and it has been impossible at times thoroughly to enforce the statutes.

GEO. B. BILLINGS,
Commissioner.

REPORT OF COMMISSIONER OF IMMIGRATION AT NEW YORK, IN CHARGE OF DISTRICT NO. 3, COMPRISING NEW YORK AND NEW JERSEY, AND THE IMMIGRATION STATION AT ELLIS ISLAND, NEW YORK HARBOR.

As a result of another period of heavy immigration there have been inspected under the immigration law at the port of New York approximately 1,033,000 aliens during the past fiscal year. The practice has continued of inspecting those traveling as first and second cabin passengers on the vessels between the quarantine station and the dock, ordering to Ellis Island such of them as were not "clearly and beyond a doubt entitled to land" or could not be conveniently and fully inspected on board. Of these there were a large number, composed mostly of second-cabin passengers, many such passengers requiring quite as careful inspection as do those traveling in the steerage, commonly known as immigrants. All of the latter were brought to Ellis Island for inspection as a matter of course. On a great many days during the last year the arrivals at Ellis Island have numbered from four to five thousand, taxing to the utmost its facilities for examination and detention. Over 60,000 cases have

---

[1] Other details regarding Chinese transactions in the New England district are shown in the bureau's report.

been considered by boards of special inquiry. Many additional cases were "temporarily detained," usually for the receipt of funds, to verify addresses, or to hear from relatives. The monthly percentages of exclusions have been as high as 1.90 and as low as 1, the variations being due principally to the differences in the classes of immigrants brought during the several months. In considering such figures it must always be borne in mind that they alone do not furnish a correct index of the work of the service in keeping ineligible aliens out of the United States, for they fail to show the large numbers of such aliens who refrain from taking ship through knowledge of the fact that under the prevailing standards of inspection they would be unable to secure admission.

It is impracticable here to do more than indicate some of the larger matters arising out of or related to the peculiar and interesting work done at Ellis Island, and that is all that this report purports to do. Some of these matters were so fully dealt with in the last annual report that nothing further will be said concerning them here. This is true as to "Cabin passengers and the immigration law," "Fraudulent use of ships' articles to land ineligible aliens," "Alien criminals," "Fraud and deceit practiced by and on behalf of immigrants," and "Reports of Ellis Island cases."

THE MEDICAL EXAMINATION OF IMMIGRANTS.

The officers of the Public Health Service are required to "certify for the information of the immigration officers and boards of special inquiry any and all physical and mental defects and diseases" observed by them in arriving immigrants. The magnitude of this task as applied to some eight or nine hundred thousand immigrants a year speaks for itself. Some of these defects are obvious, but many of them can be detected only upon thorough and painstaking examinations. Included in these are arterio sclerosis, chronic progressive diseases of central nervous system, double hernia, locomotor ataxia, psoriasis, lupus, valvular disease of the heart, varicose veins, and poor physical development and numerous other physical defects, which while not being grounds for exclusion per se (as are loathsome and dangerous contagious diseases) yet when present in aggravated form seriously affect the immigrant's ability to earn a living and thus operate to bring him within one of the excluded classes. Hence it is of great importance that where these defects exist they be detected. A thorough physical examination of immigrants ought to be regarded as a very necessary incident to a correct enforcement of the law, in fact without such examination there can be no real enforcement of the same. The conduct of examinations necessary to disclose mental defects is usually even more difficult than where physical defects are concerned. For both kinds of examinations it goes without saying that there must be an ample corps of medical officers with adequate quarters in which to do their work, yet there are at Ellis Island only 26 medical officers. The number should be at least 60. Nor will these officers be in a position to conduct mental examinations in a thorough-going manner until they are able (as is not now the case) to command the services of interpreters. The statute excludes idiots, imbeciles, insane persons and feeble-minded persons, and it is often a most delicate task to ascertain whether or not an immigrant comes within one of these classes, especially where the question is as to feeble-mindedness. It is well to realize that Ellis Island is not as fully equipped as it should be to do this work thoroughly. Nothing is gained by closing one's eyes to this fact, on the contrary, a great deal of harm is done. In the face of every effort on the part of the executive authorities to prevent the entry of the insane and the feeble-minded, unquestionably a number of immigrants of this class do enter the country every year who would be detected and excluded if the medical officers were able to conduct a more comprehensive examination. A word as to the feeble-minded. Not only are they likely to become a public charge on the community, but they are also quite likely to join the ranks of the criminal classes. In addition they may leave feeble-minded descendants. Many immigrant children who are feeble-minded or mentally backward may be found in the public schools of our large eastern cities. In both of my last annual reports (to which I refer) I dealt with this subject, with the result that numerous chambers of commerce throughout the United States passed resolutions calling upon Congress to furnish the executive authorities with all means necessary to enable them to execute the law. These means, however, are in part still lacking.

THE INSPECTION OF IMMIGRANTS BY IMMIGRANT INSPECTORS.

Correctly and promptly to "inspect" an immigrant is an art of which not all of the officials known as immigrant inspectors are masters. Under this term is included both what is known as primary inspection and examination by boards of special inquiry. To inspect means to view closely and critically; and to do this as to some

900,000 immigrants a year under a statute which requires the detection of such difficult matters, amongst others, as pauperism, likelihood of becoming a public charge,
what physical defects will affect ability to earn a living, criminality and contract
labor, is a task truly gigantic, calling for industry, intelligence, ability to examine
and cross-examine with a view to ascertaining relevant and (what is almost equally
important) omitting irrelevant facts, some knowledge of human nature, and constant
exercise of sound judgment.   This work would be difficult enough if it could be done
through the medium of the English language, in place of which it must be performed
through some forty foreign languages and dialects; also it is usually done under heavy
pressure, especially during periods when the monthly arrivals are from 80.000 to 100,-
000.   The work of the boards of special inquiry is perhaps even more difficult than
that of the primary inspectors.   Annually they dispose of over 60,000 cases.   Often
8 boards are in session, calling for the services of 24 inspectors (in addition
to clerks, stenographers, interpreters, and messengers).   It is believed that a correct
execution of the immigration law, with its indefinite tests applicable to human
beings, calls for work as difficult as that required of any executive officers in any
country; and yet the inspectors available both for primary inspection and special
inquiry duty are too few, with the result that they are required to work too rapidly
and sometimes during too long hours.   Also the primary inspectors are burdened with
too many clerical duties while "inspecting" immigrants; for instance, they are, for
lack of proper assistance, required to make corrections in long hand on the manifests
for as many as six hours a day, thus rendering it impossible for them to put their
whole mind on the larger matters before them.   And yet these men are executing a
statute which the Supreme Court has declared to be one of "police and public security."   (Japanese Immigrant Case, 189 U. S., 86, 97.)   We have here another instance
of Congress creating the work, but persistently neglecting to furnish many of the facilities required for its correct execution.
   While our immigrant inspectors as a body are able, conscientious, and intelligent,
yet it is not unnatural that there should be amongst them some who lack the peculiar
talent necessary to inspect immigrants.   This is something for which civil-service
examinations alone do not determine their fitness.   They are a very proper preliminary, but those who, having passed them, become immigrant inspectors should
thereafter be subjected to frequent tests by experienced officers with a view to determining whether or not they are really doing inspection work and are able and willing
to assume the responsibility for exercising the judgment which the statute calls for,
or whether (when acting as primary inspectors) they are principally engaged in regis-
tering the immigrant's answers, often at the outset false, to the questions on the
manifest; or (when sitting on boards of inquiry) whether they fail to do independent
thinking and merely join in the decisions suggested by others.   The men who are found
fit and competent to do real inspection work should receive better remuneration
than is now given men of this class.
   There is a general impression that the primary inspector errs only by passing the
unfit.   He is just as likely to err the other way and through unwillingness or inability
really to inspect to delay the admission of the eligible immigrant and transfer to the
board of special inquiry work which he should do.   In this connection I desire to
point out something that is very often overlooked, namely, that the protection which
the immigrant receives against improper exclusion is infinitely greater than that
which the Government receives against improper admission, for an immigrant can
be excluded only as a result of the concerted action of a number of officials, whereas a
single official has power to admit.   If this be right, it is a most convincing argument
in favor of placing none but competent and reliable officials at primary inspection
work.   If a proper number of inspectors were available I should be in favor of placing
two at each line, one of them charged with the power to act as examining inspector
and the other to be there to exercise the statutory privilege which every inspector has
of challenging an admission at primary inspection, which privilege, through lack of
officials, is now exercised only a few times in each year.

THE EXPULSION OF ALIENS ALREADY IN THE UNITED STATES.

   This occurs under sections 20 and 21 of the immigration law.   Concerning the same
the Supreme Court has said that "the power to exclude aliens and the power to expel
them rest upon one foundation, are derived from one source, are supported by the
same reasons, and are in truth but parts of one and the same power," and that "deportation is the removal of an alien out of the country simply because his presence is
deemed inconsistent with the public welfare." (Fon Yue Ting v. United States,
149 U. S., 698.)
   The law and procedure applicable to this class of cases is widely different from that
applicable to aliens seeking admission, but the two have this in common, that they
both cast upon the authorities a great deal of difficult and delicate work.   Aliens who

have become established here resent being disturbed in their residence and are often in a position to command the sympathy and support of their neighbors. The statute is silent as to any hearing to be granted before expulsion occurs, but under a decision of the Supreme Court they are entitled to and always receive one. Of this hearing it has been said (Japanese Immigrant Case, 189 U. S., 86):

"It is not necessarily an opportunity upon a regular set occasion and according to the form of judicial procedure, but one that will secure the prompt, vigorous action contemplated by Congress and at the same time be appropriate to the nature of the case upon which such officers are required to act."

During the past year there have occurred over 1,100 such hearings, and they have related to insane persons, criminals, inmates of reformatories, persons who have become public charges, prostitutes, and others found in the United States in violation of law. Deportation was subsequently ordered by the department in about 90 per cent of these cases. Sometimes the conduct of the hearings is simple, but often it is complicated, partly through the efforts of counsel for the alien to treat it as a judicial trial, whereas, in fact, it is merely an executive hearing, and to introduce matter which is irrelevant or inconclusive upon the only issue, which is whether the alien should be deported. It is not usually practicable for the commissioner to preside in person at these hearings and it is necessary for him to delegate this duty to some official who has a grasp of the nature of these proceedings and who will act with fairness to both sides and yet with firmness, so that they may be kept within proper limits and a record created which shall on its face justify the action subsequently taken thereon.

This office has frequently called attention to a serious defect in one of the statutory provisions relating to this subject, namely, that which limits the expulsion of those who become a public charge to cases due to a "cause existing prior to landing." The language quoted places upon the Government a burden of proof which it should not be called upon to sustain. In the cases of those who have come down with insanity and become public charges in insane asylums it is often impossible for the Government to learn the original cause of the insanity. It is usually without means of ascertaining their mental condition abroad or their heredity, and it is likely to have arrayed against it relatives and friends who are desirous that the aliens remain in the United States at public expense. At least the burden of proof should be shifted, so that all aliens becoming public charges within a given period (five years preferable to three years, as now provided) should be subject to deportation, unless it can be affirmatively shown on their behalf that the cause arose subsequent to landing. The principal sufferers from the objectionable phraseology of the present law are the many State and municipal institutions throughout the country which are burdened with the care of aliens who are unable to support themselves or whom it is necessary to hold in confinement in hospitals, jails, and elsewhere. If these institutions were to unite in an effort to induce Congress to change the law to meet the requirements of the situation, it can hardly be doubted that such effort would be crowned with success.

DEFECTS IN THE LAW.

There is great lack of precision on the part of those who speak of the law as defective. The layman who says that it is usually means that in his opinion it fails to designate enough classes of immigrants as excludable. He has no knowledge of the defects which inhere in the administrative machinery of the law and render it difficult for administrative officers to exclude those who under the terms of the law as it is are subject to exclusion. There will always be differences of opinion (many of them honest) as to whether or not there should be additional excluded classes. That is a subject which concerns primarily the legislators. But there can be no honest differences of opinion as to the necessity for perfecting the machinery through which the present law is to be enforced. My last annual report mentioned a number of the defects of this class which I shall not repeat here. They will be found discussed in that report under the headings "Mentally defective immigrants," "Fraudulent use of ship's articles to land ineligible aliens," "Alien criminals," and "Important defects in the law." Legislators perform only a part of their duty when they place laws on the statute books without providing executive officers with adequate means to enforce them. The machinery for the collection of customs duties is far more complete than that through which the immigration authorities are expected to enforce a much more difficult and delicate law. Speaking for myself, I have never been able to see why the differences of opinion as to whether or not there should be more excluded classes should be permitted to delay remedying the obvious defects in the administrative machinery of the present law. With these defects cured and adequate appropriations a great deal could be accomplished for the benefit of the country under this law (excellent so far as it goes) which is now necessarily left undone.

HOLDING IMMIGRANTS WITH LOATHSOME AND CONTAGIOUS DISEASES FOR HOSPITAL TREATMENT.

The law excludes immigrants of these classes from admission, yet their resident relatives frequently urge that they be held at Ellis Island for cure and not deported. It is easy to phrase these requests in language which will appeal to one's sympathies, but there is another side to this matter to which executive officials must give serious consideration. The diseases usually involved are trachoma and tinea tonsurans (ringworm of scalp), and as a rule these are either ineradicable or they yield to treatment only after a very long period. In the meantime the patients, who are in other respects bodily sound, become discontented; in fact, almost from the start they make bad hospital patients, and as time goes on confinement becomes more and more irksome. They become a disturbing element and add to the difficulty of maintaining hospital discipline. Their relatives employ physicians who, acting the part of advocates, often seek to raise false or irrelevant issues with the Government medical officers. In many cases the hospital expenses become burdensome to the relatives, who after a while decline to make further payments. As a matter of fact it has often happened that after six months the same relatives who at the outset were most anxious to have the executive authorities stretch their discretionary powers to the limit to save the immigrant from deportation change their attitude and beg to have him returned to his home country.

Petitions for hospital treatment are addressed to the discretion of the department, and there are now being held at Ellis Island for treatment under its orders 14 cases of the foregoing character. Some of them have been under treatment as long as 10 months without cure having been effected, and unless in the meantime deportation occurs several may be here another year. Each case of this class held for treatment invites attempts to bring here other immigrants with loathsome and contagious diseases in the hope that the executive authorities may be induced to show them a similar favor. Indeed, it is extremely difficult to know where to draw the line without showing partiality.

This office does not desire to take the position that no case of loathsome or contagious disease should ever be held for treatment, but in its opinion no case should be held which does not come within the plain terms of section 37 of the law. This would exclude holding any case where our medical officers have declared that treatment will at best be prolonged and tedious, with the final outcome uncertain, and this would be in accordance with the intent of the law. Abroad is the place where cure in such cases should be effected, if it can be effected at all. If the presence here of the diseased person's relatives is to be made the test of detention, an easy way is indicated to embarrass the authorities. The healthy members of the family have merely to come here first, leaving the diseased member to come later with some friend, and that this course has been frequently pursued for.the express purpose of bringing pressure to bear on the authorities the records amply show. In considering this subject the importance must be borne in mind of not permitting the hardship of individual cases to break down a correct administration of the law—though it is very questionable whether it is really a hardship to an immigrant to refuse to detain him at Ellis Island for nine months or a year with the possibility of eventual deportation even after such lengthy detention.

ADDITIONS AND IMPROVEMENTS TO PLANT.

In each of my last three annual reports much has been said on this important subject. Partly out of specific appropriations and partly out of the general allotment many additions and improvements to the plant have been made during the last three years. The main building in particular has undergone numerous and important changes. A fine new story has been erected on its west wing, the special inquiry detention room has been completely remodeled and eight appropriate board rooms now exist where formerly there were only three. The information office, to which thousands come every year from New York City and elsewhere to inquire concerning immigrants, has been quadrupled in size and the new area tiled and wainscoted so that it presents an attractive appearance. Immigrants marked for "temporary detention" are now for the first time held in a large and well ventilated room, which has been newly floored, partly wainscoted, and provided with adequate and modern toilets. Adjoining this room is an open courtyard, which has been cemented and made available for the reception of detained immigrants out of doors during warm weather. The registry or main inspection floor has been completely remodeled in appearance by removing the pipe railing partitions along which immigrants had to pass and substituting therefor appropriate benches, also by removing the stairway, which created a large opening in the middle of the floor, and installing a new one at the easterly end. At the same time the medical offices have been removed from this floor, the whole of which is now available for the inspection of immigrants, its capacity therefor having been thus doubled. New medical offices have been created on the ground floor, and while for lack of space they are still far from being what they should be, yet they are at least four times as large as the former ones and of better appearance. The whole main building has been rewired within and repointed without, the steam-heating apparatus has been repaired at an expense of $40,000, the old copper roof has been replaced with a new one of tile, and a new passenger elevator has been instal-led. A number of further changes have been made in the main building which need not be recited here. Improvements elsewhere consist in the installation of a new and more powerful electric apparatus in the power house, a new floor, wainscoting and ceiling, an automatic oiling system, a new hot-water circulating system, and an ash conveyor.

Near the powerhouse there have been erected a complete ice plant and a garbage crematory. The oldest hospital building has been repointed. Much dredging has been carried on, the great quantity of silt deposited by the waters surrounding Ellis Island rendering it necessary frequently to dredge our channels. Approximately $50,000 have during the last three years been spent for this purpose. A most important contract now being executed concerns the erection at a cost of $115,000 of a cement sea wall with granite facing at a section of Ellis Island. Eventually it will be desir-able in the interest of economy thus to encase the three islands, the life of the existing crib work above high water being very limited. An improvement of the first order will be the erection of an additional story on the dormitory building with outside porches at a cost of $350,000. Bids for this work were recently opened and the contract will be awarded shortly. This improvement will greatly ameliorate the conditions in both the day and night quarters of detained immigrants and permit the substitu-tion of two-tier for three-tier beds. Continued effort has been made to add to the attractive appearance of the grounds by setting out additional privet hedges and hardy plants. A small greenhouse has been erected by our own mechanics from old material, so that the Government is now able to propagate nearly all of the flowering plants needed for beds. The recent sundry civil bill makes appropriations for several important improvements, including a new story on the east wing of the main building, a fireproof carpenter shop, paint shop, and bakery, renovation of interior of the old hospital, and inclosure in glass of long passageway connecting the various units of the contagious disease hospital plant on No. 3 island. Two important additions for which Congress still declines to grant appropriations, though repeatedly urged to do so, are (a) for the creation of quarters in which cabin passengers may be detained (so that they need not be confined with what are commonly known as immigrants—many of them persons of filthy habits); and (b) an additional ferryboat; these are matters which have been specifically mentioned in both of my two last annual reports and I refrain from repeating what is there said concerning them. Since the Govern-ment derives a large annual revenue from aliens arriving at New York (this year over $3,800,000) there is no reason why Congress should refuse to grant for the use of Ellis Island any reasonable appropriation requested. Even with the best of facilities the work of Ellis Island will always be a difficult one to transact, and the executive officers should not be hampered by lack of any tools they may require. It is unfortu-nate that so few legislators visit Ellis Island during the periods of great pressure. Were they to do so they would obtain a realizing sense of the vast amount of business which must be dispatched, and it is hardly to be supposed that they would thereafter withhold any necessary appropriations.

In closing this topic I desire to mention two things: (a) The Ellis Island plant is a costly one, subject to extraordinary wear and tear and, owing to the situation of Ellis Island, its buildings are exposed to the action of the weather to a greater extent than are most Government structures. A great deal more money should be spent on general upkeep than is now the case under the inadequate appropriations available for general maintenance and repairs. While the condition of the plant is on the whole good, yet a great many things are necessarily left undone which would be done if it belonged to private individuals intent on maintaining it at the highest condition of efficiency, all of which is in the end poor economy; (b) we have always experi-enced great difficulty in securing temporary draftsmen to assist our regular force in preparing the plans and specifications for extraordinary improvements. There seems to be a great lack of properly trained men who will accept short terms of employ-ment at the salary which the department has thus far been willing to pay. The result is poor work, which must be gone over at great trouble by the chief engineer and superintendent of repairs before bids can be solicited thereon. This in turn means delay where expedition is often important.

CLEANLINESS AND SANITATION.

I know of no other Government institution where the maintenance of cleanliness is a more important consideration than at Ellis Island, and no effort is spared to bring this about. But the problem is a difficult one, not only because of the thousands of immigrants and other persons who pass through or come to Ellis Island daily, but (principally) because it is so often necessary to detain overnight from 1,200 to 1,800 immigrants, many of them possessing low standards of living and habits which are truly filthy. The most difficult portions of Ellis Island to keep clean are, therefore, the rooms in which immigrants of this type are detained. These rooms have tile flooring and wainscoting, and a large force of laborers is engaged in cleaning them as many times a day as seems necessary, including scouring them with hot water and disinfectants at least once each day. Their condition, all things considered, is remarkably good. Blankets used by immigrants are cleaned and disinfected daily. From time to time, however, some one discovers that a detained immigrant has been bitten by vermin and critics proceed to blame the immigration authorities for allowing vermin to exist in the detention quarters, overlooking the fact that they do not originate here but are brought by immigrants both on their persons and in their baggage, some of which contains perishable food. Considering the characteristics of many of the people who occupy the detention rooms every night, it is rather surprising that complaints of this nature should be as rare as they are. One thing is certain: So long as immigration continues certain classes of immigrants will continue to arrive with vermin, and the question before the Government is how far it will go in its efforts to exterminate such vermin. I think it should adopt all reasonable means to do so. One such means is to compel detained immigrants to take baths appropriate to exterminating the vermin on their bodies and by fumigating their clothing and baggage at the same time. To carry out these measures a special plant will be required. It can and should be erected. With such a plant in existence the likelihood of transmission of disease would be reduced to a minimum, detained immigrants accustomed to cleanliness would not run the risk of contamination from immigrants of filthy habits, and complete cleanliness could be maintained in all detention rooms.

PROTECTION OF IMMIGRANTS.

The statute makes it the duty of the immigration authorities to protect immigrants "from fraud and loss." This is a high duty and the opportunity to perform it should be regarded as a privilege. Few persons are more contemptible than those who will exploit the ignorant immigrant, and yet an immense amount of such exploitation occurs, particularly by the immigrants' own countrymen in the United States. Until widely different facilities are provided by Congress it will be beyond the power of the immigration authorities to afford the immigrant much protection after he is landed, though in the long run most protection of this character must come from State and municipal authorities, some of whom could advantageously display more zeal than they do in the welfare of our newcomers. But prior to the time when they leave the control of the Federal authorities the latter have various opportunities to afford them protection. During years of heavy immigration those who pass through Ellis Island may bring with them as much as $30,000,000, and there are various devious ways in which they will be relieved of a portion thereof unless great vigilance is exercised on their behalf by the commissioner and his subordinates. One of the ways in which, in the past, this has occurred was through the false missionary, who, after receiving immigrants at Ellis Island, thereafter conducted them to boarding houses where they were detained unnecessarily at high charges and subjected to numerous other impositions. To these matters reference has been made in my annual reports of 1909, 1910, and 1911. Now the false missionary has been banished, and it is not believed that any missionary now at Ellis Island would act in a manner detrimental to an immigrant. Furthermore, the practice gradually instituted during the past four years of detaining here those whose inspection can not be completed until some responsible person shall call for them, or until addresses can be verified or corrected, works very well indeed and has reduced materially the number whom it is necessary to send to mission houses.

At Ellis Island there are many contractors or privilege holders with numerous employees. One of the most important is the contractor for the privilege of furnishing food, and in times past much exploitation of immigrants has occurred through maladministration of his office. The best guaranty that the Government can have that they shall receive proper meals, that the boxes of food sold them shall contain full measure, and that they shall neither be overcharged therefor nor forced to buy excessive amounts is the presence here of a contractor of standing and character. But it is desirable also that the food furnished at meals be frequently tasted and the contents of the boxes frequently investigated (both before and after they have been sold) by Government agents in order that the authorities shall have positive and direct knowledge of what is done under the contract. Twice (in 1902 and again in 1909) the present commissioner found that the food furnished immigrants at meals was bad and that they were systematically overcharged for the contents of the boxes. The action taken against the then privilege holders is a matter of record. Similarly it has twice been found that the contract for the delivery of immigrants' baggage was being maladministered, a subject upon which this office in 1902 and 1911 had occasion to make some pointed remarks.

There are other ways in which immigrants may be imposed upon at Ellis Island. It is now a large place, and sometimes it may be necessary to permit as many as 2,000 persons to come here in one day in connection with the arriving immigrants. Notwithstanding the exercise of all reasonable care some unscrupulous strangers find their way to the island, and while there, as well as on the ferryboat, seek in various ways to exploit the ignorant immigrant bound for New York. A class of person who does little credit to his profession is the lawyer who charges immigrants or their relatives (often recent immigrants themselves) exorbitant sums for services he does not render, and who sues out writs of habeas corpus in bad faith and where there is no chance of success. Happily most of the "guides" and "runners" who used to waylay the immigrant at the Barge Office have been driven to cover, and this is due in part to the establishment by the North American Civic League for Immigrants of its excellent guide and transfer system at Ellis Island.

It is not the purpose hereof to do more than point out the great necessity for the exercise of vigilance at many points if Ellis Island is to be what it should be, namely, a place where justice under the law shall be done both to the people of the United States and to the immigrants and where the latter shall receive proper general treatment and protection against extortion. While, as already stated, most of the protection required after landing should properly come from State and municipal authorities, yet the immigration authorities should at least be put in a position where from time to time they may send out officials on the trains, even to considerable distances from New York, so as to obtain accurate knowledge at first hand of what happens to the immigrants on their journey westward and whether or not they reach their destinations safely. There is a great opportunity for evil-minded persons to deflect from their destinations some classes of immigrants, particularly young girls. Again, many girls arrive with addresses of improper places, some of which we uncover by timely investigations, but many of them necessarily pass unnoticed. Officials have occasionally been sent out on trains by this office and their reports filed, but the practice should become an established one, and that can only be in case of larger appropriations.

CONCLUSION.

While the duties of the commissioner at Ellis Island are purely executive, yet it is impossible for anyone to hold this position for a number of years without forming an opinion as to whether or not the present law reaches all undesirable aliens who seek to enter this country. That this is not the case must be the inevitable conclusion of any disinterested observer; nor is this surprising when the low requirements of the law are considered. It is good so far as it goes, but excludes only manifestly objectionable classes, such as idiots, imbeciles, the insane, paupers, persons likely to become a public charge, persons with loathsome or dangerous contagious diseases, persons whose physical or mental defects prevent them from earning a living, criminals, procurers and prostitutes. At the same time that the requirements of the law are low, a large portion of the immigrants are from backward races and from the poorer classes of some of the poorer countries in Europe; the best laborers and artisans of the best countries and races are not coming to us in large numbers. To enact a statute which shall reach the undesirables now permitted to enter the country will be no easy matter. Many of them are illiterate, but others are not. Still less is it possible to state accurately what proportion of the present immigration is made up of such undesirables, though it is believed to be small as compared with the number of immigrants of the right sort who are coming to our shores. It is precisely because the undesirable minority comes as a part of and is mingled with a lot of desirable immigrants that it fails, unfortunately, to attract the attention it deserves and is thus still permitted to enter. The writer is one of those who believe that in determining what additional immigrants we shall receive, we should remember that our first duty is to our own country. These are matters which I discussed at some length in my last annual report under the heading "Some aspects of immigration," and another year's experience confirms me in the correctness of the views therein expressed.

WILLIAM WILLIAMS, Commissioner.

REPORT OF CHINESE INSPECTOR IN CHARGE, DISTRICT NO. 3, COMPRISING NEW YORK AND NEW JERSEY.[1]

I have the honor to submit my report covering the fiscal year ended June 30, 1913, appending for statistical purposes three schedules, marked A, B, and C, respectively, showing the disposition of cases arising under the jurisdiction of this office during the said period. The work of this office in enforcing the Chinese exclusion law may be considered as of two classes, administrative and judicial.

Schedule A appertains to cases included in the administrative class, and shows that there were 47 applicants for admission at this port, of whom 33 were admitted and 14 denied admission, 13 of the latter number being actually deported and 1 awaiting deportation at the close of the year; also, that the privilege of transit through the United States was granted to 398, and the departure verified of 744 to whom a like privilege was granted at other ports. In addition to the work involved in connection with these cases, Schedule B shows that there were 10 applications for return certificates for departure via this port (the small number being by reason of the fact that we have no direct line of vessels leaving this port for China), while there were 297 applications for return certificates filed in and investigated by this office for departure via other ports and investigations made in 201 cases where Chinese were applying for admission to the United States at other ports. making a total of 555 cases of this character, necessitating the examination of from 1,200 to 1,500 witnesses.

In the judicial class may be included the cases covered by Schedule C, which shows the disposition of cases of Chinese persons arrested in this district upon the charge of being unlawful residents, and from which it will be noted that there were 36 arrests made during the year, which, with the 26 pending from the previous year, make a total of 62 considered by the courts, of which number 11 were discharged, 19 actually deported, 20 pending, and 12 awaiting deportation at the close of the year. Of the latter 12 cases, however, only 1 defendant is in custody, the other 11 having been released several years ago upon their personal recognizance and nominal bail through an arrangement entered into by their counsel and the United States attorney at Buffalo whereby they were used as witnesses against the parties who assisted in smuggling them into the United States, since which time no further action has been taken in their cases.

During the past year, as during the previous fiscal year, no Chinese submitted to arrest at the Canadian border for the purpose of having their alleged citizenship passed upon by United States commissioners, as had been the custom for years prior to that time. This, of course, is accounted for by reason of the Wong You decision of the Supreme Court holding that Chinese are amenable to the general immigration laws and that they could therefore be taken into custody upon warrants of arrest issued by the Secretary and deported to the trans-Pacific or trans-Atlantic port of original embarkation, on the ground of having entered the country without inspection. Notwithstanding this decision, however, in a number of cases in which the Chinese had entered the country from Canada and were therefore taken into custody upon Secretary's warrants and later ordered deported to China, writs of habeas corpus were secured; and while the district court dismissed them, the circuit court for the second circuit, on appeal, recently reversed the action of the lower court, sustaining the writs on the ground that while there was sufficient evidence to show that the petitioners had entered the country unlawfully from Canada and were therefore illegally within the United States, they could not be deported to China for the reason that there was no evidence in the record to show that they originally embarked from that country for the United States, and directed that the warrants of deportation be amended to deport them to Canada. We will be unable to carry out the mandate of the court to deport them to Canada, for the reason that that country requires a $500 head tax, and hence I presume we will be compelled to file complaints and have the cases finally passed upon by a United States commissioner. I understand that the Attorney General has under consideration at the present time the question of applying to the Supreme Court for a writ of certiorari for a review of this decision, and unless it is reversed I am reasonably certain that the conditions, at least in the Northern District of New York, of Chinese submitting to arrest and having their cases established before United States commissioners by fraudulent testimony to the effect that they were born in the United States, will soon be revived, as the Chinamen will naturally be instructed by the local attorneys and "steerers" engaged in this work to stand mute, knowing that we will then be unable to establish the fact that they embarked from China. This situation I feel can be effectually met only by new legislation.

---

[1] The magnitude of the work in district No. 3 necessitates conducting the Chinese separately from the immigration portion thereof.

This office is also called upon to verify the arrival and departure of all vessels at this port having aboard Chinese crews, of which during the past year there were 239, having aboard 4,277 Chinese. Of this number 39 escaped, and while the circumstances of each case were investigated by this office and reported to the United States attorney for the proper district, we were invariably advised that in view of decisions rendered in both the Southern and Eastern Districts of New York the facts were not considered sufficient to warrant the prosecution of the master. As the bureau knows, United States Judge Hand, sitting in this district, has held that the Chinese exclusion law does not apply to seamen, and while United States Judge Chatfield, in the Eastern District, has held to the contrary, United States Judge Veeder, in that district, following the decision of Judge Chatfield, has held that it is necessary for us to show an actual landing, which is almost impossible, and, further, that being a penal statute, it should be construed strictly, and consequently it would be necessary to establish that the act was committed with the knowledge of the master. The present statute is therefore inadequate, and I can not too strongly urge the necessity of new legislation, imposing a fine upon the owners, agents, masters, etc., for every alien Chinaman brought into this port on their vessels as a member of the crew and who is not aboard at the time of departure.

All of the officers serving under my direction have been faithful in the performance of their duties, and I have received the hearty cooperation of each, which accounts for the results obtained.

H. R. SISSON, *Inspector in Charge.*

SCHEDULE A.—APPLICANTS FOR ADMISSION TO AND THE PRIVILEGE OF TRANSIT THROUGH THE UNITED STATES AT THE PORT OF NEW YORK, N. Y., FISCAL YEAR ENDED JUNE 30, 1913.

Class.	Before inspector.			Before Department.			Summary.		
	Applicants.	Admitted.	Denied.	Appealed.	Sustained.	Dismissed.	Admitted.	Deported.	Awaiting deportation.
American citizens	2	2					2		
Wives of American citizens	1	1					1		
Section 6, travelers	4	4					4		
Section 6, students	14	12	2	1		1	12	2	
Section 6, merchants	7	7					7		
Other merchants	1		1					1	
Officials	7	7					7		
Miscellaneous [1]	11		11	1		1		10	1
Total	47	33	14	2		2	33	13	1

Applicants for transit by land 373
Applicants for transit by water 25
Transits passing out 744

SCHEDULE B.—TABLE SHOWING DISPOSITION OF CASES OF RESIDENT CHINESE APPLYING FOR RETURN CERTIFICATES AT THE PORT OF NEW YORK UNDER RULES 13, 15, AND 16, DURING THE FISCAL YEAR ENDED JUNE 30, 1913.

Class.	Before inspector.			
	Applications submitted.	Granted.	Denied.	Pending.
Natives	3	2		1
Exempts	7	3		4
Total	10	5		5

[1] 1 Chinese holding naturalization paper; 10 stowaways.

SCHEDULE C.—TABLÉ SHOWING NUMBER AND STATUS OF CHINESE ARREST CASES IN THE DISTRICT OF NEW YORK AND NEW JERSEY DURING THE FISCAL YEAR ENDED JUNE 30, 1913.

Commissioner.	Before commissioner.						Before district court.						Before circuit court of appeals.						Summary.				
	Pending from 1912.	Arrested 1912-13.	Total.	Discharged.	Ordered deported.	Pending close 1913.	Pending from 1912.	Appealed 1912-13.	Total.	Commissioner affirmed.	Commissioner reversed.	Pending close 1913.	Pending from 1912.	Appealed 1912-13.	Total.	Lower court affirmed.	Lower court reversed.	Pending close 1913.	Awaiting deportation from 1912.	Discharged.	Deported.	Pending close 1913.	Awaiting deportation close 1913.
Shields, J. A.	7	18	25	3	14	8	1	5	6	4	1	1	1	5	6	3	...	3	1 1	3	13	12	...
Keating, G. P.		2	2	...	1	1		1	1	1	...	...	...	...	...	...	...	...	2 1 1	...	1	1	11
Block, L. W.	1	1	2	1	1	...	...	...	...	...	...	...	...	...	...	...	...	...	1	1	...	...	...
Mills, B. H.	3	1	4	2	2	...	...	...	...	...	...	...	...	...	...	...	...	...	2	2	...	...	...
Benedict, B. L.	...	2	2	2	...	...	...	...	...	...	...	...	...	...	...	...	...	...	2	...	...	...	...
Morle, R.	...	2	2	...	2	...	...	2	2	...	2	...	...	...	...	...	...	...	2	...	...	...	...
Cahoone, J. G.	...	2	2	...	1	1	...	...	...	...	...	...	...	...	...	...	...	...	1	1	...	...	...
Cochran, J. G.	...	2	2	...	2	...	...	2	2	...	2	...	...	...	...	...	...	...	2	...	...	...	...
Stockton, R.	1	5	6	...	3	3	...	1	1	...	1	...	...	...	...	...	...	...	2	4	...	...	...
Joline		1	1	...	1	...	...	1	1	1	...	...	...	...	...	...	...	...	...	...	...	...	1
Total	12	36	48	9	26	13	1	12	13	6	3	4	1	5	6	3	...	3	12	11	19	20	12

[1] This case awaiting deportation June 30, 1912, was appealed to circuit court of appeals during fiscal year 1913.
[2] These Chinese not in custody, 10 having been released on personal recognizance and 1 awaiting action on bond.

REPORT OF COMMISSIONER OF IMMIGRATION, PHILADELPHIA, IN CHARGE OF DISTRICT NO. 4, COMPRISING PENNSYLVANIA, DELAWARE, AND WEST VIRGINIA.

I respectfully submit herewith report of the workings of the immigration service at this port and in this district during the fiscal year ended June 30, 1913:

ARRIVALS.

There were examined and inspected during the year 68,424 persons from foreign ports who arrived at the port of Philadelphia. This number includes cabin as well as steerage passengers, and is itemized as follows:

First-cabin arrivals, 621; second-cabin arrivals, 8,659; and steerage arrivals, 59,144. This number includes 4,019 United States citizens; 997 aliens in transit; 32 tourists; 158 citizens of Canada, Cuba, and Mexico; 15 returning cattlemen; 23 bird men; 4 diplomatic officers; and 32 persons who arrived as passengers for the purpose of reshipping outbound as members of crews. Also 420 aliens who were excluded on arrival, and deported. However, in addition to this total number, there were 1,471 alien seamen who deserted at this port.

DEPARTURES.

During the fiscal year 7,658 emigrant aliens, 2,285 nonemigrant aliens, and 4,837 United States citizens departed from this port, making a total of 14,780.

*   *   *   *   *   *   *

BOARDS OF SPECIAL INQUIRY.

Seven thousand three hundred and forty-five persons were before the board of special inquiry, and, in addition to this number, 7,342 persons were temporarily detained for minor causes, making a total of 14,687.

In connection with these cases, there were prepared, executed, and forwarded to the bureau, under instructions from the bureau, 42 bonds that aliens shall not become public charges, Form 554; 52 children's bonds, with school and public-charge clauses, Form 579; and 51 bonds for hospital treatment in institutions other than those maintained by the Immigration Service, Form 578.

Four hundred and twenty aliens were excluded by board of special inquiry and deported.

FINES.

One hundred and thirty-seven fines, in the sum of $100 each, amounting to $13,700, were imposed upon the steamship companies for bringing in the following mentally or physically afflicted aliens:

(1) Mental afflictions:
Imbecility... 2
Idiocy.. 1
(2) Tuberculosis.. 1
(3) Other loathsome or dangerous contagious diseases:
Syphilis.. 1
Trachoma... 132

when the existence of the disease or disability might have been detected by competent medical examination at the port of foreign embarkation, and so certified by the United States Public Health Surgeon.

In addition to this number fines were imposed in 3 cases of trachoma, but were later refunded—2 on account of United States citizenship being proven and 1 on account of it being shown that the alien's father had declared his intention to become a United States citizen.

CASES OF ALIENS ACCORDED HOSPITAL TREATMENT.

Hospital treatment was granted under sections 19 and 37 of the immigration laws in 51 cases; this number does not include 4 cases pending from the previous fiscal year.

*   *   *   *   *   *   *

DESERTING AND DISCHARGED SEAMEN.

A complete record of all deserting and discharged seamen was kept by this office. Said record shows that 1,471 alien seamen deserted at this port during the fiscal year (exclusive of United States citizens); and that 413 discharged seamen were inspected, each person being examined under oath and given a medical examination by a public health surgeon before being released, 44 of them desiring to remain in this country, and 369 stating that they intended to reship.

I am informed that many seamen sign on at foreign ports for the purpose of deserting when they come to a United States port, so that they can sign on another vessel here, as the wages paid to seamen signed on in the United States are greater than those paid to seamen signed on in most foreign ports, and I am of the opinion that this method of entry into the United States, under the present regulations regarding seamen, is being employed by many aliens who are ineligible to be admitted.

*   *   *   *   *   *   *

MEDICAL INSPECTION OF ARRIVING ALIENS.

Of the total number of aliens examined on arrival, also seamen examined either for the purpose of landing or for the purpose of remaining in the United States, the Public Health surgeon on duty at this station keeping no separate record of alien passengers and seamen examined, 2,359 were certified for or noted as having physical or mental defects, 283 of whom were deported.

During the fiscal year there were 104 cases of diseased and injured aliens treated by the Public Health surgeons at the detention house at this station. There were also 1 childbirth and 6 deaths, the causes of the latter were as follows:

Pneumonia, following measles (children)....................................... 4
Pleuro-pneumonia (adult)... 1
Convulsions (infant)... 1

HOSPITAL CASES.

There were reported to this office by the various hospitals as receiving treatment 297 aliens. These were fully investigated. In numerous cases the aliens' landing could not be verified, or the cost of care and maintenance in the hospital was paid by

192   REPORT OF COMMISSIONER GENERAL OF IMMIGRATION.

the alien or relatives or friends, or they did not appear to be proper subjects for treatment under the Immigration Laws and Regulations, and the hospital authorities were so advised. However, those cases were reported to the bureau in which, after investigation, the facts warranted such procedure, and 79 public charges were deported on instructions contained in warrants issued by the department.

This number does not include hospital cases arising in the Pittsburgh district, which are treated separately in this report.

DEPORTATIONS.

Of the total number of arrivals at this port during the fiscal year there were 420 aliens excluded and deported. With the exception of the North German Lloyd arrivals, these excluded aliens were deported from this port.

*   *   *   *   *   *   *

There were 208 aliens deported under departmental warrants of deportation, issued as a result of investigations conducted by this office—114 via this port, 84 via the port of New York, 7 via the port of Baltimore, 1 via the port of Norfolk, 1 via the port of Boston, and 1 via Toronto. This number does not include the deportations arising in the Pittsburgh district, which are treated separately in this report.

*   *   *   *   *   *   *

CONTRACT LABOR.

There were 24 cases (involving 124 aliens) of suspected violations of the contract labor law investigated in this district during the fiscal year, 19 cases prior to the admission of the aliens, they being detained at port of arrival pending investigation at destination, and 5 cases subsequent to the admission of the aliens, as a result of which 2 aliens were deported.

"WHITE-SLAVE" TRAFFIC, PROSTITUTES, AND PROCURERS.

There were 85 cases of prostitution, importation, and immorality investigated by this office during the fiscal year. As a result of these investigations 51 warrants of arrest were issued by the department, and 29 aliens deported, exclusive of 1 alien who died while under order of deportation. This does not include cases arising in the Pittsburgh district, which cases were included under heading "Pittsburgh sub-station."

This number, when compared with that for the previous fiscal year, shows an increase of over 30 per cent in cases investigated, over 100 per cent in warrants of arrest executed, and almost 300 per cent in deportations of prostitutes and importers effected. This increase should be ascribed to the hearty cooperation of this office with the local office of the Bureau of Investigations of the Department of Justice, whose increased activity during the past fiscal year developed many of the cases. The number of deportations of prostitutes could have been still further increased, but several cases offered opportunity for testing a policy of giving them another chance to demonstrate their fitness to remain in the United States, and it must be said that, with the exception of two or three, they are doing so. * * * It is believed that the action of this office in securing the deportation at Government expense of a number of prostitutes who had been in the United States for a period longer than three years has caused a considerable number of foreign prostitutes to seek other employment.

During the year there were 2 prosecutions brought against procurers or importers. Each received a sentence of one year imprisonment and $100 fine.

GENERAL INVESTIGATIONS.

Miscellaneous investigations to the number of 170 were conducted by this office during the fiscal year. This number includes cases of alleged criminals, persons likely to become public charges, persons who entered the United States without inspection, etc., and alleged to be in the United States in violation of law, reported to this office direct, or referred to this office by the bureau or other stations, and also includes cases of aliens detained at other ports pending investigation in this district as to their eligibility to be admitted. It does not include cases arising in the Pittsburgh district.

PROSECUTIONS.

During the fiscal year there were instituted by this office the following prosecutions in connection with immigration cases, in which decision was rendered favorable to the Government:

(1) Case of Piotr (Peter) Czeslicki, for having brought one Helene Dombek into the United States for immoral purposes; sentenced to one year's imprisonment and fine of $100.

(2) Case of Donato Scarano, for having imported and harbored one Matilda Tartaglia for immoral purposes; sentenced to one year's imprisonment and fine of $100.

(3) Prosecution of the International Mercantile Marine Co. and the North German Lloyd Steamship Co. for permitting escape of aliens from detention house; fine of $100 imposed.

(4) Prosecution of Theodore Rzepski, steamship agent, subornation of perjury in connection with the case of Mateusz Ciupak and Maryanna Gryzb; reprimanded by the United States commissioner and discharged.

(5) Prosecution of Pavlo Lesciak, for having imported one Kataryna Krawczuk for immoral purposes; held by United States commissioner, but United States attorney agreed to defendant's offer of self-deportation at own expense.

PITTSBURGH SUBSTATION.

*   *   *   *   *   *   *

(1) *Investigations prior to admission of aliens.*—These investigations usually originate at the various ports of entry, and are conducted with a view to determining the admissibility of the applicants for admission. There were 238 cases of this class investigated during the year.

(2) *Investigations subsequent to admission of aliens.*—There were 313 investigations subsequent to the admission of the aliens, consisting of 141 public-charge or hospital cases and 172 cases of alleged illegal entry, such as suspected alien contract laborers entered without inspection, aliens afflicted with loathsome or contagious diseases, persons of alleged immoral character, prostitutes, procurers, criminals, persons likely to become public charges at the time of entry, etc.

There were 128 aliens deported during the year from the Pittsburgh district—91 via New York, 27 via Philadelphia, and 10 via Baltimore. Following are the causes of deportation:

Alien contract laborers	2
Entered without inspection	4
Criminals	2
Pulmonary tuberculosis	17
Favus	[1] 2
Likely to become public charge at time of entry	41
Prostitutes	13
Procurers	2
Insanity	22
Other mental conditions	7
Pregnancy	1
Physical conditions	6
Syphilis	7
Other causes	2
Total	128

This number does not include 11 American-born children accompanying alien parents who were deported.

GENERAL ADMINISTRATION AND PROJECTED IMPROVEMENTS IN STATION.

Since last report the new detention building was opened and occupied, although not entirely equipped at the time, August 19, 1912, and after nearly a year's experience in caring for detained aliens, including emergency hospital treatment, it is more than gratifying to be able to report the success of the new arrangements. The new detention building is absolutely sanitary, and, while it was an entirely new proposition for this office to assume the care and responsibility of aliens, yet by earnest effort and constant work all difficulties have been met and overcome, so that at the present time it can be safely said that the detained aliens are being cared for at the Philadelphia Immigration Station in the best possible manner. * * * An emergency disinfecting plant has been in operation for the purpose of disinfecting blankets after the departure of detained aliens, and emergency hospital rooms have been fully equipped. The services of an additional commissioned officer of the United States Public Health Service, who resides in Gloucester City, and who is available day or night, have been secured. A nurse has also been detailed for duty at the station, also an assistant nurse. Experience has shown that certain changes are imperatively necessary—in-

---

[1] Includes 1 case deported after having been admitted for hospital treatment.

stallation of an electric light plant, ice plant, elevator, suitable disinfecting plant, laundry facilities, and additional plumbing and heating facilities, and sinking an artesian well—and recommendations along these lines will be duly submitted for the approval of the bureau. Since the opening of the detention building all aliens who are excluded or who must be detained temporarily pending investigation after inspection at the respective piers of the trans-Atlantic steamship lines, which are located on the Pennsylvania side, have been delivered by the steamship companies at the new detention house, using special ferryboat to Gloucester City and suitable busses from Gloucester Ferryhouse to this station. Owing to the failure of the contractor to finish the new pier at the station within the contract period (and even at the close of the fiscal year it was still unfinished), this system of delivering detained aliens is still continued, but as soon as the pier is completed the special ferryboat carrying the detained aliens will land them on the pier of this station, thus avoiding the transfer by busses from the Gloucester ferry, through the streets, to this station.

It is very much to be regretted that the Supervising Architect's Office could not see its way clear to prepare plans for the inspection building to be erected upon the new pier until an additional appropriation of $15,000 was secured from Congress, and it is hoped that every effort will be made by the department to secure the needed amount in order that the completion of the entire plant may not be retarded, or at least placed on a working basis, so that the inspection of arriving aliens may be made at this station instead of, as now, at the several wharves of the trans-Atlantic lines on the Pennsylvania side.

The cordial relations which have heretofore existed between the officials of the customs service at this port and this office still continue. I desire to especially commend the Surgeon General of the United States Public Health Service for his valuable assistance in the establishment of emergency hospital quarters in the detention building by detailing an assistant surgeon to reside in Gloucester City and by the appointment of a nurse and an assistant nurse for hospital duty.

In closing this report it is very gratifying to be able to state that the rank and file of the employees at this station have by their faithful, earnest, and efficient work been of inestimable assistance in making the new station (so far as completed) an undoubted success.

JNO. J. S. RODGERS, *Commissioner.*

REPORT OF COMMISSIONER OF IMMIGRATION, BALTIMORE, MD., IN CHARGE OF DISTRICT NO. 5, COMPRISING MARYLAND AND DISTRICT OF COLUMBIA.

There is submitted herewith annual report of the port of Baltimore for fiscal year ending June 30, 1913:

INWARD PASSENGER MOVEMENT.

United States citizens (including 5 stowaways)	1, 106
Alien passengers	33, 912
Alien stowaways	41
Alien deserters	328
Total arrivals	35, 387

DEPORTATIONS.

Likely to become public charge	74
Favus	12
Trachoma	34
Other loathsome contagious diseases	21
Surgeon's certificates	45
Contract laborers	4
Section 11 (guardians)	15
Convicted of crime	5
Immoral purpose	2
Assisted aliens	1
Under 16 years of age	3
Prostitute	1
Feeble-minded	1
Tuberculosis	1
Insane	1
Total	220

APPEALS.

Number of cases forwarded to bureau on appeal, including applications for special permission for hospital treatment.................................... [1]113

Appeals sustained, aliens admitted outright.............................. [2]23
Appeals sustained, aliens admitted, school bond......................... 11
Appeals sustained, aliens admitted, straight bond....................... 12

Total admitted... 46

Applications for treatment granted...................................... 7
Application for treatment denied, alien deported........................ 1
Appeals denied, aliens deported.. 53
Cases pending close of fiscal year...................................... 6

Total... 67

*   *   *   *   *   *   *

As against 15 cases for the previous year, there was granted during the fiscal year just closed special permission for hospital treatment in 7 cases, involving 11 aliens, 2 of whom were suffering with favus, 5 with ringworm of scalp, and 4 with trachoma. The 2 favus cases have been cured and admitted; 2 of the trachoma were cured and admitted and 2 are still under treatment; all 5 certified for ringworm of scalp are still under treatment, very slow progress toward a cure having been effected.

At the close of last year there were undergoing treatment in the hospitals of Baltimore, Md., Pittsburgh, Pa., Chicago, Ill., Columbus, Ohio, and Dickinson, N. Dak., 8 cases, involving 14 aliens. Of this number, during the year 13 have been landed, leaving Sure Gecht, at Pittsburgh, Pa., the only pending case from the fiscal year closing June 30, 1912. In this girl's case there has been some difficulty in obtaining prompt payment of the hospital expenses. In addition to the pending Gecht case at Pittsburgh, it will be noted that the following cases are still under treatment: Marta Zirotzki, at Jackson, Mich.; Solomon children, Stanislaw Bialek, Barszis children, at Baltimore, Md.

It is interesting to note the expense involved in the treatment of the various diseases, and there are tabulated hereunder some of the cases where the cost has been large:

3 Solomon children (pending).. $1,728
3 Katz children (cured)... 869
Berl Talpis (cured).. 517
2 Barszis children (pending)... 390
Itzig Sobelmann (cured).. 281
Stanislaw Bialek (pending)... 270

The Solomon case is a striking example of the enormous expense which is likely to be encountered by interested relatives and friends when they undertake to guarantee the payment of the cost of treatment.

The hospitals of this city are loth to accept cases of favus and ringworm of the scalp and, as stated in my last annual report, generally refuse to receive them. I understand that the Hebrew Hospital, where the Solomon children are, would be very glad to be relieved of their care, as other patients object to being in the same hospital with such diseases.

*   *   *   *   *   *   *

Another year's experience but emphasizes the inadvisability of granting hospital treatment except in cases of exceeding merit, where the assurances for payment are beyond question.

Another feature of the hospital cases, which it seems almost impossible to make the interested relatives and friends understand, is that payments must be made 15 days prior to the expiration of the time the last remittance covers. Practically, without exception, every time a payment is due it is necessary, in order that the hospital charges may be promptly paid, to write (what should be needless) letters urging the parties to comply with the requirements of the bond.

I would like to say at this point that, in my judgment, much of the suffering and distress caused by these cases would be obviated if the steamship companies were required to make a more efficient and careful medical inspection prior to embarkation.

[1] In addition to the 113 cases forwarded there was 1 case (covering 3 aliens) transmitted in which the following action was taken by the department: One alien admitted outright, one alien admitted on school bond, one alien deported.
[2] Included in the 23 cases admitted outright are the following: One feeble-minded landed by department, one favus landed by department, one alien admitted upon adoption.

CHINESE TRANSACTIONS.

Total cases investigated... 59

At Washington:
Merchants.. 13
Natives.. 10
Laborers... 2
Students.. 1
Wives and minor children of merchants..................................... 4

Total.. 30

At Baltimore:
Merchants.. 3
Natives.. 9
Laborers... 14
Sons of natives.. 2
Duplicate certificates... 1

Total.. 29

There were 11 Chinese seamen brought to this port under bond to reship and 15 taken from Baltimore to other ports under bond for the same purpose.

During the year there were 4 Chinese arrest cases taken before United States commissioners, of whom 2 were returned to the jurisdiction of this office for the action of the board of special inquiry, and deported; the other 2 are still pending, 1 in Baltimore before the United States commissioner and 1 in Washington before the United States court.

There arrived 95 vessels with a total of 1,370 Chinese seamen members in crew, all of whom were checked in and out and descriptive lists prepared, being an increase over last year of 29 ships and 499 seamen. Quite a number of investigations have been made of matters referred to this office from other districts. One Chinese seaman died in a local hospital.

*   *   *   *   *   *   *

Four Chinese stowaways were brought to this port from Jamaica and deported thereto. These 4 Chinese were evidently smuggled aboard fruit steamers at Jamaican ports by stevedores loading bananas, but were discovered by the captains before reaching the United States and reported as stowaways. Masters of these fruit steamers are fully aware of the penalty imposed in Chinese smuggling cases and I believe their ships are now thoroughly searched before leaving foreign ports to avoid legal proceedings should any smugglers be discovered by us upon arrival. A strict watch has also been kept by the immigration officers here, the customs officials cooperating with us in this respect, and steamers have been searched for Chinese and stowaways.

*   *   *   *   *   *   *

FINES IMPOSED.

For violation of section 9, bringing diseased aliens to the United States, there were 9 cases certified to the collector of customs, and the amount involved, $900, was covered into the Treasury.

One conviction was secured under section 24 for perjury before a board of special inquiry in connection with the landing of an alien.

STOWAWAYS.

Total number of stowaways arrived.............................. 46
United States citizens arriving as stowaways................................. 5

Alien stowaways landed.. 4
Alien stowaways deported.. 36
Alien stowaways escaped... 1

Total alien stowaways arrived... 41

While negro stowaways from the West Indies continue to come, their prompt exclusion and deportation has largely discouraged the practice.

DESERTING ALIEN SEAMEN.

There were boarded and inspected during the year 1,024 vessels; 328 seamen were reported as having deserted, of which number 42 were apprehended. As stated in previous annual reports, statistics with regard to alien seamen prove of very little value, for it is a known fact that many seamen desert when by so doing they can reship to advantage and avoid being caught or identified as deserters, and there is yet to be devised a practical way or method by which they may be traced. It is claimed that over 95 per cent of deserting seamen reship for various reasons.

*   *   *   *   *   *   *

MEDICAL INSPECTION.

Baltimore is fortunate in having an able, painstaking and congenial medical examiner who is always willing to cooperate in every way for the prompt and efficient dispatch of the public business of the port.

*   *   *   *   *   *   *

There were 454 aliens detained in the detention house and local hospitals for observation, care, and treatment, this being an increase over the previous year of nearly 50 per cent. It is obvious that the entire time of one surgeon is taken up in visiting the detention house and hospitals in order that the aliens may be promptly certified or released, as the circumstances warrant. * * *

As set forth in my last report, the small capacity of Suydenham Hospital, of Baltimore, for the care of cases of infectious diseases leaves no other alternative but to treat them at the detention house, as no other hospitals in Baltimore accept such cases.

DETENTION HOUSE.

The detention house at Locust Point is kept in as cleanly and sanitary condition as possible, when we consider the habits and absence of hygienic standards of the majority of the aliens necessary to detain. Good and wholesome food is served, and there have been no complaints during the past year worthy of consideration.

LANDING STATION.

Passengers are still disembarked at the Baltimore & Ohio Railroad pier, Locust Point, generally known as the "Landing station." The pier is kept clean; and while the registration floor is ample for our needs, we should have more space for detention rooms and for a second board of special inquiry. The pier is, however, more or less of a "fire trap," it being of wooden construction, with corrugated iron sides and no exterior fire escapes or adequate provision for getting out in case of fire.

SPECIAL-INQUIRY CASES.

There were approximately 1,604 special-inquiry cases tried by your boards, exclusive of rehearings which oftentimes develop situations requiring investigations that result in voluminous records. This is an increase of nearly 400 cases over last year.

The operation of the law with respect to children under 16 years of age, unaccompanied by either parent, has been widely circulated by the steamship companies and their subagents, with the result that fewer children are detained.

In the matter of affording treatment to diseased aliens, where certification makes exclusion mandatory under the law, I am quite satisfied the clear-cut position taken by the new administration has materially decreased much unprofitable correspondence, with advantages to this office in the prompt disposal of such cases, and also eventually as beneficial to the aliens themselves.

Just how many aliens traveling as man and wife, although not lawfully married, enter the United States every year is difficult to estimate, but every effort is made to determine the bona fides of the marital relationship.

*   *   *   *   *   *   *

HABEAS CORPUS CASES.

During the year the records show there were two cases in which writs of habeas corpus were taken out in behalf of aliens, as follows:

Noach Katz, aged 21, Russian Hebrew; certified for favus; excluded and ordered deported; on the day deportation was to be effected this office was served with a writ, returnable two days thereafter; the case came on for a hearing before Judge Rose, in the United States district court; writ was dismissed and alien deported.

Chaim Moische Batlin, aged 20, Russian Hebrew; excluded as assisted alien and physically defective; appealed to department and deportation ordered; writ of habeas corpus taken out June 10, returnable June 11; Judge Rose continued hearing until June 16, 1913, at which time writ was dismissed and deportation effected.

The attitude of our Federal judge with regard to writs of habeas corpus is becoming so well known that attorneys are rather reluctant to take cases of this character before him.

WARRANT CASES.

There were handled 40 warrants of arrest and 56 warrants for deportation. State and city officials, charitable associations, missionaries, and others, reported numerous cases where they thought deportation should occur. All were fully looked into, but in many instances the facts developed proved the aliens to have been in the United States over three years, and therefore warrants could not be asked for.

*　　*　　*　　*　　*　　*　　*

PERSONNEL.

On June 30, 1908, under the former commissioner, considered an economical executive, the force numbered 24, with a total immigration of 32.296. Since then there has been a gradual reduction in the number of inspectors, interpreters, etc., until I am at the present time reduced to 17 employees, with a total immigration of 35,387. During these five years there has been a steady tightening up and a more strict inspection required, entailing longer hearings before the Boards of Special Inquiry, whose cases have increased approximately 33 per cent. Boarding of vessels has increased 24 per cent; verifications of landing, 40 per cent, and immigration 49 per cent. This work at times has severely taxed every employee, we having been on various occasions at the Locust Point Dock, four miles from the center of the city, from 7 in the morning until 8 and 9 o'clock at night.

*　　*　　*　　*　　*　　*　　*

WHITE-SLAVE TRAFFIC.

There have been practically no cases of white-slave traffic, in the usually accepted term, under the immigration laws. The nearest were the following:

Alien woman, inmate of house of prostitution in Baltimore; reported to this office; found to have been in United States less than three years; deported. The keeper of the house, in the United States over five years, likewise deported, but at expense of our appropriation.

A young woman was brought to Baltimore from Philadelphia by a pimp; woman arrested by this department and man by Department of Justice; man was sentenced to but three months' imprisonment owing to girl's refusal to tell all she knew; girl was deported at New York expense of our appropriation, having been here' over three years. A brother of this girl, who seemed horrified at her having anything to do with the pimp, was himself, prior to his sister's deportation, sentenced to 18 months in the Eastern Penitentiary, Philadelphia, for violating the Mann white-slave act.

The Federal white-slave act and the Maryland State pandering act are still being vigorously enforced and the convictions secured have had a most beneficial effect.

This office continues to receive the support and cooperation of the Department of Justice and the local police officials, and it is believed that the coming year may be productive of still greater results in the purifying of the moral atmosphere.

*　　*　　*　　*　　*　　*　　*

GENERAL.

The figures will show that immigration through Baltimore has increased almost 50 per cent, and the demand for passenger accommodations on westbound vessels from Bremen has been so great that two of the North German Lloyd steamers have returned from Baltimore practically in ballast in order to relieve the congestion at Bremen, and the local agents of the North German Lloyd predict a heavy immigration.

Coming principally from Northern and Eastern Europe, via Bremen, the general quality of immigration through this port is good and has improved somewhat over last year, there being a large percentage of women and children coming to join husbands and fathers who have been successful here and intend to make the United States their permanent home. Families prefer to come to Baltimore for the reason that, while the steamers are slower and fares consequently less, they are disembarked, inspected by both the immigration and customs officials, procure their steamship tickets and food, and are entrained on one floor. This advantage has been largely advertised, to the benefit of the port.

Practically, this port does not get first-cabin passengers, receiving only second-cabin, third-class, and steerage. Therefore, while the amount of money per capita brought makes a fair average it can never hope to compare with those where the large liners bring so many wealthy first-cabin passengers.

That there are undesirables admitted because we are unable to exclude them under the present law is conceded by all students of immigration—backward races and those of a low order of intelligence, difficult of assimilation with our own people. A more rigid statute with respect to physical examination would, in my opinion, go far toward solving this serious problem. Who can say the part this tremendous influx of aliens landed during the fiscal year is to play in the future of our country?

NEW SITE FOR IMMIGRATION STATION.

It is my pleasure to report that at last Baltimore has an ideal site for an immigration station, the War Department having turned over to the Treasury Department a portion of the grounds of Fort McHenry for that purpose and of which I am now the custodian. In this connection I quote from my last annual report:

"My understanding is that eventually the fort will be turned over to the city of Baltimore. Might it not be well to take this matter up with the War Department with a view of obtaining the necessary land that is absolutely needed if the port of Baltimore is to hold her own as a place of entry for alien passengers?"

At the close of the fiscal year, June, 1912, the bill for the sale of the site purchased at Locust Point was pending in the Senate. It was enacted during the year and the Treasury Department will no doubt now sell it.

Owing to the efforts of the Maryland Representatives, the War Department, as stated above, ceded for our use a strip of the Fort McHenry land, facing on the main water channel, of sufficient size upon which to erect a pier, office buildings, detention quarters, and hospital. There is yet to be provided an outlet from this site to the nearest city thoroughfare, but this has already been taken up and can unquestionably be arranged.

The most urgent need is for the hospital building, and if at the same time the office building could be erected, our present quarters in the Stewart Building could be vacated and the Government saved $3,000 per annum rental.

    *   *   *   *   *   *   *

In closing I wish again to commend the officers and employees at this station for their fidelity and application to their duties and painstaking care in the performance of the same.

BERTRAM N. STUMP,
Commissioner.

REPORT OF INSPECTOR IN CHARGE, DISTRICT NO. 6, COMPRISING VIRGINIA AND NORTH CAROLINA, WITH HEADQUARTERS AT NORFOLK.

The following is a brief report of the transactions of the immigration service in the sixth district:

At this station (Norfolk), where there is but little immigration, the greater part of the work is confined to seamen, European and Asiatics. During 1913 1,271 foreign vessels arrived at Norfolk and 900 at Newport News, a total of 2,171, or 35 less than 1912. Among this number were many with Chinese aboard, and other aliens—such as those excluded at ports south of Norfolk—the vessels on which they were being deported stopping at Norfolk for coal. All of these classes had to be checked on departure of the vessels. There is a great deal of such work to be done here.

From the foregoing vessels 307 seamen deserted, 177 at Newport News and 130 at Norfolk—9 less than in 1912. It is to be noted that, while Newport News had 571 vessels less than Norfolk, they had 47 more deserters. This condition is due to a determined effort here to bring desertions down to a minimum, a work which will be carried out at Newport News should the occasion arise.

The passenger movement in this district is confined to one line from Norway. The admission of aliens in this district, counting those arriving as seamen (together with those brought by the above-mentioned line) was 390, an increase of 13 over 1912. The collections of head tax in accordance therewith totaled $1,500, an increase of $120 over 1912.

There were 18 exclusions, or about 4½ per cent of arrivals.

There were 17 department warrants of arrest executed, 11 aliens being deported for the following causes:

Likely to become a public charge at time of entry (1 under 16)................ 5
Insane prior to landing.. 3
Prostitute.. 1
Entered for immoral purpose... 1
Procurer (male)... 1

Five warrants were canceled after hearing and one warrant not served on account of disappearance of alien.

Arriving United States citizens totaled 71.

The arrival of Chinese seamen during the past year has been unprecedented. On 185 vessels there arrived 3,351 Chinese, and there were in port at Norfolk one day (June 27) 6 foreign vessels with a total of 144 Chinese. Of this great number but 3 escaped during the year and these were apprehended.

We have been exceptionally fortunate in keeping Chinese crews intact and not having one escape. Twenty-four hours is the longest period a Chinese seaman has been at large. It would not be exact justice to say that fortune favored us entirely in the apprehension of Chinese deserters; the modus operandi calls for quick and effective action, to wit, the master of the vessel concerned is called to the office with his agent and requested to authorize the payment of $50 reward. A complete description of the deserter is given in the first paper published after the desertion takes place, and a great number of typewritten descriptions are immediately prepared by this office and distributed at the various railroad and steamship agencies and to private detectives. Every patrolman is telephoned to on his beat. The result has been, so far, that with so many strings out the deserter will come to a point of contact, and that in a comparatively short time.

There were 5 preinvestigations made in the cases of departing Chinese, of which 1 was disapproved.

The Chinese population in this district is growing all the time, and I feel sure that some of those who come here have been made to feel that the chances of staying are good should they be brought into court.

There were no fines under section 9, and but one fine under section 15.

*   *   *   *   *   *   *

I want to say a word for the faithful and efficient support given the inspector in charge by the force here. It has been all that could be reasonably expected.

W. R. MORTON,
Inspector in Charge.

REPORT OF INSPECTOR IN CHARGE, DISTRICT NO. 7, COMPRISING SOUTH CAROLINA, GEORGIA, FLORIDA, AND ALABAMA, WITH HEADQUARTERS AT JACKSONVILLE.

In accordance with the usual custom, I have the honor to inclose, in tabulated form, a report of the principal immigration transactions in this district for the fiscal year 1913, the same having been prepared from data contained in reports submitted to the Jacksonville office by officers stationed at the various subports in district No. 7.

IMMIGRATION TRANSACTIONS IN DISTRICT NO. 7, DURING FISCAL YEAR 1913.

Ports.	Aliens admitted.		Total.	United States citizens arrived.	Aliens debarred.	Total inward passenger movement.	Aliens returned.	Stowaways.	Alien seamen deserted.	Head tax collected.	Fines.	
	Immigrants.	Nonimmigrants.									Section 9.	Section 15.
Jacksonville	4	0	4	22	0	26	0	0	47	$12	0	0
Key West	1,165	3,140	4,305	14,627	38	18,970	7	1	4	4,124	$100	$120
Miami	1,312	1,526	2,838	270	15	3,123	1	0	0	11,140	0	10
Tampa	1,344	1,289	2,633	1,886	16	4,335	8	4	104	2,880	100	30
Mobile	82	125	207	302	15	524	2	19	363	400	0	60
Charleston	13	2	15	3	5	23	1	5	92	52	0	0
Pensacola	10	0	10	25	0	35	1	0	246	40	0	20
Savannah	7	0	7	30	3	40	0	3	138	28	0	0
Brunswick	0	2	2	8	0	10	0	0	20	0	0	0
Boca Grande	2	1	3	7	0	10	0	1	3	8	0	0
Fernandina	2	0	2	0	0	2	0	0	25	8	0	0
Port Inglis	3	1	4	0	0	4	0	4	0	16	0	0
Total	3,944	6,086	10,030	17,180	92	27,302	20	37	1,042	18,708	200	240

NOTE.—Fines under Section 9 segregated as follows: (1) Mental afflictions, $000; (2) tuberculosis, $000; (3) other loathsome or dangerous contagious disease, $200.

It will be seen from this report, as compared with the report for the fiscal year 1912, that there is a considerable increase in the number of alien arrivals and also in the number of United States citizens arriving—the total inward passenger movement for district No. 7 for the fiscal year 1913 being 27,302.

When the volume of business done in this district is taken into consideration, I am sure that the bureau will agree with me that the service in this district has been economically administered.

The special attention of the bureau is called to the increase in immigration business at the port of Key West. The business at that port is rapidly on the increase, due to the fact of the completion of the Florida East Coast Railroad to that point, and also to the direct passenger service during the winter season between Key West and the Canal Zone. There are only two immigration officers stationed at Key West, and the appointment of another inspector for duty at that port will be an absolute necessity by the first of October next. Even at the present time, which is regarded the dull season at Key West, there is, by regular schedule, a passenger boat from Havana, Cuba, arriving at Key West every day in the week except Sunday.

* * * * * * *

No aliens have been admitted in this district for hospital treatment under the provisions of section 19 or section 37.

Under the Chinese-exclusion laws, 18 investigations have been made during the year, and it has been necessary to check in and out of the various ports and prevent violations of law by 2,058 Chinese seamen.

I am gratified to state that the relations existing between this office and the immigration officers throughout the district have been pleasant and harmonious for the entire year.

THOS. V. KIRK,
Inspector in charge.

REPORT OF COMMISSIONER OF IMMIGRATION, NEW ORLEANS, IN CHARGE OF DISTRICT NO. 8, COMPRISING LOUISIANA, MISSISSIPPI, ARKANSAS, AND TENNESSEE.

In submitting my report for the fiscal year ended June 30, 1913, I am much impressed with the belief that the actual operation of a modern and thoroughly equipped station at New Orleans is a marked advancement toward a solution of, and will in the near future play an important part in, the economic and industrial as well as social problems involved in the question of immigration and alien distribution. From information at hand, the new order of affairs has already caused much comment, and it is believed will attract many of those contemplating migrating to this country to select this as a port of entry.

There is still another phase attached to the inauguration of this new and modern method of receiving aliens at Southern ports that appeals strongly to me, and is, I believe, worthy of consideration. It will prove an object lesson and an educational feature to those heretofore unacquainted with the immigration laws and the manner pursued by our service in handling aliens. Having been so closely identified in and intimately connected with its development, I have kept in constant touch with the intense interest its construction has created amongst the people in the territory embraced in this district, from which I feel warranted in expressing the belief that many of those heretofore antagonistic to immigration are now awakening to the belief that what is most needed is people to populate lands now idle and vacant, and immigration will thenceforth prove an important factor in this particular form of development. * * *

* * * * * * *

The classes of aliens needed in this country at this time are the agriculturist, the home seeker, the dairy and truck farmer. The problem of curtailing immigration to this country and its distribution is one of the most vital and live questions before the people to-day. It is a subject that has its friends and foes. It is quite evident the present immigration law does not satisfactorily fulfill its intended mission, and we are striving to bring about a solution of this question through new and additional legislation. In my opinion, the greatest feature of all is not so much the reduction of immigration as the proper distribution and strict examination, the separating the wheat from the chaff. * * *

We have arriving in this country approximately 1,000,000 aliens annually, the great majority passing through the port of New York. It is admitted the facilities at that port for handling this enormous influx are inadequate, in lack of space, inspectors, surgeons, and the like. Still, let all of the deficiencies be supplied, would the problem be solved? I very much doubt it. Would it not be much more effective to limit each steamship line to a certain number of passengers yearly, and to arbitrarily limit the number that should be permitted to pass through any one port? Take the period of June 9-27, this year, there passed through the port of New York 36,785 steerage passengers. Give proportionately to Galveston, New Orleans, and other ports with immigration stations a pro rata from this enormous number of aliens, and why should not their examination be much more thorough and the country at large profit thereby? Would not such legislation at least tend to reduce to a minimum the evils that now exist? And would not the class of aliens seeking admission to these shores improve accordingly?

*   *   *   *   *   *   *

STATION—CONSTRUCTION AND PLAN.

The station proper is situated on the west bank of the Mississippi River, in the limits of the city of New Orleans, but some 3 miles below its commercial center. Its construction is on the unit system, and is composed of three units—the immigration building proper, containing primary examination hall, information room, doctor's office and laboratory, railroad ticket office, money exchange, railroad and State agents' and missionary societies' rooms, and toilets. The administration building is the left wing on entering, and contains the executive offices, two board rooms, witness rooms, private hearing rooms, attorney's consultation room, showers, lockers, and toilets. The right wing, known as the detention quarters, contains male and female dormitories, two private wards, matron's quarters, roof garden, dining hall, kitchen, pantry, cold storage, employees' dining room, infirmary, and strong room, and ample toilet facilities.

The construction of the building is fireproof, being composed of brick and reinforced concrete. The entrance to the main building for aliens is through a long runway, or pier, leading to the dock, thus affording easy access without recourse to stairs. In front of the property is located a dock 450 feet long, with a steel shed extending over most of its length. In the main examination hall 200 aliens can be accommodated at one time. Along the runway and dock there is sufficient space to properly handle at least 2,000 persons. Sleeping quarters are provided for 144 persons, and under emergency 150 may be quartered overnight. In the dining halls 75 aliens may be seated at one time. Ventilation throughout the entire plant is excellent, and all sanitary requirements have been carefully provided.

Since the opening of the station we have examined 369 steerage passengers, 48 of whom were detained; 14 detentions under warrant, and 99 Chinese in transit. From March 15 to June 30 there were 998 first-class passengers entering the port, who were examined on shipboard.

As a result of the station, the Sea Navigation Co. (Ltd.), of Budapest, Hungary, will shortly operate a passenger line to this port; and, in September, a committee from the various States comprised under district 8 will proceed to New York for consultation with the steamship conferences, with the view of diverting certain lines to New Orleans.

*   *   *   *   *   *   *

STATISTICS REGARDING NEW ORLEANS.

Immigrant aliens admitted	1,446	
Nonimmigrant aliens admitted	1,941	
		3,387
Aliens debarred		62
Deserting alien seamen		673
Section 41		66
Aliens from Porto Rico		3
Total aliens arrived		4,191
United States citizens:		
Male	5,832	
Female	2,802	
		8,634
Total inward movement		12,825
Total arriving vessels		1,350

Emigrant aliens departing................. 516
Nonemigrant aliens departing.... ...... 1, 933
United States citizens departing.......... .. 8, 955

 Total outward movement.............. .... 11, 404

Number of board of special inquiry cases................ 148
Appeals from decisions of boards of special inquiry.......... 17
Alien seamen discharged to re-ship................. 3, 960
Number of vessels arriving...................... 710
Number of passenger vessels arriving................. 636

ALIEN STOWAWAYS ARRIVING.

Admitted.............. 6
Excluded............. 24

 Total......................... .. 30
Miscellaneous investigations.................... 17

FINES.

For improper manifesting................ $450
For bringing diseased aliens:
 Trachoma..................... $200
 Carcinoma (cancer).................. 100
   300

 Total........................... 750

DEPARTMENTAL WARRANTS.

Pending at close of fiscal year 1912............. 34
Received during fiscal year 1913............. 72

 Total.......................... 106

Canceled...................... 57
Deported...................... 20
Pending at close of year................. 29

In addition to the above it has been necessary to dispose of 21 applications made by Chinese for admission at the port of New Orleans; to pass upon the cases of 276 Chinese passing through New Orleans in transit; to check in and out and prevent the landing of 3,187 Chinese seamen; and to make a large number of other investigations connected with the enforcement of the Chinese exclusion laws at the ports of and within Immigration District No. 8.

SMUGGLING.

There is no denying the fact that the patrol boat formerly used in these waters did much to reduce and keep under control smuggling, both of Chinese and other aliens. The moral effect alone of this little cutter proved sufficient to repay the service and country three times over its value in original cost and maintenance. If a city is policed but indifferently, quarters less frequented by municipal guards will develop a class of criminals that will soon be beyond control. Just so, in a section situated as is Louisiana and the southern coast of Mississippi, where waterways are in abundance, fairly inviting the irregular trader to carry on his vocation, if proper means are not furnished to safeguard the coast and waterways and keep in control these evaders of the law, disregard for the law will become more manifest and abuses increase in landing of immigrants.

In a former report I was careful to elaborate on the conditions to be found along the coast of Mississippi and Louisiana. I went thoroughly into this question, descriptively and practically, supplementing my opinions by maps, charts, and data which were indisputable. It is not a question where any doubt can possibly exist—it is simply a matter staring one in the face of controlling or condoning a situation. If those who are suspected of carrying on this illicit traffic know that they are under constant surveillance, they will be cautious, and in turn become inactive. But permit the fact to become known that we lack the means of combating them on an equal footing, and they are ready to resume operations.

  *   *   *   *   *   *   *

THE CONTRACT-LABOR LAW.

It seems very generally conceded throughout the service that the contract-labor law is constantly being violated, and that under the present law it is impossible to prevent the entrance of many aliens coming under promise or agreement to perform labor. It is not believed, however, that violations of this law are so frequent at this port, comparatively speaking, as they are perhaps at some others, where examining officers are necessarily compelled to work hurriedly on account of the great volume of business to be disposed of in a given time. Aliens arriving at New Orleans are carefully examined in every instance, and it follows that a better opportunity is afforded to detect violations of the contract-labor law, or discover other facts that may exist rendering them inadmissible. Undoubtedly aliens enter at this port as a result of encouragement or promise of employment, as it is impossible to detect all such cases. Many aliens who have been induced to come are thoroughly posted concerning the law and are prepared for any grueling ordeal to which they may be subjected, with the result that, in most instances, it is impossible to find facts sufficient to warrant exclusion. The detection of such cases becomes more difficult, seemingly, from day to day, as a result of the campaign of education among aliens of all nationalities with regard to the provisions of the law.

We have succeeded in working up a case in this district involving a number of Swedes, who seem to have been induced to come to this country to accept employment at Moss Point, Miss. Suit for recovery of the penalty provided by section 5 of the act is being instituted, and there appears to be good reason to hope for the best results. The aliens involved entered through the port of New York and proceeded direct to Moss Point, and were immediately placed at work by the company by whom imported.

An investigation has also been conducted in connection with Greek shoe shiners in Nashville, Tenn., within the past few weeks; and while it appears from the facts obtained that some of these boys were imported for the purpose of engaging in the work they are now doing, it was found impossible to secure evidence that would warrant the prosecution of the importer or justify the deportation of the aliens.

The subject of contract labor is a very broad one, and undoubtedly will require additional legislation before the evil sought to be remedied can be controlled.

WHITE-SLAVE TRAFFIC.

The past year has been one of extreme importance in activities under the white-slave laws. Fifteen prosecutions in the Federal court alone are reported. In addition, the State white-slave law has been actively supported and has proven extremely beneficial in effect throughout this district.

An inspector from this office has been assigned to this particular duty, and I am pleased to report that his activities have met with considerable success, and the number of foreign prostitutes registered in this city has materially decreased. I am of the opinion, however, that in other large cities in this district, should the appropriation warrant, considerable good could be accomplished and many cases of importance developed. I have particularly in mind Memphis, Nashville, and Chattanooga, in Tennessee, and Shreveport, La.

DESERTING ALIEN SEAMEN.

The number of deserting alien seamen apprehended, admitted, and deported shows a decrease from that of last year, owing principally to the fact that the patrol boat formerly at this port has been withdrawn. Forty-five were admitted on application, and over 40 warrants of arrests issued in such cases, most of whom were later admitted. Of those apprehended, 1 was excluded on account of trachoma, and another, a Spaniard, for poor physique and as likely to become a public charge. It is earnestly hoped and recommended that the patrol boat at this port will be restored at an early date, as the services of such an agency is of the greatest importance, and its need and usefulness as logical as the mounted patrol on the Mexican border.

DIVISION OF INFORMATION.

Over 238 persons of various nationalities were given employment through the agency at this office, at compensations varying from straight per diem of $1 to $2 up to $45 per month, including board and lodging.

The work of this division has been very satisfactory and of considerable value. The inspector having this work in charge has been diligent and active. Thanks are also due to the secretary of the Louisiana State Board of Immigration for the valuable assistance he has rendered to this branch of the service.

*　　*　　*　　*　　*　　*　　*

SUDPORTS.

GULFPORT.

*   *   *   *   *   *   *

The Gulfport office has reached a high standard of efficiency, owing to the industry and intelligent activities of the inspector in charge. It is hoped that the high standard of efficiency and results will be sustained in the future.

A new railroad project is about to be launched in Mississippi, having a terminal at Gulfport, thus bringing additional rail facilities to the port, which, it is reported, will have as a connecting link steamship lines in the banana trade, with the added possibilities of passenger business from certain Central American ports.

PASCAGOULA.

Records and a personal inspection at this port and its immediate territory disclosed a condition of a most gratifying nature. Shipping, it is true, remains about equal to past years, but, through the constant painstaking, energetic efforts of the inspector in charge, illegal entries have been reduced to a minimum, and his territory stands to-day as clean as is possible under existing conditions.

*   *   *   *   *   *   *

CONCLUSION.

In closing this report it gives me pleasure to be able to say that the officers and employees in this district have performed the duties assigned to them during the past year in a very satisfactory and efficient manner; and I am glad to share with them any credit due the district for results accomplished.

Finally, I wish to thank the bureau for the unvarying support and hearty cooperation accorded me in my efforts to administer the affairs of the service at New Orleans during the past year, and trust that my efforts in this respect may meet with its approval.

S. E. REDFERN,
Commissioner.

REPORT OF INSPECTOR IN CHARGE, DISTRICT NO. 9, COMPRISING SO MUCH OF TEXAS AS IS CONTIGUOUS TO GALVESTON, THE DISTRICT HEADQUARTERS.

I hereby submit the following brief summary of the work of this office for the fiscal year 1913:

	1912	1913	Increase (+) or decrease (−).
Immigrant aliens admitted	4.758	5.468	+710
Nonimmigrant aliens admitted	311	281	− 30
United States citizens arrived	859	1,263	+404
Aliens debarred	346	249	− 97
Total	6,274	7,261	+987

	1912	1913
Aliens deported:		
Likely to become public charges	43	96
Accompanying aliens (sec. 11)	1	2
Contract laborers	254	104
On medical certificates—		
Trachoma	42	33
Venereal diseases	1	1
Favus	1	
Insanity	1	1
Mentally defective	1	1
	2	11
Tuberculosis		1
Total	346	249

	1912	1913
Fines imposed by the department on account of:		
Mental afflictions..		
Aliens with tuberculosis..		$100
Other loathsome and dangerous contagious diseases—		
Trachoma..	$2,100	3,900
Venereal bubo..		100
Nonmanifesting..	40	180
Total..	2,140	4,280
Fines pending at close of fiscal year..		1,040

No aliens were landed for hospital treatment under authority vested in the Secretary in sections 19 and 37 of the immigration law, but one case remained pending from last year, in which treatment was continued until August 8, 1912.

The seamen question is still a matter that entails a great deal of work of a most unsatisfactory nature, and there appears to be an increase in the number of desertions, as, while during the fiscal year ending June 30, 1912, there were 277 desertions reported at this port and 54 at Port Arthur; during the fiscal year ending June 30, 1913, 318 were reported here and 110 at Port Arthur. However, in this connection it might be well to call attention to the fact that while during the former fiscal year 560 foreign vessels were boarded at the port of Galveston, 799 were boarded during the latter fiscal year; and this is especially important as showing the large percentage of increase in the class of work our boarding officer was called upon to perform, not only on account of the large number of vessels, but also due to the fact that at present a great many Chinese crews enter this port, requiring checking in and out, while up until comparatively recently very few foreign vessels entering this port carried Chinese crews.

The careful, painstaking, and thorough medical examination of arriving aliens by our medical surgeon is highly appreciated by this office, as it is realized that he is not only a very competent and experienced medical officer, but that he is by training, experience, and temperament especially and peculiarly fitted for this class of work.

There has been considerable delay in the opening of the new immigrant station here, due to the defects in the water main and telephone cable between the station and the city of Galveston; but the water main was finally repaired, and money secured from the Treasury Department, through the Marine-Hospital Service, for the repair of the telephone cable, and everything put in readiness for the opening of the station upon the arrival of the North German Lloyd S. S. *Cassel*, July 8, 1913, with 744 aliens.

With the assistance of the watchmen amd laborers detailed for duty at the station a great many improvements and alterations in same have been made at a comparatively moderate cost, so that it is believed, for the money expended, the station will prove one of the most practical and best-arranged stations we have in the service, though the location is not at all satisfactory.

While the running of the station will largely increase the amount of funds needed for this district, it must not be overlooked that during the fiscal year ending June 30, 1913, there was collected at this port $22,560 in head tax and $4,280 in fines, and the indications are that a much larger amount will be collected here during the present fiscal year.

While the work connected with the division of information entails considerable correspondence, the results have not been very satisfactory, only 33 persons having been directed to employment through said agency during the last fiscal year.

I again beg leave to urge upon the department the importance of bulkheading and filling in around the station, not only as a measure of protection for same, but especially with the view of insuring as far as possible the safety of detained aliens and others in case of high water and fire at the same time.

During the year there was no material change as regards Chinese in district No. 9 from the conditions reported for the fiscal year ending June 30, 1912, for, as previously stated, the Chinese in this district are, with very few exceptions, old-time residents who are provided with genuine certificates of residence and who not only travel but little within the district, but very rarely make trips outside of the district.

Very few rumors were received indicating that any Chinese were attempted to be smuggled into the United States through this district. However, there was one such attempt made by certain seamen on the S. S. *Alabama*, of the Gulf Coast Fruit & Steamship Co., which arrived at this port on April 14, 1913, which attempt was frustrated by our officers, The four Chinese involved were taken into custody and four seamen who were implicated in attempting to smuggle the Chinamen into this country were duly apprehended and indicted by the Federal grand jury, and when the hearing came up pleaded guilty and were sentenced to six months each in the Fort Bend County, Tex., jail, in addition to the two months that they spent in jail prior to sentence in this city. It is believed that this is the only attempt made to smuggle Chinese into the United States through this district within recent years, and the fact that the smugglers were apprehended and received punishment will have a very salutary effect upon others who might desire to enter into the Chinese smuggling business.

Formerly very few Chinese crews entered this port, but during the last year a large number of ships have arrived with Chinese crews and the handling of the Chinese seamen, under their present status, is most unsatisfactory and at times very annoying.

While rule 7, Chinese regulations, provides that shore leave shall not be granted Chinese seamen at ports of the United States except upon the giving of a bond with approved security in the penalty of $500, the decision of the Federal courts as to the status of Chinese seamen is so different in different districts that it is not always possible to get the Chinese to put up bonds, and in some instances even the captains of vessels authorize their Chinese seamen to take shore leave without the furnishing of said bonds.

In conclusion, it gives me pleasure to express my appreciation of the cordial support given me by the officers and employees stationed in this district and of their active and intelligent interest in the effective enforcement of the immigration laws.

ALFRED HAMPTON,
Inspector in Charge.

REPORT OF INSPECTOR IN CHARGE, DISTRICT NO. 10, COMPRISING OHIO AND KENTUCKY, WITH HEADQUARTERS AT CLEVELAND.

I beg to submit the following report of operations for District No. 10 during the fiscal year ending June 30, 1913. While the bulk of the work in this district during the year past has been in connection with the arrest and deportation of aliens unlawfully here, there has been an increasing number of miscellaneous investigations and inquiries of varied sorts. The work in general is of such a varying nature that it is well-nigh impossible to indicate adequately by any set of figures the actual amount of work performed and the effort expended by the officers and employees in discharging their duty. This is accounted for largely by the fact that many investigations take a wide range of inquiry and painstaking effort in order to accomplish the desired results, while conclusions in other cases of similar nature may be reached with comparative ease.

  *   *   *   *   *   *   *

STATEMENT OF ACTION UPON WARRANT CASES.

Warrant cases pending at beginning of year	26
Applications for warrants of arrest during year	217
Warrants received after requests by other offices	13
Total	256

DISPOSITION.

Class.	Warrant refused.	Escaped.	Died.	Not located.	Sent elsewhere.	Canceled.	Deported.	Pending.	Total.
Contract laborers						3	3	1	7
Public charges						1	9		10
Tuberculosis		2	3			4	14	4	27
Liable to become public charge	3			6	2	15	59	8	93
Insanity			1			3	20	2	26
Epilepsy							1		1
Criminals				2	2	3	4		11
Anarchists	2					2			4
Prostitutes	1					4	12	1	18
Females for immoral purposes				2	1	3	7	2	15
Imported woman for immoral purposes						4	8	1	13
Receiving proceeds of prostitution						1	1	2	4
Employed in house of prostitution						1	10		11
Contagious disease							5	2	7
Entry without inspection		1		1		3	3		8
Convicted under section 3								1	1
Total	6	3	4	11	5	47	156	24	256

There has been a considerably smaller number of Chinese cases handled during the past fiscal year than in years previous. This is unaccounted for, but I have been informed that many of the older Chinese are now returning to China without preparations for return.
The following indicates approximately the cases of the various classes handled:

	Cleve- land.	Cincin- nati.	Toledo.	Total.
Laborers; preinvestigation for visit to China............................	5	1	2	8
Natural born; preinvestigation for visit to China..........................	5	2	4	11
Merchants; preinvestigation for visit to China.............................		1		1
Wives and minor children, merchants; arriving................;	4	2		6
Natural born; investigation for readmission...............:	3	1	1	5
Miscellaneous..	10	1	2	13
Son of native; arriving.......................................	1			1
Student (arriving)..	1			1

CHINESE ARREST CASES.

Under immigration law:
Pending at beginning of year.. 1
Arrested during year.. 3
                                                        ———
                                                          4
Deported... 2
Escaped... 1
Pending, United States Supreme Court............................... 1
                                                        ———
Under Chinese exclusion law:
Pending at beginning of year.................................... 2
Arrests during year....................................... 5
                                                        ———
                                                          7
Deported.. 2
Pending in district court................................ 4
Pending in circuit court of appeals 1

The best reference I can make to the efficiency of the service in this district as at present organized is to compare the work with that of previous years, the warrant cases being taken as a basis therefor.
During the fiscal year of 1910, there were 95 warrants handled in this district; during 1911, 126; during 1912, 190; and for the year just closed, 256. Although the proportion of warrants to deportations is about the same for 1912 and 1913, the ratio of deportations is higher for these years than previously. During the fiscal year ending June 30, 1910, there were 47 aliens deported from this district; during 1911, 72; during 1912, 120; and during the fiscal year closing the aggregate is 156 aliens. It will therefore be noted that with the same number of officers and employees, the number of aliens deported during the year ending June 30 was more than three times greater than for 1910, more than twice the number for 1911, and 33⅓ per cent increase over 1912. And, parenthetically, it may be of interest to the bureau to know that for the calendar year 1912, the deportations for this district exceeded 200.
During the year investigations have been made at Cleveland in 194 cases where relatives or friends of detained aliens have called voluntarily, or with telegrams from the detained aliens, 15 investigations in similar cases at Toledo, and 51 at Cincinnati. At Cleveland there have been 117 investigations made at the request of officers at ports or of the bureau, in cases of arriving aliens; at Toledo 7 such investigations, and at Cincinnati 11. There have been 18 bond cases handled in the district in the cases of detained aliens.
Primary-inspection data has been sent to Montreal, or other border office, in the cases of 22 aliens who have entered the United States without the proper inspection at the border. Twenty investigations have been made concerning United States citizens in Canada whom the Dominion authorities have sought to deport back to this country.

This office has been instrumental in securing indictments against 5 persons during the fiscal year, 1 under the white-slave law, 3 of prostitutes returning to the United States after deportation, and one for importing a woman for an immoral purpose. The white-slave case was that of Davis Freedman; two of the returning prostitutes were given suspended sentences in the workhouse and were deported, in the third case that of Josephina Drago, an indictment was secured and a temporary plea of not guilty given in court when the department vacated the original order by which the alien was deported and thus restored her to the status she enjoyed before deportation, consequently the indictment was nolled. The alien was ordered released upon her own recognizance, reports to be made quarterly by this office, but within two or three weeks after her release she left for parts unknown and is now said to be living in adultery with an Italian named John Monaco. The conviction for importing a woman for immoral purposes was that in the case of John Cerko. This alien is now serving a sentence in the penitentiary at Moundsville, W. Va., and has been ordered deported at the expiration thereof.

Examinations of aliens for "certificates of arrival" for naturalization purposes have been made during the year as follows: At Cleveland, 18; at Toledo, 3; and at Cincinnati, 4. It may be worthy of note to say that the courts in Cleveland have held that the so-called certificates of arrival issued by this office are not sufficient to comply with the requirements of the naturalization act.

Miscellaneous unclassified investigations have been made in 110 instances. Of course, as regards the latter, there are hundreds of inquiries coming into the three offices of this district and minor investigations made of which no file or record is kept. These cover inquiries as to almost every phase of the immigration problem and matters outside the service itself, the latter ranging from the name of the secretary to the name or location of some American consul in Zanzibar. An endeavor is always made to give the inquirer the best information at hand.

*　　*　　*　　*　　*　　*　　*

Investigations have been conducted in 9 separate cases in which 62 aliens were involved as suspected contract laborers. Department warrants of arrest were issued in 7 cases, resulting in 3 deportations. Three warrants were by request canceled by the department. Depositions of the 3 aliens involved were taken and suits entered against the importers, which are now pending in the United States Court for the Northen District of Ohio. After the depositions had been taken and the aliens released upon their own recognizance they went to Canada. It was found desirable to have the warrants canceled in order that the men may return and appear as witnesses against the importers without fear of deportation to England. One warrant case in which proceedings were instituted against the importer is also pending. Action looking toward the deportation of the alien involved was deferred by the department pending a decision by the court. These four cases will come up for trial during the fall term of court.

During the month of June the Cleveland and Buffalo Transit Co. inaugurated a steamship service between this city and Port Stanley, Ontario, with four arrivals weekly. This work has been handled by our office at some inconvenience since it necessitates trips to the dock at a very early hour in the morning and also at night. The inspectors have handled this work, however, in addition to their regular duties, and the inspection data reported to the Montreal office, and will be taken up in the statistical reports of that office.

I understand that some of the officials have been advocating an annual meeting of commissioners and inspectors in charge of districts, and it would seem that such meetings would be highly beneficial, and would go far toward a coordination of efforts and systematizing of work, which the service now lacks.

In conclusion I beg to say a word in behalf of the faithfulness and devotion of the various officers and employees of this district to their duties and to the service in general. Our work requires unusual tact, patience, and resourcefulness, and while we are all liable to an occasional mistake, I am confident there is no district similarly situated whose officers outrank our force in loyalty and all-around ability.

J. A. FLUCKEY,
Inspector in Charge.

REPORT OF INSPECTOR IN CHARGE, DISTRICT NO. 11, COMPRISING ILLINOIS, INDIANA, MICHIGAN, AND WISCONSIN, WITH HEADQUARTERS AT CHICAGO.

I have the honor to submit the following report concerning the work of District No. 11 during the fiscal year 1913.

The following table shows the classification and action taken in 238 public charge cases investigated during the year:

PUBLIC CHARGES.

Cause.	Re-ported.	Action taken.		
		De-ported.	Not deported.	Pending.
Insane	88	55	26	7
Tuberculosis	26	11	13	2
Epileptics	3	1	2	
Imbeciles	3	2		1
Other causes	118	52	53	13
Total	238	121	94	23

NOT DEPORTED—REASONS.

Landing not verified 5
Sufficient grounds for issuance warrant of arrest not established 40
Department canceled warrant of arrest 17
Time limit expired before deportation proceedings instituted 2
Death 2
United States citizens 1
Returned Europe prior to termination deportation proceedings 10
Deportation deferred indefinitely 1
Kept under surveillance for period and warrant canceled 9
Escaped prior to execution warrant of deportation 2
Left institution before issuance warrant of arrest 3
Alien unable to travel without danger to life and warrant canceled 1
Left State after proceedings instituted 1

Total 94

In addition to the foregoing, the following 168 cases have been investigated for the purpose of ascertaining whether the facts justified the institution of deportation proceedings:

Class.	Action taken.			
	Investi-gated.	De-ported.	Not deported.	Pending.
Prostitutes, procurers, etc.	127	69	49	9
Dependents thereon [1]	2	2	0	0
Illegal entry	39	21	14	4
Total	168	92	63	13

[1] Children dependent for their support upon arrested aliens.

NOT DEPORTED—REASONS.

Not located 3
Department canceled warrants of arrest 25
Sufficient grounds not established for issuance warrant of arrest 21
Kept under surveillance for period and warrant canceled 4

Landing not verified.. 6
Returned Europe prior to termination deportation proceedings.................. 3
United States citizens.. 1

    Total.. 63

*   *   *   *   *   *   *

It should be understood that the foregoing does not include deportations from the Chicago district by Canadian border offices and the St. Louis station.

*   *   *   *   *   *   *

In addition to work in connection with deportation cases, investigations have been made in 794 miscellaneous cases, consisting principally of cases of aliens detained at sea and land border ports.

*   *   *   *   *   *

INVESTIGATIONS.

Laborers, departing... 51
Merchants, departing.. 10
Natives, departing.. 32
Students, departing... 5
Traveler, departing... 1
Minor son of native, departing.. 1
Merchant status preinvestigated, account application of wife or minor son
    for admission... 3
Natives, arriving... 2
Merchants, returning.. 2
Applications for duplicate certificates of residence.......................... 6
Application for duplicate certificate of identity............................. 1
Investigations at the request of other cities................................ 38
Examination of application for Chinese interpreter............................ 1

    Total.. 153

CASES IN COURT.

Arrest cases pending July 1, 1912... 50
Arrests... 27

    Total.. 77

DISPOSITION OF CASES.

Ordered deported by United States commissioners............................... 9
Discharged by United States commissioners..................................... 3
Ordered deported by department.. 12
Ordered deported by United States district courts............................ 21
Discharged by United States district courts.................................. 19
Case dismissed by United States district court because of death of defendant.. 1
Ordered deported by Circuit Court of Appeals.................................. 3
Forfeited bond.. 2
Deported on department warrant.. 7
Deported on court order of deportation.. 22

CRIMINAL CASES.

Convicted of personating the proper holder of certificate of residence......... 2

HABEAS CORPUS CASES.

Appealed by Government (reversed by Circuit Court of Appeals)................. 1
Appealed by alien (affirmed by Circuit Court of Appeals)..................... 1
Application for writ denied by United States District Court.................. 1
Cases pending July 1, 1913... 20

The past year has shown a still greater increase than the previous year in the number of requests received from ports of entry for investigations concerning arriving aliens. Particular attention has been given to ascertaining the living conditions and general environments at addresses to which aliens are destined. The necessity for the exercise of care in this respect is considered quite essential in cases of unaccompanied female aliens, as well as children under sixteen years of age not accompanied by either parent or guardian. It has been the policy of the office to determine, if possible, whether such aliens are to be under the surveillance of a responsible person of decent character. Not infrequently a false claim of relationship is made by arriving aliens with the hope of facilitating admission.

In connection with investigations at interior points to which aliens are destined, it has been noted that a uniform policy does not prevail at the different ports of arrival. It would appear that if the practice of having these investigations made is worthy of the time and labor involved it should be generally followed. There would doubtless be no difference of opinion as to the importance of examining officers at the ports of arrival being placed in possession of reliable information concerning the conditions under which inexperienced aliens are to live. With respect to cases of the class referred to, department's Form 547 (sworn statement submitted by relative of arriving immigrants) is now extensively used by relatives and friends in anticipation of the arrival of aliens. There would appear to be some doubt, however, whether the form referred to serves as reliably and completely as first-hand investigations made by immigrant inspectors upon request of the officer in charge at the port of entry after the alien has actually arrived and applied for admission. Form 547 provides for detailed information concerning both the expected immigrant and the relative or friend executing the statement, which is subscribed to under oath. When this statement is submitted, this office undertakes to verify the relationship claimed, as well as income, property holdings, and savings. Should there arise doubt concerning living conditions, investigation is made with reference thereto. It has been noted that a large number of relatives appear at this office to make use of Form 547, in response to telegraphic notifications sent from the port of entry by the steamship office of the line bringing the detained alien. It is believed that signing under oath a statement such as provided for in Form 547 serves to impress the person signing with a moral responsibility that serves for the protection of the Government and contributes to a more careful supervision of the alien, particularly in the case of children under sixteen.

An astonishing situation concerning living conditions in Chicago among immigrants has recently been brought to light with reference to Armenian laborers, a large number having been found occupying a building of 13 rooms, the size of each room being 6 by 8 feet, with a storeroom on the first floor 25 by 30 feet. From 3 to 5 men were sleeping on wooden beds in each of the small rooms, while from 20 to 30 men slept on the floor of the storeroom. Also, at South Deering in a storeroom 25 by 40 feet there were found 15 beds, with 2 tables for eating purposes and a cookstove. It is unnecessary to state that at both of these places a condition of squalor existed. The presence of immigrants living under such a standard discredits both the men themselves and the Government. The situation may well be regarded as a disgrace to the community. Any concern or individual employing laborers living under such conditions might well give serious consideration to providing suitable housing accommodations for its employees.

Further, concerning alien children under 16 years of age, my attention has been called, through the work of private agencies, to the fact that school attendance of immigrant children is sadly neglected. It is believed that cooperation with State authorities, whereby the latter might be supplied with the names and destination of immigrant children, might result in a more complete school attendance.

DEPORTATIONS.

This branch of the work presents an interesting study. There are seen the tragic failures of men and women in their attempts to make themselves self-supporting. Defective physical equipment renders not a few incapable of success; others succumb to the development of mental defects and, becoming hopelessly insane, are returned to be cared for by the country of which they are citizens. Another unfortunate deserving of our sympathy is the tubercular immigrant who begins life in the new country full of hope and with bright prospects, but is forced finally to give way to the insidious progress of that dread disease, the germs of which lay dormant in his system when he first landed on American soil. It then becomes necessary to return him to his home country.

"WHITE-SLAVE TRAFFIC."

In dealing with the sexually immoral class, not infrequently there develops evidence, in the process of deportation, of an appalling character, showing the influences which have resulted in the tragic wrecking of human lives. We consider it fortunate that it has been possible to remove from this immigration district, and particularly from Chicago, a number of men found operating extensively in commercial prostitution. It is encouraging also that convictions have been secured calculated to lessen the number caring to risk their freedom by engaging in this nefarious traffic. The establishment of a morals court in Chicago has served to assist the Government in the application of the immigration laws; also, valuable assistance has been given through the cooperation of the bureau of investigation of the Department of Justice; likewise, by other organizations working for the betterment of moral conditions. Disappointment has been met with in the failure to deport prostitutes by reason of their marriage to United States citizens subsequent to their arrest and prior to being given a hearing. The purposes of the immigration law have in this manner been defeated in a number of aggravated cases. Such marriages invariably are contracted for the sole purpose above indicated, and do not serve to cause the women in the cases to discontinue the practice of prostitution. There would seem to be a serious need of legislation intended to make it impossible for a woman of the confirmed prostitute class to obtain citizenship in the manner indicated, either by marriage to a native or naturalized citizen of the United States.

SURREPTITIOUS ENTRY OF ALIENS.

Recent developments appear to show Chicago the first destination of aliens who have succeeded in eluding the vigilance of the border inspectors at the north of this district and have accomplished surreptitious entry. It may reasonably be assumed that such aliens belong to the inadmissible class and may be regarded as totally undesirable. Effort is being made to disclose the plans followed in accomplishing unlawful entrance in this manner.

* * * * * * *

ADMINISTERING THE CHINESE-EXCLUSION LAW.

The work performed in this district during the last fiscal year in connection with the investigation of Chinese applying for return certificates as lawfully domiciled laborers, or members of the exempt classes, presents no unusual features. A smaller number of these applications were filed than during the preceding fiscal year. It is not believed that this is to be accounted for upon the basis of a decreased Chinese population. As the investigations in the past in this district have been conducted with great care and many frauds were detected on that account, it is my belief that the Chinese with fraudulent claims have, to a considerable extent, filed their applications at other ports, where their antecedents were not known and where, on that account, their cases would more likely pass inspection. It is a practice prevalent among Chinese, and particularly among laborers posing as merchants and those who claim American nativity, to go to the larger ports, such as San Francisco and Seattle, and there, with the aid of the local Chinese, establish fraudulent claims as members of the exempt classes or as natives. It is my opinion that an effort should be made, by close questioning of applicants and by cooperation between the various districts, to determine whether they are residents of districts where they make application, and if it be shown that they had recently come from another jurisdiction, the matter should be referred for investigation to the place of their former residence.

A total of 77 cases of arrested Chinese have been handled during the year. We were successful in all Chinese cases brought before the Circuit Court of Appeals during the year, both under the exclusion act and on habeas corpus. This court rendered an opinion in the case of United States v. Sue Lung of great value in our work and of far-reaching effect. This opinion is not only in accord with other decisions of the same court upon the question of the finality of the decision of the Secretary in warrant proceedings, but is of peculiar value in that it holds that a statement made by an arrested alien before he has consulted friends or counsel is of greater weight than his testimony given at the hearing, after he has been advised by an attorney. We have met with success in the cases handled before United States commissioners. The most difficult situation to meet in connection with the prosecution of Chinese cases before the courts in Chicago is found in the district court. The calendar of this court is always overcrowded, and this situation has been aggravated during the past year because of an unfilled vacancy on this bench. On this account it has been found difficult to bring Chinese cases to trial. Last spring some 58 cases had accumulated before the district court. In order to dispose of them a special calendar was made up. Three outside judges heard the cases. * * * Out of the calendar, more were ordered deported than where discharged. Our experience each year demonstrates more clearly that a thoroughly effective enforcement of the law through the courts is next to impossible, especially in a congested center. The long delays, which appear to be inevitable when cases are appealed, gives time for the coaching of witnesses and for the arrested Chinese to become conversant with the English language. It will, of course, continue to be necessary to bring a certain class of cases under the exclusion law before the courts, but our experience shows that in such cases as can be brought before the department under the immigration law much more satisfactory results follow. The department has ordered 12 Chinese deported during the past year and none discharged. More Chinese were deported during the present year than the preceding one, there being a total of 29 deportations.

The smuggling of Chinese from the border points into Chicago is still carried on, and doubtless so long as there is a law prohibiting their entry a way will be found to enter. It is, of course, impossible to cover all the avenues of entry through so large a center as Chicago, especially when it is taken into consideration that only one inspector devotes his attention entirely to the Chinese work in this district; but, judging from the statements contained in Chinese letters seized in the various raids and on the persons of those who have recently arrived, it is apparent that Chinese realize their entry is not without danger of apprehension. I believe that more inspectors should be assigned to Chinese work in this city and at the border point of Detroit, which is the principal place of entry for those destined to Chicago. The Chinese population of this city is so large that practically the only limit upon the number of arrests made is the ability of the officers and the courts to dispose of the cases. With a considerable volume of office work necessary in the handling of applications and investigations, only a fraction of the time of the officer assigned to Chinese work can be given to the enforcement of the law in the field.

I believe that, considering the situation as a whole, the administration of the exclusion law in this district is well in hand.

CONTRACT LABOR.

Activities directed toward the enforcement of the contract labor laws have been attended with extreme difficulties. However, investigations made at the request of different ports of arrival have resulted in the exclusion of many aliens coming under inducements or solicitations to perform labor. Important investigations involving the cause and method of immigration of large numbers of laborers coming from certain quarters of Europe and destined to the same general locality in this country are now in progress and give promise of disclosing evidence of value. A close study of conditions indicates the possible existence of an invisible system whereby employers are now supplied with alien laborers direct from Europe.

One of the most conspicuous contract labor cases handled in this district was that of the Wilson Bros., of Woodstock, Ontario. This is a Canadian ship timber concern and is found operating extensively in Wisconsin and West Virginia. During the progress of the investigation the company admitted bringing to the United States 29 Canadian workmen from the Province of Quebec, Ontario. / The return of all of these men was accomplished and a satisfactory monetary settlement secured with the concern involved in their importation. The publicity given this case so stirred certain other employers as to cause a hasty exit to Canada of a considerable number of aliens who had migrated under similar conditions.

Another noteworthy case was that of Superintendent Cochrane, of the Kewanee Boiler Works, Kewanee, Ill. The superintendent wrote a former employee, one Alidor Wanchet, in Belgium, telling him "to bring as many men as he could, up to 50," and offering $2 per day. Wanchet, subsequent to the sending of this letter, arrived at Ellis Island accompanied by 23 alien workmen, all of whom were excluded. The evidence in the case is now before the proper United States attorney.

In our last report we referred to inquiry being made into the conditions under which numerous Greek boys were employed in Chicago and other cities in this district. Attention given this situation, we believe, has served to diminish the number of victims of a padrone system, notwithstanding it having been found impossible to secure evidence of a character necessary to convict certain proprietors of shoeshine establishments, hotels, restaurants, and other branches of business employing Greek boys. It was ascertained that wages had been withheld from boys and that they were made to submit to conditions of living that were disastrous to the proper development of the individual. We were successful in securing for a number of such boys suitable employment where living wages would be promptly forthcoming. Good results have followed this humane effort.

CONCLUSION.

The diversified nature of the work required of officers at the Chicago station makes it essential that such officers be persons of ability and training. It is important also that officers be qualified and disposed to take the initiative in disclosing violations of law. The work to be accomplished is by no means routine and officers inclined only to interest themselves in regular duties are apt to be a burden to the station. Not all officers may be qualified along the same lines but each may develop work along particular lines in which they possess aptitude. It has been our effort to maintain a high degree of efficiency.

P. L. PRENTIS,
Inspector in Charge.

REPORT OF INSPECTOR IN CHARGE, DISTRICT NO. 12, COMPRISING MINNESOTA AND NORTH AND SOUTH DAKOTA, WITH HEADQUARTERS AT MINNEAPOLIS.

I beg to submit the following summarized report of immigration work, district No. 12:

DEPORTATION CASES.

Deportation cases pending in local office or before the department at close of fiscal year ended June 30, 1912.. 31
(Deportations ordered, 14; awaiting final department decision, 8; warrants of arrest issued but not served, 2; warrants of arrest served, but hearings not completed, 3; cases pending in local office before submission to department, 4.)
Aliens reported during the year for investigation and deportation................ 115

Total cases considered.. 146

DEPORTATION CASES NOT REPORTED TO DEPARTMENT AND DISPOSITION OF SAME.

Awaiting additional evidence before submission of cases to bureau.............. 9
Cases dismissed because of expiration of time limit............................ 12
Cases dismissed because of insufficient evidence.............................. 14
Died before report to department... 2
Committed suicide... 1
Dismissed account American citizenship...................................... 1
Aliens not located in district.. 1
Cases dismissed and deported by friends..................................... 2
Referred to Duluth office.. 2
Referred to Chicago office... 1

Total... 45

DEPORTATION CASES REPORTED TO DEPARTMENT AND DISPOSITION OF SAME.

Deportations accomplished during fiscal year (including 3 delivered by Chicago office).. 36
Deportations ordered but not accomplished at close of present fiscal year, June 30, 1913 (including 6 carried over from previous year)........................... 16
Deportations ordered but not accomplished at close of present fiscal year—aliens, Leavenworth Penitentiary; warrants to St. Louis office for execution.......... 2
Deportation warrant issued to Des Moines office—alien escaped and reported to Minneapolis... 1
Deportation warrants canceled by Secretary................................... 2
Deportation warrants canceled by death...................................... 2
Arrest warrants issued but not served at close of present fiscal year........... 2
Arrest warrants served, but hearings not submitted to department at close of fiscal year... 4
Arrest warrants served, decision on hearings not received from department at close of year.. 1
Arrest warrants canceled by Secretary after hearings......................... 27
Arrest warrants canceled by Secretary without hearings, on recommendation.... 1
Arrest warrants canceled on issuance of bonds................................ 2
Arrest warrants issued to Minneapolis office and referred to Duluth............ 2
Arrest warrants denied by Secretary.. 3

Total... 101

Total deportations from district No. 12... 51

The foregoing report, by comparison with the one for fiscal year ended June 30, 1912, shows a decrease in the Minneapolis office of 21 deportations. Reports of deportations from this district by the Duluth and Winnipeg offices also show a decrease of 22, making a total decrease of 43.

Investigations to the number of 134, exclusive of those made with respect to a large number of local affidavits (Form 547) submitted prior to arrival of aliens, were conducted.

There has been a notable increase in the number of immigration examinations for naturalization purposes. However, 29 such cases were ending in this district at close of year. Most of the applicants live in remote or sparsely settled sections, and it is very uncertain when such cases will be reached, official business seldom, if ever, taking an inspector to those neighborhoods. This new branch of immigration work has added considerably to the volume of local correspondence. At times it is very difficult to make applicants realize that such examinations are accorded by this service as an accommodation, and that no expense can be incurred therefor. Such examinations, moreover, are seldom satisfactory to the examining officer, as there is little or no corroborative evidence obtainable as to time and port of entry. Certificates of arrival (Form 526) are necessarily based on applicant's sworn statement. Occasionally these examinations develop the fact that applicant deserted from ship's crew or came under an assumed name.

CONTRACT LABOR.

Three contract-labor cases from last year, which had been set for trial, were dismissed by the Government, two by direction of the department and one by direction of the district attorney.

One contract-labor case in Iowa was continued from term to term. The bureau recently directed a reinvestigation of this case.

So far as I can ascertain (or believe) there are few violations of the contract-labor law in this district. This is primarily an agricultural district, with iron mining in northern Minnesota and principal manufacturing industries in Minneapolis, St. Paul, and Duluth, the three largest cities.

*   *   *   *   *   *   *

CHINESE.

Preinvestigations have been made in 28 cases, and investigations of arriving Chinese in 6 cases. In addition 8 miscellaneous investigations have been conducted.

*   *   *   *   *   *   *

Of three arrested Chinese in Minnesota whose appeals from commissioners' decisions were pending June 30, 1912, two were discharged by the United States district court, and one, failing to perfect appeal to United States circuit court of appeals, stands ordered deported (effective on filing mandate 60 days from June 20, 1913).

Sue Lung, arrested at Duluth, Minn., under Chinese exclusion law, was ordered deported, appealed, appeal dismissed, and later deported under previous immigration warrant, originally issued to Chicago office. (Effective on decision of Circuit Court of Appeals from District Court, Northern District of Illinois.)

Other Chinese arrested during last fiscal year in Minnesota under exclusion law discharged, 3; ordered deported, 1; appealed to district court and pending, 1.

In this connection would state that the district judges and commissioners in Minnesota (with the exception of one commissioner) are seemingly inclined to favor the defendants in Chinese exclusion proceedings, and it is almost impossible to obtain an order of deportation. With this apparent antagonism to the present Chinese exclusion law, it is almost useless to make any arrests in this district. The cases which we have lost this year were believed to be unusually good ones. In our opinion, the testimony for defendant, while uncontradicted, has not been sufficiently conclusive to warrant discharge. Similar opinion was expressed in annual report for fiscal year ended June 30, 1911.

CHAS. W. SEAMAN,
Inspector in Charge.

REPORT OF INSPECTOR IN CHARGE, DISTRICT NO. 13, COMPRISING MISSOURI, IOWA, KANSAS, AND OKLAHOMA WITH HEADQUARTERS AT ST. LOUIS.

I have the honor to submit herewith a report of the transactions of this office covering particularly all important investigations, inquiries, etc., coming before the central office at St. Louis and our branch offices at Kansas City and Des Moines, relating to immigration and Chinese cases arising in the thirteenth district and referred to our offices from other districts, during the fiscal year ended June 30, 1913.

Owing in part to the nature of the work and still more to the smallness of our official and clerical force, it is impossible to record in formal manner all of the multitudinous items of business transacted by our officers, but the more important are regularly recorded and systematically filed, and while the greater number are cases which upon investigation develop little importance they are handled merely by memoranda.

Approximately 2,600 cases have had the attention of this office during the past fiscal year, while very many other cases of minor importance have been passed upon in the district by our branch offices and our inspectors in the field. The transactions of particular importance are set forth in statistical form on the following pages:

IMMIGRATION CASES INVESTIGATED DURING FISCAL YEAR ENDING JUNE 30, 1913.

A total of 218 cases were reported to the St. Louis office for deportation by the State, county, and municipal authorities of the district during the year, concerning which the following shows the classification and action taken:

Cause.	Reported.	Deported.	Not deported.	Pending.
Insane	39	25	6	8
Professional beggar	2	1		1
Tuberculosis	15	9	6	
Other causes	162	55	83	24
Total	218	90	95	33

From other sources there were reported 382 cases which have been investigated with a view to deportation proceedings. These are classified and recorded as follows:

Class.	Investigated.	Deported.	Not deported.	Pending.
Prostitutes and procurers and persons sharing in, etc	110	?4	52	24
Contract laborers	35	14	21	
Criminals	39	14	18	7
Illegal entry	27	10	15	2
Insane	8	2	4	2
Likely to become public charge time entry	140	21	108	11
Warrants of deportation received for aliens sent to United States penitentiary at Leavenworth, Kans., from other districts	23	1		22
Total	382	96	218	68

NOT DEPORTED.

Above-mentioned cases were not deported, for the reasons set forth below:

Aliens not apprehended	33
Insufficient grounds for institution of warrant proceedings	139
Evidence insufficient for deportation, though warrant of arrest issued	36
Alien left country before service of warrant of arrest	2
Died	2
United States citizen	6
Total	218

218   REPORT OF COMMISSIONER GENERAL OF IMMIGRATION.

Aliens deported whose cases were pending at close of last fiscal year............   20
Aliens deported, current fiscal year cases.....................................   186

Aliens actually deported, current fiscal year...............................   206

In addition to above-mentioned deportation cases, special investigations have
been made in 462 cases of importance, and there were between 1,200 and 1,500 cases
of minor character which required more or less investigation but which were not
formally recorded.

Departing Chinese...   17
Arriving Chinese..   4
Applications for duplicate certificate............................   2
Other investigations..   22

Total...   45

Cases in court.

Cases pending July 1, 1912: Before United States district courts.................   1
Arrests:
    For being unlawfully in the United States............................   3
    For being unlawfully in the United States (immigration warrants)......   1
                                                                              ----   4

Total...   5

Disposition of cases:
    Ordered discharged by United States commissioners..................   1
    Pending before United States district courts on appeal..............   2
    Deported...   2

RECAPITULATION OF CASES INVESTIGATED DURING FISCAL YEAR.

Reported by State, county, and municipal authorities for deportation.........   218
Reported otherwise than above for deportation................................   382
Miscellaneous immigration cases..   462
Chinese cases..   45
Court cases..   5

Total recorded cases... 1,112
Minor investigations requiring careful consideration and more or less outlay of
time and effort, but not recorded in official files, approximately........... 1,500

Grand total—all cases passed upon.................................... 2,612

The foregoing résumé of official transactions in the thirteenth district shows a
large increase in immigration work and a very slight increase in Chinese work over
previous years. While there is a large Chinese population in the thirteenth district
and it is well known that a considerable number—possibly 200 or 300—of Chinese depart each year for China, very few file applications for return certificates or preinvestigation of status with our offices, although it is well known that the greater number of
them expect to return and do return to this section. For some reason these Chinese
prefer to leave the country without credentials or take their chances in being certified as residents of other districts, the latter being a well-established custom, as is
generally recognized. The actual work in this district in Chinese cases constitutes
a very small percentage of the volume of our business, and immigration cases of various
classes predominate to an enormous degree.
The number of cases actually referred to our officers involving inquiry, examination, investigation, correspondence, deportation proceedings, etc., is constantly
increasing and during the past year has greatly exceeded our past record. Our
deportations during the past year numbered 206, with a considerable number of cases
pending on July 1, 1913, and the prospect is that deportations for the ensuing year
will run nearer 300. Inquiries from ports of entry requiring investigation, the passing upon affidavits prepared by the friends and relatives of detained aliens, and

work of this character, which is urgent and compelling, occupies a large portion of the time of our officers and employees.

I can not too highly commend the faithful and zealous efforts of the inspectors assigned to this district and the employees of this office, whose earnest devotion and cheerful compliance with the unusual demands upon them have rendered possible the results attained.

At this point I respectfully and most urgently renew my request and recommendation for the transfer or appointment of two capable and experienced immigrant inspectors for immediate service in this district, to be assigned primarily to the St. Louis office, and for the appointment or transfer to the branch office at Kansas City of a capable clerk and stenographer.

The work at Kansas City is of immense importance and constantly increasing. Local conditions are such that at least all of the time of one inspector is required for investigations which necessitate absence from the office more than half the time, while the number of callers at the office is so great that considerable confusion, loss of time, and extra work are caused by the closing of the office in the absence of the inspector. Moreover, the expenses for clerk hire and stenographic services are very heavy, while of course, the inspector's work is hampered by the necessity for employing outside stenographers, as at present. By all means there should be a clerk and stenographer on duty in the office at all times.

I have endeavored in previous reports and special requisitions, as well as in my very pleasant personal conferences with the officials of the bureau at Washington, to impress the great need of the services of two additional inspectors for this office. As a matter of fact, I very seldom have the assistance of an inspector for local St. Louis work and am obliged, in addition to conducting our voluminous correspondence and directing all the office affairs, to handle all local examinations and investigations personally. This is cheerfully done to the limit of my capacity, but it is utterly impossible for one man to handle all such work, hence many cases must be neglected, and at all times there is the unpleasant and unfortunate condition of a mass of back work, much of which rightfully demands prompt and careful attention in justice to the persons involved and the interests of the Government. Without egotism I frankly say I do not believe that it is physically and mentally possible for any officer personally to handle a greater volume of business than is transacted by the inspector in charge under this constant and growing pressure.

* * * * * * *

The erection of an office at Des Moines during the past fiscal year was a measure which I long have hesitated to recommend because of the paucity of our working force and because comparatively very few cases arise at Des Moines calling for local investigation, although there is a very large and growing business to be handled in the State of Iowa. I think I am safe in saying that since Inspector Stretton has been assigned to Des Moines he has not been in that city one-sixth of his time. In Iowa the governor, board of control, the heads of numerous State institutions, and the police authorities generally report cases arising at various points in the State, all calling for prompt action, and mostly at points distant from the Des Moines office. For these reasons there is no present need of a clerk or stenographer for the Iowa office, but at times—as, for instance, at the date of this report—I have been obliged to assign three inspectors to work at various points in that State.

* * * * * * *

I respectfully renew a previous recommendation that the bureau issue for the information of all its field officers and others interested a monthly or weekly bulletin containing decisions and opinions which have the force of instructions as to methods of procedure, together with special and general orders, matters of departmental interest and suggestions, recommendations and bits of information which will tend to acquaint the field with the bureau's plans and intentions, its progressive methods and new developments in practice. Great good would result from the greater community of interest and the harmonization and systematization which would be prompted by such publication.

JAMES R. DUNN,
Inspector in Charge.

REPORT OF INSPECTOR IN CHARGE, DISTRICT NO. 14, COMPRISING COLORADO, WYOMING, NEBRASKA, AND UTAH, WITH HEADQUARTERS AT DENVER.

There is herewith submitted the annual report of immigration and Chinese transactions in the fourteenth district for the fiscal year ending June 30, 1913:

Alien prostitutes:
```
    Pending June 30, 1912.....................................................   4
    Arrested.................................................................   9
    Deported................................................................   4
    Discharged..............................................................   6
    Pending June 30, 1913...................................................   3
```
Procurers:
```
    Pending June 30, 1912...................................................   1
    Arrested................................................................   2
    Discharged..............................................................   1
    Deported................................................................   1
```
Supported by proceeds of prostitution:
```
    Pending June 30, 1912...................................................   6
    Arrested................................................................  27
    Discharged..............................................................   5
    Deported................................................................  18
    Pending June 30, 1913...................................................  10
```

Eight of the above-pending cases, named as follows, have also been indicted and tried for violating the "White-slave traffic act," and are now serving terms in the Federal penitentiary at Leavenworth, Kans. (warrants of arrest and orders of deportation were forwarded to St. Louis office for execution when their terms expire): Paul Gaye, Gazasimos Couloubis, James Theodorsan, Juan Mendez, Harry Loukas; Paul Onfant alias Verne Gabriel; Joseph Edward Rapken alias Joe Edwards; Anthenasios Kaimenakis.

Oreste Paganini, another one of the pending cases, is now serving a term in the Federal penitentiary at Leavenworth, Kans., for impersonating a Government officer. (Warrant of arrest and order of deportation were forwarded to St. Louis office for execution.)

White-slave traffic act:
```
    Pending June 30, 1912...................................................   6
    Arrested................................................................   5
    Convicted...............................................................   3
    Discharged..............................................................   1
    Deported................................................................   1
    Pending June 30, 1913...................................................   8
```
Insane aliens:
```
    Pending June 30, 1912...................................................   3
    Arrested................................................................   4
    Discharged..............................................................   1
    Deported................................................................   6
```
Alien public charges:
```
    Arrested................................................................   7
    Deported................................................................   7
```
Criminal record prior to entry:
```
    Pending June 30, 1912...................................................   1
    Arrested................................................................   2
    Deported................................................................   1
    Pending June 30, 1913...................................................   2
```

One of the above aliens now serving a term in Federal penitentiary at Leavenworth, Kans., to be deported after his term expires.

Contract labor cases:
```
    Arrested................................................................  31
    Discharged..............................................................  31
    Investigated............................................................ 280
```
Surreptitious entry:
```
    Arrested................................................................   1
    Discharged..............................................................   1
    Investigated............................................................   3
```
Miscellaneous... 167

CHINESE TRANSACTIONS.

Chinese persons:
Arrested.. 6
Deported... 1
Discharged... 5
Application for laborer's return certificate................................. 31
Application for merchant's return certificate................................ 5
Investigations for admission of alleged sons of domiciled merchants.......... 4
Investigations for admission of domiciled merchants.......................... 1
Investigations for admission of alleged natives or children of alleged native born. 6
Certificates forwarded to the bureau for cancellation........................ 11
Applications for duplicate certificates...................................... 7
Preinvestigation of native born.. 8
Investigations for other offices... 11
Miscellaneous investigations... 33

LOUIS ADAMS,
Inspector in charge.

REPORT OF INSPECTOR IN CHARGE, DISTRICT NO. 15, COMPRISING MONTANA AND IDAHO, WITH HEADQUARTERS AT HELENA.

I submit herewith report of work done by this office during the fiscal year ending June 30, 1913:

It will be noted that there is again a falling off in the number of cases of immoral aliens handled; but in view of the fact that it has, during the past year, been thoroughly settled that the three-year limit in this class is abolished, this falling off is due to but one cause, and that is that these aliens are becoming less numerous each year. If we had more cases to report, the showing on paper of the amount of work done would be greater, of course, than it is; but with the falling off in the number of cases comes the fact that it requires more work to discover and develop a case, so that the amount of work done by the officers is approximately the same. In the deportations reported under "Illegal entry" (not otherwise classified) I would say that 2 were aliens who admitted having committed a crime before entering; 2 were wanted by their own government as fugitives, and 2 had been convicted of crime in this country.

The number of Chinese arrests reported is small and the results very unsatisfactory; but until a law is passed authorizing these cases to be handled by departmental warrants the result will always be so unsatisfactory as to raise a question whether it is advisable to make an arrest except where it is practically forced upon us.

The number of investigations for certificates of arrival, Form 526a, for naturalization purposes, have materially increased this year and will probably continue to increase. The great number of former American citizens who went to Canada in past years, attracted by cheap land, are now beginning to return to take up land in this section of the United States. This number will unquestionably increase for the next few years, as it seems to be common report among them that the lands of this section of the country are better adapted to farming than those of Canada. These aliens, having been once American citizens, are quite apt to be careless of inspection upon their entry, many of them apparently thinking that they still retain their American citizenship. Owing to the great distances between immigration stations and customs offices along the northern border of Montana quite a few aliens drive over the line rather than go to the trouble and expense of shipping their goods by rail through a regular customs or immigration port. Without doubt this class of work will continue to increase until all the agricultural land of Montana is settled upon.

STATUS OF IMMIGRATION CASES (OTHER THAN CHINESE), FISCAL YEAR ENDING JUNE 30, 1913.

PROCURERS.

Criminal proceedings instituted fiscal year................................... 2
Convicted... 2
Deportation proceedings:
Pending deportation June 30, 1912 (warrant issued)............................ 1
Proceedings in progress June 30, 1912... 1
Cases handled fiscal year... 6

Total... 8

Deportation proceedings—Continued.
Disposition—
Deported 3
Pending deportation June 30, 1913................... 1
Proceedings in progress June 30, 1913.............. 3
Lack of evidence for warrant process............... 1

Total... 8

PROSTITUTES.

Proceedings in progress June 30, 1912............................ 2
Investigations fiscal year.. 14

Total.. 16
Disposition:
Deported... 3
Pending deportation June 30, 1913........................... 3
Warrant arrest or deportation canceled...................... 3
Lack of evidence for warrant process........................ 7

Total.. 16

PUBLIC CHARGES.

Deportation proceedings in progress June 30, 1912.............. 2
Cases handled fiscal year...................................... 4

Total.. 6
Disposition:
Deported... 3
Lack of evidence for warrant process........................ 3

Total.. 6

ILLEGAL ENTRY.

Pending deportation June 30, 1912 (warrant issued)............. 3
Under investigation June 30, 1912............................. 2
Cases handled current fiscal year............................. 30

Total.. 35
Disposition:
Deported... 8
Under investigation June 30, 1913........................... 8
Warrant arrest or deportation canceled...................... 11
Escaped [1].. 2
Lack of evidence for warrant proceedings.................... 5
Not apprehended... 1

Total.. 35

NATURALIZATION.

Certificates arrival, Form 526a:
Pending investigation June 30, 1912......................... 1
Cases of current fiscal year................................ 66

Total.. 67
Disposition—
Certificates granted or issuance recommended................ 41
Under investigation June 30, 1913........................... 23
Referred to other districts................................. 1
Application withdrawn....................................... 2

Total.. 67

---
[1] From city or county jails.

VARIOUS.

Referred to or from other districts for data [1]............................. 29
Unclassified... 2

   Total... 31

   Total immigration... 165

STATUS OF CHINESE CASES FISCAL YEAR ENDING JUNE 30, 1913.

CASES IN COURT.

Arrests made during fiscal year...................................... 3
Disposition:
  Discharged by United States commissioners...................... 2
  Pending before United States commissioners..................... 1

   Total... 3

DEPARTMENT WARRANT PROCEEDINGS.

Cases fiscal year (warrant canceled)................................. 2

INVESTIGATIONS.

Laborers:
  Pending investigation June 30, 1912............................ 3
  Cases of fiscal year... 52

   Total... 55
Disposition—
  Departing.. 48
  Duplicate certificates residence............................... 4
  Investigations pending... 3

   Total... 55
Merchants:
  Pending investigation June 30, 1912............................ 1
  Cases of fiscal year... 24

   Total... 25
Disposition—
  Departing.. 18
  Returning.. 1
  Sons applying for admission.................................... 3
  Sons applying for preinvestigation status...................... 1
  Investigations pending... 2

   Total... 25
Natives:
  Pending investigation June 30, 1912............................ 1
  Cases of fiscal year... 17

   Total... 18
Disposition—
  Departing.. 14
  Applying for admission... 1
  Sons applying for admission.................................... 3

   Total... 18

   Total Chinese.. 103

[1] Not otherwise included.

224 REPORT OF COMMISSIONER GENERAL OF IMMIGRATION.

STATUS OF INVESTIGATIONS UNDER "WHITE SLAVE ACT" FISCAL YEAR ENDING JUNE 30, 1913.

```
Pending prosecution June 30, 1912 (indictment returned)..................   3
Cases handled fiscal year.................................................  15
                                                                           ----
    Total.................................................................       18
Disposition:
  Criminal proceedings—
    Held to Federal grand jury by United States commissioners....   6
                                                                   ===
    United States district court—
      Convicted...............................................   8
      Pending prosecution June 30, 1913 (indicted)...........   1
                                                                ----
        Total.................................................       9
Investigations made which, when completed, would not justify com-
  plaint..................................................................   3
Referred to Department of Justice for investigation....................   3
Referred to or from other districts for investigation ¹.................   3
                                                                          ----
    Total.................................................................       18
```

LORENZO T. PLUMMER,
Inspector in charge.

REPORT OF COMMISSIONER OF IMMIGRATION, SEATTLE, IN CHARGE OF DISTRICT NO. 16, COMPRISING THE STATE OF WASHINGTON.

In submitting my report of the work of the immigration service in this jurisdiction for the fiscal year ending June 30, 1913, I wish to say in the beginning that there has been the most perfect cooperation from officers throughout the district, and by combined harmony and energy and singleness of purpose we have the pleasure of reviewing a year of accomplishment with the least possible expenditure of money. It has been our constant aim to accomplish as much as possible with the least possible expenditure, and we find much satisfaction in reviewing our work to find that our aim has been rewarded by much success. Our union of purpose and effort has been to so conduct the work of this jurisdiction, under the general supervision of the Washington authorities, to the end that the aim of the law would be satisfied to the limit of possibility, namely, to accomplish all possible consistent with the allotted amount of funds. We are much indebted, of course, to the supervising authorities at Washington for direction in general, and in many special knotty problems arising from time to time in particular cases for the degree of efficiency shown in the work of our officers.

CHARACTER OF IMMIGRATION.

The Chinese and Japanese comprise the chief bulk of immigration through this district. A few of a substantial class of Russians arrive from time to time, almost uniformly of the admissible classes. Other European arrivals are admitted occasionally only, there being few of such arrivals. The Hindus are arriving from the Philippine Islands, and in numbers to cause more or less apprehension; this is a matter, however, of sufficient importance for special attention further on in this report. It may be of interest to note that there are no Hindu laborers admitted through this district, excepting those arriving from the Philippines. Our officers have most effectively applied the existing law as against the admission of Hindu laborers arriving from their native country, and so effective has been the application of the law that there are no more arriving.

HOSPITAL TREATMENT.

The question of hospital treatment, which for a time it seemed would completely overtax the capacity of our building, seems to have been favorably adjusted to such an extent that we are now able to accommodate all who are certified. Arriving aliens suffering from the disease known as "hookworm," or unicinariasis, were permitted

---
¹ Not otherwise included.

to receive treatment in the immigration building and when all the arrivals were examined here for this disease for the first time it was found that the number certified to be so afflicted as compared with the number of arrivals was very great. This was presenting a serious problem when the matter was favorably adjusted through the bureau bringing about the arrangement whereby aliens are examined for this particular disease before embarkation. The matter has been so satisfactorily adjusted that no further serious problem is anticipated because of this disease. The prevalence of this disease, however, has caused difficulties in more ways than one. For a time it was thought that the disease should most always be detected by careful examination before embarkation, and our medical examiner at this port, acting upon this belief, certified in a number of cases that the presence of the disease could have been detected by a careful medical examination before embarkation, upon which certificate, of course, action was taken looking toward the collection of fines from the steamship companies bringing the aliens. It was finally determined that this, as a general rule, was unjust to the steamship companies for the reason that even after the most skillful examination just prior to embarkation the presence of this disease might be detected at the port of arrival. This being the case, the medical examiner has been slow to certify that the disease in any particular case could have been detected before embarkation, which accounts for the small number of fines as compared with the number certified as having the disease. It seems that the medical examiner is slow to determine and decide whether the presence of the disease might have been detected even after the most skillful examination just before the date of embarkation. However, should the percentage begin to increase materially over that of the present our medical examiners might feel that it was due to lack of proper medical examination prior to embarkation, and they might, in such event, determine to make certificates adverse to the steamship companies' material interests.

IMMIGRATION BUILDING.

In August, 1912, there was completed certain changes in our immigration building which included one additional large room and which has proven of much benefit in accommodating greater numbers, and also in making proper segregation in certain cases which seemed almost impossible before the changes and added rooming accommodations. However, this building is utterly inadequate to properly accommodate the service at this station, and in this I am satisfied that the bureau and department are in full accord with my views. It seems that this is an important matter that should be most energetically urged upon Congress at the very earliest practicable moment. Upon the opening of the Panama Canal, should immigration increase through this port to any considerable extent it will be a physical impossibility to make this building do at all. While the increase in immigration upon the opening of the canal is problematical, yet it is the part of wisdom, it seems to me, to be prepared for an increase of a few thousand each year at least. I am not anticipating any very great increase, but it is only reasonable to presume that there will be a slight increase, and with our present accommodations we are illy prepared for any increase whatever. The Seattle harbor is in process of reconstruction at the present time and an early appropriation by Congress for a new immigration building here will enable our service to get a proper location at reasonable figures. It is quite an item to be located satisfactorily from a viewpoint of expense as well as general convenience for all parties concerned. I can not too strongly urge vigorous action looking to an early appropriation for the location and erection of a suitable immigration building at this port. It will save much inconvenience, expense, and embarrassment in the near future. Quick action in this matter is imperative if Congress considers the interest and welfare of our service in this district.

GENERAL ADMINISTRATION.

The work of the district has increased in both volume and efficiency. Each officer has accomplished a little more and with a greater degree of skill. It is but just and fair to our officers who have rendered such valuable service to take proper notice of it in this report. This district has enjoyed every blessing that results from full, loyal, and forceful cooperation; the full measure that is the product of perfect harmony; this, together with the direction and support from Washington, allows us to point with pride to the accomplishments of the past year. Our officers have often been taxed to the limit in order to do what was necessary to be done within the required time and with the required skill, but to their credit it may be said no failure has been recorded— none made to record. The character of the work which confronts our officers in this district often requires the most careful thought and greatest skill in finally determining what action to take. It often takes much research to determine all the facts necessary to ascertain the exact status of a case as well as much skill in making the research. To properly appreciate the work of the district there must be taken into account not only the volume of work but also the character of the work, with emphasis on the character. When this is emphasized and the few officers who are employed in doing it there is much room for congratulation.

UNLAWFUL ENTRIES.

One phase of our work which makes but little show and yet is very important is the efforts of our officers to prevent unlawful entries from Canada. The figures will show that this number is comparatively very great. The number of aliens apprehended and returned to Canada by the few officers we have indicates two things, namely, that our officers are very active and that their presence and activity prevents an invasion of undesirable aliens—aliens who add nothing desirable to our life. To prevent undesirable immigration at every point is certainly of the highest degree of importance. It is the sifting process which must be a prominent factor in determining the future of our national life. A part of this process is in apprehending after unlawful entry as well as at the port upon application for entry. While our officers have returned a creditably large number of unlawful entries, it is only an index to the number which would be silently recorded by mingling with our people and finally leaving a lasting impress upon the character of our industrial and social fabric, and that which would tend to lower rather than to elevate; retard rather than hasten the goal of our standard, were it not for the deterrent effect of the presence of the officers as well as the important results of their activity. The energy and skill of these officers is worthy of mention and results in the satisfaction of feeling that this important task is in the care of those who are highly trustworthy in every sense. While this work does not require the same character of skill as other work of immigration officers it does require a certain character of skill and diplomacy which the officers assigned to duty there possess in a high degree, and hence the flattering record each has made for himself.

UNDESIRABLE PERSONS.

The question of certain undesirable persons who require much of our time and attention is as old as man, and I presume will be a question as long as man is, or at least as long as he is constituted as he is. So long as human nature remains as at present there will doubtless be those who, for hire, will act as go-between for male and female who seek unlawful cohabitation. The procurers and prostitutes are as old as human history and we presume that time will not efface them. This being the case, it is an ever-present evil which will require ceaseless attention in order to prevent the undermining of the social fabric. There possibly is no other evil so far-reaching or so deadly in its ultimate results, and consequently there is no other evil which requires such constant vigilance. We have left no leaf unturned that would aid in the detection and apprehension of those responsible for this blighting evil. While the record speaks volumes it is only a poor index to the labor which has been spent in an attempt to keep at the lowest possible ebb this loathsome blight so far as this district is concerned. Constant attention to this one evil should never cease. To cease activity against this social crime or to permit it to abate in the least is incompatible with any desire of suppression, for our only hope of even comparative suppression is tireless pursuit. It is true that burglaries are often prevented by noise. This is by reason of the fact that crime is always afraid of detection and therefore trembles at noise or light; for this reason as much noise as possible should follow the result of the activities of our officers. Persons of normal minds naturally take more pleasure in preventing crime than in apprehending it. Carrying out this idea I deem it wise to have published broadcast the net results of the activities of our officers in the suppression of this particular evil, the results so far as it relates to the number of prosecutions, convictions, etc., of those engaged in this unlawful practice. The more difficulties thrown in the way of crime checks it just so much, and every check, however small, does some good.

STOWAWAYS.

Year after year we are required to spend much time and money in preventing the landing of stowaways. Some of the steamship companies cooperate with us in trying to prevent the landing of the stowaway, but others do not. It seems to me, as I have said before, that it should be made the duty of the steamship companies to detect these people and to deliver them, upon arrival, to the immigration officials. The company's officials in charge of a vessel should know who is on board. These officials are in absolute charge and control and they should be expected to detect the presence of stowaways more easily than any other person, and as a matter of fact they can. Were the law so amended that responsibility would attach immediately upon the apprehension of a stowaway by an immigration officer there is no doubt in my mind but the stowaway would have little chance of ever landing. The officers of the vessels should be required to apprehend and deliver to the immigration officers, upon arrival, all stowaways, or at least before they are apprehended by our officers. Should they be apprehended by our officers a fine should attach at the discretion of the Secretary. The question of the fine in any event, in my judgment, should be left to the Secretary and not to the court. Had the Secretary full power to assess fines in such cases there would be few stowaways landed. By reason of the fact that as the law now is there is little chance of penalizing anyone connected with the landing of stowaways, there is little or no effort on the part of the officials of the steamship companies to put a stop to the business; hence it requires constant vigilance on the part of our officers, while little or no attention is paid to it by those directly responsible.

THE ANARCHIST.

In my judgment there is no more important question confronting our people than the question of anarchy. That the anarchist is among us and silently but steadily and surely laying his plans of destruction there can be little doubt. The outspoken enemies of all forms of organized government are those, most always, who have been in this country more than three years. The anarchist of foreign birth, and most all are, remains very quiet, as a rule, until the time limit protects him from deportation, and then he is loud and boisterous and begins his maniac cry against all forms of organized government; excepting, perhaps, some form of government suggested to him through his unbridled, formless, hallucinari, and degenerate brain, which is always incapable of logical thought. In my judgment, there is no room in this country for this class of mental degenerates, and there should be no time limit to their deportation. We doubtless all welcome those who are willing to reason with us on the question of the form and limits of government, but he who seeks to destroy rather than to aid in construction has no place in the affairs of men. He is a dangerous criminal and each country should take care of its own criminals. There should be no time limit to the deportation of these criminals, because of their dangerous character, and should one remain in hiding sufficiently long to become naturalized he should, at the first symptoms, be shorn of his cloak and forthwith deported. If this destructive type of humanity, if such characters can be regarded as human in the strictest sense, found no comfort or protection from any source it would at least aid in suppressing the scourge.

SMUGGLING.

So long as the immigration question is a live one, just so long will the question of smuggling also be a live one. Restriction of immigration necessarily means that there are those who do not fill all the requirements necessary for admission; in other words, they do not meet the full measurement required by the law for aliens entering this country; consequently, for some cause enumerated in the law, there are those who are eliminated. By this process of elimination there are a great many who can not lawfully enter, and hence the constant attempt to make successful entry by smuggling. There are doubtless many who enter each year in this way whom our officers are unable to apprehend. As heretofore referred to in this report, our officers apprehend a great many who attempt unlawful entry by land, but the more difficult problem which constantly confronts us is the smuggling by water. While our officers at the various Sound Stations do all possible to keep smuggling via this avenue at the minimum, it is doubtless true that there is more or less of this unlawful traffic carried on. The most effective way, of course, would be a vessel commanded by our officers which could stand the weather among the islands at all times and be in the waters at that place constantly. A properly constructed vessel for this purpose would be the most, if not the only effective method, of entirely eliminating this unlawful traffic, or keeping it to the lowest possible minimum. It is problematical, however, whether the added expense would be justified, for we must depend on rumor in a very large degree as to the number securing unlawful entry in this manner. With our present efforts and equipment there is nothing left unturned to prevent the smuggling of those not entitled to lawful entry, and it is probable that but little added expense would be justified in making a more complete defense against this unlawful traffic.

THE HINDU.

It is the generally accepted idea, as I understand it, that immigration should be so regulated that those arriving will not lower our standards of life; that no internal dissensions or troubles will result by their admission, but that ultimately those admitted will be an added blessing. This being the case, it is for Congress to so frame laws relating to this most important subject that only those who will ultimately aid rather than retard our progress can be admitted. In this connection I wish to again refer to those arriving here from certain Asiatic territory that threatens trouble from the time of arrival. I am open to argument on any debatable question, but to my mind there is no debatable ground so far as the admission of the Hindu is concerned. If his presence here can add aught but trouble, I am unable to see in what possible way. In the first place, he is caste ridden to such an extent that he is unyielding in all his manners, customs, etc. He is almost absolutely aloof in all things with one exception, and that is the question of securing possession of the dollar. In order to secure this he underbids all of our laboring people to such an extent that he can undermine them. As a matter of fact, he stands little show of work except by underbidding other laborers, for as a rule employers of labor refuse to employ the Hindu laborers excepting at a low wage. The Hindu stands little or no chance for work at the same price as our laborers and consequently he becomes a professional underbidder, and herein lies one of the chief dangers of his presence. He adds to labor disturbances as a natural consequence. In this connection I wish to quote from the brief of an attorney of this city, which was offered in behalf of certain Hindus who were applying for admission at this port. This attorney, who was using his efforts to convince the Washington authorities that his Hindu clients would not become a charge on the public, said, in part, "In the East a man might perhaps not be able to make it go, and an American, who requires more money to live on, might not be able to keep his head above the water with so small an amount of money, but with these Hindus things are entirely different. They eat fruit and vegetables, all of which they can get very cheaply. Their life in India has led them to keep together, and they all live together in one or two houses, and they have one of their party do their cooking for them, and he gets no salary, and by buying in large quantities the cost of their vegetables is small. They can live nicely on 25 cents per day, and when they make $2 they can save $1.75," etc. This is a true statement, made by an attorney friend of the Hindus. Imagine our laboring classes coping with a Hindu laborer who can and does, according to his attorney friend, live on 25 cents a day. I have no reason to doubt the correctness of the statement.

I will close my remarks on this subject by quoting my answer to that part of the attorney's brief: "The fact that Hindus now in this country are securing employment by undermining their fellow-laborers of other nationalities is only brewing trouble for the near future, and the ultimate result will be that the Hindu will be out of work and a charge on the public. The attorneys for these aliens call attention to the fact that they can live nicely on 25 cents a day and they save money and send it home. These attributes, which it must be admitted they possess, do not endear them to the American people."

SEAMEN.

Aside from Japanese laborers, I do not believe that there are many aliens of the inadmissible classes accomplishing entry through this district under the guise of seamen. Approximately 27 per cent of the alien seamen who left their ships in this district during the past fiscal year were Japanese, and I have no doubt that the greater part, if not all of them, deserted with the intention of remaining in the United States rather than reshipping in the course of their pursuit, as is the custom of seamen of other races.

Chinese seamen are giving some trouble, but during the year there were but three desertions. Beginning with the change in the form of Government of their country, they have maintained that they should be treated in the same manner as seamen of other races. They object to the surveillance which is maintained over them and contend that they are entitled to all privileges granted seamen, including shore leave. The shipping concerns have so far managed to hold their crews by employing special watchmen for the purpose of keeping them on board their vessels.

*　　　*　　　*　　　*　　　*　　　*　　　*

The following is a detailed statement of the work performed in this jurisdiction during the last fiscal year:

INWARD PASSENGER MOVEMENT.

	Male.	Female.	Total.
Immigrant aliens admitted	1,224	1,180	2,404
Nonimmigrant aliens admitted	1,931	89	2,020
United States citizens arrived	625	176	801
Aliens debarred	92	8	100
Aliens whose cases are pending either before this office or the bureau	24	14	38
Grand total			5,363

The inward passenger movement for the year 1913 exceeded that of the year 1912 by 1,006. The increase was largely due to the arrival of a greater number of Japanese. The increase in the number of Japanese alone was 787.

Of the 2,404 immigrant aliens admitted, 1,723 were Japanese; 600 males, and 1,123 females.

Of the 2,020 nonimmigrant aliens admitted, 1,256 were Japanese; 1,199 males, and 57 females.

Of the total (2,979) Japanese arrivals, 1,420 were former residents.

During the current fiscal year there were 517 Japanese proxy brides arrived; during the fiscal year 1912 there were 511 arrived, or an increase of 6 proxy brides.

ARRIVALS FROM INSULAR POSSESSIONS.

[Not included in statistics.]

Of the total 438 arrivals from insular possessions, 406 were East Indians.

STOWAWAYS.

Total number of stowaways for the year, 45; Japanese 30, Chinese 7, others 8.

OUTWARD PASSENGER MOVEMENT.

	Male.	Female.	Total.
Emigrant aliens departed	580	53	633
Nonemigrant aliens departed	2,104	176	2,280
United States citizens departed	518	258	770
Grand total			3,689

Of the 633 emigrant aliens departed, 175 were Japanese, 141 males, and 34 females.

Of the 2,280 nonemigrant aliens departed, 1,561 were Japanese; 1,416 males, and 145 females.

DEBARRED ALIENS.

	Males.	Females.	Total.
Japanese	32	3	35
Chinese	56	5	61
West Indian	2		2
English	1		1
Welsh	1		1
Grand total	92	8	100

ALIEN SEAMEN.

Vessels arrived	1,348
Alien crew (Chinese, 13,353; other, 12,986)	26,339
Certified by marine hospital surgeon	54
Certified seamen, deserting	1
Deserting seamen	[1] 249
Discharged (admitted to the United States)	326
Discharged (passed to follow their vocation)	525

WARRANTS OF ARREST—RECEIVED.

Issued during the fiscal year 1913	183
Issued in previous years executed during the fiscal year	11
Total handled	194

WARRANTS OF ARREST—DISPOSITION.

Executed	163
Unexecuted June 30, 1913	12
Canceled	18
Sent to other districts for execution	1
Total	194

ACTION ON WARRANTS OF ARREST EXECUTED DURING THE FISCAL YEAR 1913.

Deportation ordered	131
Release ordered	22
Pending before department	2
Pending before this office	8
Total	163

Orders of deportation entered	131
Orders of deportation canceled	2
Released on recognizance after order of deportation entered	2
Orders of deportation forwarded other districts for execution	2
	6
Net orders of deportation	125

DEPORTATIONS.

Net orders of deportation issued during the fiscal year 1913, based on arrests made during that year	125
Orders of deportation, based on arrests made previous years, executed during the fiscal year 1913	33
Total	158

Deportations direct from this district	53
Deportations from Atlantic United States seaports	47
Deportations from Canadian seaports	11
Deportations from all other seaports	4
Orders of deportation, based on arrests made during the fiscal year 1913, pending June 30, 1913	43

Deported after landing, arrests made in this district	158
Deportations through this district, arrests made in other districts	6
Grand total of all deportations	164

[1] Of the 249 deserting seamen, 65 were Japanese.

PROCURERS, ETC.

Deported... 10
Awaiting deportation... 10
Released... 1
Orders of deportation forwarded other districts............................ 2

Arrests during the fiscal year 1913....................................... 23

PROSTITUTES, ETC.

Deported... 8
Awaiting deportation... 1
Released... 5
Pending before this office... 2

Arrests during the fiscal year 1913....................................... 16

Procurers arrested during previous years deported during the fiscal year 1913.... 1
Prostitutes arrested during previous years deported during the fiscal year 1913.. 2

*   *   *   *   *   *   *

CRIMINAL PROSECUTIONS.

Fifty-seven prosecutions have been instituted for violations of penal provisions of the immigration and white slave traffic acts. Convictions have been had in 34 cases, defendants were acquitted or indictments dismissed in 13 cases, and the balance are pending at the close of the year.

BOARD OF SPECIAL INQUIRY CASES HELD AND THE ACTION TAKEN THEREON.

Admitted by board.. 431
Excluded by board.. 417

Cases held during the year... 848

APPEALS FROM DECISION OF BOARD OF SPECIAL INQUIRY.

Sustained.. 1
Dismissed.. 4
Referred back for action under the Chinese exclusion act on account of Nakashima decision... 1

Appeals taken... 6

CHINESE TRANSACTIONS.

During the year just closed 1,276 applications for admission were considered, an increase of 203 over the previous year, and 1,081 applications of domiciled Chinese for return certificates, a decrease of 38. The increase in arrivals was due entirely to returning domiciled Chinese, a larger number than usual having been called home last year on account of the unsettled conditions then existing in China. A slight decrease in the number of "new arrivals" will be noted.

*   *   *   *   *   *   *

Departing Chinese to whom there were issued return certificates all took passage at the port of Seattle, except one who boarded a steamer of the Osaka Shosen Kaisha Line at Tacoma. Blue Funnel steamers, while entering at Tacoma, all clear from Seattle. Those Chinese leaving without first securing return certificates are not included in this report.

APPLICATIONS FOR ADMISSION.

Disposed of as follows:
Admitted... 1,177
Passed in transit.. 3
Returned... 61
Died... 1

Pending:
Awaiting deportation.. 6
On appeal to department... 4
Before inspectors.. 23
Before court on writ... 1

Total cases of all classes before commissioner during fiscal year......... 1,276

DIVISION BY CLASSES.

Laborers:
Cases pending from previous year....................................... 3
Applications for admission current year................................ 437

Total... 440

Disposed of as follows—
Admitted... 430
Returned... 5
Awaiting return.. 5

Total... 440

Increase over 1912, 79.

Domiciled merchants, etc.:
Cases pending from previous year....................................... 1
Applications for admission current year................................ 209

Total... 210

Disposed of as follows—
Admitted... 205
Returned... 3
Pending before inspectors.. 2

Total... 210

Increase over 1912, 62.

As practically all domiciled exempts now have their status determined under rule 15 of the regulations, before departure from the country, it follows that but few of this class are denied admission on return. Occasionally it is discovered that an alleged exempt secured his return certificate through fraud, and consequently admission is denied him if he seeks to reenter the country. As a rule, however, these frauds are discovered before the person returns, and notice of inadmissibility is then sent to him in China.

AMERICAN-BORN CHINESE (CITIZENS).

Gradually this class, together with the wives and children of its members, has become the most important of all in connection with the enforcement of the exclusion law, and the indications are that the movement of "citizens" is in its infancy. The thousands of Chinese who were adjudged citizens by United States commissioners, by the courts, and by this service some years since are now bringing to this country their alleged children, who under section 1993 of the Revised Statutes are also citizens. These applicants are often married men, so in time their children born abroad may also come in as citizens, and so on ad infinitum. Citizens are also bringing in their wives, hence the number of children actually born in the United States is on the increase. It has been the practice for some years to secure from each applicant, for future use, a description of his family. For a time this plan worked well, but its purpose has now been defeated in many instances; the Chinese appreciating the situation provide themselves in their testimony with a family of boys and thus lay a foundation for future admissions. It is remarkable how many "citizens" living in the Eastern States, principally in Boston and vicinity, testify to their having three boys and no girls in their families. No doubt collusion exists among these persons. These are principally Chinese who entered the country surreptitiously some years ago via Canada and northern New York and who on arrest were found to be American-born by certain United States commissioners, on testimony adduced by unscrupulous attorneys and others. Here is presented a question for the consideration of the bureau. Citizens admitted may be classified as follows:

Cases pending from previous year	7
Applicants for admission current year	350
Total before commissioner	357

Disposed of as follows:

Admitted	318
Returned	25
Pending on appeal to department	3
Pending before inspectors	11
Total	357

Further subdivisions:

"Raw" natives:

Admitted	1
Returned	8
Total	9

Record of departure—prior landing:

Admitted	291
Returned	2
Pending	1
Total	294

Prior residence—status not determined:

Admitted	7
Returned	3
Pending	1
Total	11

Children of citizens:

Admitted	19
Returned	12
Pending	12
Total	43
	357

Increase over 1912, 70.

"SECTION 6," EXEMPTS.

The number of "section 6" applications decreased from 141 in 1912 to 130 in 1913. All were admitted, except 1 rejected medically and 31 paroled to a Presbyterian clergyman of this city. Not one altered certificate was found, though in previous years a number were detected.

The movement, originated in 1912 by certain profit-seeking Americans to bring alleged students to this country for a consideration, landing guaranteed, and which resulted in an increased number of applications, as heretofore reported, has not made much headway the past year, though a number of persons are still working along the same line. The failure of the movement is due to the careful inspection of all applications for visé by special officers of this service now attached to the offices of the consuls at both Hongkong and Canton, and to the fact that the Chinese Government itself, judging from reports received, has undertaken to see that "section 6" papers are issued only to bona fide students, and that a suitable guaranty is given that the applicant will remain a student for a certain length of time in this country. Of the students admitted 28 are to be supported by the Canton Government; all spoke English and were destined to different leading educational institutions in this country; those attending a school in the West are to receive $800 gold a year for expenses;

those going to the universities in the Middle West, $900, and those going to eastern colleges, $960. The recipient of assistance is required to pay back but half of the money advanced if on completion of his education he return to Canton Province to settle; if he settle elsewhere he must repay all within 10 years.

EXEMPTS OTHER THAN "SECTION 6."

The number of applications of this class was the same as in 1912; there was, however, a decrease in the number of minor sons of exempts presenting themselves, and a corresponding increase in the number of wives and minor daughters, as follows:

Cases pending from previous year	10
Applications for admission current year	126
Total	**136**

Disposed of as follows:

Admitted	98
Returned	27
Awaiting return	1
Pending on appeal before department	1
Pending before inspectors	9
Total	**136**

This class may be further divided as follows:

Minor sons of merchants:

Admitted	51
Returned	22
Awaiting return	1
Pending before department	1
Pending before inspectors	8
Total	**83**

Minor daughters of merchants admitted	7

Wives of merchants:

Admitted	21
Returned	2
Pending before inspectors	1
Total	**24**

Wives of citizens:

Admitted	10
Returned	3
Total	**13**

Miscellaneous admissions	9

TRANSITS.

By land	1
By water	2
Total	**3**

There was during the year but one application for release on bond by a Chinese of the exempt class, pending final determination of right to enter the United States.

*　　　*　　　*　　　*　　　.*　　　*　　　*

WRITS OF HABEAS CORPUS.

During the past year but one case was taken into court on writ of habeas corpus, that of Mac Fock. Mac Fock is a Chinese who entered the country surreptitiously in 1896; he was arrested, and on hearing before United States Commissioner McGettrick was discharged as an American citizen. Recently, on return from a visit abroad, he admitted on examination that he was born in China and that his crossing the line at Richford, Vt., was his original entry into the United States. The excluding decision of this office being sustained by the department on appeal, the court was petitioned to stay deportation, on the ground that the status of the applicant was res adjudicata, he having been found to be an American citizen by a court of competent authority, which decision had never been set aside and, therefore, can not now be ignored by the immigration authorities. The matter has not yet been heard.

ARRESTS UNDER THE EXCLUSION LAW.

Cases pending July 1, 1912	1
Arrests during fiscal year	5
Total	6

Disposed of as follows:

Deported	2
Discharged	2
Pending before court on appeal	2
	6

It has been deemed inadvisable to make arrests under the exclusion law unless reasonably sure that a claim of citizenship will not be set up as a defense. There seems to be in the country a large number of young Chinese who claim birth in the United States and who have never had their status passed on by this service or the courts. These Chinese are probably unlawfully here, but in a hearing before a United States commissioner they are very likely to be discharged as citizens on evidence which would not be accepted by this service. It is a fact that certain persons of this class when refused return certificates have invited arrest on the charge of being unlawfully within the United States. The status of a citizen is very valuable to a Chinese, hence he will pay much money to secure one, employing attorneys of standing and influence to defend him. To effectively rid the country of contraband Chinese the enforcement of the law should be placed in the hands of the Secretary and arrests made on department warrants. A number of Chinese who had entered without inspection within three years were arrested under the general immigration law. These were surreptitious entries from Canada apprehended near the border.

PREINVESTIGATED CASES.

A phase of the work which is of much importance is the investigation of applications for return certificates of those desiring to go abroad temporarily. Under the regulations according privilege of having their status predetermined many Chinese laborers who are without certificates of residence undertake to qualify either as domiciled merchants or as citizens. These persons are believed to have gained admission originally as stowaways or by surreptitious entry from either Canada or Mexico, and consequently, being unable to show by parol evidence a lawful residence here, attach themselves to some mercantile establishment for a short time and then apply for a return certificate as a domiciled exempt, this class not being required under the law to show affirmatively a lawful residence in the country, it being sufficient if the applicant prove by two witnesses other than Chinese that he has been a merchant for the previous year and has not performed any manual labor except such as was incident to his business. Under the law, therefore, contraband laborers are able to gain a status to which they are not entitled, and one which enables them later to bring in their wives and minor children, after which they can again become laborers without fear of arrest. Many applicants admitted as "minor sons," though actually laborers, join this class on reaching their majority so as to visit China, a laborer's return certificate being denied them on the ground that they were originally admitted to join their fathers in some exempt pursuit.

In addition to the class just referred to there are a large number of Chinese in the country between the ages of 21 and 35 who claim to have been born here and never to have been out of the country. Some of these young men are believed to have been admitted at one time as "minors," but the majority of them are surreptitious entries. Being without documentary proof of birth they undertake to establish their claimed status by parol evidence, and it is remarkable how much assistance they can get from white persons, some of whom accept compensation therefor. Chinese of this class on getting into the country usually Americanize themselves as much as possible in dress and by attending some mission school for a time to learn English and to make the acquaintance of white persons whose assistance they may later need. An instance is recalled of a young Chinese about 27 years of age who claimed citizenship and who presented as a witness in his behalf a white woman, of Portland, Oreg., a public-school teacher and a mission worker. This woman swore that she had known the applicant since his childhood, having taken a number of eastern visitors to Chinatown to see him when a baby in his mother's arms, which was a rare sight for them, and to have kept track of him ever since. The truth as to the original entry having been gleaned from other sources, the applicant on being confronted with it confessed that he was born in China and that he first came to this country when about 15 years of age, entering surreptitiously from Canada, and that he had never seen the woman referred to until he attended her class in the mission school about one year after entry.

Applications for return certificates under rules 13, 15, and 16 of the regulations to the number of 1,081 were handled.

  *   *   *   *   *   *   *

Respectfully,

ELLIS DE BRULER,
Commissioner.

REPORT OF INSPECTOR IN CHARGE, DISTRICT No. 17, COMPRISING THE STATE OF OREGON, WITH HEADQUARTERS AT PORTLAND.

I submit herewith annual report for district 17 for the fiscal year ended June 30, 1913:

The immigration service at Portland, Oreg., still occupies rooms in the Railway Exchange Building, at an annual rental of $2,028. The new Federal building, to which our service will be assigned, has been projected, but beyond acquisition of land for same nothing has been done and it will be several years no doubt before said building is commenced and completed.

While there are several plans on foot for the establishment of foreign passenger lines at this port, none has yet materialized.

During the fiscal year just passed there entered this district 178 steam and sailing vessels, carrying 4,809 alien seamen, 8 alien stowaways, 151 seamen claiming American citizenship, and 1 stowaway claiming American citizenship. Of these there were:

Immigrant aliens admitted 50
Nonimmigrant aliens admitted... 2
Alien seamen deserted.. 426
Head tax collected and covered into the general fund....................... $1,536

Fines under section 9 of the immigration law, aggregating $200, were inflicted in the cases of two alien seamen, a Chinese and a Japanese, who were certified as being afflicted with trachoma, which disease might have been detected by means of a competent medical examination at the port of embarkation.

Departmental warrants were issued for the arrest of 70 aliens (including Chinese) as follows:

	Warrants of arrest issued.	Warrants of deportation issued.
Entered without inspection...	9	6
Insane from prior causes..	24	16
Admits crime or misdemeanor involving moral turpitude prior to entry and entered without inspection...	4	3
Likely to become public charge at time of entry.........................	4	4
Imported woman for immoral purpose.....................................	2	1
Prostitutes...	9	5
Women who entered the United States for immoral purpose...............	3	2
Likely to become public charge at time of entry and entered without inspection.	11	6
Found public charge in United States from causes existing prior to entry.....	1	1
Insane within five years previous to entry and likely to become public charge at time of entry...	1	....
Connected with management of house of prostitution......................	1	2
Anarchist...	1	....
Total...	70	46

Of above deportations, 16 cases were from the Oregon State Insane Asylum, 1 from the State Tuberculosis Sanitarium, 9 were inmates of the Oregon State Penitentiary, 3 were Chinese who entered without inspection and were arrested under immigration law, and 2 were Japanese deserters from vessels in Portland Harbor. Shortage in our district allotment during the latter part of the current year curtailed to some extent activity in the arrest and prosecution generally of certain classes, such as prostitutes, Chinese, etc. * * *

During the year there were made the subject of investigation 269 Chinese cases.

* * * * * * *

Forty-five steamers carrying Chinese crews called at this port during the past year and remained for periods of from one to three weeks. The total number of Chinese crewmen brought on these vessels was 1,248. Three of this number deserted and were not apprehended. During the same period 30 Japanese crewmen deserted the vessels which brought them to this port.

The use of Form 547 by local residents desiring to bring their relatives and friends to this country from abroad has materially increased, the number of said forms filed and investigated by this office during the fiscal year amounting to 85. Careful investigation of these cases involves much time and research and requires the almost constant attention of one inspector.

In common with other Pacific coast ports, Portland expects much activity along immigration lines with the opening of the Panama Canal. While the results of this great event can not be safely predicted, it is not believed that the local influx from Europe by way of the canal will be felt for some years, or until a readjustment of conditions is effected. At the outset the new route will no doubt be used principally for the importation of unskilled labor employed by railroads, irrigation and water-power projects, lumbering enterprises, etc. From such there is always a fluctuating demand for foreign help, varying with the seasons.

Local employment agencies report a constant call for the newly arrived unskilled and green immigrant laborer. This demand will no doubt be promptly exploited by agents familiar with the profitable traffic. The certainty of securing directly and at first hand laborers fresh from Europe will make such enterprises exceedingly attractive, and great care and discrimination should be exercised in admitting bodies of newcomers of this class. The Pacific Coast States desire most of all agricultural immigrants, and are striving here and abroad to attract the attention of this element. The greatest fear of the coast communities is the establishment of slums and lower social standards through an overwhelming influx of the unlettered and unskilled common laborer. Much will depend upon the manner in which the Immigration Service, as represented at its western ports, handles the situation. The bureau, no doubt, out of its experience, will evolve standard qualifications for admission, but must at the same time see that the application of these standards is exactly uniform at each of the six Pacific coast ports of entry.

J. H. BARBOUR,
Inspector in Charge.

REPORT OF COMMISSIONER OF IMMIGRATION, SAN FRANCISCO, IN CHARGE OF DISTRICT NO. 18, COMPRISING NORTHERN CALIFORNIA AND NEVADA AND THE ANGEL ISLAND IMMIGRATION STATION.

I have the honor to submit the following report regarding transactions under the immigration and Chinese-exclusion laws at San Francisco and in District No. 18:

APPLICATIONS FOR ENTRY.

New applications of Chinese for admission to the United States at this port fell off during the year, but so slightly as to be insignificant. Indeed, in work under the laws relating to the exclusion of Chinese, the year developed little of the unusual and disclosed little more than what may be regarded as the routine movement of people of the Chinese race to and fro through this port. Of a total of 3,750 applications for admission considered during the fiscal year, only 220, or 6 per cent, were primarily denied admission. Of these 170 were deported, only 4.5 per cent of the total number applying for admission.

The number of alleged merchants' and natives' children applying for admission during the year showed substantial increase, but presented the possibly significant feature of a large addition in the percentage of children of tender years. This might indicate that those who are entitled or plan to bring their families to the United States are exhausting their supply and must now bring forward the youngest members of their families. If this theory be correct, it would seem that a falling off in the arrivals of this class might be expected before a great while, unless the older "children" who have entered in the last few years themselves start a new influx—the children of sons of natives and the children of sons of merchants who have acquired a mercantile status after their entry.

This office feels that many of the cases which are dependent upon a mercantile status would fall if a really searching investigation as to the honesty of the claim of mercantile pursuit were in each instance conducted. Collateral circumstances, especially those surrounding "country" cases frequently indicate that rigid inquiry would disclose fraud on the part of alleged fathers in so far as their claims to be a merchant is concerned. Such inquiries, however, are absolutely prohibited by the limited number of officers available for investigating work; and, while we feel almost certain that the law is being violated in this class of applications, we can do but superficial work under present conditions with respect to force and funds.

"Section 6" applications have, on the whole, been much more satisfactory than during the previous year, the department's firm attitude toward "personally conducted" student parties having had a good effect. Toward the end of the fiscal year, however, a new form of undertaking presented itself in a number of applications for admission of students who in preparation and appearance fully qualified but, when closely questioned as to the arrangements made for their maintenance, acknowledged that they expected by various methods to work their way through college. Investigation indicated a considerable movement of this character supported in most instances by missionaries and teachers connected with semicharitable institutions.

Applications of alleged citizens, while in their number presenting high figures, have been very largely confined to "prior-landed" and "court-record" cases, and, while during the year we considered only four applications of what has come to be known as "raw native" cases, one only of those four was granted admission.

APPEALS.

The total number of Chinese appeal cases considered by this office during the year was 199, only 124 of which, however, were passed upon by the department, the others having been withdrawn, reopened, or being still pending at the end of the fiscal year. Of the 124 passed upon by the department, this office's excluding decision was affirmed in 85 cases and decisions in favor of the applicants were rendered in 39, or 31 per cent. To say that the procedure which has been built up in the handling of appeal cases is remarkable is mildly expressing it. It permits of importunity, reexamination, reconsideration, etc., from the very inception of the case until it reaches the appellate authority; and the records, when final action is recorded, are often little more than a mass of conflicting opinion with no real basis for certain judgment. It would seem that more satisfactory and expeditious judgment of cases would be reached if hearings to attorneys were absolutely confined to that granted by the commissioner's office at the time the case is to be passed upon at the port of entry. This appears to be the logical time and place for the hearing and consideration of anything which is to be offered on behalf of an applicant, and any hearings granted at other periods in the procedures are ill-timed, illogical, and confusing.

TRANSITS.

During the year almost 1,800 Chinese applied at this port for the privilege of passing through the United States or its waters to foreign territory. Of this number over 200 were denied the privilege. The larger part of this movement was due to an extraordinary demand existing in certain parts of Mexico for farm laborers. While this was the excuse for the unusually heavy influx, unquestionably a large number of those applying for the transit privilege sought only thus to reach a point contiguous to United States territory, thereby being enabled easily to smuggle over the borders of this country. This fact was fully appreciated by the service; but, on the other hand, it was argued that if this Chinese movement were not permitted on American line steamers it would be diverted to vessels sailing directly from China to Mexico, the American line thus losing the revenues, the Government losing opportunity to secure the basis of identification of those who thereafter smuggled into the United States, and the cost of the deportation of such smuggling Chinese being visited upon the Government; whereas, if the movement through this port were permitted, deportation could be required at the expense of the steamship companies. These were strong reasons, and the movement was therefore permitted under restrictions whereby careful arrangements were to be made to prevent the dissemination of the disease uncinariasis, or hookworm, during the trip through the country by the transits, a large percentage of whom were afflicted with said disease.   Near the end of the fiscal year, however, circumstances indicated that unexpected complications would render a liberal attitude toward the movement impossible and that it would have to be stopped.

PREINVESTIGATIONS.

Over 2,000 preinvestigations were made during the year under rules 13, 15, and 16, 1,963 applications being finally granted and 86 denied.   Out of the total number of applications 922 were made by Chinese who claimed to have been born in the United States or to be sons of fathers who were so born.   No great percentage of these applications, however, were made by Chinese whose cases had not previously had some form of investigation and adjudication, and the instances wherein mature Chinese undertook to establish a "native" claim without any documentary or other substantial evidence of the truth of the claim were more rare than formerly, a result believed to be due to this office's action in undertaking prosecutions of fraudulent witnesses in such cases.

MISCELLANEOUS WORK AND GENERAL COMMENT.

During the year our officers made 2,973 miscellaneous Chinese investigations; they checked out 4,818 departing Chinese and checked in and out 11,047 Chinese crew men. Adding these to the 2,049 Chinese preinvestigations made, the 1,795 "in transit" cases considered, and the 3,750 applications for admission which we were called upon to dispose of, it is shown that we handled 26,432 transactions under the laws relating to the admission of Chinese, an average of about 88 per working day or 500 per week.

As general comment upon the results achieved in the administration of the laws relating to the admission of Chinese, this office feels that considering the limited facilities which are at the disposal of the service undue attention is being given to the work of handling applications for admission at ports of entry as compared with the handling of Chinese who are gaining or have gained entry by surreptitious methods. Contemplate the figures referred to in the foregoing, especially those regarding applicants for admission.

To achieve the rejection and return to China of 190 Chinese applicants has required an enormous volume of work for a whole year by probably 50 inspectors, stenographers, interpreters, and watchmen.   Meanwhile, observation by those who were equipped intelligently to judge of the situation indicates that there are thousands of Chinese undisturbed in the United States through surreptitious entry, and that hundreds of others are coming in by the same methods each year.   A ridiculously small portion of the employees whose entire time is devoted to the handling of Chinese applicants at this port alone, if properly organized into what might be termed "arrest crews" and assigned exclusively to Chinese arrest work at various points in the country, could within a few months make it so unsafe for Chinese who smuggled in that the incentive to smuggle would practically be destroyed.

GENERAL IMMIGRATION AND EMIGRATION.

The aliens admitted during the year amounted to 8,935, an increase of over 800 over the previous year; and those departing numbered 8,641, practically the same as last year.   The total passenger movement through the port during the year approximated 30,000, a substantial increase over the movement of the last fiscal year.   Informal statements and reports are persistent that steamship companies and others interested are satisfied that with the Panama Canal made fully available within the next year or two a large increase of European immigration direct to this coast may be expected. Present facilities are at times employed to their maximum in taking care of the work handled at this time, and proper consideration for the possibilities demands that the service shall not ignore what seems clear to everyone else in the nature of coming conditions which will call for greatly increased facilities.

During the year 266 aliens were returned to their foreign ports of embarkation.

JAPANESE.

The total number of Japanese arriving reach 3,477, an increase of over 25 per cent. During the same period the Japanese departing numbered 3,633, or a falling off of about 2 per cent.   Of the total arrivals during the year, 1,910 were males and 1,567 females, the former showing an increase of 574 and the latter an increase of 131.   The total number of Japanese debarred was only 24—16 males and 8 females.

240 REPORT OF COMMISSIONER GENERAL OF IMMIGRATION.

As will be suggested from the foregoing totals, the Japanese "bride" continues to increase in numbers in the United States. Many of them are destined to ranches in California, Oregon, and Washington, really to engage as farm laborers. This fact, however, does not make them any less the housewives that they say they are to be, and practically all such applications for admission are flawless under the immigration laws.

HINDUS.

The full strength of the immigration laws continued to be applied against East Indian arrivals during the fiscal year, and we were called upon to decide only a total of 83 applications of people of that race, of whom 46 were admitted and 37 deported, these figures having no significance other than to show that the immigration laws are usually effective against undesirable immigration if fully applied. Late in the fiscal year, however, a few Hindus arrived from Manila, P. I., and in connection with the handling of their cases it was disclosed that the service was soon going to be confronted with a systematic effort on the part of both the transportation companies and the Hindus themselves to make the Philippines a "back door" entrance to the mainland of the United States. Steps to meet the situation were being taken as the year closed.

ARREST AND DEPORTATION OF IMMORAL CLASSES.

During the year this office has undertaken deportation in 117 cases of aliens connected with immoral occupations under the act of 1907 as amended March 26, 1910. This was almost double the number of such proceedings inaugurated in the previous fiscal year. Of these 75 were completely disposed of during the year as against 37 the previous year. In 34 cases deportation was accomplished, and 42 cases were still pending at the close of the year, the warrants having been canceled in the remainder. This is many times the work formerly done in this district, and although practically every case has been bitterly fought, our efforts have been so fruitful as to have a salutary influence on the general moral standing of the community. The Immigration Service is now recognized by those connected with prostitution as a serious factor to be dealt with, and, whereas efforts of the service were at one time belittled, those aliens who persist in their illegal practices are forced to do so under cover against discovery by our officers, with a much smaller number concerned in the evils as a result.

ARREST AND DEPORTATION OF INSANE ALIENS.

Northern California and Nevada have been relieved of 38 insane aliens during the year through the operation of the immigration laws, this number of deportation procedures being successful out of 48 undertaken, with 8 cases pending at the close of the year. This against only 12 such deportations during the fiscal year of 1911-12. The State institutions have only recently come to a full appreciation of the value of the immigration law in relieving them of many of their burdens, and we are now getting the maximum of cooperation from all State hospitals. There is still much that needs attention, however, some of which has been permitted to rest because of an insufficient appropriation, some 200 cases of insane Chinese being a conspicuous instance of this.

OTHER ARRESTS AND DEPORTATIONS.

In "warrant" cases for illegal entry and under the public charge provisions of the statutes, this district has dealt with 95 cases during the year, an increase of almost 200 per cent. In 64 cases deportation was accomplished, and a total of 78 cases was disposed of, with 17 pending at the end of the year. It is noteworthy that with each year it is increasingly difficult to meet the importunity and sympathetic obstruction which is put forth on behalf of aliens falling within this class, and, when it is considered that probably no other district in the United States presents more sharply conflicting interests than exist in this district, the showing made in the figures set forth is gratifying to those held responsible for results in administrative work. All told, 260 immigration warrant cases were undertaken during the year, and 193 were disposed of—136 by deportation—with 67 cases still pending at the close of the year. The increase in deportations was almost 100 per cent, marking a much larger percentage of successful work than the previous year.

ARREST AND DEPORTATION OF CHINESE.

The result of the year's efforts in the deportation of Chinese under court procedure was that of a total of 70 cases inaugurated, 44 were disposed of, and of the latter number deportation occurred in 28 cases. The contrast between this result and that obtained where the immigration law procedure was followed should be noted. Of a total of 80 cases instituted under the immigration laws, 45 were deported during the year. Total Chinese deportation cases undertaken during the year were 150, in 73 of which deportation was accomplished—the largest number for many years in this district.

It is believed that many Chinese communities in northern California and Nevada are teeming with Chinese who have gained illegal entry to the United States and are resting secure because the limited facilities of this service prevent their being given attention under the law. Of course more attention could be given them with resultant neglect of the work now done on Chinese applicants for admission at this station. As I have previously indicated in this report, I am of the impression that it would be good administration to more equally distribute our Chinese forces on the two classes of work. Such a proposal, however, is so revolutionary of the long-established practices that I would not feel free to carry it out unless specifically ordered so to do by the department.

*　　*　　*　　*　　*　　*　　*

PROSECUTIONS.

A total of 33 criminal prosecutions were considered during the year in this district, only 14 being disposed of, 10 convictions being secured. There remained pending at the close of the fiscal year 19 cases. No class of work with which this office has to deal is subject to such delay, congestion, and injury as a result as that which requires the use of the courts. The officers under the district attorney give us every cooperation which their facilities afford, but at times are so helpless to meet the demands made upon them that it is discouraging and seems useless to institute proceedings which it is felt are likely to fail for lack of proper attention. In so far as the work of this service is concerned, this could be largely corrected by the assignment from this service of an officer qualified to handle court cases arising under the immigration and Chinese-exclusion laws. Such a suggestion has frequently been made by the district attorney's office, and if the department could find some means for carrying it out it would surely prove a valuable aid in the effective enforcement of the law in this jurisdiction.

FINES.

During the year seven fines were certified against incoming vessels for the bringing of diseased aliens to this port and nonmanifestation. All fines certified were finally assessed, excepting one—a total of $520 presumably being collected.

*　　*　　*　　*　　*　　*　　*

HOSPITAL CASES.

A total of 1,086 persons were in the hospital during the year, for periods varying from one day to 13 weeks each. Of the total number, 840 patients were treated for uncinariasis, or hookworm, 539 being cured within one week, 756 within two weeks, and 806 within three weeks. It will be noted that to this disease a very large part of our total hospital treatment is chargeable. Early in the fiscal year the number of certifications for the ailment had reached such a high point and the hospital treatment applications were so many that it was found necessary in some way to reduce the number of patients. Steps taken to meet the situation reduced the average treatment days from 1,996 in July, 1912, to 282 in February, 1913, and the highest point since reached was 700 in May of this calendar year. Whereas the daily average of hospital charges in July, 1912, was $64.40, they fell in the early months of this year to $8 and $10 and have not since reached over $22.58. The average daily charges for the year were $29.32—the total for the year, $13,175. The actual cash earnings, however, were $13,112.35 and the expenses of maintenance of the hospital $6,085.28. The latter sum proved a constant drain on our allotment, and no portion of the earnings referred to was returnable to our fund as reimbursement of the expenses incurred.

CONSTRUCTION AND MAINTENANCE WORK.

The year has seen many improvements at the station, chief among which was the completion of a new concrete lavatory and toilet building with the most modern fixtures especially designed to meet the needs of the peculiar class of immigration handled at this port. It has met the most crying demand existing and has done more to remove the tenable grounds for criticism of the station than anything else which could have been done.

7686°—14——16

Concurrently with the erection of the lavatory building, a 300,000-gallon concrete tank for the conservation of surface and spring water was built, with a resultant saving in the amount of water to be carried from Sausalito in barges. As the fresh-water storage capacity of the station was only 50,000 gallons, it was also deemed advisable to erect two additional 50,000-gallon tanks, thus raising the fresh-water storage capacity to a total of 150,000 gallons. That all of these improvements were made has proved a most fortunate circumstance, for with the opening of the new lavatory building the demand on our water supply unavoidably increased by leaps and bounds. Every effort has been made to harbor the supply, but with an increased number of detained inmates the consumption has almost doubled. Through protracted negotiation we were finally able to arrange for the furnishing of water at 65 cents per 1,000 gallons, ultimately to be reduced to 30 cents. The previous price for many months had been $1.50 per 1,000 gallons delivered, but, as the use of our cutter *Inspector* for delivering water under the new arrangement also enabled the establishment of a night boat schedule between the city and the station, the cost of hauling water was very small and the economy in the new arrangement was substantial.

A further improvement of importance has been the enlargement of the concrete powerhouse and the installation of an additional boiler. While the former boiler capacity had not proved insufficient it had been found that the demand made upon it would soon put us in the position of having frequently to shut down to make repairs, and the increased facilities now provided will undoubtedly prove wise.

The wharf has been substantially strengthened during the year by the concreting of some 60 foundation piles and the mooring facilities greatly improved by the addition of spring piles.

BRANCH OFFICES.

During the year branch offices have been opened at Sacramento, Eureka, and Monterey, Cal., with three employees at the first-named and one each at the other two. The amount of work conducted through these offices and the expedition with which it has been handled have more than proved the wisdom of the action.

In conclusion, I am pleased to report that our relations with other departments of the Government service, with the peace officers of the communities of the district, and with the public are pleasant and such as to secure for us a great measure of cooperation. We all endeavor to reciprocate. The relations of the employees of the force are harmonious, and, considered as a whole, I feel that all employees are giving their duties faithful and intelligent attention.

SAMUEL W. BACKUS,
Commissioner.

REPORT OF INSPECTOR IN CHARGE, DISTRICT NO. 20, COMPRISING ALASKA, WITH HEADQUARTERS AT KETCHIKAN.

I submit the following report of work done in the district of Alaska during the fiscal year ended June 30, 1913:

Port.	Aliens admitted with certificates No. 524.	Aliens examined and admitted without certificates.	Aliens in transit recorded.	Aliens debarred.	Aliens arrested and deported.	Citizens admitted.	Aliens inspected and admitted but not recorded in statistics.	Head tax collected.
Ketchikan	68	359	11	5		1,965	1,255	$68.00
Skagway and White Pass	16	33	30			2,464	2,825	24.00
Eagle						1,600	45	
Nome		1						4.00
Valdez					4			
Total	84	393	41	5	4	6,029	4,125	96.00

COMMENTS AND RECOMMENDATIONS.

The number of admissions of aliens shows considerable increase over the previous year. Aliens in transit recorded in the above table are all Japanese. Aliens debarred are all likely to become public charges and excluded as such. Of the aliens arrested and deported all were Japanese seal poachers who had served their sentences.

There were 11 deserting alien seamen at Port Armstrong, a whaling station, and 1 at Ketchikan.

Two Chinese persons were arrested under United States commissioner's warrants for being unlawfully in the United States.   Their cases are still pending.

There were 3 Chinese in transit from one port in Canada to another.

One Chinaman made application for a return certificate under rule 13, which was granted.

The principal duty of this office is the inspection of aliens arriving from the south from British Columbia at the port of Ketchikan, and from the north from British Columbia and Yukon Territory at the summit of White Pass, near Skagway; and from Dawson, Yukon territory, to Eagle, Alaska, and from the Siberian coast and Vladivostok, Russia, to the port of Nome.   This latter port is of least importance, as the arrivals, which are very few in number, occur only during the summer season.

Therefore, it will be seen that there are 3 principal ports of entry from contiguous territory with only 2 regularly appointed inspectors to enforce the immigration law in the district of Alaska.   Both these inspectors are stationed at Ketchikan, where the most of the work of the district is being done.   The other ports are being covered by deputy collectors of customs who are appointed to act as immigrant inspectors. Of course, at some of these ports the volume of immigration business is too small to warrant appointment of a regular immigrant inspector.

  *   *   *   *   *   *   *

At the subport of Nome also has been noted a falling off of business, hence a regular inspector was not sent there last summer.

At the port of Eagle during the summer season the arrivals occur upon the opening of the navigation, on or about June, and lasting until about the middle of October. During the winter season some aliens arrive on dog sleds.   Two prostitutes thus coming were excluded and deported to Dawson two winters ago.

In order properly to enforce the immigration law in Alaska, this office has adopted the following plan: One inspector will make a tour to the interior every summer, to wit, on or about the middle of July, or as soon as the navigation opens.   He will proceed via Dawson, Yukon Territory, to Eagle, Alaska, and there inspect the rush of passengers coming from Dawson.   Thence, and after the rush is over, he will proceed to Nome and remain there, say, about two months.   Thus an inspector, being on temporary duty either at Eagle or Nome, would be available for urgent duty that may arise in the interior of Alaska.   At the close of the navigation season he will return to his permanent station.   In making such tours he will observe how the customs inspectors designated as immigrant inspectors are discharging the duties of the Immigration Service, and at the same time instruct them.

With reference to the projected improvements in station, I recommend that suitable immigration quarters, with offices and detention rooms, be erected at Ketchikan. Past experience has sufficiently demonstrated the wisdom of such recommendation. The immigration service in Alaska was established 10 years ago, and since its inception there has been expended in rentals for the office quarters about $3,000.   At present time the rates in rents are steadily increasing.   Therefore, in my opinion, an appropriation of $10,000 would be a wise investment and of great benefit to the service.   Or, if this should be impossible, why not cooperate with other branches of the Government maintaining offices and paying rent at Ketchikan, to wit, the Customs, Forest, Lighthouse, and Postal Services.   Such state of facts alone justify the erection of a Federal building for the accommodation of those offices, including the Immigration Service, in view of the fact that the Department of Justice alone owns its offices here.

DOMIANUS MASKEVICZIUS,
Inspector in Charge.

REPORT OF COMMISSIONER OF IMMIGRATION, SAN JUAN, P. R., IN CHARGE OF DISTRICT NO. 21, COMPRISING ISLAND OF PORTO RICO.

I have the honor to submit the following general report of transactions and conditions in district No. 21 for the fiscal year ending June 30, 1913:

The beginning of this year found business in Porto Rico in a paralyzed condition owing to the prevalence of bubonic plague in this island, and immigration was practically at a standstill during the first six months of the period covered by this report. All transactions, therefore, show a decrease for the year from those of the preceding year, while for the period between January 1 and June 30, 1913, an increase is visible over the corresponding period of last year.   Immigration is now in a healthy condition.   The total passenger movement for the year amounted to 8,143, not including the large number of tourists, both native and alien, who came to remain in Porto Rico usually but a few hours and departed by the same ships which brought them here. Nor does the above figure include the natives and aliens who arrived in and departed from Porto Rico via the mainland of the United States. The total alien arrivals in Porto Rico from foreign ports direct during the year were 2,301, as against 3,336 of last year. The total arrivals from foreign ports, 3,941, as against 6,098 last year, show a decrease of 35.3 per cent.

INWARD PASSENGER MOVEMENT.

	Immigrants.	Nonimmigrants.
Males	556	998
Females	328	419
Total	884	1,417

Aliens departing for foreign countries direct, 1,783; and citizens of the United States and Porto Rico so departing, 2,175.

CHARACTER OF IMMIGRATION.

Very few Syrians have arrived in Porto Rico during the past year. Spaniards and West Indians predominate. Immigration from the islands to the westward is very similar in race, customs, and habits to the native race in Porto Rico and easily fuses therewith, making no change in standards or economic conditions. Islands to the eastward produce African blacks of English, Danish, and French nationalities, who are of very low moral standards and who form an undesirable addition to the population of the island. English-speaking women come as servants and find ready employment among English-speaking families in Porto Rico at much higher wages than are paid native servants, but a large percentage of this immigration from the eastward ultimately finds its way to the mainland.

Spanish immigration is very desirable to Porto Rico in many ways. They are an industrious race of a higher moral standard than are the West Indians, but they are nearly all merchants or mercantile employees. Virtually, the entire mercantile business of the island is in the hands of the Spaniards, who, instead of employing Porto Rican young men in their establishments, bring over their young relatives and friends from Spain to work in their stores. Most of these Spanish boys come to work under the old Spanish system of compulsory savings and investment, so that there is a continuous stream of retired merchants returning to Spain with their fortunes made and another stream of young boys beginning at the bottom and gradually working up. This is a most excellent system, but it shuts out the Porto Rican young men from the mercantile life, as they have no opportunities to learn. Therefore, the poorer class must bring their children up either as common laborers or skilled mechanics, and the richer class send their children to the States to learn professions, so that the island is now oversupplied with young doctors, lawyers, dentists, and civil engineers.

FINANCIAL CONDITION OF ALIENS.

Most steamship lines accepting aliens for Porto Rico require a deposit of $50 with the purser of the vessel before ticket is sold. This is done colorably to insure that the alien will not be rejected for lack of funds, but it is believed that in many cases where deportation is effected the expenses of the return voyage is taken out of this deposit by the steamship companies.

Aliens arriving in Porto Rico during the year brought $238,315, or a per capita of $103.57.

MEDICAL EXAMINER.

The medical examination of aliens at the port of San Juan has been eminently satisfactory. At the port of Mayaguez no certifications whatever have been made during the past year, which is something remarkable in view of the prevalence of the hookworm, venereal diseases, tuberculosis, and trachoma in the West Indies. The Syrians have quit using Mayaguez as a port of entry, but there is a large Syrian colony in Santo Domingo, many of whom are known to have trachoma and it would be remarkable if the disease has not spread among the Dominicans. The same condition exists in St. Thomas.

*   *   *   *   *   *   *

DETENTION FACILITIES.

In this district neither the Government nor any of the steamship companies maintain detention quarters for aliens who are not immediately landed. This is very unsatisfactory. Aliens in the temporary charge of steamship companies are sometimes detained in hotels and sometimes in the homes of their relatives, and at other times are practically given their liberty on their promise to return for board hearing. Under the peculiar conditions existing in Porto Rico the writer does not see any particular harm in this somewhat loose method, except in the cases of diseased aliens, criminals, prostitutes, and procurers. Some method should be devised for the actual physical detention of these aliens in such a way that they can not do harm to the community during the long periods which often elapse between sailings. It is believed that steamship companies in San Juan will eventually unite to provide a suitable place for the detention of aliens.

BOARDS OF SPECIAL INQUIRY.

This district labors under the disadvantage of having but a few immigration officers and employees qualified as members of boards of special inquiry, making it necessary in almost every case to call upon duly qualified Government officers in other branches of the Government service to act as members of the various boards. These outside members in nearly all instances respond cheerfully and willingly, and perform their duties to the best of their knowledge and ability. There is a noticeable tendency toward leniency, however, on the part of most of these gentlemen, they being more inclined to be influenced by sympathy for the transgressions or infirmities of the aliens than are immigration officers of long experience. There is no particular incentive for any of these gentlemen to make an exhaustive study of the immigration laws and regulations, decisions and rulings, but, nevertheless, they are due great credit for their work on the boards, which, in many cases, is at the sacrifice of their duties in other branches or of their personal time.

During the year 64 aliens were detained for board hearings, 45 of whom were finally landed, 17 deported, and 2 were pending at the close of the year. Two aliens pending at the beginning of the year were deported. Thirteen aliens appealed from excluding decisions, 4 of whom were finally deported by order of the Secretary and 9 landed. Seven of the aliens who were landed on appeal were school-bond cases in which the boards were obliged to formally vote for exclusion, although feeling that the aliens should be admitted under school bond; therefore, the free and untrammeled decision of a board of special inquiry has been reversed but twice by the Secretary during the year just closed.

Nineteen aliens were deported during the year as a result of board decisions for the following reasons: Admits the commission of crime, 4; under 16, unaccompanied, 4; contract labor, 2; likely to become a public charge, 2; tuberculosis, 2; trachoma, 1; procurer, 1; insane, 1; assisted alien, 1; accompanying alien, 1. Thirteen excluded aliens did not appeal.

*   *   *   *   *   *   *

DESERTING ALIEN SEAMEN.

Most of the deserting alien seamen from foreign ports during the year were from small schooners and were natives of the Dutch West Indies. Seventeen in all were reported, only one of whom was apprehended, although in all cases the assistance of the insular police was solicited in an effort to locate them.

One class of alien seamen who cause considerable trouble, not only to the Immigration Service, but to other branches of the Federal Service in Porto Rico, are those discharged or deserting from vessels coming from the mainland. There is very little opportunity for them to ship back to the United States during certain seasons of the year. A great many of these are stranded in Porto Rico and become, for the time, professional beggars or public charges.

Under the present regulations this office can do nothing for these people, unless it can be ascertained that their original entry into the mainland of the United States was illegal and that the statutory period has not elapsed. If steamship companies could be required, by regulation, to return to the mainland all alien seamen left in Porto Rico by them, who become public charges or professional beggars, the difficulty would be solved, for the reason that at almost any mainland port the seamen could find ready employment.

WHITE SLAVE CASES.

Systematic traffic in native and alien women was carried on to some extent from and to this island prior to the passage of the act of June 25, 1910, although it was always difficult to secure sufficient evidence to warrant prosecution. During the preceding fiscal year one conviction was secured under the new law, and since that time it is doubtful if the business has been carried on to any great extent, especially from other countries to this island. Concubinage, however, is about as common in the West Indies as legal marriage, and there are frequently recurring cases of men transporting both alien and native women for their own personal use.

*   *   *   *   *   *   *

HOSPITAL TREATMENT.

One application for hospital treatment was made at the port of Ponce and was granted. However, the alien was unable to secure the bond specified by the bureau and was ultimately deported.

OFFICE QUARTERS.

The new Federal building, in which the Immigration Service has been assigned quarters, is still in course of construction. The Immigration Service now occupies very desirable and commodious quarters in the old naval station, San Juan. The service also has a good office at Ponce and one at Mayaguez in the customhouses at those places.

SUBPORTS.

Experienced and competent immigrant inspectors are stationed at the principal subports, Ponce and Mayaguez, and at the other subports, where aliens arrive only occasionally, the work of this service is performed by customs officers.

WARRANT PROCEDURE.

Four aliens were arrested on departmental warrants during the year, one of whom was deported and three pending deportation at the close of the year.

OFFICERS AND EMPLOYEES.

The immigration force in Porto Rico has worked contentedly and harmoniously during the past year. The men are experienced and competent, and, above all, earnest and enthusiastic in their work. None of them is now seeking transfer to the mainland, which is an unusual state of affairs with the force in Porto Rico. Living conditions for the Americans in Porto Rico are anything but satisfactory. Rents are high, the food required by Americans very expensive, and climatic conditions are such that married officers are put to considerable expense from time to time sending their families to the States to recuperate.

*   *   *   *   *   *   *

CONCLUSION.

The most cordial relations exist between this service and all other branches of the Federal establishment in Porto Rico. The Immigration Service stands as high in public esteem as could well be, considering the restrictive nature of our duties. The undersigned is proud of the fact that neither during the year just closed nor during any previous year of his administration has an official complaint been made against him by anyone.

GRAHAM L. RICE,
Commissioner.

REPORT OF INSPECTOR IN CHARGE, DISTRICT NO. 22, COMPRISING TERRITORY OF HAWAII, WITH HEADQUARTERS AT HONOLULU.

I have the honor to submit herewith annual report for the year ending June 30, 1913:

Aliens admitted	8,559
Aliens departed	3,729
Excess of admitted	4,830
Citizens admitted	1,242
Citizens departed	2,002
Excess of departures	760

Alien certificates issued for mainland, 2,398, of which 1,570 were for Spanish and Portuguese, being about double the number issued for these races in the preceding year. During the year 2,554 Spanish and Portuguese immigrants were brought in by the territorial board of immigration. A large number of Portuguese who were citizens have departed for the mainland. The tax for territorial assisted immigration has been greatly reduced, and to such an extent that there is little likelihood of a shipload of aliens being imported in the coming year. The indications are that there will be a decrease of Spanish and Portuguese residents.

The Sugar Planters' Labor Bureau has brought in during the year 5,742 Filipinos and are erecting a $25,000 detention station for future arrivals, where Filipinos may be kept until physically prepared to go to the plantations. In the month of April there were working on the plantations 7,916 Filipinos, of whom only 84 were women and 48 minors; 5,362 Spanish and Portuguese, of whom 390 were women and 1,072 minors; 25,073 Japanese, of whom 1,847 were women and 231 minors; 2,495 Chinese, of whom 5 were women and 3 minors; 106 Russians, of whom 21 were women and 15 minors; 643 Americans; 1,034 Hawaiians; 1,538 Porto Ricans; 1,581 Koreans; all others, 299, making a total of 46,047. The Filipinos are rapidly replacing all except the Japanese, and their percentage is increasing as compared with the Japanese.

The percentage of murders, assaults, and thefts committed by Filipinos exceeds that of other races. Three were hung to-day. The bringing of these Filipinos is justified on the grounds of economic necessity; but many of them are of a low order and social defectives, tending to debauch and degrade the social condition of this outmost bound of our integral country, which ought to strive to present an attractive and wholesome civilization, even though it be at the expense of curbing insatiate greed. It may be still possible by scouring the back streets of civilization to obtain some cheaper and as objectionable immigration. Recently one prominently connected heretofore with recruiting laborers asked me as to the possibilities of Hindus being admitted here.

In regard to the Filipinos there is a perceptible tendency among them to come to Honolulu, and we now see the faint beginnings of a movement toward the mainland, which will be accelerated as they become used to our social life.

During the year 4,860 alien Japanese were admitted, an increase of about 50 per cent over last year. Of these admitted 1,572 were so-called "picture brides." Alien Japanese departures were 2,546, being 47 less than last year. Excess of arrivals over departures, 2,314, as against an excess of 791 last year. This excess is to be accounted for by the fact that formerly passports were seldom granted to Japanese laborers who had been absent over one year, but now the time limit seems to be practically removed. The local Japanese press has demanded that passports be given to any who were here before, and without the usual formalities and delay due to consular certification. There has been a perceptible increase in able-bodied males. As the issuance of passports is restricted to former residents, parent and child, and husband and wife to join each other, in order to bring in brothers the aged father or mother is called by a son, and after arrival requests are made by the father that his sons in Japan be granted passports to join him.

No further comment is necessary to set forth the remorseless displacement of white labor by Asiatics.

The Japanese press, stimulated by the Japanese Merchants' Association, has conducted an earnest propaganda to induce laborers to stay in the islands; and its success is seen by the excess of arrivals over departures. Of the 82,000 Japanese in the islands, those who are not on the plantations, together with the Filipinos, are crowding white labor to the water-front, whence, through poverty and privation, having secured the means of embarkation, they depart for the mainland.

High taxes in Japan and business uncertainty have helped to firmly fix the policy to stay in Hawaii. Heretofore the Yokohama Specie Bank has received money to transmit to Japan, and made conservative loans to merchants, and refused loans for real estate. There has now been established, it is said, through the aid of Mr. Asano, president of the Toyo Kisen Kaisha Steamship Co., and Baron Shibusawa of Tokyo, a Japanese bank with the fixed policy of encouraging investment here. Japanese during the past year have bought a great deal of real estate in the Territory, and native-born Japanese have taken up many homesteads. The shifting tide shows that Hawaii will become less of a place where they seek temporary gain and more one of permanent residence and profit.

Certificates of Hawaiian birth are issued by the secretary of the Territory of Hawaii for the most part to Japanese and Chinese. A large number of these certificates are issued to persons who are alleged to have been born here and left in infancy or when they were of tender years. These certificates are issued nunc pro tunc in some cases when the beneficiary is supposed to have left here as long as 25 years ago.

There are Chinese persons in Honolulu now endeavoring to secure the names of all Chinese who left here years ago. I am satisfied that there is an organized movement to obtain these certificates for use here or at other ports. These certificates of course are conclusive upon the Territory as to the citizenship of their possessors. In the case of the possessor of one of these certificates who was denied a landing and for whom habeas corpus proceedings were taken, Judge Clemons decided adversely to the petitioner, who has taken an appeal, and the purpose of the attorneys is to carry the case to the Supreme Court, seeking to obtain a decision that these certificates are conclusive against the United States. The parties who are behind this are wealthy and unscrupulous Chinese. These certificates are very valuable for territorial purposes, as their possessors are able to homestead on the public lands.

Chinese aliens:

Laborers admitted	241
Exempts admitted	142
Total admissions	383

Chinese citizens admitted:

Hawaiian born	272
Naturalized citizens	10
Wives of citizens	30
Children of citizens	24
Total	336

Chinese deported:

Alleged Hawaiian born	24
Alleged Hawaiian born on appeal	37
Laborer	1
Merchants' wives	5
Merchants' children	5
Citizens' children on appeal	2
Citizens' wives on appeal	4
Section 6, students	2
Total	80

Of the above 10 were certified as having trachoma, and 1 as having gonorrhea.

Certificates:

Form 430, native born—

Granted by officer in charge	46
Denied by officer in charge	1
Total	47

Form 431, exempts—

Granted by officer in charge	65
Denied by officer in charge	2
Denied by department	2
Total	69

Certificates—Continued.
Form 432, laborers—

Granted by officer in charge	279
Denied by officer in charge	8
Denied by department	2
Total	289

Deportations (other than Chinese):

Trachoma	187
Likely to become public charge	15
Hookworm	11
Insane	1
Unlawfully in United States	1
Accompanying alien	2
Total	217
Chinese	80
Total deportations for year	297

FINES.

Four fines of $100 each have been covered into the Treasury for bringing in aliens with a dangerous contagious disease which might have been detected before embarkation. One was a case pending from last year, and there is one case now pending. In the early part of the year the Japanese consul took up with his Government the matter of the examination of aliens on Japanese vessels, with the result that there were 50 per cent less certifications here for disease. The Pacific Mail Steamship Co. lately has taken action, and on the last boat, over 100 aliens, there was no certification for disease. The examining surgeon here has made comparatively few certifications on the day of arrival, and many cases are apparently old cases which have been treated and break out on the voyage or after a few days detention.

The strong policy of the present Public Health surgeon is beginning to bear good fruit, and the rejection of questionable or possibly dormant cases, or of those who may be considered by some surgeons to have arrived at the so-called "benign condition" is becoming the rule, in view of which ships' doctors will take no chances.

*   *   *   *   *   *   *

GENERAL ADMINISTRATION.

The volume of work has been greater than in former years. In the Chinese department we are greatly hampered by the fact that there are no complete, and in many cases no reliable records of departures before annexation. In view of this we have a correspondingly abnormal number of "raw native" cases to deal with, and in the face of an effort to bring in many of this class our inspectors have worked with zeal and persistence. The volume of testimony taken in a given case is larger than heretofore, and we have found an increase of bad cases. I am able to assign but one inspector exclusively to Chinese work, and in order to finish warrant cases pending he is not able to give now over half of his time to the Chinese. As this is the slack season in Chinese work I am making an effort to keep the work up with urgent help of the other inspectors. There is a large work that ought to be done here under the "white-slave act," on this and other islands. Inspector Brown is exceptionally well informed and qualified to handle such cases. I have already asked for another inspector to act as boarding officer, and there should be another stenographer to be assigned exclusively to Chinese work.

Considering the number of "picture brides," all of whom come before the board of special inquiry, and the number of wives and children, and other detained aliens who come before the board it will be apparent how much of the time of the clerk is taken up by service on the board. I respectfully emphasize the need of an additional inspector and stenographer. We are putting all the force and vigor we can into the administration of the law. The assurances of prominent citizens or aliens or attorneys that a case is good are not considered; the law and the testimony alone are conclusive. There is no one in office who states unofficially that what is needed is the admission of more Chinese laborers. We are not moved by a desire for public praise nor depressed by abuse, and we are highly gratified that in cases where the alien and local press have attacked this office we have been sustained by the department. The administration of the law here has been as temperate, kindly, and firm as at other ports.   If the added help desired is granted, I am confident that the coming year will show better and truer results, wider in their influence and beneficial to the State.

Our immigration station was erected eight years ago, on July 4.   There have been some additions, but little of repairs.   I had hoped that it might have been taken over by the Quartermaster Department of the Army and a more suitable building erected on Sand Island near the quarantine station.   However, certain additions and alterations are now necessary.

*   *   *   *   *   *   *

A number of habeas corpus cases have been started and some are still pending, having been under advisement for over four months.   There is a determined and self-announced effort to contest in the courts cases denied by the office or the department on the ground that the hearings are not fair.   This office and the department alike are made the subject of virulent abuse by attorneys in court, to the evident delight of their Asiatic clients.   To allow such abuse of a coordinate branch of the Government is not calculated to inculcate in the oriental mind a respect for our Government.   We have obtained some favorable decisions, but in others it seems to me there has been a broadening of the Nakashima case.   The steamship companies complain of the expense for maintenance of aliens held so long under habeas corpus proceedings.   Where an appeal to the United States circuit court of appeals has been taken the judges have released the petitioner on bail, holding in Chinese cases that the provision as to "no bail" applies only to the time prior to their decision.

*   *   *   *   *   *   *

RICHARD L. HALSEY,
Inspector in Charge.

REPORT OF THE SUPERVISING INSPECTOR, DISTRICT NO. 23, COMPRISING TEXAS (EXCEPT DISTRICT NO. 9), NEW MEXICO, ARIZONA, AND SOUTHERN CALIFORNIA.

There is submitted herewith report covering the administration of the immigration and Chinese-exclusion acts in the Mexican border district for the year ended June 30, 1913.

ALIEN ARRIVALS OTHER THAN CHINESE.

During the period covered by this report 85,132 aliens were inspected.   Of this number 80,510 were admitted on primary inspection.   The remainder, 4,622, were held for investigation by boards of special inquiry, and of those so detained 1,135 were eventually permitted to enter and 3,487 rejected, or 4.095 per cent.   Owing to the peculiar and it may be said unparalleled conditions obtaining along the Mexican border, a bald presentation of figures showing the number admitted and excluded would, without some analysis of the character of the immigration thereby represented, be incomplete and susceptible of erroneous deductions.   Of the total number of aliens presenting themselves for admission at the southern frontier the largest proportion is at all times naturally composed of Mexicans, forming in the main a vast migratory element, which, coming with no definite intention of remaining permanently, adds only in a limited degree to the sum total of our permanent population.   Such aliens, broadly speaking, fall within the class known as nonstatistical, and of the 85,132 applicants 67,972 belonged to this class, leaving 17,160 who might reasonably be considered as potential citizens, or at least permanent residents.   Of the 67,972 nonstatistical applicants 1,612 were debarred, or 2.37 per cent.   Of the 17,160 statistical aliens 1,875, or 10.9 per cent, were rejected.   A decided decrease in the number of the latter class applying this year, as compared with the year preceding, will be noted, while on the other hand the volume of nonstatistical or transitory applicants has more than doubled.   This striking change in the character of immigration from and through Mexico is in a large measure traceable to the continued political unrest in that country.

During the past year a large number of aliens of the better classes, particularly those of the Mexican race, have, as a result of this condition, taken up a temporary abode in this country, and while these are in the main, broadly speaking, refugees, and will with but relatively few exceptions ultimately return to their native land, records have been maintained concerning them.   During the fiscal year preceding, out of a total of 28,288 statistical aliens (including various races) 1,715 were debarred, or 6.01 per cent.   Of these 5.18 per cent were Mexicans and 0.83 per cent other races.   In the year just closed, as previously stated, but 17,160 statistical aliens applied for admission, of which number 1,875 were debarred, or 10.9 per cent, of which 8.2 per cent were Mexicans and 2.7 per cent other races. It will be seen that the greatest increase in the number of rejections has occurred in the statistical class and that the greater part of said increase has been of Mexicans. The net increase in the percentage of rejections of statistical aliens this year, as compared with last, is 3.02 per cent Mexican and 1.87 per cent all other races. As pointed out in the report for the fiscal year 1912, it was then difficult to make comparisons of a satisfactory and conclusive character, owing to the varied influences had upon immigration by the revolution in Mexico. A similar condition has existed practically throughout the entire past year, and while, as the figures show, there has been an increase in the number of debarred, as compared with the preceding year, it may be said that humane considerations have led to the admission of a considerable number of refugees who would doubtless have been more rigidly dealt with had they applied as other than such. Taken as a whole, the immigration over this border during the past year has not averaged up in quality with that of the previous year.

ILLEGITIMATE IMMIGRATION.

In each annual report since the establishment of this district more or less discussion has been had of immigration under this heading. With the exception of arrivals of the Syrian race there has been an inconsiderable volume of what might be termed illegitimate immigration during the past year. Information gathered from various sources in the past has conclusively demonstrated that the diversion of Syrian immigration by way of the Mexican border is largely due to representations made by unscrupulous persons located in Marseille, France, and other transoceanic points in effect that the same rigid examinations are not conducted on the border as prevail at seaports, and that if excluded there always remains the opportunity for the immigrant to enter surreptitiously. Such representations have without doubt had their weight in persuading aliens of this race, particularly those physically disqualified, to proceed by the longer and more expensive route. During the latter part of the preceding fiscal year the practice was inaugurated, and has since been continued with gratifying results, of instituting searching investigations at the destinations of these applicants before finally taking action in their cases, in consequence of which out of a total of 408 Syrians who sought admission 217 were debarred, or a percentage of 53.1, as contrasted with 22.5 per cent rejected the year previous. Forty-nine of those debarred subsequently effected surreptitious entry, of which number 43 were deported. It is unquestionably true that the average immigrant of this race seeking entry by way of Mexico is of the very lowest and most undesirable type, thus rendering a firm enforcement of the law not only justifiable but imperative if hope is entertained of ever teaching these unfortunates that the Mexican border does not offer an easy means of access to our country.

* * * * * * *

REFUGEES.

The number of alien refugees has been greater during the past year than in the two preceding years, and no inconsiderable portion thereof consisted of people possessed of some means, intending merely a temporary sojourn if conditions in their native country would, within a reasonable period, permit return. Many of these, underestimating the duration of their enforced exile, have found their means insufficient to tide them over the period of waiting and have sought employment. Refugees will be found in almost every city and town in this district, a considerable number of whom are unfit to perform hard manual labor, and as their funds become exhausted it will be difficult for them to maintain themselves, and unless conditions in Mexico become settled in the near future a satisfactory disposition of the refugees may become a serious problem.

JAPANESE.

Immigration of Japanese through this district has been practically negligible. During the year last past 78 applied for admission, of which number 18 were debarred. Forty-seven were arrested, 45 of whom were charged with illegal entry and 2 with illegal residence. Of the total number 40 were deported. 2 warrants were canceled, 1 escaped, and the the cases of 4 remained pending at the close of the year. Practically all of the illegal entries were effected over the southern California land boundary, and the apprehension of aliens of this race who enter clandestinely continues to engage earnest attention.

Numerous gardens and ranches conducted by Japanese in immediate proximity to the southern California boundary afford employment and refuge to the newcomers until opportunity presents to proceed to the more thickly populated towns and cities where the chances of arrest are even more remote. In the absence of evidence that these aliens are illegally in the country, their stories of long residence, often corroborated by their employers, must, perforce, be accepted. On various occasions Japanese with maps in their possession have been arrested by officers of this district. These maps indicate routes of travel from Ensenada to points in California and are almost invariably accompanied by detailed instructions, indicating the presence of persons in the United States interested in assisting aliens of this race to effect surreptitious entry. It is difficult to fasten upon anyone criminal responsibility for the introduction of such aliens, as the contraband are rarely directly assisted in crossing the boundary, but instead rely upon the maps referred to, nor will they, with rare exceptions, furnish evidence against the person or persons criminally liable.

The officers of this district have been extremely diligent in their efforts to break up the smuggling of Japanese, a task which, though fraught with many difficulties, has met with encouraging results.

APPEALS AND BONDS.

*   *   *   *   *   *   *

During the year 321 aliens appealed from the decisions of boards of special inquiry or applied for admission under bond, of which number the department directed the exclusion of 219 and the admission of 86, leaving 16 pending at the close of the year

ARRESTS UNDER DEPARTMENT WARRANTS.

*   *   *   *   *   *   *

Including cases pending from the preceding year, there were under arrest during the period covered by this report 780 aliens, of which number 647 were actually deported; 54 warrants were canceled; 13 aliens escaped, and the cases of 66 were pending at the close of the year. A considerable number of aliens found unlawfully in the United States in the immediate vicinity of the border were, after having signified a desire to return to Mexico, permitted to do so, in some instances the only disqualification apparent being that of entry without inspection. It is considered that this procedure is in line with good administration, as it not only relieves this service of much needless expense, but avoids inflicting hardships incident to arrest and detention.

In the case of practically every alien arrested there is a more or less important principle involved, and consideration is at all times had primarily of the mischief evidently sought to be remedied by Congress. In other words, quality rather than quantity is held to be the chief desideratum.

*   *   *   *   *   *   *

PROSECUTIONS.

*   *   *   *   *   *   *

The following brief summary of criminal prosecutions and civil suits instituted for violations of either the Chinese exclusion or the immigration laws will be of special interest:

Criminal.	Number of persons.	Number of indictments.
Indicted and awaiting trial July 1, 1912...	57	72
Indicted during fiscal year 1913..	70	79
Awaiting action by the grand jury, July 1, 1913.....................................	3	....
Total..	130	151
Convictions during fiscal year 1913 (involving prison sentences aggregating 27 years 8 months and 12 days, and fines amounting to $1,922, and bonds forfeited to the amount of $1,200)...........................	35	43
Acquittals, or indictments quashed..	13	15
Deceased defendants under indictment.......................................	1	1
Awaiting trial under indictments.......................................	1 82	92
Awaiting action by the grand jury.......................................	3	....
Total..	134	151

¹Includes 4 defendants who were convicted or acquitted during the fiscal year 1913.

CIVIL SUITS.

Pending July 1, 1912 (involving penalties aggregating $76,000)................   3
Instituted during fiscal year 1913 (involving penalties aggregating $41,000).....   5

  Total.   8

Tried and verdicts rendered in favor defendants (involving penalties aggregating
  $29,000)...   3
Dismissed under instructions of Attorney General (involving penalties aggregating
  $20,000)...   1
Pending July 1, 1913 (involving penalties aggregating $88,000)................   4

As will be seen from the foregoing, the usual success has attended the prosecution of offenders against the immigration and Chinese exclusion acts. There is no one phase of the work in this district which demands greater skill, perseverance, and intelligence than that which has for its object the collection of evidence in contemplated criminal proceedings. In the early history of the district the means employed by smugglers to evade detection were more or less crude. With time, however, their methods have undergone a marked change. It is a resourceful criminal indeed who can for long escape the just consequence of his evil doing. Many persons heretofore engaged in violating our laws have realized this, and noting the vigor of the prosecutions waged against the fraternity have turned their attention to pursuits which, if no less unlawful, at least possess the merit of being less dangerous. Those who remain among the ranks of the smugglers do so by virtue of refinement of methods, which to say the least makes their apprehension an interesting and it may be said fascinating study.

Prosecutions in this district are largely directed against persons in conspiracy to violate the laws. The evidence in such cases is usually a matter of slow development, often originating with some incident or circumstance apparently trivial and innocent in itself but significant and suggestive to the mind of the trained and experienced officer.

While the number of criminal convictions during the year just past has been slightly less than that of the year preceding, the results obtained have been highly satisfactory.

CHINESE TRANSITS.

The privilege of transit at border ports was granted 346 Chinese. This is a slight increase over the preceding year, due to the hardships attendant upon the continued unsettled conditions in Mexico. Transits to the number of 976 passed through this district into Mexico. It will be observed that the number of transits who passed into Mexico during the past year is more than double that of the preceding year. Of the 976 referred to, 646 proceeded to Lower California through Calexico, Cal.

The passing of Chinese transits into Lower California has been the subject of more or less discussion during the past year with both the bureau and the commissioner at San Francisco. Investigations so far conducted indicate that this movement is fostered by powerful financial interests having as their object the development of large tracts of land in Lower California. Events have proven also that a considerable number of such Chinese have sought the privilege with the purpose in view of ultimately effecting surreptitious entry into the United States. Investigations have likewise disclosed that the number of transits to Lower California during the past year has been greatly in excess of the demand for such labor, in consequence of which the unemployed, as the only alternative, are awaiting favorable opportunity clandestinely to enter this country. It is reasonably well established that no inconsiderable number of such Chinese have proceeded to Lower California under a misapprehension as to wages paid in that country. These have naturally become dissatisfied and have further augmented the numbers already referred to awaiting opportunity to secure illegal entry. Authentic advices have been received since the close of the year that from 2,000 to 5,000 additional Chinese are to be brought from Hongkong to Lower California.

It is apparent that a serious problem confronts our officers in the vicinity of Calexico, and that only by the most strenuous efforts may we hope successfully to cope with it. It is anticipated that a material strengthening of the force in that locality will be necessary before the close of the fiscal year 1914 by reason of the conditions described,

254   REPORT OF COMMISSIONER GENERAL OF IMMIGRATION.

INVESTIGATIONS (CHINESE).

The following is a summary of investigations conducted in connection with Chinese matters other than those relating to deportation and criminal proceedings:

Departing laborers (provision for return)	112
Departing exempts	112
Departing natives	67
Returning and initial exempts	105
Returning natives	60
Departing laborers (no return provisions)	55
Duplicate certificates	58
Suspected alteration or wrongful possession of certificates of residence by holders	106
Miscellaneous	104
Total	779

*   *   *   *   *   *   *

During the year the cases of 272 Chinese were considered by the courts or awaiting deportation by virtue of orders issued in the previous year; 59 of these were new cases. Of the total first mentioned 53 were discharged; 83 deported; 22 were awaiting deportation or disposition of their cases on appeal, and 114 were pending at the close of the year. Three hundred and forty-six Chinese were arrested under departmental warrant during the year, which number added to the 272 above mentioned makes a total of 618.

The benefits resultant from handling Chinese cases under departmental warrants have been far-reaching in their effect. It was formerly the custom of many Chinese to enter from Mexico without formality and deliberately court arrest, secure in the knowledge that a free trip to their native land would be the inevitable result. The effect of deporting aliens of this character to Pacific coast points in Mexico has, it is believed, gone a long way toward eradicating this evil. While the number of Chinese arrested during the past year has fallen off somewhat, as compared with the preceding year, it is undoubtedly a fact that of the number apprehended a larger proportion than ever before were desirous of effecting permanent lodgment in this country.

PENDING CASES.

Chinese deportation cases pending in the courts within this district number 114, of which 80 are in the western district of Texas. Progress has been made during the year in reducing the formerly congested calendars, * * * but the results still continue far from satisfactory. Administrative proceedings offer a partial remedy for this condition, but until such time as it is possible to remove all illegally resident Chinese by this means, regardless of length of residence, the law's delays will continue to afford a measure of protection to a class of aliens whose expulsion from the country should be accomplished in a summary manner.

CERTIFICATE CHINESE.

It is gratifying to be able to report that satisfactory progress has been made during the year toward breaking up the long standing practice whereby Chinese laborers possessed of valid certificates of residence seek to effect return at El Paso after a temporary sojourn abroad. During the year 478 Chinese, a majority of whom were of the class described, were checked out of El Paso to interior points of the United States, as compared with 647 for the preceding year. It is safe to say that practically all of those checked out of this district effected surreptitious entry from Mexico, but affirmative proof of such entry was lacking. This pernicious practice, forming as it does one of the principal sources of revenue of the smuggling ring, will doubtless continue, though never again in so flourishing a manner as obtained in the years when the only recourse was the commissioners' court. As repeatedly pointed out, Congress alone can remedy this condition. It is of interest to note in this connection that certificates of residence to the number of 93, as compared with 56 for the year previous, have been invalidated and canceled during the year, largely by reason of the departure and return of their holders without having first made proper provision.

GENERAL.

The enforcement of the provisions of the Chinese exclusion act continues one of the most difficult and perplexing problems met with on this border. The same general tactics described in preceding reports are followed by persons interested in assisting contraband Chinese to reach the interior of the United States, though, as suggested elsewhere in this report, there is a noticeable refinement in the methods employed by such persons, and their connection with the actual introduction of the Chinese is so remote that evidence justifying criminal prosecution is procured with increasing difficulty. The duties of inspectors within this district were never more exacting, and to locate and successfully overcome the obscure, unlawful influence at work requires energy, earnestness, and intelligence of the highest order.

The value of the automobile as a fairly safe and rapid means of transporting contraband Chinese from the border to interior points has been recognized by the smugglers, and the time is not far distant when the service on this border will be virtually powerless to cope with them unless it is equally progressive.

The smuggling of contraband Chinese by water continues a most vexing and difficult problem. There is every reason to believe that a considerable number of these are being landed at points along the Pacific coast. For a short period during the past year this service had at its disposal a small high-power launch which unfortunately was lost at sea. During the period when this vessel was in commission it is believed that the traffic was at a standstill, but since the loss of the *Elizabeth* persons engaged in smuggling by water have had almost full sway. The service can not satisfactorily handle this situation without proper equipment, and in order to keep pace with our needs no reasonable means to that end should be neglected.

Recommendations heretofore made looking to the purchase of automobiles, a suitable boat, and to an increase of the clerical force, the necessity for all of which has been conceded, are herewith renewed, and it is earnestly hoped that a way may be found which will render possible favorable action thereupon.

In concluding the writer wishes to specially commend the officers and employees within this jurisdiction for their loyal support. It is due to their zealous cooperation that the very gratifying results obtained in this district have been possible of attainment.

F. W. BERKSHIRE,
Supervising Inspector.

APPENDIX IV

OPERATION OF THE PRESENT IMMIGRA-
TION LAW

OPERATION OF PRESENT IMMIGRATION LAW—A STATEMENT IN REGARD TO THE OPERATION OF THE PRESENT IMMIGRATION LAW PREPARED BY THE RETIRING COMMISSIONER GENERAL OF IMMIGRATION.

The present immigration law has but little effect in reducing or checking the great influx of aliens. In fact, it scarcely excludes any except those who are afflicted with serious mental of physical defects. Indeed, if it were not for the few debarred on these grounds, and the occasional contract laborer, anarchist, criminal, or immoral person turned back, the effect of the law would be almost negligible. Notwithstanding the mandatory provisions of the law, it has been difficult in the past to deport even when the aliens are mentally or physically defective. It has become customary for friends or philanthropic societies to appeal in behalf of rejected aliens, and in taking such appeals little or no consideration is given to the merits of the cases, the desire being in any event to land the alien. The endeavors of all parties concerned are frequently directed toward persuading the department that the boards of special inquiry (composed in each instance of three experienced immigrant inspectors, who personally examine and observe the aliens and their witnesses) and the public health surgeons (doctors of training and experience whose only interest, of course, is to perform their duty) are mistaken in their conclusions, and in the event of their failure to have the aliens landed writs of habeas corpus are sought in an effort to have the courts set aside the decision of the administrative officers.

During the fiscal year ended June 30, 1912, 1,033,212 aliens applied for admission, of whom only 1.4 per cent were excluded for all causes. Present indications are that for the fiscal year ending June 30, 1913, there will be approximately 1,375,000 applicants for admission and that the percentage of exclusions will not exceed that of the previous year. This great influx, composed largely of unskilled laborers, undoubtedly is due largely to the activities of ticket agents and others, who solicit and induce aliens to migrate.

Notwithstanding the small percentage of rejections, there are those who constantly criticize the Immigration Service on every conceivable ground, even to the extent of asserting that the law is being so enforced as to reduce the labor supply at a time when there is a great demand for labor, especially in connection with agricultural pursuits. Much of this criticism is not honest; such as is honest is usually based upon ignorance of the law and conditions. Thus those who say the farm-labor supply is being interfered with seem to assume that immigrants from southern and eastern Europe go on the farms, whereas practically none of them do, although they may have been farm laborers in their native countries. As a matter of fact, over 80 per cent of the immigrants of to-day come from southern and eastern Europe or western Asia, and very few of these have any intention of performing or could be induced to perform farm work in the United States, and in the main dependence must be had upon the 18 or 20 per cent from northern or western Europe for the farmers' labor supply, so far as it can be expected to come from overseas. What the bulk of these aliens do is either to enter unskilled city occupations or engage in common labor in manufacturing, mining, or construction work. As a matter of fact, our immigration is poorly assorted in the industrial sense, and unquestionably it is having a disastrous effect on American unskilled labor.

It being obvious that the existing law is not sufficient to meet the serious situation from an economic point of view, growing out of the fact that about 80 per cent of our immigration is composed of aliens belonging to races not of the same stock as the original settlers or the voluntary immigration previous to 25 years ago, it would seem to be incumbent upon Congress to adopt an immigration measure that will be sufficient.

The Burnett-Dillingham bill, passed at the last session of Congress, but vetoed by President Taft, was an excellent measure, not only in the improvements it would have effected in the administrative features of the law, but because it contained the illiteracy test, a provision that would have gone a long way toward reducing the economically undesirable portion of our immigration.

Although I was in favor of the illiteracy test (and undertook to indorse it in my last annual report), I am not at all sure it goes far enough in restricting immigration of the class against which it is especially directed. At any rate, I am clearly of the opinion that the restriction of immigration of the physically, mentally, and morally unsound should be made more thorough, as has been repeatedly suggested in my annual reports. The physical standard for male aliens who are to do manual labor should be raised to approximate that enforced by the Army and Navy in securing recruits. It should also be possible for the United States authorities to exercise a wide discretion with regard to the admission or rejection of large numbers of aliens who, for reasons existing at the time of application or in the locality where the aliens propose to go, would be an undesirable addition to the population on economic grounds.

However, in my opinion, the best suggestion that has yet been made regarding the further restriction of immigration is that recently proposed as a substitute for the illiteracy test, although I can see no reason why the illiteracy test should not be placed in the law simultaneously with it. The suggestion in question is that the number of aliens of any nationality, exclusive of temporary visitors, admitted to the United States in any fiscal year should be required by law not to exceed 10 per cent of the number of persons of such nationality resident in the United States at the time the next preceding census was taken, but the minimum number of any nationality admissible in any fiscal year should be not less than 5,000. It is not contemplated that this provision shall apply to Canada, Newfoundland, Mexico, or Cuba. Nationality under this plan would be determined by country of birth, and colonies and dependencies would be regarded as separate countries. If there had been admitted from any particular country its yearly quota, all aliens of that nationality thereafter applying would be rejected unless it should be shown that they were returning from a temporary visit, or were coming to join near relatives, or were members of clearly defined professional and business classes.

Analysis of the statistics of foreign population given in the last census and a comparison of the figures representing 10 per cent, respectively, of the various nationalities concerned with immigration statistics showing average annual immigration for the 10 years 1903 to 1912, inclusive, indicates some very interesting results that would flow from the adoption of this suggestion, and it is apparent that in the main the reduction in immigration that would be accomplished would be constituted of reductions from countries of southern and eastern Europe and western Asia. Thus under this plan 134,312 Italians could come annually, while the average number per year during the past decade has been 207,152; from Austria-Hungary, 167,053 could come, against an annual average for the past decade of 219,782; from Greece, 10,128, against 20,118; from Turkey in Europe, 5,000, against 10,832. On the other hand, 250,133 natives of Germany would be entitled to come annually, while the average annual immigration of such people during the past decade has been only 35,139; Denmark could send 18,165, compared with 6,971 that have been coming; and the United Kingdom would be allowed a maximum of 257,353, against 95,826.

After four and a half years' connection with the Immigration Service, I feel that, while of course somewhat more could be accomplished toward keeping out the undesirable if more money and more inspectors and doctors were available, no very considerable increase in rejections can be expected unless and until the law is materially improved and strengthened. I have been interested and somewhat amused to observe in the public press statements asserting or predicting that since the Immigration Service has been placed under the new Department of Labor the law will be much more rigidly enforced than heretofore—suggestions which usually carry an imputation of unfairness. The truth of the matter is that the maximum percentage of rejections possible under existing law is so small that, no matter what the desires of administrative officers might be, it is not possible materially to increase rejections. My term of service has covered three months of the new administration. I feel perfectly sure that the Secretary of Labor will administer the immigration law in a thorough and fair manner, and will wherever proper temper justice with mercy. In this connection it is interesting to note that the figures for the several months last past show that the percentage of rejections is lower than that shown for the same months of the previous year.

The Immigration Service is thoroughly and efficiently organized, and its employees quite generally are of a very high grade and will compare favorably with those in any other branch of the Government service, notwithstanding they are charged with the performance of very difficult duties, which involve the handling of human beings and the application to concrete cases, often of a very complicated nature, of the various provisions of the laws on immigration. It has indeed been a great pleasure to me to be associated as commissioner general with an organization of such excellence, the personnel of which I have learned to respect and honor for their sterling qualities.

DANL. J. KEEFE.

INDEX.

261